INDIGENOUS PEOPLES,
NATIONAL PARKS,
AND PROTECTED AREAS

Indigenous Peoples, National Parks, and Protected Areas

A New Paradigm Linking Conservation, Culture, and Rights

EDITED BY
STAN STEVENS

THE UNIVERSITY OF
ARIZONA PRESS

TUCSON

The University of Arizona Press
www.uapress.arizona.edu

© 2014 The Arizona Board of Regents
All rights reserved. Printed 2014

Printed in the United States of America
19 18 17 16 15 14   6 5 4 3 2 1

Cover photo: Tenzing Tashi Sherpa gesturing to highlight the extensive forests, grasslands, and sacred places conserved by the Sharwa (Sherpa) people in their territory of Khumbu. This region is now incorporated into Sagarmatha (Mt. Everest) National Park and World Heritage Site. Photo by Stan Stevens. Reprinted courtesy of IUCN, Natural Justice, and United Nations University—Institute of Advanced Studies.
Cover design by Lori Lieber Graphic Design, Inc.

Library of Congress Cataloging-in-Publication Data are available from the Library of Congress.

♾ This paper meets the requirements of ANSI/NISO Z39.48-1992 (Permanence of Paper).

*To the memories of
Bernard (Barney) Q. Nietschmann, P. H. C. (Bing) Lucas,
and Konchok Chombi Sherpa, with thanks for their friendship
and for sharing their visions of linking culture,
social justice, and conservation*

Contents

Acknowledgments ix

Abbreviations xi

Introduction 3
Stan Stevens

Part I. Rethinking Protected Areas and Indigenous Peoples

1. Indigenous Peoples, Biocultural Diversity, and Protected Areas 15
   Stan Stevens

2. A New Protected Area Paradigm 47
   Stan Stevens

3. Community-Oriented Protected Areas for Indigenous Peoples and Local Communities: Indigenous Protected Areas in Australia 84
   Marcia Langton, Lisa Palmer, and Zane Ma Rhea

4. A Tale of Three Parks: Tlingit Conservation, Representation, and Repatriation in Southeastern Alaska's National Parks 108
   Thomas F. Thornton

Part II. Complexity and Critiques

5. National Parks in the Canadian North: Comanagement or Colonialism Revisited? 133
   John Sandlos

6. State Governmentality or Indigenous Sovereignty? Protected Area Comanagement in the Ashaninka Communal Reserve in Peru 150
Emily Caruso

7. Green Neoliberal Space: The Mesoamerican Biological Corridor 172
Mary Finley-Brook

8. "Bargaining with Patriarchy": Miskito Struggles over Family Land in the Honduran Río Plátano Biosphere Reserve 197
Sharlene Mollett

Part III. Moving Forward: Opportunities, Constraints, and Negotiations

9. Mutual Gains and Distributive Ideologies in South Africa: Theorizing Negotiations between Communities and Protected Areas 217
Derick A. Fay

10. Conservation and Maya Autonomy in Guatemala's Western Highlands: The Case of Totonicapán 241
Brian W. Conz

11. Indigenous Peoples' and Community Conserved Territories and Areas in the High Himalaya: Recognition and Rights in Nepal's National Parks 261
Stan Stevens

12. Advancing the New Paradigm: Implementation, Challenges, and Potential 283
Stan Stevens

References 313

Editor and Contributors 361

Illustration Credits 365

Index 367

Acknowledgments

I am grateful to the ten geographers and anthropologists from the United States, Canada, the United Kingdom, and Australia who have contributed to this book. I give special thanks to Allyson Carter, editor-in-chief at the University of Arizona Press, for encouragement and guidance. I also appreciate the assistance at the University of Arizona Press of Amanda Piell, Leigh McDonald, Abby Mogollon, Lela Scott MacNeil, Julia Balestracci, and Scott De Herrera. The book benefitted from the copyediting of Lisa DiDonato Brousseau, close reading and comments from two anonymous reviewers, and Piper R. Gaubatz's assistance with maps, diagrams, and graphs. I thank the publishers who gave permission for several authors to adapt earlier versions of their case studies or to use previously published illustrations, as acknowledged in their chapters. I also appreciate the timely assistance of the University of Massachusetts, Amherst, which provided a UMass Amherst Book Subvention Program award.

Abbreviations

ABC	Atlantic Biological Corridor
AC48	Alcaldes Comunales de los 48 Cantones (the Communal Mayors of the 48 Towns)
ACHPR	African Commission on Human and Peoples' Rights
ANILCA	Alaska National Interest Lands Conservation Act of 1980
ASCR	Ashaninka Communal Reserve (Peru)
AT files	Files held by André Terblanche, Ncise, Mthatha
CAFTA	Central American Free Trade Agreement
CARE	Ene Ashaninka Federation
CBD	Convention on Biological Diversity
CBNRM	community-based natural resource management
CCAD	Central American Commission on Environment and Development
CONAP	Protected Areas Council (Guatemala)
COP	Conference of the Parties
DLA	Department of Land Affairs (South Africa)
DLMAC	Dhimurru Land Management Aboriginal Corporation
DNPWC	Department of National Parks and Wildlife Conservation (Nepal)
ECNC	Eastern Cape Nature Conservation (South Africa)
GEF	Global Environment Facility
GIS	geographic information system
GtZ	Deutsche Gesellschaft für Technische Zusammenarbeit (Society for Technical Cooperation)
ICCA	Indigenous Peoples' and Community Conserved Territories and Areas (also Indigenous and Community Conserved Areas)

ICDP	integrated conservation and development project
ICT	Indigenous Conservation Territory
ILC	Indigenous Land Corporation
ILO 169	International Labour Organization Convention 169 Concerning Indigenous and Tribal Peoples in Independent Countries
INAB	Guatemalan National Forestry Agency
IPA	Indigenous Protected Area
IUCN	International Union for Conservation of Nature
LNP	Langtang National Park
MBC	Mesoamerican Biological Corridor
M-BNP	Makalu-Barun National Park
MP	Mesoamerican Project
NAGPRA	Native American Graves Protection and Repatriation Act
NGO	nongovernmental organization
NPB	National Parks Board (South Africa)
PoWPA	Programme of Work on Protected Areas
PPP	Puebla-Panama Plan
RAP	Rapid Assessment Programme
RAYAKA	"life," Miskito organization
RMP	regional municipal park
RPBR	Río Plátano Biosphere Reserve
SANP	South African National Parks
SERNANP	Servicio Nacional de Areas Naturales Protegidas (Peru)
SNP	Sagarmatha National Park
S-PNP	Shey-Phoksundo National Park
TASBA	"land," Miskito organization
TVP	The Village Planner (South Africa)
UCJ	Ulew Che' Ja' (Earth, Trees, and Water; Guatemala NGO)
UN	United Nations
UNDRIP	United Nations Declaration on the Rights of Indigenous Peoples
UNEP	United Nations Environment Programme
UNESCO	United Nations Educational, Scientific, and Cultural Organization
WCC	World Conservation Congress
WCPA	World Commission on Protected Areas
WDPA	World Database on Protected Areas
WPC	World Parks Congress

INDIGENOUS PEOPLES,
NATIONAL PARKS,
AND PROTECTED AREAS

Introduction

Stan Stevens

The fortunes and futures of Indigenous peoples and national parks and other protected areas are entwined across vast areas of the world.[1] Indigenous peoples' lands and waters have provided global conservation with many of its most intact ecosystems and biologically richest regions. Large parts of Indigenous peoples' customary territories are now national parks and other kinds of protected areas dedicated to the long-term conservation of biodiversity. Indeed, Indigenous peoples' lands comprise most of the area in the global protected area network. Although the value of this contribution to global conservation and sustainability is beyond measure, the costs to Indigenous peoples have been high. Many peoples have been coercively dispossessed and displaced, often without compensation, when their territories were expropriated to create uninhabited nature reserves. Others have managed to remain in their homelands, but they have been deprived of self-governance, denied access to livelihood resources, and prevented from maintaining their cultural practices, social solidarity, and relationships with their territories and "nature."[2] It is not surprising that many Indigenous peoples consider protected areas to be threats to their welfare and denounce them as colonialism and human rights violations (chapters 1 and 2; Stevens 1997a; Colchester 2003; Dowie 2009).

Many of the national parks and other protected areas created at such great cost to Indigenous peoples have failed to meet conservation expectations. Effective protected areas require long-term commitment to biodiversity conservation goals and defense against incompatible use. In international conservation circles, it was once widely assumed that this could only be achieved by removing resident Indigenous peoples and entrusting protected areas solely to state administration. From a conservation standpoint, this practice has had three adverse consequences: (1) loss of Indigenous peoples' custodianship and care of what have long been cultural landscapes and culturally shaped ecosystems rather than uninhabited wilderness (Gomez-Pompa and Kaus 1992; Anderson and Barbour 2003); (2) loss of their guardianship and defense of territories and ecosystems against environmentally destructive settlement, extractive industries, and large-scale infrastructure development (Stevens 1997a); and (3) reliance for the protection, maintenance, and restoration of protected area ecosystems and biodiversity on state authorities who often have lacked the necessary capacity, resources, or political will to achieve these outcomes.

In retrospect, it seems that this faith in an ecologically responsible state was naïve, and that the displacement of Indigenous peoples was often an ecological as well as a moral mistake.[3] Many states' conservation records generate little confidence in their ability to protect and manage protected areas effectively in the near term, much less for centuries. In many cases, this has as much or more to do with ideology and political priorities than with capacity or available resources. Protected areas often are far from secure or effectively governed and managed, even in wealthy countries. Many are vulnerable due to states' promotion of extractive industries or regional development and infrastructure projects. This is the case even in the United States, the birthplace of the concepts of both the national park and wilderness area. Protection of the ecological integrity of the largest U.S. terrestrial protected area and wilderness, the Arctic National Wildlife Refuge in Alaska, for example, has required what Peter Matthiessen (2012: 366) has called "the longest and most acrimonious environmental fight in American history" to prevent oil exploration and development.[4] Whether the Arctic Refuge can continue to be protected is far from certain, nor are any of the crown jewel national parks secured against future extractive activity and other inappropriate use should Congress choose to authorize it.[5] The status of protected areas is even more precarious across much of the global South. In many countries, protected areas remain "paper parks" decades after their declaration because state authorities have little or no on-the-ground management presence and do not implement plans and regulations. In at least a dozen countries, the downgrading, downsizing, or degazettement of protected areas is a current issue. The first international study of such practices identified eighty-nine cases in twenty-seven countries since 1900 (Mascia and Pailler 2011; see also Bertzky et al. 2012).

The future of protected areas remains precarious in countries whose mainstream societies seem ambivalent about biodiversity conservation or prioritize economic development at all costs. The security of national parks and other state-administered protected areas becomes even more tenuous when the state itself is entwined with extractive industries. Confidence in the long-term ecological integrity of protected areas cannot be high in countries—Peru, Ecuador, Belize, Indonesia, South Africa, and Botswana among them (a full list may be quite long)—whose national laws and policies call for strict protection of protected areas but have proved unable to prevent state agencies from authorizing mining, oil and gas extraction, logging, big dams and reservoirs, highways, and other projects that conflict with protected area conservation goals. In many countries, protected area goals themselves are an issue because they do not prioritize biodiversity conservation. Countries establish protected areas, including national parks, for many purposes, among them the protection of scenery and natural wonders, national cultural and historical heritage, recreation, tourism, and international acclaim and support. As has been the case for many U.S. national parks, biodiversity conservation often is not foremost among these goals (Sellars 2009).

Marcus Colchester (2003: 51), an anthropologist and former director of the prominent international conservation and social justice organization Forest Peoples Programme, observed that "if the track record of the State is that it cannot be relied on to defend biological diversity, the question that then occurs to conservationists is whether any other institutions, such as indigenous ones, can." National park and protected area policies and practices that have dispossessed, disempowered, and alienated Indigenous peoples raise many further questions:

- Would the future ecological integrity of these areas be more secure if Indigenous peoples' ownership of them were assured rather than denied?
- Might conservation goals be more likely to be met over the long term if Indigenous peoples had an effective role in decisions about protected area goals and management?
- Can Indigenous peoples contribute to the success of protected areas by bringing to them their values, knowledge of local ecology, environmentally and place-attuned land-use and management practices, protection of sacred places, and commitment to defending their territories?
- Are there alternatives to wilderness preserves governed by state agencies and based solely on non-Indigenous techno-managerial and scientific expertise?

- Has international conservation and conservation funding focused too narrowly on a single, problematic model for protected areas? Have other kinds of protected areas been underfunded?
- Have states and international conservationists squandered invaluable opportunities for conservation alliances, mutual learning, and shared efforts with the very peoples whose knowledge, values, and commitment may be vital to the success of many protected areas?
- Has conservation unnecessarily caused some of the world's poorest and most marginalized peoples even greater suffering and impoverishment?
- Can Indigenous peoples benefit from protected areas? Can they be a means to realize territorial, livelihood, and cultural integrity and security? Can they provide economic opportunities and be a means of avoiding unwanted, culturally and environmentally destructive "development"?
- Can past mistakes and injustices be rectified, relationships reconstituted, and conservation put on a more effective, enduring, equitable, and just basis?
- Can protected areas become places where states and international conservation organizations respect Indigenous peoples' rights, responsibilities to their territories and peoples, and conservation contributions and provide support when asked to, including helping buffer external threats?

Such questions have catalyzed much discussion and debate in international conservation circles over the past several decades. International acknowledgment of the conservation importance of Indigenous peoples' knowledge and practices, together with new recognition of their collective rights as peoples, has transformed thinking about conservation and protected areas. While only a few years ago "fortress conservation" and state governance of uninhabited protected areas were nearly universally taken for granted by conservationists and state conservation agencies as the only legitimate form of conservation, it is increasingly understood that ignoring Indigenous peoples' existence, conservation contributions, and rights has been an enormous mistake and injustice. The violent historical displacement of so many Indigenous peoples over the past 150 years to create national parks and other protected areas is now widely regretted in international conservation circles. Once-standard policies and practices are now repudiated by many conservationists and conservation nongovernmental organizations (NGOs) and intergovernmental organizations, challenged by Indigenous peoples and social justice organizations, investigated by national and international human rights monitoring institutions, and found to violate national and international laws by national and international courts.

This does not mean that past injustices have been remedied, that new ones are not being perpetrated, or that Indigenous peoples' contributions to the biological and cultural richness of their homelands are no longer ignored or dismissed. In many places, strict nature preservation and exclusionary protected areas continue to be created and maintained without the free, prior, and informed consent of Indigenous peoples, fair compensation, participation in protected area governance, equitable share of financial and other benefits, or provision for their continuing access to and custodianship of cultural sites and customary activities. No state has yet apologized for their past treatment of Indigenous peoples in the name of conservation. Coercive displacements continue in a number of countries in Africa and Asia. Many peoples worldwide continue to endure ecologically unjustified bans on their customary land and marine use and management practices. Many are denied their custodianship and responsibility for caring for and protecting sacred places and other cultural sites. Conservation pursued by creating exclusionary, rights-violating protected areas has been a disaster for many Indigenous peoples worldwide (chapter 1).

There is another way. A paradigm shift in international conservation may dramatically reshape the shared futures of protected areas and Indigenous peoples. A new paradigm has been developed and adopted by the International Union for Conservation of Nature (IUCN) and the Parties to the Convention on Biological Diversity (CBD) that not only repudiates many long-standing assumptions, policies, and practices but also envisions very different ways of establishing, governing, and managing national parks and other protected areas (chapter 2). This paradigm calls for affirmation of Indigenous peoples' conservation achievements, rights-based conservation, establishment of new kinds of protected areas, and reform of existing protected areas that do not meet new international standards.[6] It maintains that biodiversity conservation can be advanced by recognizing, respecting, and supporting Indigenous peoples' conservation achievements and initiatives and by working together with them in ways that respect their ownership of their territory, their sovereignty, and their rights and responsibilities. It envisions conservation that does not displace Indigenous peoples, exclude them from full and effective participation in protected area governance, impose regulations and management practices on them, violate their rights, prevent them from carrying out their responsibilities, or deny them their fair share of benefits.

The new paradigm does not (as many assume) deny the value of nature protection or wilderness. Strict nature protection can be appropriate and just if it has Indigenous peoples' free, prior, and informed consent; fully and effectively involves them in governance; and does not violate rights. Indigenous peoples may themselves wish to protect certain places as uninhabited or little used and may decide to adopt new use restrictions on parts of their territories. But the new paradigm, unlike earlier ways of thinking, does not emphasize or impose strict preservation as a protected area goal to the exclusion of others. It also values other kinds of protected areas with different goals and principles, including those that sustain customary practices that contribute to cultural and biological diversity. It values as protected areas inhabited cultural landscapes that sustain and enhance biodiversity, where conservation management relies on and supports cultural values, stewardship, and sustainable livelihood practices. Moreover, new paradigm principles support reconfiguring the governance and management of protected areas of all types within Indigenous peoples' territories, including those dedicated to strict preservation of biodiversity, to ensure that Indigenous peoples participate fully and effectively and that their rights are upheld to maintain their identities, ownership, and control over their territories, cultural values, self-governance, livelihoods, and well-being.

The new paradigm gives new prominence to rights. It takes as its standard the United Nations Declaration on the Rights of Indigenous Peoples and other international rights instruments, and it requires that these be honored in all aspects of protected area establishment, design, governance, and management. This includes acknowledging that states must recognize Indigenous peoples' continuing ownership of their territories and their relationships with it, and that territory that is now incorporated in protected areas be restituted if it was taken without their free, prior, and informed consent. Achieving such rights-based conservation will often require profound changes in societal relationships and interactions as well as in conservation law, policies, and practices (chapters 1, 2, 4, 11, and 12).

The new paradigm has enormous potential and promise. Early experience attests that protected areas based on these principles can be an important means of affirming and realizing Indigenous peoples' rights while simultaneously safeguarding biodiversity. Such protected areas can facilitate not only new conservation synergies but also social reconciliation. Indeed, the new paradigm offers a means for protected areas to become a way of reconstituting and decolonizing relationships between Indigenous peoples, conservationists, and wider societies. Certainly this will not happen overnight, without struggle, or completely. Powerful prejudices and conflicting interests impede implementation. Realization of the new paradigm will be uneven, partial, contested, and continually renegotiated. In many countries, the necessary legal, institutional, and social changes will be controversial and resisted. But important efforts are underway, and there have been significant accomplishments in policy and practice in a short time (chapters 2 and 12).

Book Structure and Themes

This book explores the sea change in thinking about protected areas and Indigenous peoples and examines both encouraging and cautionary experiences with implementation of the new paradigm. At its core is a conceptualization of protected areas that is attentive to social and political as well as ecological relationships and a vision of how global conservation can be enriched and made more socially just by protected areas that affirm Indigenous peoples' territories, cultures, self-governance, and rights. The book thus builds on and extends my earlier book *Conservation through Cultural Survival: Indigenous Peoples and Protected Areas* (Island Press, 1997). In that book, my fellow contributors and I documented and analyzed a number of the then most promising protected area initiatives that embodied the principles that now define the new paradigm. After nearly two decades, it is time for a reassessment based on subsequent experience with new kinds of protected areas and changes in conservation thinking, international protected area policy, and Indigenous rights recognition.

The book opens with discussion of Indigenous peoples, rights, biocultural diversity, national parks and other protected areas, and the principles of both the old and new paradigms of protected area–based conservation (chapters 1 and 2). It closes by assessing efforts thus far to implement the new paradigm and lessons learned from early experiences (chapter 12). The nine case study chapters in between are the core of the book. Geographers and anthropologists from the United States, the United Kingdom, Canada, and Australia draw on in-depth fieldwork to provide insights into protected areas that have been considered to embody new paradigm principles in Australia, the United States (Alaska), Canada (Northwest Territories), Guatemala, Honduras, Nicaragua, Peru, South Africa, and Nepal (figure I.1), including national parks in the United States, Canada, South Africa, and Nepal. Several of the case studies (chapters 3, 4, 6, and 9) provide insights into exemplary cases, and these and chapters 8, 10, and 11

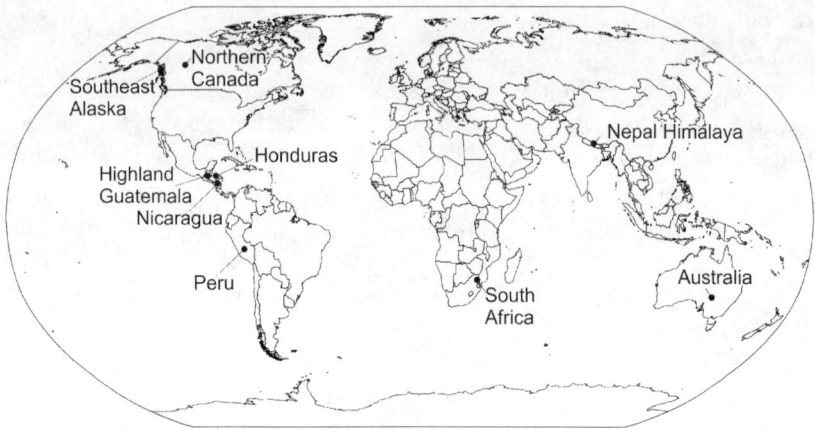

Figure I.1. Locations of chapter case studies: southeast Alaska (chapter 4), northern Canada (chapter 5), highland Guatemala (chapter 10), Honduras (chapter 8), Nicaragua (chapter 7), Peru (chapter 6), South Africa (chapter 9), Nepal Himalaya (chapter 11), and Australia (chapter 3).

illuminate how Indigenous peoples' knowledge, values, and perspectives offer ways to reconceptualize and construct protected areas.

However, a number of the chapters (particularly chapters 5, 7, 8, 10, and 11, but also chapters 4 and 9) also testify to the difficulties of achieving full and effective implementation of the new paradigm's principles. Clearly, the obstacles and challenges to reform are formidable, and there is no reason for premature celebration or mistaking potentially transformative ideas and discourse for current conditions on the ground. At the same time, it is important to appreciate the significance of the conceptual and policy breakthroughs that have been achieved, the potential of initiatives now underway, and the hope the new paradigm offers to Indigenous peoples and societies seeking to link sustainability and the protection of biodiversity with recognition of cultural diversity, human rights, and the promotion of social and environmental justice.

Most of the chapters collected here were originally presented as papers between 2004 and 2012 at sessions on Indigenous peoples and protected areas held at the annual meetings of the Association of American Geographers and sponsored by the Indigenous Peoples Specialty Group and the Cultural and Political Ecology Specialty Group (chapters 3, 5, and 9 are exceptions). The contributing authors of this book are academics, and the book speaks to colleagues and students in diverse fields, including environmental studies, development studies, geography, anthropology, natural resource management, Native American studies, Indigenous studies, and ethnic studies. We hope it will be read and valued as well by those who are engaged with conservation and protected areas, from Indigenous peoples and members of local communities to government officials, conservationists, Indigenous rights advocates and activists, and donors.

Notes

1. This book focuses on policies, practices, and issues concerning Indigenous peoples and protected areas. Many new paradigm proponents hold that its core principles (see table 2.1) also apply to local communities. Key IUCN and CBD policies and decisions that articulate the new paradigm refer to local communities as well as Indigenous peoples (Phillips 2003; Borrini-Feyerabend et al. 2004a, 2013; Kothari et al. 2012). There is disagreement, however, over how "local communities" should be identified or defined, what collective rights they hold, and whether or not the provisions of the new paradigm apply equally to all kinds of communities.

2. Many Indigenous peoples reject the concept of "resources" and particularly "natural resources." Interacting with living beings and places in this way, like the use of concepts of "ownership" of land as "property" and conceptions of "nature" and "wilderness" that separate people and the world, is often alien to Indigenous peoples' worldview or cosmovision (their shared understanding of the world and their place in it) and values. Many consider these ways of thinking and interacting as objectifying and disrespecting living beings, violating relationships based on respect, reciprocity, restraint, and responsibility. In many cases, these relationships are based on perceived kinship with other beings. Many Indigenous peoples, moreover, do not have direct equivalents of other terms in common use in international conservation circles, including "environment," "ecosystem," "biodiversity," "conservation," "protected areas," and "wilderness," and they often reject the assumptions and values that underlie contemporary Western conceptualizations of them. This includes conceptions of "conservation" and "protected areas" that are limited to biodiversity preservation and dichotomize the world into protected and unprotected areas. Our use in this book of these terms does not imply our endorsement of non-Indigenous attitudes and assumptions, but rather reflects our desire to engage with contemporary international conservation and rights thinking, literature, and policies that rely on these terms.

3. Janis Alcorn (1994) observed that conservationists who believe in strict preservation often also believe in a myth of the "noble state." A faith that the state can be relied on to champion biodiversity conservation and protected areas overgeneralizes, romanticizes, and essentializes the state as a conservation actor as much (if not more) than what Redford (1991) characterized as the myth of the "ecologically noble savage." The myth of the ecologically noble state permeates much law, policy, and funding and perpetuates state-centric power relationships and vested interests.

4. The customary territory of the Indigenous Gwitch'in and Inupiat peoples, the Arctic National Wildlife Refuge is preeminent for its size, intact ecosystems, and extraordinary wildlife. It was nonetheless targeted for priority oil development by the

administrations of three presidents. Congressional proposals to authorize oil exploration and development (the latest in 2011 and 2012) have often only narrowly been blocked, in 1995 only by a veto by President Bill Clinton (Standlea 2006; Schaller 2012).

5. The history of Yosemite National Park, one of the crown jewels of the U.S. national park system, is a reminder of the vulnerability of protected areas in the United States. A century ago, only sixteen years after one Congress had declared the national park in 1890, another excised a third of the national park's total area that was coveted by mining and timber companies (Runte 1993).

6. The new paradigm's emphasis on equity, justice, and rights extends to conservation and protected areas a "right-based approach" already underway in international development circles. An important literature is being established that explores and critiques rights-based approaches to conservation; see, for example, Alcorn and Royo (2007), Campese et al. (2009), two special issues of the IUCN Commission on Environmental, Economic, and Social Policy journal *Policy Matters* (Campese and Borrini-Feyerabend 2007; Shrumm 2010), and Sikor and Stahl (2011). Aspects of the new rights-based literature that have particular bearing on protected areas include the concept of "traditional resource rights" (Posey and Dutfield 1996; Villalba 2010), rights and restitution (MacKay 2007; Morel 2010), and recognizing Indigenous Peoples' and Community Conserved Territories and Areas (ICCAs) as a means of implementing international human law (Stevens 2009, 2010, 2013a).

PART I

Rethinking Protected Areas and Indigenous Peoples

CHAPTER ONE

Indigenous Peoples, Biocultural Diversity, and Protected Areas

Stan Stevens

In recent years, Indigenous peoples have gained new international visibility and recognition. The term "Indigenous peoples," little used in international discourse before the 1980s, has become the watchword of one of the great social and political movements of our time. "Indigenous peoples" is now a keyword in the lexicons of international politics, human rights, development, and conservation. Although it continues to be controversial and contested in some intellectual, social, and political circles, the term is well established in everyday use and in international law and jurisprudence.[1] It has become fundamental to the perceptions and articulations of the identities, social relationships, aspirations, rights claims, and political mobilizations of many individuals and peoples worldwide (Niezen 2003). The increased emphasis on indigeneity in the pursuit of social and environmental justice has great import for conservation and protected areas.

Worldwide, according to UN figures, there are more than 5000 different Indigenous peoples with a total population of some 370 million people living in seventy-two countries. They constitute at least 5 percent of the world's total population (UN Department of Economic and Social Affairs 2009; UN Permanent Forum on Indigenous Issues n.d.).[2] Indigenous peoples' cultures are a great human heritage; collectively they constitute the primary repository of global cultural diversity. Despite the loss of many Indigenous languages to assimilation processes, for example, Indigenous peoples maintain more than two-thirds of the languages of the world.

Their territories, which despite invasions and annexations still comprise at least 20 percent of the land area of the planet, are rich in natural resources and are estimated to hold 80 percent of the world's biodiversity (Sobrevila 2008; Watanabe 2008; GEF 2011).[3] It is not surprising that international conservation, which until the 1990s largely ignored Indigenous peoples, now engages them to a greater degree and on different terms.

This chapter discusses current thinking about Indigenous peoples and rights, their contributions to global biocultural diversity, and the global spatial congruence between Indigenous peoples' territories and protected areas. It concludes by discussing the old protected area paradigm and considering the consequences that this mindset has had for Indigenous peoples.

Situating Indigenous Peoples

There is no single, universally embraced definition of "Indigenous peoples." The term was not defined in the 2007 United Nations Declaration on the Rights of Indigenous Peoples (UNDRIP), and in UN circles it is now considered that "the most fruitful approach is to identify, rather than define indigenous peoples" (UN Permanent Forum on Indigenous Issues n.d.: 1).[4] Recent international identification of Indigenous peoples within UN contexts, expanding on earlier UN discussions and treaties,[5] emphasizes a set of key elements that include: self-identification; historical continuity with ancestors who inhabited their territory prior to conquest, colonialism, or the establishment of the present boundaries of the state; distinctive identity and culture, which may include their own cultural, social, political, and economic institutions; social, political, and economic marginalization by wider society; and acceptance as Indigenous peoples by other peoples in the global Indigenous peoples movement.

These identifying characteristics have not always been applied or adopted consistently. Many peoples who identify as Indigenous have not been recognized as such by the states they live in. Other peoples do not (or do not yet) consider themselves to be Indigenous and have not pressed to be recognized as such, yet meet all the other characteristics listed above. There has been considerable debate over whether the concept of Indigenous peoples is as appropriate for Asia and Africa as it is for the Americas (Niezen 2003). Some Asian states (including China and India) and several African ones consider all their citizens to be "Indigenous" in that their occupation of national territory predates earlier colonialism, but choose to recognize few or none of these peoples as being "Indigenous peoples" who have collective rights as identified in international rights instruments.[6]

The African Commission on Human and Peoples' Rights (ACHPR) recently emphatically endorsed the concept of Indigenous peoples and clarified its application in the African context in ways that also are relevant to Asia and other regions. The ACHPR (2005: 95) stated "it is our position that it is important to accept the use of the term indigenous peoples all over the world, including in Africa" and the view that "the term indigenous is not applicable in Africa as 'all Africans are indigenous,'" is a "misconception" (ACHPR 2005: 88). Instead it maintained that "the concept in its modern forms more adequately encapsulates the real situation of the groups and communities concerned" than does the term "minorities." The ACHPR approved of the term's use by "particular marginalized groups [who] use the term indigenous to describe their situation" and who employ "the modern analytical form of the concept (which does not merely focus on aboriginality) in an attempt to draw attention to and alleviate the particular form of discrimination they suffer from" (ACHPR 2005: 95, 88). The ACHPR accordingly included collective experiences of injustice as one of the distinguishing characteristics of Indigenous peoples, which it held can be identified based on "*self-definition* as indigenous and distinctly different from other groups within a state; on a *special attachment to and use of their traditional land* whereby their ancestral land and territory has a fundamental importance for their collective physical and cultural survival as peoples; [and] on an experience of *subjugation, marginalization, dispossession, exclusion or discrimination* because these peoples have different cultures, ways of life or modes of production than the national hegemonic and dominant model" (ACHPR 2005: 92–93; italics in original).

Indigenous peoples worldwide have experienced similar histories of discrimination and social, political, and economic marginalization, often rationalized and naturalized through racialized discourses that have denigrated their ethnic and cultural difference and represented them as inferior, backward, incapable, and even subhuman. They have been dispossessed of their territories and natural resources, denied self-governance and self-determination, and subjected to coercive assimilation. A vast number of Indigenous peoples in countries in both the global North and South continue to find themselves in states whose ethnic elites seek to create unitary nation-states through conquest, control, and the assimilation of Indigenous peoples to a single culture. This has often involved the theft of Indigenous peoples' territories and natural resources, social denigration and exclusion, political marginalization, and the active suppression of

Indigenous peoples' cultures, including outlawing their use of their own languages and maintaining their distinctive cultural and religious practices, community institutions and events, land and marine use, and collective land and marine management practices. Such coercive national integration and nation building has been denounced as a form of internal colonialism, so prevalent in countries of the First, Second, and Third World alike that it has been referred to as the "Fourth World" (Manuel and Posluns 1973; Nietschmann 1994). Indigenous nations (in the sense of peoples with their own customary territories) that lack autonomy within nation-states dominated by other peoples continue to experience a colonial present even in supposedly postcolonial states.

Geographer Bernard Nietschmann (1994) suggested that the Fourth World plight of Indigenous peoples "explain[s] persistent global patterns of ethnocide and ecocide." The destruction of Indigenous peoples' cultures and the loss of the biological diversity and ecological integrity of their homelands seem to be frequently simultaneous, entwined, and driven by social, political, and economic dynamics in which state policies and practices figure prominently.[7] State implication in ethnocide is well known, including through making Indigenous languages and cultural practices illegal and requiring attendance in national schools that use education as a means of assimilation. The creation and development of unitary nation-states also increase the vulnerability of Indigenous peoples and their territories to unwanted economic exploitation that is both environmentally and socially destructive. States often disregard Indigenous peoples' ownership of their territories, preferring to regard them as unclaimed and unowned land (*terra nullius*) that it can "discover," nationalize, administer, sell, disburse, or lease as it sees fit.[8] State expropriation of Indigenous peoples' lands transforms them into resource and settlement frontiers that are often central to national economic growth. Expropriated Indigenous peoples' territories are the sites of agrarian colonization, mining, oil and natural gas extraction, logging, fisheries, and plantation and ranching operations, as well as infrastructure development such as hydroelectric dams, reservoirs, oil and gas pipelines, and roads. States, in close coordination or collusion with corporations, encourage and facilitate frontier resource rushes on Indigenous peoples' lands, often giving little regulatory attention to either environmental degradation or the adverse impacts on Indigenous peoples' autonomy, social cohesion, livelihoods, cultures, or health. In *The New Imperialism*, geographer David Harvey (2003) identified this process as "accumulation by dispossession"; Nietschmann (1986) condemned it as "development by the destruction of [Indigenous] nations."

The annexation and expropriation of Indigenous peoples' territories also has political significance. Indigenous peoples' sovereignty, in the sense of their inherent authority over their affairs—including living in and maintaining a relationship with the world according to their own worldview, values, and aspirations—is often impeded by state territorialization, the process of state extension of administrative control over areas within their claimed boundaries (Vandergeest and Peluso 1995).[9] In Fourth World conditions, state territorialization typically refuses to recognize the legitimacy of Indigenous peoples' territories, systems of governance, customary laws and institutions, or cultural distinctiveness. Forcing Indigenous peoples to conform to national standards makes their institutions and practices more "legible" (Scott 1998), and hence more easily administered by the state, but undermines their rights as peoples to their territories, cultural integrity, self-governance, and self-determination. Protected areas have become a vehicle of state territorialization in many countries (see the discussion below of the old paradigm of protected areas) and often have been used by repressive states as a means to seize greater control of Indigenous peoples' territories and lives (Nietschmann 1994; Neumann 2004).

In many parts of the world, Indigenous peoples have resisted Fourth World dispossession and territorialization. This resistance has taken many forms, from efforts to counter the colonization of the mind to contesting state law and cartographies to armed struggles seeking greater autonomy within states or the creation of their own nation-states.[10] In the late twentieth century, such armed resistance movements accounted for a high percentage of violent conflicts worldwide, what Nietschmann (1987) called a "Third World War" between Fourth World nations and states. These diverse struggles are grounded in culture as well as in defense of territory, identity, and self-determination. They are frontier wars over homelands and resource wars over the natural wealth on Indigenous peoples' lands. But they are also what Mander and Tauli-Corpuz (2006) call "paradigm wars," collisions of different worldviews, ways of life, and values.[11] Protected areas, particularly those that fit the old paradigm, have been central sites of Fourth World conflict.

Indigenous Rights and Conservation

The global Indigenous peoples' movement has sought international recognition for Indigenous peoples' individual and collective rights. Much progress has been made in the articulation of these rights and their embodiment in international law. Two major milestones were the 1989 entry into force of a UN treaty on Indigenous rights (International Labour Organization Convention 169 Concerning Indigenous and Tribal Peoples in Independent Countries; hereafter ILO 169) and the 2007 adoption by the UN General Assembly of UNDRIP. UN adoption of UNDRIP by an overwhelming vote capped more than twenty-five years of negotiations and strong resistance from a number of states, including the United States, Canada, Australia, and New Zealand.[12] Together ILO 169 and UNDRIP affirm that Indigenous peoples have both individual and collective rights and fundamental freedoms that include territorial, tenure, political, economic, development, cultural, environmental, civil, and legal rights. The rights acknowledged in UNDRIP are considered to be the "minimum standards for the survival, dignity and well-being of the indigenous peoples of the world" (UNDRIP, Article 43).[13]

From the perspective of international law, Indigenous rights are not conditional privileges granted by states but are rather universal, inherent, indivisible, and interdependent rights. States are rights duty-bearers and have an obligation to affirm, ensure, and facilitate Indigenous peoples' enjoyment of these rights. Indigenous rights are not considered to be special rights held only by them, but rather their right to the individual and collective rights held by all peoples. Their rights as "peoples" distinguish them from "populations," "ethnic groups," "minority groups," "communities," and "local people." Crucially, as *peoples* (with a critical final "s") they hold the collective right to self-determination as affirmed by multiple international treaties and UNDRIP (Niezen 2003; Anaya 2004).[14] As bearers of collective rights to sovereignty, self-governance, and the ownership and control of their customary territories, Indigenous peoples are rights-bearers rather than simply stakeholders in all matters concerning the administration, conservation, and development of their territories.

A number of the specific rights affirmed in ILO 169, UNDRIP, and other international human rights instruments and jurisprudence have strong bearing on the establishment, governance, and management of protected areas (MacKay 2007, 2011; Campese et al. 2009; Greiber et al. 2009; Stevens 2009, 2010, 2014; Morel 2010; Villalba 2010; Lausche and Burhenne 2011; Sikor and Stahl 2011).[15] Most of the articles of both ILO 169 and UNDRIP are relevant. These can be conceptualized as seven broad, indivisible, mutually reinforcing sets or bundles of rights,[16] each of which is supported by multiple articles of ILO 169 and UNDRIP (chapter 11; Stevens 2009, 2010, 2014):

1. human rights and freedoms, including the individual and collective rights of women and men, elders, youth, and children;
2. self-governance, sovereignty, self-determination, and participation in decision-making, including the requirement of providing free, prior, and informed consent to legislation, administrative actions, or projects that affect them and their territories;
3. ownership, use, and management of territory, land, and resources including collective ownership and stewardship, restitution of land taken without consent, no forced removals, access to natural resources and to their own means of subsistence and development, and engagement in traditional and other economic activities;
4. culture and religion, including the use, development, revitalization, and transmission of their languages, histories, knowledge, traditions, and customs; maintaining and protecting sacred and other cultural sites; and maintaining their spiritual relationships with their territories;
5. customary institutions and the exercise of customary law;
6. environment, including appropriate assistance in maintaining the environmental integrity and capacity of their territories; and
7. development, including defining their own development goals consistent with their identities, cultures, needs, and aspirations.

The right to free, prior, and informed consent—including the right to withhold consent—is inherent or explicitly indicated in UNDRIP for many of these sets of rights. It has considerable bearing on protected area establishment, design, and planning. Indigenous peoples' right to participate in decisions affecting their lives and territories is pertinent not only for individual protected areas in their territories but also in the development of national protected area law and policies. Rights are associated with responsibilities, including not only legal and moral obligations but also the "right to responsibility" (Jonas et al. 2014), Indigenous peoples' inherent right to be responsible for maintaining what they see as proper relationships with their territories, the life in them, and the welfare of their peoples. This includes, among other things, their spiritual relationships, their care and defense of their territory, cultural and conservation obligations, and obligations to ancestors and future generations. UNDRIP (2007) Article 25 affirms Indigenous peoples' right "to maintain and strengthen their distinctive spiritual relationship with their traditionally owned or otherwise occupied and used lands, territories, waters and coastal seas and other resources and to uphold their responsibilities to future generations in this regard." The ability to be accountable in these ways requires recognition of territorial ownership, self-governance, cultural integrity, and many other rights affirmed in UNDRIP.

Although Indigenous peoples' rights are now established international law and policy, ensuring that these rights are honored and facilitated is a huge challenge. Some states have declared themselves to be plurinational, but no country has yet achieved a truly pluri-national society that fully recognizes and respects Indigenous peoples' cultural difference and integrity, territorial ownership or stewardship, and self-determination.[17] The IUCN and the CBD have made rights-based conservation a central principle of the new paradigm (see chapters 2 and 12), but many protected areas continue to violate rights. States continue to designate new protected areas that do not appropriately recognize rights, reflecting states' determination to assert territoriality, including their sole authority for protected area governance as well as their ownership of expropriated territory and natural resources. Struggles over rights in protected areas, as Ribot (2008: iv in Nelson 2010: 329) observed for forest governance and use in Senegal, constitute a "last frontier of decolonization" and can require new negotiations of both citizenship and statehood.

Indigenous Peoples and Biocultural Diversity

Over the last twenty-five years, there has been increased interest in the concept of biocultural diversity. Research suggests that cultural and biological diversity may be interlinked, often interdependent, and perhaps coevolved (Chapin 1990, 1992; Dasmann 1991; Nietschmann 1992b; Alcorn 1994; Harmon 1996, 2002; Nabhan 1997; Stevens 1997a; Posey 1999; Oviedo et al. 2000; Maffi 2001, 2007; Anderson 2006; Pretty 2007; Pretty et al. 2009; Maffi and Woodley 2010). Beginning with Mac Chapin's (1992) work in Central America, regional and global patterns of overlapping biodiversity and cultural diversity have been mapped and display striking correspondences between the geography of Indigenous peoples' territories and remaining areas of high biodiversity and relatively ecologically intact regions.[18] Although it was once assumed that many of these areas of high biodiversity were uninhabited wilderness, they are now widely understood to be Indigenous peoples' homelands, livelihood use areas, and cultural landscapes.[19] The World Wide Fund for Nature (2008) has observed, for example, that "most of the remaining significant areas of high natural value on Earth are inhabited by Indigenous peoples." The IUCN's World Commission on Protected Areas (2003b) similarly affirmed that "indigenous peoples, including mobile indigenous peoples, and local communities live in most of the world's biodiversity-rich regions," and the most recent IUCN World Conservation Congress (WCC) declared in the preamble of Resolution 5.094 that "a considerable part of the Earth's biological and cultural diversity is concentrated in the customary territories and areas of indigenous peoples and traditional communities, including both mobile and sedentary peoples" (IUCN 2012d). According to Nietschmann:

> Representing the Earth's primary natural and human resources and evolutionary potential, biological and cultural diversity appear to be interdependent, geographically coterminous, and almost everywhere threatened or endangered.... The vast majority of the world's biological diversity is not in gene banks, zoos, national parks, or protected areas. Most biological diversity is in landscapes and seascapes inhabited and used by local peoples, mostly indigenous, whose great collective accomplishment is to have conserved the great variety of remaining life forms, using culture, the most powerful and valuable human resource, to do so (Nietschmann 1992, quoted in Stevens 1997a: 26).

As a result, as Mac Chapin (2004: 29) noted, "Indigenous peoples live in most of the ecosystems that conservationists are so anxious to preserve." Indeed, a preliminary analysis carried out by the World Wide Fund for Nature and Terralingua (Oviedo et al. 2000) found that Indigenous peoples and "traditional peoples" inhabit 95 percent of the 238 ecoregions (of a global total of 895 terrestrial ecosystems) that the World Wide Fund for Nature considers critical for global conservation.[20]

The strong correspondence between biological diversity, relatively intact ecosystems, and Indigenous peoples' territories is not likely to be a coincidence. These regions may remain ecologically rich in large part because of the way that Indigenous peoples have lived in them. This is not simply a matter of low population densities or limited technologies. It also reflects the conservation contributions of Indigenous peoples' values and institutions, including their spiritual beliefs, relationships with other life forms, customary laws, collective systems of tenure, and collective management and care of lands, waters, and sacred places. In many cases, the continuing ecological integrity of their homelands testifies as well to their defense of them—on the ground and in government, media, and court—against resource extraction, infrastructure, and other development pressures they have rejected as unwelcome and incompatible with their vision of the future of their peoples and territories.

Exploration of the relationships between cultural diversity and biological diversity is only beginning and remains a challenging area of research. But there are abundant indications that Indigenous peoples' cultural and place-based values, institutions, and practices are a key foundation of biocultural diversity (Nietschmann 1992b; Stevens 1997a; Pretty et al. 2009; Borrini-Feyerabend et al. 2010; Maffi and Woodley 2010). Although skeptics remain, it is now widely affirmed in international conservation discourse that Indigenous peoples make major contributions to global biodiversity, ecosystem health and benefits, and the climatic stability of the planet.[21] Some question whether Indigenous peoples practice "conservation" (particularly when it is narrowly defined as biodiversity preservation for its own sake), suggesting that the richness of biodiversity in their territories is an unintended outcome of factors such as low population density, low-intensity land and marine use with "limited" technologies, and lack of integration with national and global market economies. But there is also much evidence of Indigenous peoples' deliberate protection and sustainable use of natural resources, species, and ecosystems, including through customary law and collective institutions and actions as well as through individual practices based on attitudes and values that foster care and respect for their territories and for other forms of life.

Indigenous peoples' testimonies as well as decades of research in cultural ecology and political ecology, including large bodies of work on socio-ecological systems, traditional ecological knowledge, and commons management (collective management of common property resources), indicate that Indigenous peoples' knowledge, values, institutions, and practices strongly contribute to conservation.[22] Much research has documented the conservation achievements of community forest management (Agrawal and Chhatre 2006; Hayes 2006; Chhatre and Agrawal 2009; Bowler et al. 2010; Persha et al. 2011) and community marine management areas (Johannes 2002; Govan 2009). The conservation significance of the protection of sacred natural sites and sacred natural species now also is better appreciated and documented (Posey 1999; Lee and Schaaf 2003; Wild and McLeod 2008; Verschuuren et al. 2010; for a survey of one hundred pertinent scientific studies in Asia and Africa, see Dudley et al. 2010).

Recent research has also corroborated Indigenous peoples' conservation achievements through comparative analyses of ecological conditions in Indigenous peoples' territories and adjacent protected areas. Studies from Mexico, Guatemala, Brazil, and India report that Indigenous peoples' territories and self-governed protected areas are as well or better conserved than strictly protected, state-governed protected areas.[23] Bray et al. (2008), for example, found that Maya community-managed forests in Mexico and Guatemala were as or more effective than government-administered protected areas in avoiding deforestation (see also Duran et al. 2005; Ellis and Porter-Bolland 2008). Nepstad et al. (2006) concluded that Indigenous reserves in the Brazilian Amazon—then numbering 361 and constituting 20 percent of all of the Brazilian Amazon—were more effective than state protected areas in preventing deforestation and burning, despite being more often situated on the edge of the "arc of deforestation" that marks the advancing colonization and deforestation fronts in the southern Amazon. The extraordinary contrasts in this region between forested Indigenous reserves and deforested areas immediately outside their boundaries are dramatically evident in satellite imagery (see also Stocks et al. 2007 on Nicaragua's Bosawás Biosphere Reserve). A study examining 292 protected areas and Indigenous peoples' lands in the Brazilian Amazon also found that "Indigenous lands appeared particularly effective at curbing high deforestation pressure, relative to both strictly protected and sustainable use areas" and concluded that these territories are "at least as effective [in protecting forests against deforestation] as strictly protected areas at moderate levels of pressure and more effective than any other protection type at high levels of pressure" (Nolte et al. 2013: 4958–4959).

Global analyses of the effectiveness of Indigenous peoples' and local communities' conservation of forests as compared to state protected areas also have found that Indigenous peoples' conserved territories and areas in general are as or more effective than state-administered protected areas. One study (Hayes and Ostrom 2005; Hayes 2006), using standardized data from eleven countries in the Americas, South and Southeast Asia, and East Africa, compared eighty-seven community-managed forests with seventy-six protected areas. This study concluded that the "non-parks" were at least as effective in maintaining vegetation density as protected areas. Nelson and Chomitz (2011), in a study carried out by the World Bank Independent Evaluation Group, found that community-managed forests—and particularly forests controlled and managed by Indigenous peoples in Latin America—were much better protected against deforestation than national parks and other Category I–IV protected areas (see sidebar 1.1 for an explanation of IUCN protected area categories). They concluded (2011: 9) that "in Latin America, where indigenous areas can be identified, they are found to have extremely large impacts on reducing deforestation." Indeed, their data suggest that forests managed by Indigenous peoples are up to six times better protected against deforestation than strictly protected areas, even though Indigenous areas "are disproportionately located in areas of higher deforestation pressure." Porter-Bolland et al. (2012: 9), in a meta-analysis for the Center for International Forestry, reviewed data from seventy-three case studies in sixteen countries (mostly in Latin America) of community forests and strictly protected Category I–IV protected areas and concluded that "community managed forests may be at least as, if not more, effective in reducing deforestation as PAs [protected areas] at the pantropical scale." In a study of eighty-four protected areas in Asia and Africa, Persha et al. (2011) found that community participation in forest governance was associated with higher biodiversity richness.

Although Indigenous peoples' stewardship and conservation of their territories should not be romanticized, recent research strongly challenges long-common assumptions by state officials and international conservationists that Indigenous peoples are threats to protected areas. Indigenous peoples' knowledge, institutions, and practices can no longer be assumed to have no conservation value, and it cannot be taken for granted that their displacement from protected areas or exclusion from participation in protected area governance has scientific legitimacy.

Protected Areas and Indigenous Peoples Territories: Valuing Diversity

A protected area, according to the CBD, is "a geographically defined area which is designated or regulated and managed to achieve specific conservation objectives." In 2008, the IUCN developed a more detailed definition, according to which a protected area is "a clearly defined geographical space, recognized, dedicated and managed, through legal or other effective means, to achieve the long-term conservation of nature with associated ecosystem services and cultural values" (Dudley 2008).[24] These conservation areas span hundreds of different types, among them national parks and forests, wildlife refuges, state parks, NGO-owned and -governed preserves, Indigenous peoples' protected areas, and—depending on how the term protected area is interpreted—community forests and grazing lands, locally managed marine areas, sacred natural sites, entire Indigenous territories, and many other places where the protection of nature or the practice of sustainable livelihoods fosters ecosystem integrity, biodiversity, and other conservation values. As of 2011, there were more than 177,500 nationally designated protected areas worldwide (figure 1.1)

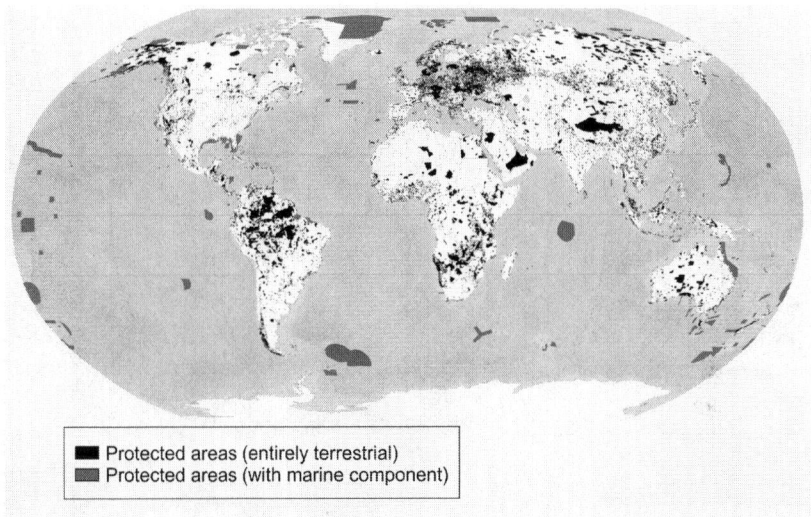

Figure 1.1. The global distribution of the 177,547 nationally designated protected areas in 2012.

that encompass 17 million square kilometers, 12.7 percent of the Earth's land surface and inland waters outside of Antarctica (an area nearly the size of South America), and 1.6 percent of the world's oceans (including 4 percent of waters in national jurisdiction and 7.2 percent of coastal waters) (Bertzky et al. 2012).[25] The number and area of nationally designated protected areas have increased dramatically since 1960 and have continued to grow strikingly since 1990, when only 8.8 percent of the Earth's terrestrial area was in protected areas (figures 1.2 and 1.3).[26]

Protected areas are foundations of global conservation and sustainability efforts.[27] Both the CBD and IUCN have made protected areas central to their programs. One of the oldest IUCN commissions (today the World Commission on Protected Areas, WCPA) focuses on protected areas, and the programs of several others also engage with them. Protected area policies are elaborated through the IUCN WCC resolutions, the recommendations of the IUCN's decennial World Parks Congresses (WPCs), action plans, IUCN guideline volumes, and other means (chapter 2). The CBD similarly has emphasized protected areas, focusing on them from its outset as the primary site of its *in situ* conservation efforts. CBD protected area policies are adopted through decisions of the state Parties; a Programme of Work on Protected Areas (PoWPA) was adopted in an annex to a 2004 decision (Conference of the Parties to the CBD 2004a, 2004b). Major

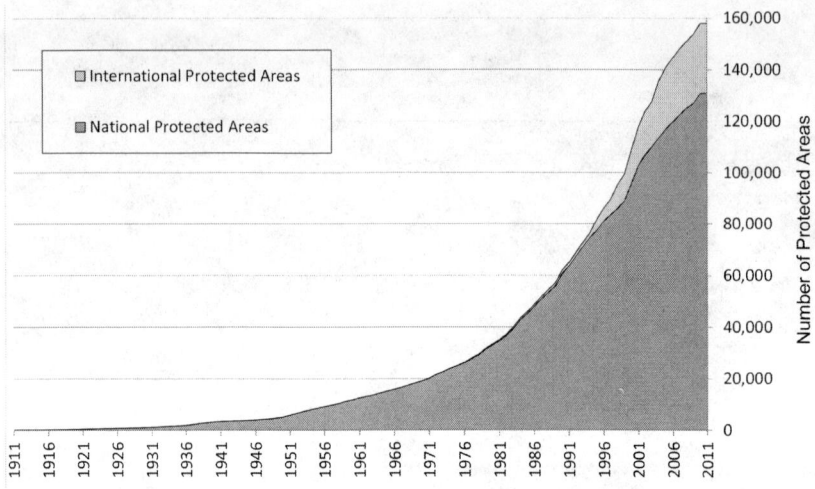

Figure 1.2. Changes in the number of protected areas from 1911 to 2011.

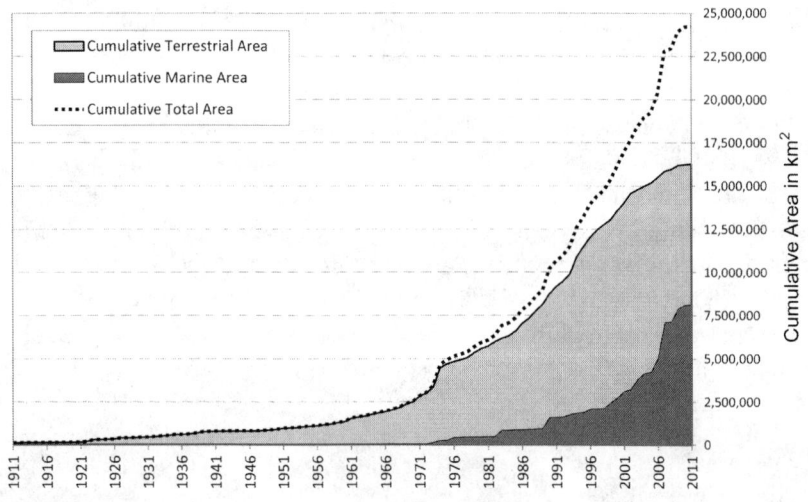

Figure 1.3. Changes in the area of protected areas from 1911 to 2011.

international funding is devoted to expanding and improving national protected area networks, in part because the Global Environment Facility (GEF) is directed to do so by the Parties to the CBD, for which it functions as the main financial implementation mechanism. Since 1991, about 60 percent of GEF biodiversity conservation funding has supported protected areas, with GEF investing $2.2 billion in protected areas and leveraging another $7.35 billion in cofinancing. This has supported 324 protected area projects (Executive Secretary of the CBD 2012), funding the establishment or management of 2400 protected areas covering 6.3 million square kilometers. The World Bank spends $275 million per year on protected areas, including $100 million of its own funds, $60 million from GEF, and $115 million in cofinancing.[28] The UN Development Programme used $456 million in GEF funds and $1.4 billion in cofinancing in support of 147 protected area projects in more than one hundred countries between 2003 and 2012, while the UN Environment Programme (UNEP) has channeled another $135 million in GEF funds to protected areas since 2006. Major investments are also made by states, including through bilateral aid, and by international conservation organizations. As of 2007, total global investment in protected areas was between $7.5 billion and $12.1 billion per year, with an estimated $1 billion to $2 billion of this from Indigenous peoples and local communities (Bertzky et al. 2012).

Not long ago, the IUCN had a narrow conception of the governance and goals of protected areas. Until the 1970s it recognized only uninhabited "national parks and equivalent reserves," and until 1994 it maintained that only the central governments of countries should establish and govern protected areas. The concept of national park adopted by the IUCN (1969) at its Tenth General Assembly in 1969 in New Delhi defined them as places "where one or several ecosystems are not materially altered by human exploitation and occupation" and "where the highest competent authority of the country has taken steps to prevent or eliminate as soon as possible exploitation or occupation in the whole area." This excluded many existing national parks, including the national park system of England and Wales. Since the 1970s, however, the IUCN has dramatically revised its perspectives on both appropriate protected area goals and governance. For forty years, it has valued not only national parks but also diverse other kinds of conservation areas with varying goals. Indeed, the IUCN deliberately adopted the term "protected area" in the 1970s to counter overemphasis on national parks. Since 1994, the IUCN has also validated diverse forms of protected area governance.[29]

The IUCN now recognizes six protected area management categories (see sidebar 1.1). These categories vary considerably in their goals and policies, ranging from the more strictly preserved Category I–IV protected areas, which place considerable restrictions on settlement and land and marine use, to the protected landscapes and seascapes (Category V) and areas dedicated to sustainable use (Category VI), which recognize the conservation importance of many societies' customary relationships with nature and sustainable use of natural resources. Indigenous peoples' settlement and land use can be compatible with the management goals of protected areas of all categories (IUCN CNPPA 1994; Stevens 1997a; Dudley 2008). Category V and VI protected areas accounted for 49 percent of the total global extent of protected areas for those protected areas for which management category data were available in 2010.[30] Globally, there was a greater area in Category VI protected areas (32 percent), which are dedicated to sustainable use of natural resources, than in Category II national parks (27 percent) (Bertzky et al. 2012).

The IUCN and the CBD further recognize four types of protected area governance arrangements, all of which they consider to be equally legitimate. Besides governance by governments of all types (Type A), protected areas can also be governed by private individuals and NGOs (Type C), by Indigenous peoples and local communities as forms of Indigenous Peoples' and Community Conserved Territories and Areas (ICCAs) or Community Conserved Areas (Type D), and through several kinds of shared governance arrangements (Type B). Governance Type D identifies two forms of protected areas: ICCAs governed by Indigenous peoples and Community Conserved Areas governed by local communities (these are collectively referred to in international conservation circles as ICCAs).[31]

Figure 1.4 illustrates how some of the protected areas discussed in this book would be situated in the IUCN matrix of management categories and governance types. They cover a greater range of management and governance types than is typical of most countries' national protected area systems. As the matrix makes clear, the IUCN and the CBD emphasize that all of the four governance arrangements can appropriately administer protected areas from the full range of management categories. Indigenous peoples may thus appropriately govern or cogovern not only Category V and VI protected areas, which allow for higher levels of human habitation and use, but also Category I strict nature reserves and wilderness areas (such as highly protected sacred natural sites), Category II and III national parks and monuments, and Category IV wildlife reserves.

Indigenous Peoples, Biocultural Diversity, and Protected Areas • 31

Governance types / Protected area categories	A. Governance by government	B. Shared governance	C. Private governance	D. Governance by Indigenous peoples and local communities
I a. Strict Nature Reserve				
Ib. Wilderness Area				9, 10
II. National Park	1, 2	4, 5		8, 9, 10
III. Natural Monument				8, 9, 10
IV. Habitat/Species Management		6		8, 9, 10
V. Protected Landscape/Seascape	3			8, 9, 10
VI. Protected Area with Sustainable Use of Natural Resources		7		8, 9, 10

1 Sagarmatha National Park and other high Himayalan national parks (Nepal)
2 Glacier Bay National Park (Alaska)
3 Klondike Gold Rush International Historical Park (Alaska and Yukon Territory, Canada)
4 Kluane National Park Reserve, Gwaii Haanas National Park Reserve, and other northern national park reserves (Canada)
5 Kruger National Park and Dwesa-Cwebe Nature Reserves (South Africa)
6 Los Altos de San Miguel Regional Municipal Park (Guatemala)
7 Ashaninka Communal Reserve (Peru)
8 Indigenous Protected Areas (Australia)
9 Tribal parks, USA and Canada, including Mission Mountains Tribal Wilderness, Sinkyone Inter-Tribal Wilderness, Tla-o-quiaht First Nation tribal parks
10 ICCAs overlapping with or within Nepal national parks

Figure 1.4. IUCN protected area matrix. Categories and governance types are estimated for some protected areas.

The number of protected areas governed or cogoverned by Indigenous peoples has increased markedly over the past twenty years, although precise figures are not available. The World Database on Protected Areas (WDPA) has governance-type data on only 51 percent of nationally recognized protected areas, and many other areas meet IUCN and CBD definitions of protected areas without yet having been nationally recognized as such. According to available data, the percentage of the total global area in protected areas governed by Indigenous peoples and local communities increased from 3.8 to 9.3 percent between 1990 and 2010, while protected areas with shared governance increased from 0.1 to 13.5 percent. The WDPA, maintained by the IUCN's World Commission on Protected Areas and UNEP's World Conservation Monitoring Centre, now includes some 700 ICCAs encompassing 1.1 million square kilometers, but this is considered "likely to represent only a fraction of the total area of these types of sites" (Bertzky et al. 2012: 32).

Sidebar 1.1. IUCN Protected Area Management Categories and Governance Types

Management Categories

Ia. Strict nature reserve: Strictly protected for biodiversity and possibly geological/geomorphological features, where human visitation, use, and impacts are controlled and limited to ensure protection of the conservation values.

Ib. Wilderness area: Usually large unmodified or slightly modified areas, retaining their natural character and influence, without permanent or significant human habitation, protected and managed to preserve their natural condition.

II. National park: Large natural or near-natural areas protecting large-scale ecological processes with characteristic species and ecosystems, which also have environmentally and culturally compatible spiritual, scientific, educational, recreational and visitor opportunities.

III. Natural monument or feature: Areas set aside to protect a specific natural monument, which can be a landform, sea mount, marine cavern, geological feature such as a cave, or a living feature such as an ancient grove.

IV. Habitat/species management area: Areas [dedicated] to protect particular species or habitats, where management reflects this priority. Many will need regular, active interventions to meet the needs of particular species or habitats, but this is not a requirement of the category.

V. Protected landscape or seascape: [Areas] where the interaction of people and nature over time has produced a distinct character with significant ecological, biological, cultural, and scenic value, and where safeguarding the integrity of this interaction is vital to protecting and sustaining the area and its associated nature conservation and other values.

VI. Protected area with sustainable use of natural resources (managed resource protected area): Areas which conserve ecosystems, together with associated cultural values and traditional natural resource management systems.

> Generally large, mainly in a natural condition, with a proportion under sustainable natural resource management and where low-level nonindustrial natural resource use compatible with nature conservation is seen as one of the main aims.
>
> ### Governance Types
> A. Governance by government: Federal or national ministry/agency in charge; subnational ministry/agency in charge; government-delegated management (for example, to an NGO).
> B. Shared governance: Collaborative management (various degrees of influence), joint management (pluralist management board), and transboundary management (various levels across international borders).
> C. Private governance: By individual owner, non-profit organizations (NGOs, universities, cooperatives), and for-profit organizations (individuals or corporate).
> D. Governance by Indigenous peoples and local communities: Indigenous peoples' conserved areas and territories, community conserved areas [that are] declared and run by local communities.
>
> Source: Borrini-Feyerabend et al. (2013).

Protected Areas and the Territories of Indigenous Peoples: Convergent Geographies

A large number of nationally designated protected areas in all management categories and governance types—and likely most of their total global area—are in the customary territories of Indigenous peoples.[32] As Nigel Dudley (2008: 30) observed in the IUCN's *Guidelines for Applying Protected Area Management Categories*, "Especially in regions such as Latin America, North America, Oceania, Africa, Asia, and the Arctic, many formally designated protected areas are at the same time the ancestral lands and waters of indigenous peoples, cultures and communities." A publication by the Global Environment Facility has referred to this as a "remarkable spatial convergence" (Watanabe 2008: 9).

This pattern of spatial convergence is striking in the Americas. In Central America the overlap between protected areas and Indigenous lands may exceed 90 percent (Herlihy 1997; Negi and Nautiyal 2003; Colchester 2004). South America's national parks are a similar story: an early 1990s study found that 86 percent of 158 national parks were inhabited

(Amend and Amend 1995). Data on the overlap of national parks and other protected areas with Indigenous peoples' territories are available for some countries. About half of Colombia's fifty-six national parks, for example, overlap with Indigenous peoples' reserves (*resguardos indígenes*) or those of Afro-Colombian communities (these Indigenous reserves encompass 34 million hectares, nearly 30 percent of the total area of Colombia) (Riascos et al. 2008; Borrini-Feyerabend et al. 2010; Kothari et al. 2012). Extensive areas of Bolivia's protected areas overlap with recognized or prospective Tierras Comunitarias de Origen (since 2009 referred to as Territorios Indigena Originario Campesinos); fourteen of the first forty-four titled Tierras Comunitarias de Origen overlap with protected areas, and thirty overlap with protected area buffer zones (Borrini-Feyerabend et al. 2010). Unofficial estimates put the overlap of protected areas and Indigenous peoples' territories in Chile as high as 90 percent, although official numbers suggest this is the case for only eighteen of Chile's ninety-four protected areas (Kothari et al. 2012: 52). As of 2005 in the Brazil Amazon, where 361 Indigenous reserves encompassed a full 20 percent of the region—more than five times the area then in state-declared protected areas—five national parks, sixteen national forests, two biological reserves, and an ecological station overlapped entirely or partly with Indigenous peoples' territories that totaled nearly 110,000 square kilometers (Nepstad et al. 2006; Rylands et al. 2008).

In both Canada and the United States, a high percentage of protected areas, including national parks, are situated in Indigenous peoples' customary territories. In Canada much of the present extensive national parks system is established in the customary territories of First Nations, Inuit, and Métis (Deardon and Langdon 2009). As of 2010, a full 68 percent of the lands in Parks Canada administration were associated with formal agreements with these peoples (Langdon et al. 2010). The crown jewels of the U.S. national parks system, including Yellowstone, Yosemite, Glacier, and Grand Canyon, are all customary Indigenous territories. So, too, are the Alaskan national parks (which constitute two-thirds of the total area in the U.S. national park system) and the protected areas of Hawai'i (Keller and Turek 1998; Spence 1999).

Overlap is also strong in Australia, New Zealand, and Oceania. All of Australia's protected areas are established in the customary territories of Aboriginal and Torres Strait Islander peoples. Sixty Indigenous Protected Areas (2013) comprise more than a third of the total area in the national reserve system, and many national parks, including Kakadu National Park and World Heritage Site (Australia's largest national park) and Uluru-Kata Tjuta National Park and World Heritage Site, are largely or entirely on lands whose Aboriginal ownership was recognized in the 1970s and 1980s (chapter 3; De Lacy and Lawson 1997; Australian Government, Department of Environment n.d.). Papua New Guinea's thirty wildlife management areas, which constitute 84 percent of the extent of the national protected area system, are all Indigenous peoples' territories (Eaton 1997; Department of Environment and Conservation 2010). Many marine protected areas in Pacific Island countries overlap with Indigenous peoples' territories (Govan 2009; Leenhardt et al. 2013), and New Zealand's national parks overlap the customary territories of Māori *iwi* (tribes) (Ruru 2008).

Data are lacking for many countries of Asia and Africa, but overlap appears to be strong in several countries. In Asia, for example, almost all of India's protected areas include territories of *adivasi* (Indigenous peoples) or other local communities; all of Nepal's national parks overlap with the customary territories of Indigenous peoples; and sixty-nine of ninety-nine protected areas in the Philippines, a total area of nearly 1 million hectares, overlap with Indigenous peoples' ancestral domains (chapter 11; Kothari et al. 2012). Kenya, Tanzania, Botswana, Namibia, and South Africa are among the African countries in which large parts of the protected area systems overlap with Indigenous peoples' customary territories.

The importance of Indigenous lands to the global protected area system, moreover, is likely to increase as conservation organizations and governments concentrate efforts to expand protected area systems in priority global eco-regions. A high percentage of these are inhabited by Indigenous peoples. Extensive areas are legally recognized as Indigenous reserves or other collective lands, and others are subject to title claim. Ceded areas may still be subject to reserved treaty rights, and Indigenous peoples retain rights throughout their customary territories under provisions of UNDRIP and ILO 169. Moreover, while not all Indigenous peoples' territories may currently meet international criteria for recognition as protected areas, many do. Indigenous peoples' territories, including protected areas established in them with their participation and consent and governed by or with them, may prove to be vital to achieving more comprehensive coverage of threatened ecosystems in national protected area systems as well as establishing larger conservation landscapes that create conservation connectivity among multiple protected areas and their surroundings (chapter 7).

Old Paradigm Legacies

It was long widely assumed in international conservation circles that protected areas should be declared and administered by states as uninhabited wilderness preserves. This distinctive form of protected areas, often called the "Yellowstone model" because of its development in U.S. national parks during the nineteenth and early twentieth centuries (Stevens 1997a), is also referred to as the "protection" paradigm or the "old" paradigm. Although it was never universal—the national parks of England and Wales and the regional parks of France, for example, both celebrate rural cultural landscapes and traditional livelihood practices—the old paradigm has influenced the protected area laws, policies, and practices of many countries.

Such protected areas are based on four key assumptions: (1) protected areas should be created and governed by states; (2) the goal of protected areas should be strict nature preservation and particularly biodiversity conservation; (3) effective protected area management requires protected areas to be uninhabited and without any human use of natural resources, because Indigenous peoples and local communities are threats to the objectives of protected areas; and (4) coercive force is legally and morally justified to remove resident peoples and protect biodiversity. Because of its frequent association with militarized defense of protected area borders and ecosystems, the old paradigm is often referred to as "fortress conservation" (Brockington 2002) and as conservation through "command and control" and "fences and fines."[33]

Protected areas based on these principles have been established in vast areas worldwide, and include most national parks, national forests, wilderness areas, and wildlife reserves.[34] These assumptions have strongly shaped the character of both the U.S. national park and national forest systems since their origins (Keller and Turek 1998; Spence 1999). Although the U.S. National Park Service began to change its relationships and interactions with Indigenous peoples in positive ways in the 1970s, old paradigm principles continue to dominate U.S. protected area management.[35] The colonial European creation of uninhabited, state-governed colonial national parks and game reserves in Africa and Asia in the late nineteenth and early twentieth centuries reflected similar assumptions (see, for example, Anderson and Grove 1987; Neumann 1998; Adams and Mulligan 2003), and to a striking degree they also have characterized postcolonial conservation in many former colonies. Historically many protected areas in Canada, Australia, and New Zealand have embodied the old paradigm, although in recent decades they have also been sites of experimentation with other approaches (chapters 2 and 3; Stevens 1997a). The vast system of protected areas developed by the Soviet Union adopted similarly exclusionary policies (Pryde 1991; Weiner 2002).

The old paradigm requires the construction of uninhabited wilderness, often in places that have been the homelands of Indigenous peoples for centuries or millennia. This has created what Mark Spence (1999) called in the U.S. context "wilderness by dispossession," achieved by evicting Indigenous peoples or through their voluntary (or induced) relocation (Lasgorceix and Kothari 2009). Although a full accounting may never be possible due to lack of accurate records, there is abundant evidence that large numbers of people have been dispossessed. Estimates of the number that may have been displaced worldwide run into the tens of millions (West and Brechin 1991; Geisler and de Sousa 2000; Geisler 2002, 2003a, 2003b; Cernea and Schmidt-Soltau 2005; Brockington and Igoe 2006; Brockington et al. 2008; Agrawal and Redford 2009; Dowie 2009).[36] In a review of a small number of protected areas in ten African countries, Geisler and de Sousa (2000) found that half a million people have reportedly been displaced from fourteen protected areas alone.

It appears that most people displaced by protected areas have been involuntarily displaced without compensation or provision for their resettlement, creating a new kind of "conservation refugee."[37] Others who accepted offers of relocation have not been satisfied with the sites or terms. Some supposedly voluntary relocations, on closer inspection, prove to have been induced by threats or by false promises (Lasgorceix and Kothari 2009). Many people have been violently evicted with no compensation or relocation arrangements. Widespread coercive displacement contributes to the assessment that "the vast majority of these protected areas have been established and/or managed in violation of indigenous peoples' rights" (MacKay 2011: 33).

Most attention focuses on displacement as physical removal, and particularly on coercive displacement. Increasing attention is being devoted to economic displacement (Cernea 2006), including opportunity costs as well as impoverishment as a result of restricted access to natural resources and other exclusion. Cultural and political marginalization can also be displacement in the sense of lost connection with place and diminished authority and responsibility for territories, lands, and waters (table 1.1). Many Indigenous peoples have been culturally displaced by being prevented from caring for and interacting with cultural sites or maintaining cultural activities. In some African cases, evicted peoples have been

Table 1.1. Forms of protected area displacement and marginalization

Type	Characteristics
Spatial/physical	Forced or induced relocation; continued residence made conditional to compliance with imposed restrictions on settlement, transhumance, and migration; lack of recognition of customary territories, including collective tenure and usufruct rights
Economic	Imposed restrictions or bans on land and marine use or specific practices; loss of livelihoods and livelihood security; loss of food security; loss of access to shelter, water, and other rights; opportunity costs from foreclosed avenues of development; lack of benefits from protected area revenues or employment
Political	Loss of territorial control and self-governance; lack of recognition of customary governance and resource management institutions and practices; loss of governance authority for commons management; loss of stewardship authority for cultural sites
Cultural	Loss of shared life in homelands; loss of responsibility for the care of homelands; loss of access to and care for cultural sites and cultural resources; cultural and religious sites desecrated or untended; lack of recognition of territory and tenure; and lack of respect for customary law, customary institutions, customary livelihoods, and other cultural practices

prevented even from visiting family and ancestral burial sites or risk being shot on sight as poachers for doing so (Dowie 2009; Amend et al. 2008). Indigenous peoples have been politically displaced by being deprived of self-governance and decision-making authority in their territories even when they have not been physically relocated.

These impacts often reflect assumptions both about the necessity of establishing uninhabited protected areas and states' and conservationists' legal and moral authority to impose them in Indigenous peoples' territories. As Colchester (2003: 4) observed, "Conservationists have fought shy of admitting the underlying reason that the classical approach to protected area management has failed. For the choice that they have made is to impose their vision, their priorities and their values of landscape, nature and society on other peoples, securing their endeavours through the power of the State and its right of eminent domain. Almost by definition, therefore, conventional protected areas have been at odds with indigenous peoples' rights to self-determination and territorial control." Biodiversity conservation based on protected areas declared and governed by states, moreover, often is entangled with Fourth World interethnic and political dynamics. The establishment of protected areas can be a justification (with international legitimacy and funding) for "frontier" pacification of Indigenous peoples and expropriation of their territories. Protected areas can thus constitute a form of state territorialization from the standpoints both of the physical expropriation of land and the extension of state administrative control over formerly autonomous territory and peoples (Nietschmann 1994; Vandergeest and Peluso 1995; Bryant and Bailey 1997; Scott 1998; Peluso and Vandergeest 2001; Neumann 2004). Protected areas, like other forms of territorialization, impose new laws, new forms of surveillance and control, and new institutions. In establishing new forms of governance, they can also create forms of frontier governmentality that seek to induce Indigenous peoples to adopt new values and behaviors (Neumann 2004; Agrawal 2005).[38] In this sense, protected areas become a vehicle of coercive assimilation, a core component of what the state represents as a "civilizing mission" (Neumann 2004). Protected areas established and governed in these ways can be viewed as imperialism by Indigenous peoples who experience them as subjugation and loss of lands, resources, and self-governance rationalized through ecological as well as ethnocentric and racializing discourses that exoticize, distance, and demonize Indigenous peoples as profoundly "Other" and inferior (Said 1979, 1993).

Exclusionary wilderness preserves also can be conceptualized as a prominent form of "green grabbing" (Fairhead et al. 2012) or as a new kind of conservation enclosure movement (*The Ecologist* 1993; Bryant and Baily 1997; Neumann 2004) through which the state excludes Indigenous peoples from their territorial commons in the name of conservation. This has often been facilitated by representing Indigenous peoples' homelands as wilderness rather than as cultural landscapes, a discursive erasure of those peoples' existence and histories that makes their territories *terra nullius* from the state's perspective and legitimizes its unilateral declaration of them as strictly preserved protected areas (Langton 1998, 2012).

Another way of thinking about the process of the establishment of exclusionary, state-administered protected areas is as "modernism" or as "high modernism" (Neumann 2004). Modernism here is used in the sense of being assumed to be intrinsic to states' civilizing, social welfare and development missions by separating the wild from the human (Peet and Watts 2004) and "high modernism" in the sense of constituting a grandiose social and environmental engineering project that has had catastrophic environmental and human consequences because of ignoring local conditions, concerns, and rights (Scott 1998).[39]

Conservation's entwinement with national political projects of subjugating Indigenous peoples and expropriating their territory has resulted in many protected areas being established, governed, and managed within Fourth World contexts. Extreme interethnic power inequities, long-standing ethnocentrism and racism, and prejudices about "conservation" and the assumed threats to it posed by Indigenous peoples and local communities may account for why the process of creating protected areas has so often been carried out with such coercion and violence and with so little regard for human, Indigenous, and civil rights, international rights treaties, or IUCN and CBD protected area standards.

Notes

1. Intellectual, social, and political controversies continue over the concept and legal status of "Indigenous peoples." Critiques of the concept and its use have highlighted ambiguities, difficulties in identifying peoples and territories given complex histories and social dynamics, issues of essentialism and strategic essentialism, allegedly opportunistic claims to rights and benefits, and injustices created when even poorer and more marginalized and oppressed groups are neglected (Li 2000, 2005; Kuper 2003; Brockington et al. 2008). For discussion of the development of current conceptual and legal characterizations of Indigenous peoples, see Niezen (2003), Anaya (2004, 2009a), and UN Department of Economic and Social Affairs (2009).

2. The total number of Indigenous peoples and their cumulative population would increase considerably if more peoples in Africa and Asia begin to self-identify as Indigenous peoples.

3. The total extent of Indigenous peoples' customary terrestrial and marine territories is much greater, but no global accounting has yet been undertaken.

4. Indigenous peoples have resisted a definition because of their concerns that this could be applied unjustly to exclude some peoples from due recognition (Niezen 2003). International human rights treaties, including the International Covenant on Civil and Political Rights and the International Covenant on Economic, Social, and Cultural Rights, similarly do not define "peoples."

5. These draw on earlier characterizations of Indigenous peoples such as those developed by Jose Martino Cobo, Special Rapporteur of the Sub-Commission on Prevention of Discrimination and Protection of Minorities, and the one incorporated into International Labor Organization Convention 169 (1989). As has been widely noted, however, these early characterizations do not encompass the full diversity of situations and contexts of peoples worldwide who identify as Indigenous peoples (Niezen 2003; Anaya 2004; Langton et al. 2005).

6. In this book, in accordance with common use, the term "national" will often signify country-level institutions. "Nation" and "national," however, will also be used in the earlier meaning of these words to refer to peoples, as in Indigenous nations.

7. Although it is useful to characterize states in broad socio-economic and political terms, it is important to recognize that they are not homogenous entities (Bryant and Bailey 1997). Oversimplified representations and structural determinism can overlook important spaces and opportunities for alternative interactions and reform. This applies not only to "the state" as a whole but also to particular government agencies such as those concerned with protected areas.

8. State expropriation of these lands is rationalized by the "doctrine of discovery," which in effect holds that unowned lands (and lands not considered by states to be "properly" owned) can be discovered, claimed, and nationalized by the state. This discourse was used to justify European and U.S. colonialism and internal colonialism in former centuries. It also underlies recent nationalization of vast areas of Indigenous peoples' territories in postcolonial states in the global South.

9. For further discussion of debates about conceptions of sovereignty and Indigenous sovereignty, see chapter 6, Niezen (2003), and Anaya (2004).

10. Contesting state cartographies through "counter-mapping" (Peluso 1995) has become an important decolonization strategy employed by many Indigenous peoples and supportive NGOs (Brosius et al. 2005; Chapin et al. 2005). Much use has been made of participatory mapping, Geographic Information System (GIS), and 3-D modeling in struggles to regain territorial control, state recognition of collective land tenure, and rights to livelihood and cultural resources and management in situations of imposed protected areas, including the Kayan Mentarang National Park in Indonesia (Eghenter 2000), Bosawás Biosphere Reserve in Nicaragua (Stocks 2003), and the Campo Ma'an National Park in Cameroon (Oyono et al. 2010). Indigenous peoples have also used participatory mapping in establishing their own protected areas, including the Guna Nusagandi forest park in Panama (Chapin 1998), the Tawahka Biosphere Reserve in Honduras (Herlihy 1997), the Miskito Community Protected Territory in Nicaragua (Nietschmann 1995, 1997), and the proposed Wapichan Conserved Forest in Guyana (Forest Peoples Programme 2012).

11. On state expropriation of Indigenous peoples' territories and natural resources, and its association with economic globalization, prevailing conceptions of "development," "resource colonialism," and nation-state integration, see Nietschmann (1986, 1994), Gedicks (1999, 2001), Blaser et al. (2004), Mander and Tauli-Corpuz (2006), Bodley (2008), and UN Department of Economic and Social Affairs (2009).

12. These were the only countries that voted against UNDRIP (eleven abstained). All four have since announced their support, although sometimes with important qualifications.

13. Critics charge, however, that the rights recognized in UNDRIP are insufficient, in part because they affirm state sovereignty and frame the rights of Indigenous peoples within the context of state citizenship (Champagne 2013).

14. Indigenous peoples have had to engage in a prolonged struggle to gain recognition of their status as peoples. This struggle continues in many countries and in some international circles, as attested, for example, by the continuing use of the phrase "indigenous and local communities" by the CBD.

15. UN Special Rapporteurs on the Rights of Indigenous Peoples (prior to 2010 known as the UN Special Rapporteur on the Situation of Human Rights and Fundamental Freedoms of Indigenous Peoples) have highlighted violations of rights in

protected areas in a number of their country reports. The committee monitoring implementation of the Convention on the Elimination of All Forms of Racial Discrimination has also provided guidance on protected area and rights issues, as have regional human rights commissions and courts in the Americas and Asia (Morel 2010; MacKay 2011).

16. Darrell Posey and Graham Dutfield (1996) similarly grouped diverse bundles of rights into what they called "traditional resource rights."

17. Pluri-national states are those that value the diversity of nations (peoples with territories) within their borders, rather than attempting to coercively construct a unitary, single "nationality" nation-state.

18. Research on cultural diversity has focused on language as a proxy for culture and a key means of intergenerational transmission of locally grounded knowledge (Harmon 1996; Maffi 1998; Maffi and Woodley 2010). Recent research (Gorenflo et al. 2012) examining the co-occurrence of linguistic and biological diversity found that 70 percent of world languages (4,800 of 6,900) are Indigenous languages and localized "non-migrant" languages that are found in five high biodiversity wilderness areas and the Earth's thirty-five biodiversity hotspots, which comprise 6.1 percent and 2.3 percent of the world's land area, respectively, and are the sites of 19,000 protected areas.

19. The cultural landscape character of many supposed "natural" or "wilderness" landscapes has been understood for decades (Gomez-Pompa and Kaus 1992) and led the IUCN to reconceptualize its understanding of "natural" ecosystems and landscapes (Stevens 1997a; Dudley 2008). An effort to identify and map the world's "last wildernesses" by Conservation International (Mittermeir et al. 2003) chose not to define wilderness as a place without human use, but rather emphasized rich biodiversity, healthy ecosystems, and relatively light human habitation. Conservation International identified thirty-seven wilderness regions worldwide that met criteria that included an area of 10,000 or more square kilometers, land cover of 70 percent or more "original vegetation," and fewer than five people per square kilometer. From this perspective, wilderness continues to be found across fully 39 percent of the world's land surface. A high percentage of the wilderness areas outside of Antarctica and the interior of Greenland proved to be situated in Indigenous peoples' territories.

20. According to the World Wide Fund for Nature (Oviedo et al. 2000: 1), an ecoregion is a "large unit of land or water containing a geographically distinct assemblage of species, natural communities, and environmental conditions."

21. Skepticism by some government officials, protected area administrators, and conservation scientists about the effectiveness and long-term sustainability of conservation by Indigenous peoples is matched by many Indigenous peoples' skepticism about the effectiveness and long-term sustainability of conservation by most states and non-Indigenous peoples.

22. See Berkes (2008) for an introduction to the rich literature on socio-ecological systems and traditional ecological knowledge; Blaikie and Brookfield (1987), McCay and Atkinson (1990), and Ostrom (1990; Ostrom et al. 2002) for influential early work on collective governance and management of commons that contested Garrett Hardin's overly simplistic "tragedy of the commons" hypothesis; and Posey (1999), Lee and Schaaf (2003); Schaaf and Lee (2006), Wild and McLeod (2008), Verschuuren et al. (2010), and Pungetti et al. (2012) on sacred natural sites, conservation, and protected areas.

23. There are, however, significant limitations to such global analyses. Generalization can be problematic given the complexity of individual cases and issues of data availability, reliability, and comparability.

24. There is disagreement within the IUCN about aspects of the interpretation of the new definition. Some hold that "conservation of nature" should be taken to refer primarily or exclusively to biodiversity conservation, and interpret the phrase "recognized, dedicated, and managed" to mean that biodiversity preservation must be the explicit, preeminent management goal of all protected areas, a position adopted in the IUCN's 2008 *Guidelines for Applying Protected Area Management Categories* (Dudley 2008). Others argue that this is an overly narrow conceptualization, alien to many peoples, which ethnocentrically privileges certain cultural conceptions ("ecosystems," "biodiversity"), unnecessarily devalues other aspects of conservation, and disregards long-standing understandings that "conservation" includes environmentally sensitive, sustainable management and use of natural resources. (A conception of conservation as sustainable use, for example, guided early U.S. national forest management and was integral to the IUCN's [1980] representation of conservation as preservation, sustainable use, and ecological restoration in its *World Conservation Strategy*.) Many existing protected areas worldwide would not meet the narrow conceptualization of conservation advanced in the 2008 IUCN guidelines. Many national parks, for example, including most of those in the United States and the United Kingdom, were established to protect scenery, geological wonders, historical sites, and areas valued for recreation and tourism rather than to preserve biodiversity, as is evident in their enabling legislation and management histories. Nor was biodiversity conservation the explicit, predominate goal of the establishment of most U.S. wilderness areas.

25. There are also internationally designated protected areas such as World Heritage sites, Ramsar sites, and European Natura 2000 sites. Many, but not all of these, overlap with nationally designated protected areas.

26. On the globalization of conservation and conservation territories, including protected areas and conservation corridors such as the Mesoamerican Biological Corridor (chapter 8), see Zimmerer (2006b), Brockington et al. (2008), Chape et al. (2008), and Bertzky et al. (2012) for recent analyses of protected area geography and history.

27. It is recognized, however, that protected areas alone are not sufficient to secure global biodiversity protection and ecosystem services. They must be set within larger conservation landscapes, regional planning, and national environmental law and regulation. Achieving better global biodiversity protection and sustainability will also likely require major political and economic change together with changes in individual consciousness, lifestyles, and daily practices.

28. GEF has a responsibility to finance the implementation of the CBD, which has placed a high priority on protected areas and their effective management. It is notable, however, that relatively few GEF projects have promoted the goals of Element 2 of the CBD's PoWPA (see chapter 2), which emphasize equity, Indigenous peoples' participation in protected area governance, and recognition of diverse protected area governance arrangements (Executive Secretary of the CBD 2012: figures 7 and 8). World Bank investment in protected areas may seem out of character for an organization often criticized for funding environmentally destructive projects. Its interest in protected areas may reflect appreciation of the role of protected areas in sustainable development, including sustaining ecosystem services and "natural capital," as well

as a possible effort to "green" the World Bank's image. The World Bank's interest in protected area, land titling, and regional planning and zoning programs, however, may also be tied to promoting infrastructure and extractive development by clarifying which "frontier" areas will be recognized as Indigenous peoples' territories, which will become protected areas, and which will be open for investment and development with fewer restrictions (see chapter 7).

29. The expanded conceptualization of "protected areas" between the early 1970s and early 1990s also demanded a reconceptualization of conservation history. Clearly that history extends far before the establishment of Yellowstone National Park in 1872 or the 1864 protection of Yosemite Valley and the Mariposa sequoia grove by the U.S. federal government and the state of California (Stevens 1997a; Brockington et al. 2008).

30. The WDPA has management category data for only 75 percent of the protected areas in the database.

31. The IUCN first adopted the term "Community Conserved Areas" in 2003. In 2008 it changed this to Indigenous Peoples' and Community Conserved Areas (ICCAs) in response to the wishes of Indigenous peoples, and in 2012 adopted the wording Indigenous Peoples' and Community Conserved Territories and Areas while retaining the abbreviation ICCA. ICCAs also are often referred to as "Indigenous and Community Conserved Areas," including by the CBD.

32. Colchester (1999: 12) estimated that "as many as three quarters of all protected areas overlap indigenous territories," and in 2003 the Indigenous Peoples Ad Hoc Working Group for the World Parks Congress (2003b: 1) observed that "a majority of these protected areas overlap lands owned or claimed by indigenous peoples" and raised the concern that "most of these have been established without indigenous peoples' consent." Sobrevila (2008: 7) similarly reported that "it has been estimated that as much as 85 percent of the world's protected areas are inhabited by Indigenous Peoples." In recent years, however, a large number of European protected areas have been added to the WDPA, and this has decreased the total global percentage of protected areas that overlap with Indigenous peoples territories. As of 2011, a total of 102,084 protected areas, 63 percent of all protected areas globally, were in Europe.

33. The term "fortress conservation" (Blaikie and Jeanrenaud 1997; Brockington 2002) is now in wide circulation to refer to militaristic surveillance and defense of protected areas.

34. The assumption at the core of the old paradigm—that the state and elites can legitimately expropriate territory, claim sole governance authority over it, ignore prior ownership and prior rights held by Indigenous peoples and local communities, and exclude customary use and management—is very old indeed. State game reserves, forests, elephant reserves, and other protected areas far predate the invention of national parks and can be traced back a millennia in Europe, more than two millennia in India and China, and may have been invented in present Iraq more than four millennia ago (Blaikie and Jeanrenaud 1997; Holdgate 1999; Phillips 2003; Stevens 2007; Brockington et al. 2008; Chape et al. 2008). On the global history of the old protected area paradigm, see West and Brechin (1991), Ghimire and Pimbert (1997), Stevens (1997a, 2007), Wilshusen et al. (2002), Brechin et al. (2003a), and Hutton et al. (2005). On displacement and marginalization of Indigenous peoples by national forests, see, for example, Guha (1989), Peluso (1992), and Bryant and Bailey (1997).

35. The governance and management of U.S. national parks and other protected areas continue to fall far short of the new paradigm standards adopted by the IUCN and the Parties to the CBD. There have been important initiatives, however, since 1970. Congressional establishment of new national parks in Alaska in 1980 under the Alaska National Interest Lands Conservation Act (ANILCA), for example, authorized subsistence hunting by Indigenous and non-Indigenous residents of nearby communities and also created subsistence resource use advisory commissions (chapter 4; Sneed 1997). Hunting is also authorized in part of Badlands National Park, the South Unit of which is part of the Pine Ridge Reservation and is currently comanaged by the Lakota (Igoe 2004; Ross et al. 2011). Agreements have been reached between several tribes to recognize traditional plant harvesting in national parks, including Hawai'i Volcanoes, Mount Rainier, Zion, and Yosemite. However, as Anderson and Barbour (2003: 270) observed, the agreements made with American Indians and Native Hawaiians for recognizing traditional plant harvesting "focus on plant collection and joint monitoring, not traditional management." There is vast potential for U.S. national parks to benefit from the restoration of biodiverse "ethnographic landscapes" (Anderson and Barbour 2003) through traditional use and ecosystem management by American Indians, Alaska Natives, and Native Hawaiians. Beyond greater involvement in active management, the national parks can benefit from their stronger participation in park governance. Significant initiatives are in process. In 2012 the U.S. National Park Service recommended, following extensive discussion and public comment by Lakota, that the South Unit of Badlands National Park become the first Tribal National Park. James Anaya, the UN Special Rapporteur on the Rights of Indigenous Peoples, singled out the prospect of a tribal national park as a particularly important development in his 2012 report on the status of Indigenous peoples in the United States. Whether a tribal national park can be established, however, may depend on congressional authorization. See also Villalba's (2010) discussion of informal management collaborations in Pinnacles National Monument (now Pinnacles National Park).

36. There are significant issues with the quality of data for both historical and contemporary displacement (Brockington and Igoe 2006; Brockington et al. 2008). Documentation of displacement is often poor or lacking altogether, in part because states and conservation NGOs have often not kept careful account or do not wish to make data publicly known. Global estimates of the total number of people displaced are generalized on the basis of inadequate data and vary tremendously (Geisler and de Sousa 2000; Geisler 2003a, 2003b; Brockington and Igoe 2006; Brockington et al. 2008; Agrawal and Redford 2009). But it is clear that many different Indigenous peoples and local communities have been physically displaced and economically marginalized, that large numbers of people have been affected, and that people continue to be relocated against their wishes from protected areas.

37. The term "conservation refugee," popularized by journalist Mark Dowie (2009), was coined by sociologist Charles Geisler (2002, 2003a, 2003b).

38. Arun Agrawal (2005) discussed the creation of new "environmental subjects" in one area of the Himalayan region of India through the socialization or assimilation of individuals who adopt new conservation values as a result of participating in externally introduced institutions. He refers to this hegemonic form of governmentality as "environmentality" (see chapter 12).

39. Neumann (2004: 212) also has theorized that the reorganization of territory to separate people and nature by containing nature in uninhabited protected areas and displacing Indigenous peoples to other sites is "a generalizable process of state-building" that can be "documented in every region of European expansion." For Neumann, this makes exclusionary wilderness areas "as much an expression of modernism as skyscrapers" and "an integral part of the practice of modern statecraft" as well as an expression of colonialism and a "key focus in the continuing struggles over the commons and proprietary rights" between states and Indigenous peoples. Although national parks and protected areas have indeed been created in almost all modern states, the pattern of creating exclusionary wilderness areas and relocating residents to other rural and urban areas does not hold true in all of these. Indeed, a number of modern states (among them England, France, Norway, Sweden, Japan, Nepal, Australia, Colombia, Canada, and—in recent decades—the United States) have national parks or other protected areas that recognize settlement or land use by Indigenous peoples or local communities. It may be that displacement of Indigenous peoples to create uninhabited wilderness areas was a common component of nineteenth- and twentieth-century European and American colonialism (and attempts to create some unitary nation-states in the global South in the late twentieth and early twenty-first centuries), rather than of state-building per se.

CHAPTER TWO

A New Protected Area Paradigm

Stan Stevens

In September 2003 a remarkable—and possibly watershed—moment in conservation and human rights history took place at the IUCN's Vth World Parks Congress (WPC) in Durban, South Africa. The WPC is the most important global occasion for setting international standards and guidelines for national parks and other protected areas. It has been organized every decade since 1962 by the IUCN's World Commission on Protected Areas. The Durban WPC, the first to be held in Africa, was the largest ever, bringing together 3000 participants from 144 countries, including nearly 150 Indigenous people (Brosius 2004; Colchester 2004).[1] Taghi Farvar (2013), then chair of IUCN's Commission on Environmental, Economic, and Social Policy, observed that this "was the first time a huge number of Indigenous peoples" participated in a World Parks Congress and that it "put a tremendous imprint on conservation, probably forever." The Durban World Parks Congress became the site of a historic dialogue (at times confrontational) between Indigenous peoples and international conservationists that transformed international protected area policy. Indigenous peoples and advocates of new protected area policies used the world stage of the WPC to condemn past practices and to challenge the IUCN to require that protected areas recognize and respect Indigenous peoples' rights, responsibilities, and conservation contributions.

Durban identified a "new protected area paradigm," elevated it to a central position in IUCN policy, and for the first time established time targets for reforms.[2] The IUCN's advocacy of the new paradigm almost immediately reshaped CBD policy as well, and the paradigm was strongly incorporated in its Programme of Work on Protected Areas. This chapter discusses these revolutionary policies and the new kinds of protected areas that embody them.

Confronting and Decolonizing Colonial Conservation

At the Vth WPC, Indigenous peoples strongly repudiated the exclusionary protected areas that states, as well as international conservationists and conservation NGOs, have often imposed in the name of biodiversity conservation and wilderness protection. The Indigenous Peoples Ad Hoc Working Group for the World Parks Congress (2003a, 2003b) condemned states' confiscation of their lands, forced relocation, and the development of protected area plans and regulations without their participation or consent in two powerful statements, *The Indigenous Peoples' Declaration to the World Parks Congress* (see sidebar 2.1, figure 2.1) and their closing plenary statement to the WPC. "The declaration of protected areas on indigenous territories without our consent and engagement," the Indigenous peoples group reminded the assembled conservationists at the closing plenary, "has resulted in our dispossession and resettlement, the violation of our rights, the displacement of our peoples, the loss of our sacred sites and the slow but continuous loss of our cultures, as well as impoverishment. It is thus difficult to talk about benefits for Indigenous Peoples when protected areas are being declared on our territories unilaterally. First we were dispossessed in the name of kings and emperors, later in the name of State development, and now in the name of conservation" (Indigenous Peoples Ad Hoc Working Group for the World Parks Congress (2003b).

Indigenous peoples denounced such practices as human rights violations and as major threats to their survival and cultural integrity. Protected areas, they declared in *The Indigenous Peoples' Declaration to the World Parks Congress* (Indigenous Peoples Ad Hoc Working Group for the World Parks Congress 2003b), have been a "form of cultural genocide" responsible for the "destruction of their livelihood[s]." They demanded recognition that "Indigenous Peoples are rights-holders and not merely stakeholders" and that it be acknowledged that they have the "inherent right to self-determination" and that the "*ancestral and customary rights* of Indigenous Peoples to their *lands, territories, and natural resources* must be recognized, respected, and protected." They called for an "*immediate halt*" to their "forced expulsion and systematic exclusion" from protected

Figure 2.1. Luz María de la Torre presenting the *Indigenous Peoples' Declaration to the World Parks Congress* in Durban, South Africa, in 2003.

areas. And they called for justice, including that "in cases where our lands have been expropriated to create protected areas, these *must be restituted to us and rapid, just, fair, and significant compensation*, agreed upon in a fully transparent, participatory, and culturally appropriate manner, must be provided" (my emphasis).

Of crucial importance to the future of conservation, however, was Indigenous peoples' call for reforming protected areas rather than for ending them. As IUCN Councillor Aroha Mead (a Māori of the Ngāti Awa and Ngāti Porou *iwi*) observed in her address at the 2003 WPC's opening ceremony, Indigenous peoples' goals are often compatible with protected areas (Indigenous Peoples Ad Hoc Working Group for the World Parks Congress 2003a: 8). But the reforms that Indigenous peoples demanded constitute a fundamentally different vision for international conservation (see sidebar 2.1). They articulate a new paradigm for protected areas that respects culturally diverse ways of contributing to conservation and holds conservation accountable for affirming human rights as well as the rights of nature. This new set of assumptions makes respect for the rights of Indigenous peoples a fundamental principle that redefines how protected areas are established, governed, and managed. It distinguishes Indigenous peoples, as "rights-holders," from other "stakeholders" and acknowledges their collective rights to their territories, identity, culture, self-governance, and self-determination and their responsibilities to their territories and peoples. This includes authorizing protected areas within their territories, fully and effectively participating in those protected areas' design and governance, and ensuring that conservation is consonant with their values, aspirations, and rights.

> Sidebar 2.1. Key Statements from *The Indigenous Peoples' Declaration to the World Parks Congress* and *Indigenous Peoples' World Parks Congress Closing Plenary Statement*, Vth World Parks Congress, Durban, South Africa
>
> "When protected areas are to be established, the free, prior and informed consent of the Indigenous Peoples concerned must be obtained, an appropriate social and cultural impact assessment must be carried out and, most importantly, the Indigenous Peoples must at all times reserve the right to say 'no'" (Declaration, par. 8).
>
> "In existing protected areas, created on Indigenous Peoples' territories, the World Parks Congress should support the rapid establishment of a legal framework to ensure culturally appropriate, full and effective participation of the Indigenous Peoples concerned in all aspects of the administration and management processes of protected areas" (Declaration, par. 9).
>
> "The World Parks Congress must recognize the cultural integrity of Indigenous Peoples and ensure the integration of traditional collective management systems as a basis for the management of protected areas" (Declaration, par. 12).
>
> "[We] call upon the World Parks Congress to uphold civil, political, economic, social and cultural rights in all protected area policies, programmes, projects and activities" (Declaration, par. 6).
>
> "We want to stress our insistence for the recognition and respect of the rights of Indigenous Peoples in existing and proposed protected areas" (Closing Plenary Statement).
>
> "[P]rioritize the recognition of Indigenous-owned and community-owned territories and areas as a sound basis for conservation" (Closing Plenary Statement).
>
> "Neither Indigenous Peoples, nor our lands and territories are objects of tourism development. If tourism is to benefit us, it must be under our full control" (Declaration, par. 10).

The International Union for Conservation of Nature Responds

This new paradigm was controversial at the 2003 WPC. Some participants, including members of the IUCN's intercommission Theme on Indigenous and Local Communities, Equity, and Protected Areas and the WCPA Theme on Governance, Equity, and Rights, strongly supported Indigenous peoples at Durban and advocated for policy change. Other participants, however, expressed "culture shock" and dismay. One commented that, in his opinion, the congress offered "an irresistible global stage for propounding a political agenda that was at best only tangential to biodiversity conservation" (Terborgh 2004: 55). A prominent conservation leader charged that the conservation agenda had been "hijacked," and I was told by another conservationist that he had felt "ambushed." Many IUCN leaders and members were far from being strong supporters of Indigenous peoples and rights-based conservation. The WPC organizers had not intended for Indigenous peoples to have such high visibility at the congress. It had not been planned for Indigenous peoples' representatives to address either the opening or closing plenaries. Nor was there initially an Indigenous peoples' representative on the committee that drafted the *Durban Accord* and the *Durban Action Plan* (Indigenous Peoples Ad Hoc Working Group for the World Parks Congress 2003a).

Indigenous peoples gained greater voice because they organized and were persistent in the face of bureaucratic and other obstacles. As they observed in their statement at the closing plenary on September 17, 2003: "Too long we have been ignored in global debates about conservation. At this Congress, we have made our presence felt through our work with you, and have made sure our voice has been heard by all the different participants. . . . The presence of Indigenous Peoples in this Congress has been prominent in the different working groups, a presence that was made felt through our delegates' voices and opinions. We can say that this space was won, it was not granted" (Indigenous Peoples Ad Hoc Working Group for the World Parks Congress 2003a: 19).

The policies that ultimately came of these negotiations and dialogues presaged a new relationship between Indigenous peoples and protected areas. In its ten-year program for protected area action, the congress acknowledged that "many mistakes have been, and continue to be made" and called for "urgent reevaluation of policies affecting indigenous peoples and local communities" (IUCN WCPA 2003b: 248). It adopted policy recommendations that affirmed that Indigenous peoples' knowledge, conservation contributions, and rights must be respected and that they must fully and effectively participate in the establishment, governance, and management of protected areas in their territories. The adopted policies far exceeded the expectations many reform advocates had had for the WPC, as did their strong incorporation a few months later in the CBD's Programme of Work on Protected Areas and further endorsement by the CBD and by the IUCN in the years since.

The *Durban Accord* and the *Durban Action Plan*

The new paradigm is prominent in the WPC's key outputs, including the *Durban Accord*, the *Durban Action Plan*, "Message to the Convention on Biological Diversity," and thirty-two adopted thematic recommendations. This section provides an overview of the principles and actions highlighted in the *Durban Accord* and *Durban Action Plan*. Many of the thematic recommendations also articulate policies that promote the new paradigm. Recommendation V.24, Indigenous Peoples and Protected Areas, is a particularly important statement (see table 2.1 for key recommendations).

The Durban Accord (IUCN WCPA 2003a) announced the IUCN's adoption of a "new paradigm for protected areas." It commended Indigenous peoples for "their efforts to make protected areas places of natural, cultural and spiritual convergence," expressed "concern that many places conserved over the ages by local communities, mobile and indigenous peoples are not given recognition, protection and support," and noted that "many costs of protected areas are borne locally—particularly by poor communities—while benefits accrue globally."[3] To remedy this, *The Durban Accord* announced several commitments:

1. foster "the integral relationship of people with protected areas";
2. involve Indigenous peoples "in the creation, proclamation and management of protected areas";
3. ensure participation "in relevant decision-making on a fair and equitable basis in full respect of . . . human and social rights";
4. support "protected area management that strives to reduce, and in no way exacerbates, poverty";
5. ensure that protected areas share benefits with Indigenous peoples and local communities;
6. foster "innovation in protected area management, including adaptive, collaborative and comanagement strategies";

7. "recognise, strengthen, protect and support community conservation areas"; and
8. "value and use all protected area knowledge systems, whether scientific or traditionally based."

These pronouncements were given substance and character in the *Durban Action Plan*. The action plan, the first ever adopted by the World Commission on Protected Areas, was intended to guide a decade of work on protected areas by the IUCN and its member states and conservation organizations. It identified a set of goals to be achieved by the next decennial WPC and specific actions to attain them. Its ten major goals or desired "outcomes," fifteen time-specific targets, and many subtargets and recommendations provided a roadmap for global efforts to expand and improve protected areas. Four of its ten primary desired outcomes reflected new paradigm principles, including Outcome 5 (IUCN 2003a), which set a goal that "the rights of Indigenous Peoples including mobile indigenous peoples, and local communities are secured in relation to natural resources and biodiversity conservation."

The preamble of Outcome 5 acknowledged that "many protected areas have been established without adequate attention to and respect for the rights of indigenous peoples, including mobile indigenous peoples, and local communities, especially their rights to lands, territories and resources, and their right freely to consent to activities that affect them" (IUCN WCPA 2003b). To address this issue, it identified three main targets to attain by the next WPC:

1. Main Target 8. "All existing and future protected areas are established and managed in full compliance with the rights of indigenous peoples, including mobile indigenous peoples, and local communities by the time of the next IUCN World Parks Congress."
2. Main Target 9. "The management of all relevant protected areas involves representatives chosen by indigenous peoples, including mobile indigenous peoples, and local communities proportionate to their rights and interests, by the time of the next IUCN World Parks Congress."
3. Main Target 10. "Participatory mechanisms for the restitution of indigenous peoples' traditional lands and territories that were incorporated in protected areas without their free and informed consent are established and implemented by the time of the next IUCN World Parks Congress."

Table 2.1. Key new paradigm policies of the Vth World Parks Congress (Durban, South Africa, 2003)

Recommendation	Title	Significance
V.13	Cultural and Spiritual Values of Protected Areas	First IUCN policy on sacred natural sites; calls for restitution, self-governance and custodianship, and recognition of ICCAs
V.16	Good Governance of Protected Areas	First IUCN policy on protected area governance quality
V.17	Recognising and Supporting a Diversity of Governance Types for Protected Areas	First IUCN policy calling for recognition of four governance types, including ICCAs and shared governance of protected areas
V.18	Management Effectiveness Evaluation to Support Protected Area Management	Indigenous peoples' involvement in monitoring, assessment, and evaluation, with specific attention to adverse social impacts and to their participation in protected area governance and management
V.19	IUCN Protected Area Management Categories	Recognizes the value of diverse management goals and greater attention to culture, sustainable use, and ICCAs
V.24	Indigenous Peoples and Protected Areas	A major policy statement advancing the new paradigm (see table 2.2); extends WCC 1.53 (1996), calling for rights, restitution, governance, ICCAs, comanagement, and a truth and reconciliation commission
V.25	Comanagement of Protected Areas	Reaffirms earlier IUCN policies promoting comanaged protected areas, including WCC 1.42 (1996) and WCC 2.15 (2000)
V.26	Community Conserved Areas	First IUCN policy on ICCAs, including the definition still in use
V.27	Mobile Indigenous Peoples and Conservation	First IUCN policy on mobile Indigenous peoples; affirms collective rights, comanagement rights, and calls for recognition of ICCAs

Abbreviations: IUCN: International Union for Conservation of Nature; ICCA: Indigenous Peoples' and Community Conserved Territories and Areas; WCC: World Conservation Congress

These three targets and a set of twenty-nine supporting targets and actions envisioned rights-based reform and redress for past injustices. Target 8 clarified that the rights of Indigenous peoples apply in all protected areas. This will require the revision of many countries' laws and policies as well as reform of specific protected areas' governance and management. In many countries debates about rights recognition in protected areas have focused solely on ending evictions and violent suppression of customary land use, whereas Targets 8 and 9 clarified that Indigenous peoples have rights that pertain to both the establishment and the management of protected areas. Target 9 underscored that Indigenous peoples have the right to participate in the management of protected areas in ways "proportionate to their rights and interests." No details were specified, but a high bar for participation was implied. Diverse rights (chapter 1) are involved, and clearly the interests of Indigenous peoples are enormous given the potential of protected areas to affect their livelihoods, welfare, cultural integrity, self-governance, and the future ecological conditions of their territories. Such profound rights and interests require more than token consultation, arguing for Indigenous peoples' self-governance of protected areas—Indigenous peoples' protected areas (ICCAs)—or a strong role in shared governance arrangements.

Main Target 10 is also concerned with rights in a different sense: redress for their past violation. It responded to demands for the restitution of Indigenous peoples' traditional territories and lands that were incorporated in protected areas without their free, prior, and informed consent. No distinction was drawn between state-owned or privately owned protected areas. Restitution is sought for "traditional lands and territories" and not only for those to which Indigenous peoples can establish that they held state-recognized legal title prior to their nationalization or privatization. The ramifications of this target are vast. It may apply to tens of thousands of protected areas, including, for example, much of the U.S. national park system. Restitution will often require new national laws and procedures for the titling of collectively owned land (chapters 7 and 8). As Finley-Brook, Mollett, and Fay (chapters 7, 8, and 9) document, however, restitution may often be constrained by state reluctance to restore nationalized land, legitimize customary tenure systems, or recognize Indigenous peoples' authority over their territories (see also chapter 12). Prior to Durban there were only a few examples of such restitution, most notably in Australia and South Africa (see chapter 9). There have been few initiatives in other countries since then.

Many rights advocates expect that international mediation may be necessary for restitution, appropriate compensation, and achieving rights-based reform in protected area design and governance. An international Truth and Reconciliation Commission for Indigenous Peoples and Protected Areas was called for in WPC Recommendation V.24 on Indigenous Peoples and Protected Areas. Such a body has not yet been established, however, and it is unclear how it might be created and be effective. The IUCN currently is developing a mechanism, the Whakatane Assessments, to facilitate dispute resolution and to celebrate and promote good practices (chapter 12). Additional impetus toward remedy, redress, and reconciliation may come from greater attention to protected area situations by international rights monitoring mechanisms, including the UN Human Rights Council, the UN Expert Mechanism on the Rights of Indigenous Peoples, the UN Permanent Forum on Indigenous Issues, and the UN Special Rapporteur on the Rights of Indigenous Peoples, as well as from international human rights commissions and courts.

The three main targets of Outcome 5 were supported by a set of specific recommendations to member states, "protected area authorities," and other actors that gave further guidance on necessary actions to meet these standards appropriately.[4] Among these were recommendations to the IUCN's member states to:

1. approve the UN Declaration on the Rights of Indigenous Peoples and adopt ILO 169;
2. "review all existing conservation laws and policies that impact on indigenous peoples" and ensure that they fully recognize and respect the rights of Indigenous peoples in protected areas;
3. recognize ICCAs and the shared governance of protected areas and provide for the inclusion of such protected areas within national protected area systems;
4. ensure Indigenous peoples' full and effective participation in establishing and managing protected areas;
5. incorporate Indigenous peoples' knowledge, innovations, and practices in protected area management;
6. adopt laws and policies regarding Indigenous peoples' control of their sacred places;
7. ensure "equitable distribution of benefits, authority, and responsibility."

Beyond Durban: The International Union for Conservation of Nature, the Convention on Biological Diversity, and the New Paradigm since 2003

Many of the policies adopted at the Vth IUCN World Parks Congress have subsequently been endorsed and further developed in resolutions passed by three subsequent IUCN World Conservation Congresses (2004, 2008, and 2012). Key principles and provisions were also incorporated into legally binding decisions of the Parties to the CBD and the CBD's Programme of Work on Protected Areas (PoWPA).

International Union for Conservation of Nature Policies Post-Durban

Since the last WPC, the IUCN has convened three WCCs. These gatherings, held every four years, are the venues at which the IUCN's member governments and NGOs make IUCN policy, including enacting resolutions which call on the IUCN and its members to implement WPC recommendations. Each WCC since Durban has further endorsed and developed the new paradigm. The 3rd WCC in Bangkok, Thailand, in 2004, for example, adopted Resolution 3.055, Indigenous Peoples, Protected Areas, and the CBD Programme of Work, calling for advancing CBD policies that promote equity and rights (IUCN 2004b) and for an implementation review of Resolution 1.53, Indigenous Peoples and Protected Areas, which was adopted at the 1st WCC in Montreal in 1996. The 3rd WCC also adopted Resolution 3.049, Community Conserved Areas (IUCN 2004a), giving further weight to a key new type of protected area that had been endorsed the year before in Durban

Four years later at the 4th WCC, held in Barcelona, Spain, the IUCN's members adopted Resolution 4.048, Indigenous Peoples, Protected Areas, and Implementation of the Durban Accord. This resolution (IUCN 2008b, par. 4(a)(i–iv)) called on the IUCN to apply UNDRIP "to the whole of IUCN's Programme and operations," advance key recommendations from the *Durban Accord* and *Durban Action Plan*, and "promote the recognition of indigenous peoples' rights and systems pertaining to the use, management, conservation and governance of their territories, lands and natural resources." It specifically requested that the IUCN's state members reform their laws, policies, and practices to meet the standards of the *Durban Accord*, CBD Programme of Work on Protected Areas, and UNDRIP. These reforms should "ensure that protected areas which affect or may affect indigenous peoples' lands, territories, natural and cultural resources are not established without indigenous peoples' free, prior and informed consent and ... ensure due recognition of the rights of indigenous peoples in existing protected areas" (IUCN 2008b, par. 2(a) and (b)).

A separate recommendation, 4.127, Indigenous Peoples' Rights in the Management of Protected Areas Fully or Partially in the Territories of Indigenous Peoples, strongly seconded and expanded on this. It called on states to "make available the means necessary for the full exercise and effective implementation of the rights recognized in the United Nations Declaration on the Rights of Indigenous Peoples" (IUCN 2008d). The recommendation specifically urged states in the case of "designated protected areas fully or partially within the territories of indigenous peoples" to "respect the rights of these peoples, ensuring the full and effective participation of their representative organizations in making decisions on the management and protection of these areas" and (quoting Article 28.1 of UNDRIP) redress past injustices "by means that can include restitution or, when this is not possible, just, fair and equitable compensation, for lands, territories and resources which they have traditionally owned or otherwise occupied or used, and which have been confiscated, taken, occupied, used or damaged without their free, prior and informed consent" (IUCN 2008d).

The 4th WCC in 2008 and the 2012 WCC, held in Jeju, South Korea, continued to stress recognition of Indigenous peoples' governance of protected areas with a strong set of resolutions: Resolution 4.049, Supporting Indigenous Conservation Territories and Other Indigenous Peoples' and Community Conserved Areas; Resolution 4.050, Recognition of Indigenous Conservation Territories; and Resolution 5.094, Respecting, Recognizing and Supporting Indigenous Peoples' and Community Conserved Territories and Areas. Additional resolutions on UNDRIP, rights-based approaches to conservation, and sacred natural sites were also adopted in 2008 and 2012.

The Convention on Biological Diversity and the Programme of Work on Protected Areas

Many of the new paradigm principles that the IUCN has endorsed have also now been incorporated into the decisions and PoWPA of the Parties to the CBD. The CBD is a UN environmental treaty developed, along with Agenda 21, at the 1992 Rio "Earth Summit" (the UN Conference on Environment and Development). As an international treaty, it has force of law for those countries that have ratified it, which now number 193. The original treaty is augmented by further decisions adopted in biannual Conferences of the Parties (COPs). CBD articles and decisions are legally binding and thus have greater international weight than IUCN recommendations and resolutions. (Many CBD decisions, however, use the language of guidance, with actions suggested to the Parties, and often these recommendations are qualified further with reference to their being consistent with "national legislation and applicable international obligations.")

Two of the CBD's articles are particularly important for Indigenous peoples. Article 8(j) concerns "in-situ conservation" (for which protected areas are considered by the Parties to the CBD to be central), whereas 10(c) refers to "sustainable use of components of biological diversity." These have created spaces in the CBD to promote new paradigm principles. Article 8(j) enjoins states to "respect, preserve and maintain knowledge, innovations and practices of indigenous and local communities embodying traditional lifestyles relevant for the conservation and sustainable use of biological diversity." Article 10(c) calls for states to "protect and encourage customary use of biological resources in accordance with traditional cultural practices that are compatible with conservation or sustainable use requirements." Both require states to rethink protected area policies and practices.[5]

The Parties to the CBD also have facilitated the new paradigm through decisions reached at the biannual COPs. COP 7, held in Kuala Lumpur in 2004, endorsed rights-based approaches to protected areas in Decision VII/28 (par. 22), reminding the Parties of their obligations to Indigenous peoples under Article 8(j) and noting that "the establishment, management and monitoring of protected areas should take place with the full and effective participation of, and full respect for the rights of, indigenous and local communities consistent with national law and applicable international obligations." It also adopted, as an annex to Decision VII/28, a PoWPA that draws substantially on the policies developed at Durban. Subsequent COPs have repeatedly adopted decisions that affirm Indigenous peoples' rights; their full and effective participation in protected area establishment, governance, and management; and equitable sharing of costs and benefits (for example, COP 9 Decision IX/18, par. 6(d); COP 10 Decision X/31, par. 32(c); and COP 11 Decision XI/14, section F, par. 10(c)(i)). COP decisions have also highlighted that states should take into account Indigenous peoples' own management systems and customary uses in protected areas (COP 9 Decision IX/18, par. 19) and have specifically endorsed ICCAs in PoWPA and a number of recent COP decisions, including COP 10 Decisions X/31 (section 9, par. 31, 32, and 33), X/32 (par. 7), and X/33 (par. 8(i)); and COP 11 Decisions XI/14 (section A, par. 9) and Decision XI/24 (par. 1(e) and 10). COP 11 Decision XI/24 (par. 1(e)) on protected areas, for example, invited Parties to "strengthen recognition of and support for community-based approaches to conservation and sustainable use of biodiversity in situ, including indigenous and local community conserved areas" (Conference of the Parties to the CBD 2012b). The CBD's current Executive Secretary, Braulio Ferreira de Souza Dias (2012: 6), has advised that ICCAs are a particularly important way to implement Articles 8(j) and 10(c), remarking that "ICCAs can be the living embodiment of Articles 8(j) and 10(c) of the Convention" and that they will play a "crucial role in Implementing the Strategic Plan for Biodiversity 2011–2012" (see also Executive Secretary of the CBD 2009).

New paradigm principles were prominent in the 2004 PoWPA. Many of its four component elements, seventeen goals with their time-specific targets, and 124 suggested implementation activities called for reforming old paradigm approaches. Element 2, Governance, Participation, Equity, and Benefit Sharing, particularly promoted the new paradigm. It had two goals: "to promote equity and benefit sharing" and "to enhance and secure involvement of indigenous and local communities and relevant stakeholders." Each had a time-specific implementation target. States were advised to "establish by 2008 mechanisms for equitable sharing of both costs and benefits arising from the establishment and management of protected areas." They were also urged to secure "full and effective participation by 2008 of indigenous and local communities, in full respect of their rights and recognition of their responsibilities . . . in the management of existing, and the establishment and management of new, protected areas." The PoWPA suggested specific means to realize these goals, including Indigenous rights recognition; free, prior, and informed consent to any relocation from protected areas; recognition of ICCAs; and shared governance of protected areas.

Conceptualizing the New Protected Area Paradigm: Core Principles and Implications

The new paradigm as developed in IUCN policy and CBD decisions calls for rethinking and reforming many aspects of protected area conceptualization, design, and practice. It requires states to reestablish their relationships with Indigenous peoples and to recognize the value of their land and sea tenure, cultures, and practices for conservation. And it makes rights recognition foundational. Table 2.2 compares old and new paradigm approaches to establishing, governing, and managing protected areas. This comparison differs from previous ones (Phillips 2003; Chape et al. 2008) by focusing on those aspects of the new paradigm that relate to Indigenous peoples and by highlighting rights. Rights affirmation shapes all aspects of new paradigm thinking about protected area establishment, governance, and management. Contrasted in this way, the differences between the two paradigms are clearly many and profound. They envision not only different relationships with Indigenous peoples but also different kinds of protected areas that strikingly diverge in ownership; governance; management; goals; the process of adopting and implementing policies and management plans; habitation; access to natural and cultural resources; and the allocation of responsibilities, costs, and benefits.

In this, the new paradigm goes far beyond earlier parks and people approaches such as community-based natural resource management (CBNRM) and integrated conservation and development projects (ICDPs). Popular since the 1980s, CBNRM and ICDPs have received massive international funding and other support but have been much criticized on both conservation and social justice grounds (Western and Wright 1994; Terborgh 1999; Wilshusen et al. 2002; McShane et al. 2004; Brosius et al. 2005; Dressler et al. 2010). The differences are striking. CBNRM and ICDPs have focused on promoting development in the areas outside of protected areas in the often-unrealized hope that this will reduce customary natural resource use within the protected areas themselves. Their goal is not to change how protected areas are established and managed, and they are entirely compatible with exclusionary protected areas and fortress conservation. Ironically for programs extolled as "community-based" conservation, they have been community "sited" but not community "driven and controlled" (Langton et al. 2005: 34). Generally they have ignored Indigenous peoples' existing conservation practices, contributions, and potential, instead promoting standardized programs designed by international conservation organizations and states. They have not been concerned with affirming Indigenous peoples' residence and sustainable land use within protected areas, much less their participation in governing them or gaining full recognition of their rights. CBNRM programs and ICDPs have seldom included among their goals gaining Indigenous peoples' secure tenure to their territories; securing their right to free, prior, and informed consent in all things related to protected areas; or providing them with an equitable share of protected area benefits.

Table 2.2. Old and new paradigm contrasts

	Old paradigm	*New paradigm*
Rights	No recognition of rights	Rights are affirmed and fostered
	Rights are not considered relevant because protected areas are uninhabited and former residents have surrendered rights and claims	Indigenous rights exist in all protected areas established in the customary territories of Indigenous peoples, including those they have been displaced from
Establishment	Unilaterally declared by states	Declared by or with Indigenous peoples with their free, prior, and informed consent
Design	Designed by government agencies and conservationists; nationally standardized	Designed by or with Indigenous peoples; diverse and site/culturally particularized
Tenure	Owned by the state	Owned by Indigenous peoples
Governance	Governed by state agencies	Governed by or with Indigenous peoples
	No participation by Indigenous peoples	Indigenous peoples' full and effective participation required, including when living outside of protected area
	No recognition of ICCAs within protected areas	ICCAs recognized as protected areas and as zones or jurisdictions within them
Management authority	State agencies hold sole management authority	Management by and with Indigenous peoples
Conservation conceptions	Conservation as conceived by conservation scientists	Diverse conceptions of conservation grounded in cosmovision and culture as well as in Western science
Knowledge base	Western science	Indigenous knowledge; Indigenous and Western sciences
Goals	Biodiversity conservation	Conservation, identity, cultural values, livelihood security, ecosystem services, sustainable development, restoration, restitution
Management category	IUCN Categories I–IV, especially Categories I and II	IUCN Categories I–VI
	Emphasis on a single management goal	May have different management goals in different zones

	Old paradigm	New paradigm
Management principles	Protect ecosystems unimpaired	Protect and restore ecosystems and cultural landscapes
	Preserve or restore uninhabited wilderness	Maintain and restore cultural landscapes
	Protect and restore biodiversity	Protect and restore biodiversity
	Eliminate settlement, migration, and use of cultural and natural resources (or restrict natural resource use to authorized commercial use in the case of national forests)	Maintain settlement, migration, use of cultural and natural resources, and land and marine management practices consistent with Indigenous peoples' wishes and rights and compatible with agreed-upon protected area goals
	Tourism development only	Sustainable development
Policy development	State developed, authorized, and imposed	Developed with the full and effective participation of Indigenous peoples and adopted with their free, prior, and informed consent
Settlement and resettlement	All settlement is banned; coercive displacement is justified, although voluntary resettlement may be preferred	Continued settlement (and return in the case of involuntarily displaced peoples) is recognized as a right
		No coercive displacement or relocation
		Free, prior, and informed consent to any relocation, with agreed on, equitable compensation and Indigenous peoples' full participation in decision-making and planning
Equitable benefits, obligations, and responsibilities	All revenues and other benefits belong to the state or its designatees	Indigenous peoples have the right to an equitable share of all benefits
	All responsibility rests with the state or its delegates	Recognition of Indigenous peoples' responsibilities, including those to their peoples, ancestors, future generations, territories, beliefs, and values

Abbreviations: ICCA: Indigenous Peoples' and Community Conserved Territories and Areas; IUCN: International Union for Conservation of Nature

CBNRM and ICDP discourse emphasizes linkages between conservation and development but lacks an entire lexicon of keywords that are fundamental to the new protected area paradigm. Much is said by the discursive silence about Indigenous peoples, justice, rights, equity, territory, collective tenure, restitution, self-governance, cultural integrity, Indigenous knowledge, customary law and institutions, participation in protected area governance and other decision-making, and the requirement for free, prior, and informed consent in all aspects of protected area establishment, governance, and management. As Brechin et al. (2002: 52) have observed, it is not that ICDPs and similar approaches have tried but failed to link protected areas and social justice, but rather that "nature protection with social justice has not yet been tried as a general strategy since integrated conservation and development [projects merely] have emphasized economic incentives and compensation as a means of 'buying' constraint [in natural resource use]." These economic incentives come at a high cost that includes loss of customary territories and natural resources, culturally important livelihood practices, and customary institutions of self-governance and land management. Moreover, ICDPs and CBNRM can also be entwined with buffer-zone and landscape-scale conservation projects that spatially extend protected area authorities' administrative oversight and impose new conservation goals, land-use regulations, and management institutions on neighboring areas and peoples. From the perspectives of these critiques, CBNRM programs and ICDPs can be seen to be forms of "deep colonising" (Rose 1996). Even if the donors, states, and NGOs that promote and implement these programs mean for them to be empowering and beneficial, they can be so deeply imbued with problematic attitudes and assumptions that they become the opposite.

Achieving new paradigm goals will require a course change in a political economy of conservation that has for decades focused on the global North funding exclusionary protected areas, CBNRM projects, and ICDPs in the global South. For decades, the allocation of international funding for protected areas and conservation (including funding from the GEF, World Bank, U.S. Agency for International Development, other multilateral and bilateral agencies, and major international conservation NGOs) has created systems of protected areas and buffer zones dedicated to old paradigm principles. The new paradigm would instead redirect hundreds of millions of dollars per year of financial, technical, and legal support to establishing and supporting different kinds of protected areas and reforming existing ones to meet new paradigm standards. It will focus much greater financial attention on governance effectiveness, including equity and rights recognition. It will also challenge the practice of channeling so much of total international funding through conservation organizations based in the global North and states in the global South. Achieving the new paradigm will require much stronger participation by Indigenous peoples in decision-making about international conservation financing and the redirection of significantly more resources directly to them.

Finally, in many countries the reforms needed to achieve the new paradigm will not only require major changes in national laws, policies, and regulations concerning protected areas but also broader change in Fourth World social relationships and political dynamics. Appropriately recognizing and securing Indigenous peoples' rights and responsibilities to their territories, their customary use and management of natural resources, and their custodianship of sacred places may require significant changes to many national constitutions, laws, regulations, and practices.

Rights and Protected Areas

The new paradigm has the potential to make protected areas a key site of strong Indigenous rights affirmation rather than a prominent source of their violation. It promotes rights-based conservation as a guiding principle for all protected areas. Rights recognition establishes parameters and ground rules for appropriate protected area declaration, governance, and management. This requires more than simply ending coercive evictions and unlawful violence against Indigenous peoples or securing their free, prior, and informed consent to the establishment of new protected areas. It will mean reconfiguring who makes decisions and how they are made, changing how responsibilities and benefits are shared, and rethinking how governance and management quality are evaluated. Rights-based conservation will require that the establishment, governance, and management of protected areas aim not only to conserve biodiversity but also to do so while supporting Indigenous peoples in their efforts to maintain their identities, cultures, livelihoods, spiritual relationships with their territories, and stewardship responsibilities.

Contrary to the fears of some critics, this need not mean an end to protected areas or even to Category I–IV ones. Indigenous peoples may consider the goal of strict nature preservation appropriate for some protected areas, including those that protect sacred sites. Strict nature preservation of some areas may be entirely compatible with Indigenous peoples' values and aspirations, just as sustainable use of natural resources is in other parts of their territories. These land and marine management decisions, however, must reflect their wishes rather than being imposed on them. Under the new paradigm, all protected areas, Category I–IV as well as Category V and VI, must conform to rights standards that will require protected areas to be established, governed, and managed through structures and processes that are different from those that have prevailed in the past. Governance arrangements, management goals, and regulations will have to accord with Indigenous peoples' rights, cultures, and aspirations. In the case of already established protected areas, this will often require changes to governance structures, policies, regulations, management plans, and practices even when Indigenous peoples consider the conservation goals of the protected areas to be appropriate and acceptable. It may also require legal restitution of territory and compensation for past injustices.

The IUCN has strongly endorsed the application of UNDRIP and international human rights law to protected areas.[6] The state parties to the CBD have thus far been less enthusiastic, but have also taken note of UNDRIP in the context of protected areas. In coming years policies and decisions on implementing UNDRIP in protected areas likely will be developed in more detail and will be further elaborated by guidance from UN human rights monitoring bodies and by court decisions.[7] New IUCN policies have already specified a number of key points with regard to the application of rights to protected areas, including:

- Human rights and the rights of Indigenous peoples apply in protected areas.
- Indigenous peoples have the right to retain ownership of territory within protected areas, including national parks, and the right to restitution of land incorporated in protected areas without their free, prior, and informed consent.
- New protected areas should only be established with Indigenous peoples' free, prior, and informed consent.
- Indigenous peoples should not be coercively evicted from protected areas.
- Indigenous peoples' full and effective participation in protected area governance and management is required in all existing and new protected areas with full respect for their rights.
- Indigenous peoples have rights to livelihood and cultural use and management of natural resources.
- Indigenous peoples have rights to custodianship of sacred natural sites.

Protected Area Governance

IUCN policies make clear that rights concerns should strongly shape protected area governance and management. The importance of governance for rights fulfillment is obviously fundamental, given that it bears on matters of who has the authority to make decisions, how decisions are made, and how decision-makers are held accountable. Governance is thus "about power, relationships, responsibility and accountability" (Borrini-Feyerabend et al. 2006: 116). Management, by contrast, is concerned with implementing policies, regulations, and plans. It "addresses what is done about a given site or situation" (Borrini-Feyerabend et al. 2006: 116). Effective management, however, has come to be equated in part with good governance and equity. The World Conservation Monitoring Centre, for example, suggests that "it is widely recognized that effective protected area management requires good governance as a prerequisite" (Bertzky et al. 2012: 30). Recent IUCN guidance strongly reshapes our understanding of "good governance" and "effective management" of protected areas, promoting standards that most protected areas today do not meet.

The IUCN's conception of good governance draws on principles developed in the UN system (Borrini-Feyerabend et al. 2004a, 2006, 2008, 2013; Dudley 2008; Lausche and Burhenne 2011). Key principles identified as "IUCN principles of good governance for protected areas" (Borrini-Feyerabend et al. 2013: 12) include legitimacy and voice, direction, performance (including "subsidiarity" and "transparency"),[8] accountability, and fairness and rights (equity, justice, and rights, including upholding the collective rights of Indigenous peoples).[9]

Not all formulations of these principles give sufficient attention to the specific concerns of Indigenous peoples. For example, recognizing the importance of "human rights" for good governance does not necessarily include affirmation of the rights of Indigenous peoples. Simply recognizing individual rights, the principle of "do not harm," or even a right to "free, prior, and informed consent" fails to adequately engage with the rights of Indigenous peoples, which include rights associated with identity, culture, territory, and self-governance and self-determination (chapter 1). Inadequate conceptualization and affirmation of rights, along with failure to take rights—including the full rights of Indigenous peoples—into account in assessing fairness (or legitimacy and voice, direction, performance, or accountability) leads to flawed standards of "effective" or "good" governance and management that legitimize rights violations. Good governance of protected areas established in the customary territories of Indigenous peoples must instead take as its foundation the protection and promotion of the rights and responsibilities of Indigenous peoples as identified in UNDRIP, ILO 169, the CBD and other international rights instruments and jurisprudence, and IUCN policies. UNDRIP, as specified in its Article 43, must be considered to be a minimal set of standards. Anything less cannot be considered to be "rights-based conservation," conservation with equity, or social justice.

Both the IUCN and CBD have made reference to specific rights in their protected area recommendations. These include, for example, the right to full and effective participation in the governance of protected areas and to free, prior, and informed consent in various specific contexts.[10] The CBD (2004a, 2004b) recognizes that free, prior, and informed consent should apply in cases of the displacement or relocation of Indigenous peoples from protected areas. In 2012, the Conference of the Parties to the CBD (2012a, section F, par. 10(c)(i)) called in Decision XI/14 for implementation of Article 10(c) with best practices that include not only Indigenous peoples' "full and effective participation" but also their "prior and informed consent to or approval of and involvement in the establishment, expansion, governance and management of protected areas . . . that may affect indigenous and local communities." The IUCN also affirms Indigenous peoples' right to free, prior, and informed consent for protected area establishment and management. An important step would be for the IUCN and CBD to specify that "full and effective participation in governance" requires that Indigenous peoples have authority or shared governance authority over all protected areas in their territories and that good governance requires that the rights and responsibilities articulated in UNDRIP, ILO 169, and other international rights instruments be legally acknowledged, secured, and facilitated.

Management, like governance, must affirm, secure, and foster the enjoyment of rights. Management policies, regulations and rules, and plans and their implementation must affirm and facilitate the realization of Indigenous peoples' rights and responsibilities. Effectively and equitably managed protected areas must respect Indigenous peoples' ownership of their territories, livelihood security, and responsibilities toward their territories and the welfare of their peoples. This includes upholding rights to maintain identities, cultures, and values, including customary governance institutions, traditional and recently adopted land and marine management practices, and care of sacred sites. Ensuring that Indigenous peoples or their designees compose all or most protected area staff at all levels, including superintendents, can facilitate this. So, too, can ensuring that resident Indigenous peoples hold liaison positions with responsibility for maintaining two-way communication between their peoples and protected area administrators, including advising park staff on local protocols and perspectives.

Rights will also influence the monitoring and evaluation of protected areas. The IUCN has been working to make social assessment an integral part of evaluating management effectiveness (Hockings et al. 2006), and attention to rights is integral to the frameworks presented for assessing and evaluating protected area governance at the levels of both national systems and individual protected areas in the recent IUCN Best Practice Guidelines Series volume *Governance of Protected Areas*. In these frameworks, respect for rights, the appropriate inclusion of rights-holders in protected area governance, promotion of equity and benefit sharing, and concern with free, prior, and informed consent are key indicators for assessing governance quality (Borrini-Feyerabend et al. 2013). Facilitating Indigenous peoples' full and effective participation in assessment and evaluation, including provisions for them to report independently on their findings, may ensure their values, aspirations, concerns, and understanding of their rights will figure prominently in governance and management assessments. Nothing less is likely to be considered legitimate by them or under international law.

New Paradigm Protected Areas: Key Approaches

Respect for diversity in the governance of protected areas is a hallmark of the new paradigm, which breaks sharply from earlier thinking by emphasizing that protected areas are legitimately governed by or with Indigenous peoples. Both the IUCN and CBD affirm that Indigenous peoples have a right to participate fully and effectively in the governance of protected areas, and they call on states to include protected areas governed by Indigenous peoples (ICCAs) and those with shared governance in national protected area systems. There is important experience already with both of these kinds of protected areas in a number of countries.[11]

Indigenous Peoples' and Community Conserved Territories and Areas

Ashish Kothari (2006a: 549), former co-chair of IUCN's Strategy/Theme on Indigenous Peoples, Local Communities, Equity, and Protected Areas, observed that "perhaps the most exciting conservation development of the twenty-first century is the global recognition of community conserved areas." Indigenous Peoples' and Community Conserved Territories and Areas (ICCAs), were first endorsed by IUCN as "community conserved areas" in 2003 at the Vth WPC in Durban (IUCN WCPA 2003f). Recommendation V.26 defined them as "natural and modified ecosystems including significant biodiversity, ecological services and cultural values voluntarily conserved by indigenous and local communities through customary laws or other effective means." Since then, the term has come to have multiple meanings. As an umbrella term ICCA encompasses the many ways that Indigenous peoples and local communities achieve conservation in particular places through their culture, relationships with their territories, and self-governance. The term provides a convenient way of thinking and speaking about territories and areas conserved through such diverse institutions and practices as the collective care and protection of sacred natural sites, community management of commons, the declaration of self-governed protected areas, and ways of life and values that result in environmentally sensitive stewardship and land and marine use across customary territories. As such, it has become an important "engaged universal" (Tsing 2005, see chapter 3), a term that Indigenous peoples and their allies can use to engage in new dialogues with the state, outside NGOs, and extractive industries to gain greater traction for their efforts to secure recognition and support for their self-governance, stewardship, and protection of their territories. More specifically, the term is used by the IUCN and the CBD to refer to a particular type of protected area governance: governance by Indigenous peoples or local communities (see chapter 1).[12] The CBD (2010) now also refers to ICCAs as one of the important types of "other effective area-based conservation measures" in situations in which they are not considered to be protected areas either because they do not meet national or international criteria or because Indigenous peoples, local communities, or the state prefer they not be included in national systems.

Institutions and practices that meet the IUCN's definition of ICCAs are often concerned with much more than conservation alone. They can be central to livelihood, culture (including identity, relationships to territory, and spiritual beliefs), and, when appropriately recognized and respected, to the realization of rights.[13] They are essential to secure livelihoods, providing access to food, water, shelter, clothing, energy, and income (Dias 2012) through sustainable use of natural resources based on local knowledge, cultural values, and collective management of commons. As cultural practices, they can be fundamental to collective identities, heritage, religion, and proper ways of living in and relating with the world. They are also a primary means through which Indigenous peoples maintain control over their territories, lands, and waters and meet their stewardship responsibilities to them (Stevens 2014). ICCAs are critical to creating and maintaining biocultural diversity. Indeed, ICCAs have been described as the "bio-cultural jewels of the world" (Borrini-Feyerabend et al. 2013: 109).

Recent discussions of ICCAs in IUCN and CBD publications emphasize three core characteristics[14] (Borrini-Feyerabend et al. 2010, 2013; Kothari et al. 2012). These are: (1) a "close and profound relationship with a site"; (2) governance by Indigenous peoples or local communities who are the "major player in decision-making related to the site" and who hold "*de facto* and/or *de jure* capacity to develop and enforce regulations"; and (3) voluntary "decisions and efforts [that] lead to the conservation of biodiversity, ecological functions and benefits, and associated cultural values, regardless of original or primary motivations" (Borrini-Feyerabend et al. 2013: 1).[15]

Thus characterized, ICCAs are territories and areas in which conservation results from both de jure and de facto institutions and practices that are known by diverse local names. They can be long-standing, but there are also many examples of recently developed or adopted ICCAs. They vary tremendously in size, from very small sacred sites to entire Indigenous peoples' territories (see chapter 11). They can be terrestrial or marine. Conceptualizations and categorizations of ICCAs continue to evolve, and often include Indigenous Conservation Territories, collectively managed commons, sacred natural sites and other cultural sites, and self-declared Indigenous peoples' protected areas.

The Executive Secretary of the CBD has observed that "today, there are many thousands of indigenous territories and other areas conserved by indigenous peoples and local communities across the world" (Dias 2012: 6). It is likely that Indigenous peoples and local communities maintain tens or hundreds of thousands of territories, areas, institutions, and practices that meet the IUCN's characterization of ICCAs, although few Indigenous peoples as of yet themselves conceptualize and articulate these as "ICCAs" and very few have sought their national or international recognition as such (for example, through listing in UNEP's WDPA or its global ICCA Registry). Ashish Kothari (2006c; Kothari et al. 2013) has suggested that worldwide ICCAs collectively may equal or exceed the entire area now in protected areas. In many parts of the world documentation is only beginning.[16]

Very few Indigenous peoples' territories and areas that meet IUCN criteria for ICCAs are currently recognized by states as part of national protected area systems. Prominent exceptions include the sixty Indigenous Protected Areas (2013) that comprise more than a third of the total area in Australia's national reserve system and encompass a greater total area than the fifty-nine U.S. national parks, seventy-six communal conservancies (2012) in Namibia (which together are more extensive than the national park system), thirty wildlife management areas (2010) that comprise 84 percent of the protected area system of Papua New Guinea, community conserved areas recognized as Voluntary Conserved Areas in Mexico, and the Konashen Community-owned Conserved Area in Guyana, that country's largest protected area (see chapter 3; Borrini-Feyerabend 2010; Borrini-Feyerabend et al. 2010, 2013; Department of Environment and Conservation 2010; Martin et al. 2011; Jonas et al. 2012; Kothari et al. 2012).[17]

Many other Indigenous peoples' conserved territories and areas, including Indigenous peoples' self-declared protected areas in several countries, meet or could potentially meet international definitions of protected areas (see chapter 1), although they may not be recognized as such by states. These include more than 500 Locally Managed Marine Areas in the Pacific Island countries (Govan 2009), many of them now registered with the WDPA; thousands of forests, wetlands, wildlife reserves, and other areas collectively governed and protected by Indigenous peoples and local communities in diverse parts of India and Nepal (chapter 11; Broome 2009); a large number of sacred natural sites in many parts of the world; and the many tribal parks established by American Indian tribes and First Nations in their reserves and customary territories in the United States and Canada.[18] Tribal parks include the system of protected areas established by the Diné (Navajo); the Mission Mountains Tribal Wilderness and Buffer Zone (Confederated Salish and Kootenai); Ute Mountain Tribal Park; the four Tla-o-qui-aht First Nations tribal parks; and the Haida First Nation's Haida Heritage Sites, among others (figures 2.2 and 2.3; Keller and Turok 1998; Burnham 2000; Krahe 2005; Tanner 2008; Murray and King 2012). The Inter-Tribal Sinkyone Wilderness and the Native American Land Conservancy's Old Woman Mountains Preserve are examples of effective use of conservation trusts and cultural conservation easements to conserve territories in ways that meet protected area definitions (Middleton 2011; Rosales 2012). Whether Indigenous peoples welcome national or international recognition of these conserved territories and areas as protected areas will vary greatly. Some peoples may welcome or seek such status for

Figure 2.2. Mission Mountains Tribal Wilderness, the first tribally declared wilderness in the United States, was established by the Confederated Salish and Kootenai tribes on the Flathead Reservation in 1982.

their territories. Others may decide potential benefits are outweighed by the possibility of diminished autonomy and other ramifications.

The IUCN also recognizes Indigenous Conservation Territories (ICTs), which can be considered to be a form of ICCA.[19] These include all or parts of Indigenous peoples' territories that Indigenous peoples conserve through maintaining environmentally sensitive and sustainable ways of life. Indigenous peoples introduced the concept of ICTs in 2007 at the second Latin American Congress on National Parks and Other Protected Areas in Bariloche, Argentina (Nahuel 2009), and proposed two ICT-related resolutions that were adopted by the IUCN at the 4th WCC in Barcelona, Spain, in 2008. Although not all Indigenous peoples' territories meet the criteria for ICTs, many do, including, for example, the territories of the Kayapo and other peoples in Brazil, the Yekuana in Venezuela, territories of many nomadic peoples in Iran, and many Indigenous reserves in Colombia and Bolivia (some of which are now recognized as protected areas by those states).[20] Within ICTs there are often local, specialized ICCAs such as community-managed commons and sacred places.

Figure 2.3. Monument Valley Navajo Tribal Park, Navajo Nation. Established by the government of the Navajo Nation in 1958, this was the first declared tribal park in the United States. Tsé Bii' Ndzisgaii (Valley of the Rocks) continues to be the home of Diné (Navajo) who maintain customary livelihood practices.

ICCAs and protected areas can also overlap. Indigenous peoples may continue to conserve territories and areas that can be considered to be ICCAs, including through collective management of commons or the protection of sacred natural sites, even after these areas have been incorporated into protected areas (examples of this from Nepal are discussed in chapter 11). These ICCAs may or may not be legally recognized. They may be ignored, undermined, suppressed, or supplanted by new institutions and governance arrangements imposed by protected area authorities. For Indigenous peoples, this situation has been a major source of disempowerment, cultural loss, rights violations, and conflict in those protected areas from which they have not been physically displaced (Stevens 2009, 2010, 2013, 2014). Issues of appropriate recognition and respect of ICCAs in situations where they overlap with protected areas have attracted international attention (figure 2.4; chapters 11 and 12; Stevens 2009, 2010, 2013, 2014; Borrini-Feyerabend 2010; Borrini-Feyerabend et al. 2010, 2013; Kothari et al. 2012). In 2012 the IUCN called on states, NGOs, and

Figure 2.4. The village of Khunde and part of the Khumjung-Khunde protected community forest, Sagarmatha National Park and Buffer Zone and World Heritage Site, Nepal. These villages continue to manage all forest shown in the photograph, despite the incorporation of their collective lands into the national park. In recent years, the Khunde and Khumjung village assemblies have tightened protection by banning tree felling and gathering deadwood for fuel.

the IUCN's bodies to "recognize and support ICCAs in situations where they overlap with protected area or other designations" by adopting resolution 5.094, Respecting, Recognizing and Supporting Indigenous Peoples' and Community Conserved Territories and Areas, at the 5th WCC (IUCN 2012d). This can be done by recognizing Indigenous peoples' customary ICCAs as protected areas or appropriately recognizing ICCAs within state protected areas through such means as national laws and administrative regulations for national protected area systems and for individual protected areas, legally binding memoranda of understanding, and protected area management plans that recognize Indigenous peoples' responsibility for the governance of particular areas or zones or specific activities such as hunting, fishing, collecting, grazing, and forest use in all or part of protected areas. Recognition that requires ICCAs to meet narrow standards or undermines their autonomy, however, can diminish their effectiveness and violate rights (see chapters 11 and 12; Borrini-Feyerabend et al. 2010, 2013; Stevens 2010, 2014; Jonas et al. 2012; Kothari et al. 2012).

Shared Governance (Comanagement) of Protected Areas

Shared governance has been a central component of the new paradigm since its early formulations (Colchester 1997; Stevens 1997a; IUCN WCPA 2003b; Phillips 2003; Borrini-Feyerabend et al. 2004a, 2004b). It is now firmly enshrined in IUCN and CBD policies, which identify shared governance as one of four approved forms of protected area governance and specifically promote it. Diverse arrangements, often referred to as "comanagement," "joint management," "participatory" management, and "collaborative" or "consultative" management, are in place in many different countries. These differ enormously in institutional arrangements, participation and decision-making dynamics, and degree of power sharing (see chapters 5, 6, 9, 10, and 12; De Lacy and Lawson 1997; Sneed 1997; Stevens 1997a; Lawrence 2000; Borrini-Feyerabend et al. 2004a, 2004b, 2013; Kothari 2006a; Galvin and Haller 2008; Haynes 2009, 2013).[21] Shared governance can be envisioned as a spectrum of different approaches that constitute the middle of a continuum between state or other top-down governance by outsiders and Indigenous governance. Its variable arrangements range from informal consultation to full sharing of decision-making authority. Although shared governance of protected areas often is portrayed as an equal partnership, in practice states and NGOs often refuse to share power equitably with Indigenous peoples. Weaver (1991) and Sneed (1997) argued that shared governance (as comanagement) must include effective participation in policy formulation, planning, management, and monitoring and evaluation (see also Stevens 1997a).

Proponents conceive of shared governance as a collaboration that benefits from shared knowledge, experience, purpose, and effort. It can be a "process of collective understanding and action by which human communities and other social actors manage natural resources and ecosystems together, drawing from everyone's unique strengths, vantage points, and capacities" that can make possible "the birth of many forms of social 'syncretism' and synergy" by promoting new cross-cultural interaction and dialogue (Borrini-Feyerabend et al. 2004b: xxx). Shared work, responsibilities, and rewards can lead to greater respect, trust, and commitment to mutual aid (Haynes 2009) and facilitate social learning, the coproduction of knowledge, and adaptive management (Berkes 2009a, 2009b). At its best shared governance can be "one of the most effective ways to mobilize . . . conservation-relevant resources" that use the "substantial wealth and diversity of conservation-relevant knowledge, skills, resources and institutions at the disposal of indigenous, mobile and local communities, local governments, NGOs, resource users and the private sector" as well as national governments (IUCN WPC 2003 V.25). Full and effective participation by Indigenous peoples in shared governance arrangements, with real power-sharing and recognition of Indigenous rights, however, has been relatively rare (chapter 12).

The potential benefits of shared governance for Indigenous peoples are many, including recognition, restitution, and defense of territory; self-respect and pride; greater recognition and respect for their knowledge and institutions, including ICCAs; support for self-identified capacity building and projects; increased access to information and resources including revenue sharing from protected area entrance fees, taxes, and license fees; employment; preferential access to business licenses and protected area concessionaire contracts; and conservation funding such as ecological service payments and overhead fees for supervising NGO programs. State assistance in protecting territorial integrity from unwanted settlement and development may be particularly valued. Shared governance of protected areas can even become part of a process of reconciliation that can support Indigenous peoples' sovereignty and policies that express and sustain their values and secure their rights (Ross et al. 2011). Yet sharing governance can diminish autonomy, and many peoples have found that in practice they have been disappointed with power-sharing arrangements and the degree of respect for their cultures, concerns, and rights. Often potential intercultural and multiscale conservation synergies fail to evolve. Some of the reasons for this are discussed in chapters 5, 6, 10, and 12.

Indigenous peoples now share in the governance of protected areas in many countries, generally with state agencies (Stevens 1997a; Borrini-Feyerabend et al. 2004a, 2004b, 2013; Kothari 2006a). The earliest example dates back more than a century to the establishment of Tongariro National Park, New Zealand, in 1894 (figure 2.5).[22] Today at least some of the protected areas in countries as diverse as Australia, Canada, the United States, South Africa, the Philippines, Indonesia, Nepal, Guatemala, Colombia, Peru, and Bolivia have shared governance arrangements.[23] Indigenous peoples now share in the governance of thirteen or more Canadian national park reserves encompassing more than 18 million hectares and more than 150 Australian protected areas, including iconic Uluru-Kata Tjuta National Park and World Heritage Site and Kakadu National Park and World Heritage Site (Australian Government Department of the Environment 2012). In Europe, the Saami now comanage Laponia World Heritage Site in Sweden, which includes Sweden's oldest national parks. Kaa-Iya del Gran Chaco National Park and Integrated Management Area

Figure 2.5. Tongariro National Park and World Heritage Site and Lake Rotoaira, New Zealand. The national park was established after a Ngāti Tūwharetoa *iwi* Māori leader "gifted" the sacred mountain Tongariro to the British crown for protection in 1887. This was the first national park in the world in which an Indigenous people participated in shared governance. In 1993 it became the first natural World Heritage site to be declared both a natural World Heritage site and a World Heritage cultural landscape. Lake Rotoaira, outside of the national park, is administered on behalf of the Ngāti Tūwharetoa *iwi* owners by the Lake Rotoaira Trust.

in Bolivia (the first national park in South America created at the request of an Indigenous people), Kruger National Park (South Africa), Richtersveld National Park (South Africa and Namibia), Kgalagadi Transfrontier Park (South Africa and Botswana), and the many "cogoverned" national parks of Colombia (where cogovernance is required by national law in overlap situations) are other examples (Kothari 2006a; Kothari et al. 2012; Borrini-Feyerabend et al. 2013). Indigenous peoples also share in the governance of some U.S. protected areas, including Canyon de Chelly National Monument in the Navajo Nation. There is also a formal comanagement arrangement between Lakota and the U.S. National Park Service for the South Unit of Badlands National Park, and the Subsistence Resource Commissions provide advice on hunting, fishing, and other polices to the vast national parks established in Alaska in 1980. The third of Death

Figure 2.6. Entrance sign to Death Valley National Park, United States. This sign attests to the recognition, after long struggle, that the largest national park in the contiguous states remains the homeland of the Timbisha Shoshone tribe. In 2000, 300 acres of land within the national park were restituted to the Timbisha Shoshone by an act of Congress, and provisions were made for their use and comanagement of a third of the national park as a Timbisha Shoshone Natural and Cultural Preservation Area.

Valley National Park that is designated the Timbisha Shoshone Natural and Cultural Preservation Area is to be comanaged by the Timbisha Shoshone and the National Park Service (figure 2.6).

Taking Stock and Looking Forward

In recent years, policies have been adopted by the IUCN, the CBD, and some states that reconceptualize protected areas and the role of Indigenous peoples in conservation. As this book's case studies highlight, however, shifting paradigms is easier done rhetorically than on the ground. Many states and some conservation organizations are reluctant to fully and effectively implement the new paradigm, not only because it requires rethinking often strongly held assumptions and prejudices about conservation but also because it challenges entrenched social and political relationships and power dynamics.[24] I discuss ongoing international efforts to overcome these obstacles in chapter 12.

Yet despite the formidable challenges, it is no small matter that Indigenous peoples, the IUCN, and the CBD have developed a new vision that links conservation, culture, and rights in new kinds of protected areas. That this is now so strongly articulated in international conservation policy is a major achievement that provides a foundation for the awareness raising, capacity building, and political work ahead. There is now clarity about what aspects of protected area law, policy, and practices need to be reformed and what new principles should be upheld. Detailed guidance is being developed for appropriate establishment, governance, and management of protected areas. The nine case studies that follow examine implementation experiences in diverse contexts.

Notes

1. This was the strongest participation ever by Indigenous peoples in a WPC (Indigenous Peoples Ad Hoc Working Group for the World Parks Congress 2003a).

2. The new paradigm was developed over several decades, and many components of it were already under discussion or were IUCN policy before the Durban WPC (Colchester 1997; Stevens 1997a; Gray et al. 1998; Phillips 2003). In this account, I emphasize the aspects of the new paradigm particularly concerned with Indigenous peoples and protected areas (see also the characterization of the new paradigm in the 2008 IUCN WCC Resolution 4.048; Larsen 2006). The new paradigm is also concerned with other things, including ecosystem management, landscape-scale conservation, and the development of systems of protected areas that are representative of ecological diversity (see, for example, the fifteen targets of the IUCN Vth WPC *Durban Accord* and *Durban Action Plan* and Phillips 2003; Lockwood et al. 2006; Chapin et al. 2008).

3. Mobile indigenous peoples include nomadic and transhumant pastoralists, swidden farmers, and peoples who move seasonally between different areas for farming, hunting, fishing, and plant collecting. Their recognition at the Vth WPC was a major advance in international conservation policies toward Indigenous peoples.

4. These are further articulated in several of the recommendations adopted by the congress, including V.24, Indigenous Peoples and Protected Areas; V.25, Comanagement of Protected Areas; V.26, Community Conserved Areas; and V.27, Mobile Indigenous Peoples and Conservation.

5. The 1992 CBD, however, also contains qualifying language. Implementation of Article 8(j), for example, is to be "subject to its national legislation" and Article 10(c) should be implemented only "as far as possible and as appropriate." Moreover, both

lack any mention of rights, refer to "indigenous and local communities" rather than to Indigenous peoples and local communities, and refer to "traditional lifestyles" and "traditional cultural practices" rather than also recognizing Indigenous peoples' development of new knowledge, institutions, and sustainable practices.

6. IUCN support for the recognition of the rights of Indigenous peoples within protected areas dates to Resolution 12.5, Protection of Traditional Ways of Life, adopted by the Twelfth IUCN General Assembly in Kinshasa, Zaire, and provisions in the 1996 Resolution 1.53, Indigenous Peoples and Protected Areas, adopted by the First WCC in Montreal, Canada. Implementation of these policies by the IUCN's member states and organizations, however, has been poor.

7. The recent *Guidelines for Protected Areas Legislation* (Lausche and Burhenne 2011) produced by the IUCN's Commission on Environmental Law and its World Commission on Protected Areas, for example, mentioned UNDRIP and ILO 169 but did not explore in depth their implications for protected area law and policy. The various chapters of another recent IUCN publication, *Conservation with Justice: A Rights-Based Approach* (Greiber et al. 2009) vary considerably in their engagement with Indigenous rights issues (the chapter on rights-based approaches to protected areas does not mention UNDRIP or ILO 169). At the same time IUCN has committed to uphold UNDRIP in multiple 2008 and 2012 WCC resolutions, and the IUCN Policy on Conservation and Human Rights for Sustainable Development, adopted by Resolution 5.099 (IUCN 2012e), includes implementation of UNDRIP and attention to the targets of Outcome 5 of the *Durban Action Plan* (chapter 1) among its guiding principles for mainstreaming respect for rights in IUCN's activities.

8. *Governance of Protected Areas* (Borrini-Feyerabend et al. 2013: 72) explains that subsidiarity in the context of protected areas governance is achieved by "attributing management authority and responsibility to the institutions closest to the resources, compatible with capacities."

9. Another way of framing broad good governance principles for protected areas is as "respect for rights and the rule of law; promotion of constructive dialogue and fair access to information; accountability in decision-making; and existence of institutions and procedures for fair dispute resolution" (Borrini-Feyerabend et al. 2013: 4).

10. What the right to "full and effective participation" should mean requires clarification by both the IUCN and CBD.

11. The new paradigm also affirms the value of protected areas with diverse management goals, including Category V, protected landscapes and seascapes, and Category VI, protected areas with sustainable use of natural resources.

12. Although the term ICCA has come into widespread use, such protected areas also can be conceptualized as "Indigenous peoples' protected areas" or "community protected areas." For discussion of why some ICCAs do not meet IUCN protected area criteria, see Broome (2009), Kothari et al. (2012), and Borrini-Feyerabend et al. (2013). It is also important to note that Indigenous peoples should decide whether they wish their territories and areas to be designated as ICCAs or protected areas and whether they wish them to be included in national protected area systems or in national or international ICCA registries or databases.

13. On the importance of appropriate ICCA recognition and respect for realizing many of the rights identified in UNDRIP, ILO 169, the Convention on the Elimination of All Forms of Racial Discrimination, and other international law, see Stevens

(2010, 2014). Appropriate ICCA recognition and respect, including reestablishment or rejuvenation of ICCAs in situations where they have been destroyed or undermined by state protected area policies and practices, can be an important remedy and redress for past injustices. However, this realization of rights hinges on the character and quality of recognition. State recognition can violate rights, for example, when it recognizes ICCAs without Indigenous peoples' free, prior, and informed consent or does so in ways that co-opt, standardize, or undermine existing institutions and practices (see chapter 12; Borrini-Feyerabend 2010; Borrini-Feyerabend et al. 2010, 2013; Kothari et al. 2012). It must also be recognized that Indigenous peoples may not wish to dedicate and manage all of their lands for conservation purposes, and efforts to compel or induce them to do so violate their right to self-determination.

14. The IUCN and CBD do not yet acknowledge that Indigenous peoples' territorial ownership is essential for appropriate recognition and respect for their ICCAs. Many ICCA advocates, however, consider this to be critical.

15. ICCAs—like other conservation-associated institutions and practices—should not be romanticized. There has been considerable discussion of the many internal and external factors and contexts that can weaken or destroy ICCAs and diminish their effectiveness (see, for example, Borrini-Feyerabend 2010; Borrini-Feyerabend et al. 2010; Kothari et al. 2012). There has been less analysis of the internal and multiscale or multilevel relational and contextual factors associated with effective ICCAs (in conservation, livelihood, or socio-cultural terms; see, however, Borrini-Feyerabend 2010; Borrini-Feyerabend et al. 2010). Much work on the collective management of commons and sacred places, however, is applicable to ICCAs, including the significance of community and external relations and contexts, worldviews, values, and beliefs as well as institutional arrangements, rules, and enforcement (see, for example, Blaikie and Brookfield 1987; McCay and Atkinson 1990; Ostrom 1990; Posey 1999; Agrawal 2002; Ostrom et al. 2002; Lee and Schaaf 2003; Schaaf and Lee 2006; Wild and McLeod 2008; Verschuuren et al. 2010; Pungetti et al. 2012). It is also important to acknowledge that the governance of some ICCAs is dominated by local political, social, and cultural elites and that ICCAs' diverse benefits may not be equally realized by all community members.

16. Kothari et al. (2012) provided some preliminary data on ICCA numbers in a range of countries.

17. Under Papua New Guinea law, wildlife management areas (WMAs) are declared and governed by Indigenous peoples on their own lands. Yet while some WMAs are ICCAs (Eaton 1997), in practice others seem rather to be governed by international NGOs and the state more than by Indigenous peoples (West 2006). Mark Dowie (2009) has also raised important concerns about the appropriate participation by concerned Indigenous peoples in the recent establishment of protected areas in the territories of the Wai Wai and Wapichan. Concern over co-optation is also a factor in Mexico. Indigenous peoples and local communities in Mexico can declare their collective lands to be community conserved areas, as more than a hundred have, for example, in Oaxaca state. These can be recognized as Voluntary Conserved Areas in the national protected area system, but there is concern that this could lead to states transforming ICCAs into shared governance regimes (Martin 2010).

18. While most of these are established on Indigenous territories recognized by treaty or other legal means, some are declared in customary territories whose ownership by

Indigenous peoples is not recognized by the state (for example, the Tla-o-qui-aht Tribal Parks on Vancouver Island in British Columbia, Canada, and the proposed Wapichan Conserved Forest, Guyana).

19. In this book I use the term ICCA to include ICTs.

20. Whether an Indigenous peoples' territory is considered to be an ICT depends, however, on its conservation attributes.

21. Many countries refer to the shared governance of protected areas as "comanagement" or "joint management." In this book, in accordance with current IUCN practice, I generally will refer to these arrangements as shared governance.

22. The establishment of Tongariro National Park followed the gifting of the summits of that mountain and two other peaks in 1887 to Queen Victoria by a Ngāti Tuwharatoa *iwi* ("tribe") leader, Horonuku Te Heuheu Tukino IV. One condition of the gift was that his son was to be appointed for life to the first board established to manage the Tongariro National Park. Thereafter, the Minister of Lands was to name a successor to the son on five-year terms. The chief's representative had all the same rights as others on the board, including a right to vote (Department of Conservation/ Te Papa Atawhai, Tongariro/Taupō Conservancy [New Zealand] 2006). While this arrangement facilitated Ngāti Tuwharatoa participation in national park governance, it did not constitute an equal partnership. The arrangement, moreover, did not recognize participation by other *iwi* who live around the mountain (Ruru 2008). See Boast (2008) on the many questions raised in the nineteenth century regarding whether Horonuku Te Heuheu had authority to gift the mountains, the subsequent process by which that gift was given and received, and the eventual establishment of the national park.

23. The shared governance arrangements of many protected areas (including several of the examples cited in the text), however, are far from exemplary. Many fail to secure Indigenous peoples' full and effective participation and rights. (For a discussion of common issues with shared governance, see chapter 12.)

24. These same challenges also have slowed land restitution, administrative devolution, forest tenure reform (Sikor and Stahl 2011), recognition of Indigenous rights, and implementation of international human rights treaties.

CHAPTER THREE

Community-Oriented Protected Areas for Indigenous Peoples and Local Communities

Indigenous Protected Areas in Australia

Marcia Langton, Lisa Palmer, and Zane Ma Rhea

Across the globe, community-oriented protected areas have been recognized as an effective way to support the preservation and maintenance of the traditional biodiversity-related knowledge of Indigenous peoples and local communities (chapters 1 and 2). Our research on the federal Indigenous Protected Area (IPA) program in Australia shows that guaranteed land security and the ability of Indigenous and local peoples to exercise their own governance structures are central to the success of community-oriented protected area programs.[1] We examine the conservation and community development outcomes of the IPA program established in 1996 by the Federal Department of Environment and Heritage. This program is based on the premise that Indigenous landowners should exercise effective control over environmental governance, including management plans, and have effective control of access to their lands, waters, and resources. Most IPAs thus meet the IUCN's criteria for ICCAs (chapter 2) that are included in the national protected area system at Indigenous peoples' request and without undermining their self-governance and control over their territories.[2]

We also examine the ways in which programs such as IPAs can contribute to supporting the lifeways of Indigenous peoples and local communities, assist in the preservation and maintenance of their traditional biodiversity-related knowledge, and enable Indigenous peoples and local communities to participate in both customary subsistence and market economies. In contrast to many critiques of community-based conservation elsewhere, we argue that community-oriented protected areas are delivering significant benefits to Indigenous peoples in Australia. Along with the strengthening of traditional modes of governance and sustainable land management regimes, we argue that the benefits accruing to Indigenous peoples and local communities from participation in community-oriented and, most crucially, *community-controlled* protected area initiatives can include the preservation, renewal, and maintenance of the knowledge systems upon which Indigenous livelihoods and environmental security depend.[3]

Traditional Livelihoods and Biodiversity

A growing literature has recognized the role of traditional knowledge and practices in preserving biodiversity (Nietschmann 1992b; Ghai 1994; Mathias 1994, 1995; Matowanyika et al. 1995; Maundu 1995; Richards 1995; Maffi 2001; Ferarri 2003; Posey 2003). For Indigenous peoples and local communities, concern about the preservation and maintenance of traditional knowledge is not only motivated by the desire to conserve biodiversity as an end in itself but also by the desire to live on their ancestral lands, to safeguard local food security, and, to the extent possible, to exercise local economic, cultural, and political autonomy (see, for example, Langton 2003). In economically developed nations such as Australia, a significant proportion of Indigenous peoples in rural and remote areas are dependent on traditional knowledge and practices in caring for their traditional territories and for harvesting wild food and animals, medicines, water, and other basic needs. Hunting, gathering, and fishing continue to contribute a substantial part of the diet and basic needs for populations in rural and remote areas of Australia. Elsewhere, for example, most economically developing nation-states of the Asian region do not have the capacity for all of the people who live within their borders to fully enter the market economy. Without attention paid to the protection and preservation of the lands and waters of local communities and Indigenous peoples and to their continuing subsistence knowledge, management, and practices, these nation-states would be unable to feed their populations.

In relation to what are commonly termed hunter-gather societies, Western literature generally emphasizes "the subsistence role rather than the productivity of hunting (the production of social cohesion, the communication with the mythic countryside, and the gathering of healthy foods for the human body)" (Povinelli 1993: 60). We agree with Povenelli's contention that "hunting and gathering contributes to local cultural, economic, and sociological well-being" (1993: 62), and support for this can be found throughout the literature. We also agree with Povinelli (1993: 24) in her contention that "discussions of the Fourth World have as yet failed to describe adequately the dense network of economic, political, and cultural motivations that account for indigenous practice (in particular indigenous struggles to produce economic and cultural well-being in the postcolonial nation) or to theorize the relationship between the productivity of indigenous practice and the production of cultural identity."

These points are well borne out in the findings of both Jon Altman (1987, 2003) and Elizabeth Povinelli (1993), just two of the anthropologists whose work has described the actual food and other production of such hunting and gathering economies in Australia. Altman (2003) and Povinelli (1993) have argued that despite the impacts of modernization, which has caused accelerated change across traditional societies and their different economic systems, hunting and gathering bush foods in northern Australia continue as socially integrated aspects of Aboriginal lifestyles. Based on her work in a northern Australian Aboriginal community, Povinelli (1993: 59–60) documented, for instance, that, "at times of economic scarcity, bush foods provide an important supplement to people's diet." Altman (2003: 71) compared his earlier fieldwork findings in a remote northern Australian Aboriginal community with those of 2002: "In 1979–1980 I observed 90 animal species . . . regularly harvested and 80 plant species consumed while 56 plant species . . . were used in non-dietary ways, mainly in the manufacture of artefacts." In 2002, Altman (2003: 72) found that the harvesting practices were remarkably similar: "In ecological terms, . . . there had been no decline in the common species generally harvested. . . . Furthermore, information on harvesting levels and species stocks makes it clear that harvesting is within ecologically sustainable limits . . . this economy is structurally the same hybrid economy with customary (hunting), market (arts production and sale) and state (income support transfers) sectors in both periods."

The diverse systems of food production among Indigenous societies affect in various ways the readiness of governments to institute protected areas and the legal nature of such protected areas with respect to the recognition of subsistence rights. The readiness of nation-states to recognize the intertwined destinies of natural and cultural diversity in the areas where traditional societies continue economic subsistence practices and related knowledge systems is influenced at the highest political levels not only by the supportive provisions of the Convention on Biological Diversity (CBD), the UN Declaration on the Rights of Indigenous Peoples, and IUCN policy (chapters 1 and 2) but also by environmental NGOs, whose understanding of these issues has often lagged behind the urgent demands of the Indigenous and local peoples for protection of their traditional resource rights (see, for example, Magome and Murombedzi 2003).

Although over the last decade environmental organizations have begun to champion the link between environmental protection and the "protection" of Indigenous peoples, some writers such as Chapin (2004) argue that an apparent lack of success in this endeavor has led international environmental organizations to retract their support in practice, if not in their rhetoric. Similarly Langton (2003: 142) observed, "As well as the opposition by some governments seeking to appropriate indigenous lands and resources, conservationist organizations resist compromise on land use issues because they believe that global biodiversity preservation goals take precedence over the needs of local people." The implications of such attitudes are profound, given what often appear to be the seamless alliances forged between the rhetoric of ecological modernization and the state. In this context, the rights of Indigenous and local communities are, more often than not, limited by statutes and regulations because of the ideological stance that modern nation-states have toward these subsistence economic systems, holding them to be backward ways of life against the belief in progressive ways of life that the modern global economy is purported to offer (Li 2003; Colchester 2004).

The Emergence of Community-Oriented Protected Areas

The shift from a "fortress conservation" framework to a community-oriented protected areas approach has emerged alongside international trends seeking to combine conservation and community development, the notion of community-based conservation (chapter 2; Phillips 2003). This has paralleled shifts in the discipline of applied ecology away from reductionism to a systems view of the ecosystem, toward an inclusion of humans in the ecosystem, and away from expert-based approaches to participatory approaches to ecosystem management (Berkes 2004).

There are criticisms of the community-based conservation approach. Berkes, among others, noted that "the term *community* hides a great deal of complexity" (2004: 623). Rather than isolated and static entities, Berkes argued that communities are better thought of as "multi-dimensional, cross-scale, social-political units or networks changing through time" (2004: 623). Others have noted that uncritically linking together conservation and development objectives is often counter-productive for both objectives (Redford and Sanderson 2000; see also Agrawal and Ribot 2000; Adams et al. 2004; Agrawal and Redford 2005). An equally critical gaze needs to be cast over the reasons for the success or failure of project outcomes that arise from community-based conservation based on community-oriented participation in externally controlled conservation projects and programs and those conservation-oriented projects and programs that are themselves community driven and controlled. The critical objects of analysis here are the environmental governance frameworks employed and the location of authority in decision-making and project responsibility.

We examine developments in protected area management in Australia, specifically the IPA program, and the ways in which such programs are opening a space for the mainstream recognition of Indigenous peoples' environmental governance priorities and decision-making processes. According to Tsing (2005: 264), despite the "standard lines" pitched to funding agencies to enable such collaborations "when the grantees go home," those involved in the projects—individuals, communities, their advocates, and critics—"must work these lines into the matrix of possibilities offered by their practical situations." Tsing (2005: 5–6) deployed the "metaphorical image of friction" to remind us "that heterogeneous and unequal encounters can lead to new arrangements of culture and power. . . . The effects of encounters across difference can be compromising or empowering." In these contexts, she noted, "'Communities' are constituted in relation to other kinds of scale-making projects, including bureaucracies, nations and international bodies of power and expertise. Community-making projects may or may not empower local peoples; it all depends on just how this relation is organised: Who benefits?" (2005: 264).

It is our contention that the IPA program does offer Indigenous peoples involved in the program a way to benefit from the global conversations created by the "engaged universals" of nature conservation (Tsing 2005). We focus on the ways in which local communities can draw in outsiders through their engagements with the ideas of "nature," "biodiversity conservation," "protected areas," "sustainable use," "food security," "Indigenous people," and "human rights," invoking and drawing on the power of such "engaged universals" to enable diverse interests to come together in conversation and build relationships, despite what is often a dissonance in the meanings and priorities attributed to the concepts themselves (see Tsing 2005). In this way the IPA program can be seen as an opportunity to gain traction for, among other things, maintaining knowledge, livelihood practices, self-governance, relationships with territory, restoring country, and realizing rights.

Protected Areas in Australia

Like Indigenous peoples elsewhere, Aboriginal and Torres Strait Islander peoples living in rural and remote areas of Australia are concerned with promoting and maintaining their active involvement in the pursuit of environmental security and sustainable economic livelihoods on their ancestral lands.

In the National Strategy for the Conservation of Australia's Biodiversity, the Australian government has committed to enhancing the effective participation of Indigenous Australians in the management and protection of biological diversity. There are various legal and practical reasons for the Australian government to incorporate Indigenous customary interests into the broader Australian project of land, sea, and resource conservation. Land and water subject to Indigenous ownership and governance constitutes a significant and substantial proportion—more than 20 percent—of the Australian continent, particularly in northern and central Australia.[4] Since the High Court's finding in the landmark Mabo[5] judgment and the codification of the Native Title Act of 1993, native title rights to land, sea, and resources are now recognized in Australia's legislative landscape.[6] In 1999, some customary rights to fauna were also found to exist as a form of native title by the High Court of Australia.[7] Furthermore, Indigenous ownership and input to management of land will increase as statutory and Indigenous corporations acquire more land for constituent groups through commercial dealings and as Indigenous groups exercise their statutory and common law native title rights and acquire access to, and control of, national parks and state forests under management and cultural heritage agreements (Hassall and Associates 2003: 100).[8]

Despite the influence of the North American model on the development of its national parks, Australia has, in relation to certain key national parks, taken a lead role in the development of joint management agreements with Indigenous groups. Nevertheless, in jointly managed parks where Indigenous people maintain ownership and varied degrees of control over their estates, tensions still arise between Western and Indigenous ways of practicing land management. This is the case in the Kakadu and Uluru-Kata Tjuta National Parks, which are jointly managed by a lease agreement between traditional Aboriginal landowners and the federal government (see, for example, Lawrence 2000; Power 2002; Palmer 2004a, 2004b).

The federal government's IPA program was established in 1996 as a part of its push to establish a National Reserve System. According to the national strategy, the aim of this system was to "establish and manage a comprehensive, adequate and representative system of protected areas covering Australia's biological diversity" (Commonwealth of Australia 1996: 9). It aimed to address gaps in the kinds of ecosystems under protected area management and divided the continent in eighty-five regions under a process called the Interim Biogeographic Regionalisation of Australia, based on factors associated with climate, lithology, geology, landforms, and vegetation. The Interim Biogeographic Regionalisation of Australia provides the bioregional planning framework for developing the National Reserve System, and the data generated on existing protected areas and gaps in the protected area estate are used to inform future land acquisitions. The usual method of adding to the nation's conservation estate is through the government purchase of land for dedication as parks and reserves.

However, as the Interim Biogeographic Regionalisation of Australia planning framework was drawn up, the government officials recognized that in some instances, such as under the provisions of the Aboriginal Land Rights Act of 1976 in the Northern Territory, Aboriginal people owned whole bioregions. Moreover, the existence of native title, native title claims, and the future act regime built in the Native Title Act of 1993 were all issues that would impinge upon the government's appropriation of land for the national reserve system. In addition, the Indigenous Land Corporation (ILC), a statutory body set up to meet the needs of

Indigenous groups who because of the extent of their dispossession and the subsequent common law interpretation of the act were unlikely to achieve success with native title claims, increased the size of the Indigenous estate through sizeable land purchases.

At the same time, there were increasing interest and initiatives by Indigenous landholders to reestablish their land management traditions and cooperate with government conservation agencies to achieve their aspirations (Smyth and Sutherland 1996: 96–97). These initiatives were complemented at the international level by a new IUCN system of protected area categories (chapter 1), which substantially recognized "the rights and interests of indigenous people to own, manage and sustainably use areas of land and sea of high conservation value" (Smyth and Sutherland 1996: 96–97).

These new categories allowed for the establishment of protected areas that linked land and associated cultural values managed through legal or other effective means. This created possibilities to enable Indigenous landowners to manage protected areas on parity with the mainstream protected area estate. These combined initiatives resulted in the federal conservation agency conducting a consultation process with Indigenous organizations and state conservation agencies to discuss the establishment of what would become the IPA program (Smyth 1995).

However, when Indigenous groups and their representative bodies came together at two national workshops and expressed interest in the IPA idea as it could be applied to land owned by Indigenous peoples, this interest was subject to several conditions set by Indigenous groups:

- There would no loss of control over land by Indigenous people. There was concern that government would try to take over the management of IPA land.
- That landowners make the decisions and the plan of management on their own terms.
- That the role of government would remain one of a "good neighbor" providing advice and technical support on a needs basis on matters relating to issues such as weeds, feral animal management, and tourism infrastructure.
- That the commitment by government for the IPA program would be long term.
- That the government addresses, as an issue of equity, Aboriginal involvement in protected area management for those groups who have no land base as a result of dispossession (Steve Szabo, pers. comm., 2002).

Following these negotiations, the federal government proceeded with the establishment of an IPA program with two components: (1) the development and declaration of IPAs on Indigenous-owned land where land owners manage the land as independent bodies, and (2) a program to assist and support Indigenous people to negotiate a land management role in existing government-owned national parks and reserves with state agencies through some type of comanagement arrangement.

The IPA program, supported by the federal government's Natural Heritage Trust, began in 1996 with an undertaking to develop twelve pilot projects in diverse locations including high-density settled areas and remote areas. Some were IPA scoping projects and others were investigating comanagement initiatives. The first declared IPA was Nantawarrina near the Flinders Ranges in South Australia in August 1998. By 2005, another eighteen IPAs had been declared, eleven others had been funded to pursue comanagement arrangements in government-owned protected areas, and fourteen more groups received interim funding to investigate the possibility of establishing an IPA (figure 3.1).[9] Since then, the scheme has expanded considerably. There are now sixty declared IPAs in Australia covering 48 million hectares and making up 36 percent of the National Reserve System. In addition, the IPA area may expand further in coming years, as the program, now managed by the Indigenous Affairs Group (Department of the Prime Minister and Cabinet), includes twenty-seven consultation projects across Australia.[10]

Each IPA has a plan of management, is declared under one or more IUCN categories, undergoes a process of public declaration, and is entirely managed by Indigenous landowners. IPAs like Nantawarrina and Deen Maar in southern Australia, once significantly denuded farm and pastoral lands, are now significantly regenerated, prompting the return of a diversity of native species of flora and fauna (see, for example, Krishnapillai 2000; Muller 2003). IPA agreements are voluntary and are made between the Policy and Coordination Section of the department and Indigenous communities, land councils, and other Indigenous bodies. The security and viability of IPAs lie in the establishment of long-term land-use agreements offering financial support from the government. These take the form of contractual one-year financial assistance agreements. Average annual funding from the Department of Environment and Heritage to each IPA is A$110,000 (US$77,000) per annum (Szabo and Smyth 2003: 157). At present, however, IPAs offer only short-term funding contracts, so that Indigenous land management organizations must constantly seek ongoing and additional sources of funding.

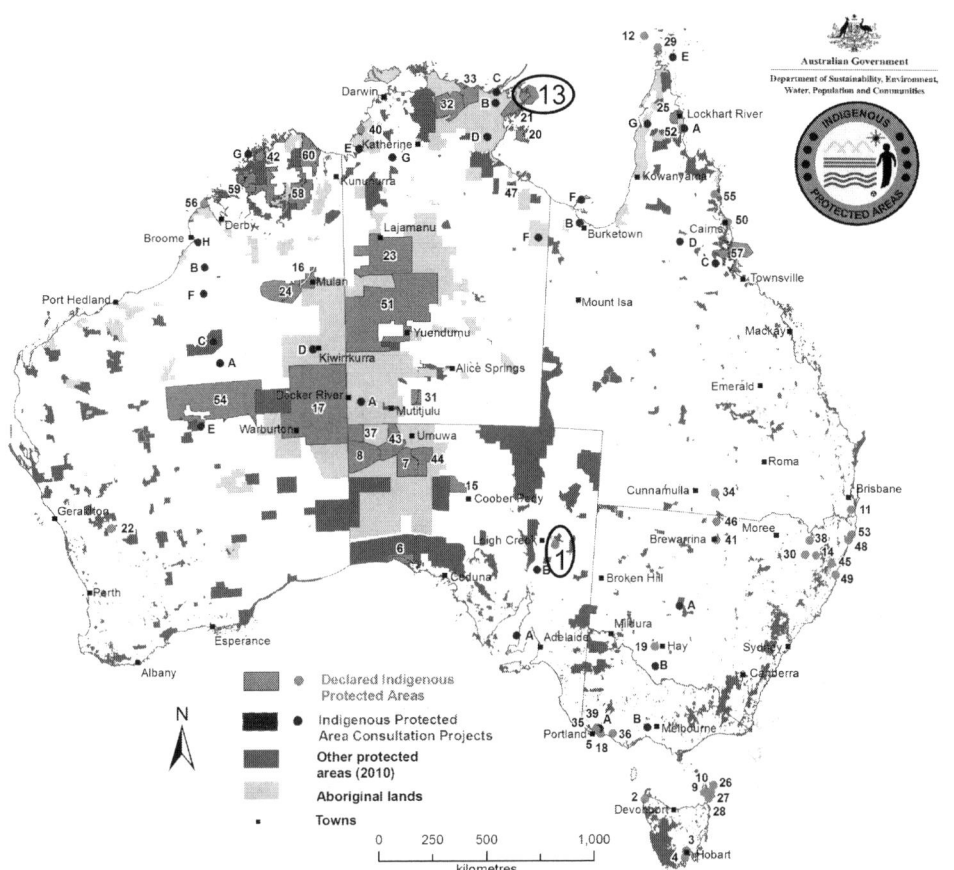

Figure 3.1. Indigenous Protected Areas of Australia, August 2013. The numbers on the map refer to declared IPAs, the letters indicate IPA consultation projects, and the two case studies in the chapter, Nantawarrina and Dhimurru IPAs, are indicated by the numbers 1 and 13.

In many cases, the declaration of IPAs and the provision of training and capacity building for IPA managers and annual financial assistance have empowered communities and provided significant environmental, economic, social, and cultural benefits. Land management activities range from tourism management and visitor interpretative services to weed and feral animal management and land rehabilitation.

Indigenous land owners participating in the program have also begun entering into conservation agreements with state conservation agencies that provide them with additional technical advice, training capacity, and access to powers relating to permits and law enforcement on their land. They are also building relationships with other state natural resource management agencies and NGOs, establishing partnerships and participating in joint projects and other activities that both attract additional funding and expand the capacities of land owners to pursue their land management objectives. In some cases, Indigenous groups are creating arrangements in which other agents such as mining and tourism companies with interests in the region contribute funds to enable the management of IPAs and surrounding Indigenous lands.

In the following sections, we discuss some of the key elements and characteristics of two IPAs. This discussion is informed by findings in project archives and the published literature in the case of the Nantawarrina IPA in South Australia and fieldwork carried out by the authors in the case of the Dhimurru IPA in the Northern Territory.[11]

Nantawarrina Indigenous Protected Area

Located adjacent to the Gammon Ranges National Park in the northern Flinders Ranges region of South Australia, the Nantawarrina IPA covers 58,000 hectares.[12] The local Adnyamathanha community living in Nepabunna numbers some eighty people, and their local land management organization manages the land for conservation and cultural values. Title to the land is held by the South Australian Aboriginal Lands Trust on behalf of the Adnyamathanha people. In South Australia, there has been a long history of negotiated settlements between Aboriginal peoples and the state government, including those involving the Anangu Pitjantjatjara and the Maralinga Tjarutja peoples (Mazel 2006). The Aboriginal Lands Trust Act of 1966 was the first statutory recognition of Aboriginal land rights in Australia. In areas where legislative title to land has not yet been secured, Aboriginal peoples in South Australia have sought to address their marginalization in innovative ways (see Davies and Young 1996; Agius et al. 2004).

In her analysis of this IPA program, Samantha Muller (2003) referred to it as a part of the ongoing decolonization of protected areas in Australia. She argued that the success of joint Indigenous/non-Indigenous land management arrangements can best be measured by the extent to which they enable community empowerment, equity, and social justice. Although the experience of joint management of national parks in Australia to date has yet to create conclusive outcomes in these areas,[13] the evidence indicates that these measures of success—empowerment, equity, and social justice—may be more readily achievable under IPA arrangements. Rather than government conservation agencies making a "space" for Indigenous involvement (Porter 2004) within the framework of their own management models, the IPA program allows for Indigenous control of the process from the outset. For example, Muller (2003) reported that the Nantawarrina IPA plan of management was not a plan presented to the community as a finished product for end-of-process consultation or negotiation. Rather, with advisory assistance from the federal environment department project officers,[14] the Adnyamathanha community in Nepabunna and other Aboriginal representatives from the South Australian Aboriginal Lands Trust went through a lengthy planning process, which allowed the community to take ownership of the plan from the outset. Following the finalization of the management plan, the allocation of resources was modeled on the plan under direct community control.

To date, the outcomes of the Nantawarrina IPA process have been successful in terms of the improved conservation of the area's cultural and natural values, particularly in relation to revegetation, weed control, and feral animal management. To employ a local idiom, "the country is coming back." The community is hoping to be able to increase the economic benefit of the land to the community by encouraging tourism. It has been developing small-scale tourism infrastructure and a tourism plan is under preparation.

The land covered by the Nantawarrina IPA was returned to the South Australian Aboriginal Lands Trust in 1966 under the provisions of South Australia's Aboriginal Lands Trust Act. This land had been extensively degraded by pastoralism, and Muller reported that this damage "has been exacerbated by exotic species, in particular goats, donkeys and rabbits" (2003: 35). Prior to the declaration of the IPA, there was significant pressure by the Upper Flinders Ranges Soil Board to improve the environmental health of the area, and the need to access resources to manage the area was a significant part of the community's decision to declare an IPA (Muller 2003). The availability of funding is a critical issue for Indigenous land managers across the Indigenous estate, and its absence feeds criticisms by state agencies about the poor environmental health of areas and the inability of Indigenous people to manage the land effectively. Such is the history of relationships between state agencies and Indigenous communities that within the Nepabunna community itself there was initially a degree of community skepticism about the IPA model, based on suspicions that it was in fact a way for the government to surreptitiously take their lands from them (Muller 2003). Despite these concerns, the community proceeded with the declaration, and two years later they won a United Nations Environment Day award for rehabilitating Nantawarrina (Muller 2003). Community self-esteem has been significantly boosted by the formal recognition of their land management capacities (Muller 2003).

This IPA has also been strengthened by several collaborative arrangements with others, including the federal and state governments' Bounceback 2000 program, which targeted feral animal control and revegetation. At the launch of the IPA in 1998, the community also signed an agreement to establish a cooperative relationship with the South Australian Department of Environment and Heritage and Aboriginal Affairs, which manages the adjacent Gammon Ranges National Park.

There have been some tensions relating to the rights and interests of Adnyamathanha resident elsewhere to access the land and benefit from the IPA (see Muller 2003). However, such issues transcend specific concerns about Nantawarrina and are being dealt with at a regional scale by Aboriginal peoples themselves (see, for example, Agius et al. 2004). Gender bias is another issue of concern in the management of the IPA, and Muller noted a general tendency for governments to fund conservation initiatives entered into with male-dominated organizations. However, Indigenous organizations engaged in land management across Australia are making a concerted effort to better integrate women into formal land management activities.

Dhimurru Indigenous Protected Area

The Dhimurru IPA was declared in October 2000. The area covers more than 101,000 hectares of Aboriginal land and sea country (held mainly under the Aboriginal Land Rights Act) in the northeastern Arnhem Land region of the Northern Territory. In August 2006, Dhimurru launched *Yolŋuwu Monuk Gapu Waŋa*, a Sea Country Plan, which set out a "Yolngu Vision and Plan for Sea Country Management in North-East Arnhem Land, Northern Territory," and received a high commendation from the Minister for the Environment in the 2006 Coastal Custodians Award.[15]

The IPA is managed by the Dhimurru Land Management Aboriginal Corporation (DLMAC) on behalf of the Yolngu traditional owners in accordance with customary law and the IUCN Category V, protected landscape/seascape, defined as a "protected area managed mainly for landscape/seascape conservation and recreation."[16]

Since bauxite mining began in the area in the 1970s, an increasingly large non-Yolngu population has moved into the region. DLMAC was established in 1992 to manage the land designated as recreational in the vicinity of the coastal mining township of Nhulunbuy.[17] The corporation was established by traditional landowners and is directly accountable to them. It has an executive committee comprised of nominated representatives from eleven clans that have an interest in the affected lands, and a quorum of five committee representatives meets regularly to make operational and administrative decisions on behalf of the members. Prior to conducting any land or sea management activity that will have significant impacts, DLMAC is required to consult with the traditional owners of the country concerned. Because DLMAC is directly accountable to traditional owners, it must also operate across its jurisdiction in a manner that is sensitive to the roles of preexisting community organizations with similar functions.

The IPA has an advisory body comprised of the federal environment department, the Parks and Wildlife Commission of the Northern Territory, the Northern Land Council (the regional body that administers the Aboriginal Land Rights Act on behalf of Aboriginal traditional owners), and two Yolngu traditional landowners. This arrangement ensures that Yolngu and their advocates have majority representation, and it is stipulated that the chair must always be a traditional owner.

The only leverage outside agencies have over the IPA is the threat to withdraw from the process. Given their long-standing interest in creating a Northern Territory–controlled national park in the region, members of the Parks and Wildlife Commission of the Northern Territory were initially reluctant participants. With the success of Dhimurru's approach, however, the agency signed an agreement with landowners and DLMAC to provide for ongoing Yolngu ranger training and the delegation of law enforcement powers.

DLMAC and the IPA are initiatives taken by traditional owners as a means to achieve their aspirations and address their concerns for the ongoing management of their lands. They provide Yolngu with ways to manage the land according to customary practices, while creating avenues for them to benefit from and learn the tools of non-Indigenous science (Robinson and Munungguritj 2001; Ayre 2002). Many of the Yolngu rangers who have been employed within the IPA are resource management graduates of an Indigenous higher education institution located elsewhere in the Northern Territory. According to the Dhimurru IPA Management Plan, the guiding principles of Dhimurru are:

> A commitment to the conservation and enhancement of the natural and cultural values of the region while ensuring future management reflects the aspirations of Yolngu (Aboriginal) estate owners;
>
> A commitment to a representative, Yolngu-controlled, sustainable and collective form of land and sea management, which seeks to devise strategies from a mutual investigation of Ngapaki (white) and Yolngu systems of knowledge; and
>
> A commitment to the continued development of positive interactions with the non-Aboriginal world and the sponsoring of cooperative, respectful, educative and mutually beneficial relationships.[18]

The Plan of Management states: "It is a first principle of the Yolngu decision that participation in an IPA arrangement will not diminish in any way their rights and responsibilities with respect to their lands."[19] The decision to enter into an IPA arrangement was taken after traditional owners carried out an investigative tour of a number of joint management and community ranger programs across northern Australia. The autonomy and flexibility offered through the IPA program appealed to the traditional owners and DLMAC because it is a model that allows estate owners to maintain their own management discretion, including being able to close areas to public access immediately should the need arise.[20] This contrasts, for example, with the situation in jointly managed national parks of Uluru-Kata Tjuta and Kakadu, where the approval of the federal director of national parks is required to close, even temporarily, popular tourist sites.[21]

The IPA includes both land and sea areas with significant biodiversity values, including feeding and nesting habitat for sea birds and several threatened species of marine turtle. DLMAC activities include managing visitor access and administering a fee-paying permit system, rehabilitating damage from past uncontrolled access, wildlife protection, participation in quarantine surveys, visitor interpretations, and research including monitoring the impact of marine debris on threatened turtle populations (figures 3.2 and 3.3; see also Langton 1998; Kennett et al. 2004; Robinson and Munuriggurit] 2001; Ayre 2002). DLMAC also manages Yolngu impacts on the area. At the direction of traditional estate owners, the organization

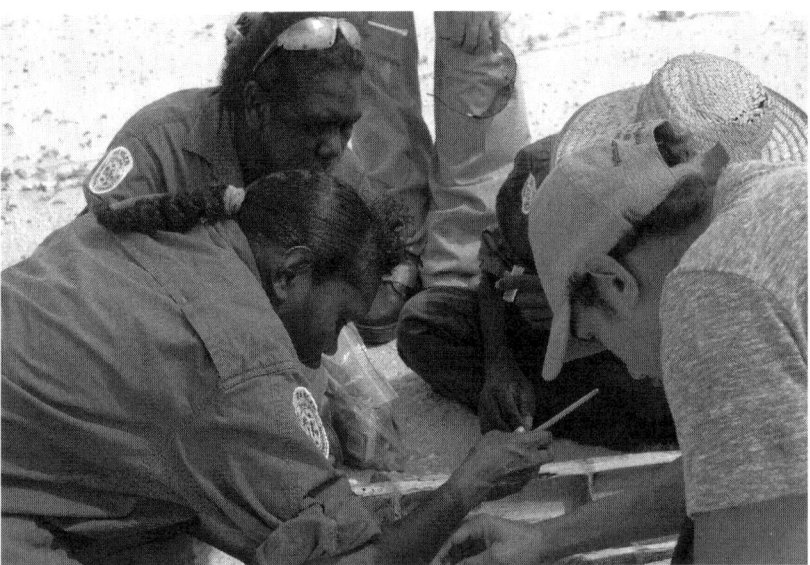

Figure 3.2. Marine debris survey in Wanuwuy conducted by the Dhimurru Aboriginal Corporation. Showing counter-clockwise: Department of Agriculture, Fisheries and Forestry Biosecurity Community Liaison Officer Nhulunbuy, Vern Patullo, and Dhimurru Rangers Bawuli Marika, Wanggawuy Manungguritj, Milika Blackie-Smith, and Ngalkanbuy Manunggurr.

has put in place mechanisms to manage sought-after resources such as turtle eggs in areas deemed by estate owners to be sensitive to, or affected by, overexploitation.

Because permit fees for use of the recreational areas within the IPA cover only a portion of operating costs, additional sponsorship provides crucial project-specific and other funding support for DLMAC and the IPA. These sponsors include the local bauxite mining company, now owned by Rio Tinto Alcan, and a range of environmental organizations such as World Wide Fund for Nature, Australian Conservation Volunteers, and the Threatened Species Network. The local estate-owning organizations initially funded the establishment of DLMAC with funding for a two-year period. Later, this show of community support and the achievements of the organization attracted other support from federally funded conservation programs and the local mining company. Dhimurru's "both ways approach" has meant that the role of the executive officer to date has been filled by a non-Yolngu man with the agreement of the Yolngu

Figure 3.3. Wanuwuy rehabilitation conducted by the Dhimurru Aboriginal Corporation. Showing left to right: Dhimurru Sea Country Facilitator Vanessa Drysdale, Dhimurru Senior Ranger Fiona Marika, Dhimurru Ranger Buduwutpuy Dhurrkay, Dhimurru Ranger Djambatj Pearson, and Dhimurru Senior Ranger Gathapura Mununggurr.

board members, while the majority of other staff is Yolngu. The executive officer's role has involved identifying alternative sources of funding, writing grant applications, and reporting on expenditures to existing funding sources. This position works alongside the director, who conversely has always been a Yolngu, and who oversees Yolngu aspects of the organizations and the critical interface between cultures. The Dhimurru IPA was formally declared eight years after the establishment of DLMAC, and one of the IPA's advantages is that it provided the organization with a relatively stable and streamlined source of funding to manage its core land management business. At the same time, it provided DLMAC with a level of financial viability and institutional legitimacy through which it could attract funding from other sources for additional activities.

The IPA program assists in the payment of the salary of Yolngu staff, including the director. Ranger positions are funded through the Natural

Heritage Trust as part of a yellow crazy ant eradication campaign. Ranger positions are also funded through other programs, including the local Community Development Employment Program (essentially a government-funded work for welfare scheme). The salaries of the executive officer, the permits officer, and the accounts officer are paid in large part by contributions from the local mining company and income from access permit fees. Although DLMAC operates on the assumption that the IPA program will continue to be funded, IPAs are funded on an annual basis. The relative precariousness of these funding arrangements compared to the formalized ongoing government commitments provided to jointly managed national parks was a trade-off considered carefully by Yolngu land owners when they made the decision to pursue the IPA model. In the face of very vocal local and Northern Territory–wide white opposition to the creation of the IPA, senior traditional landowners were adamant from the outset that this was the correct pathway.

The Significance of Community-Oriented Protected Areas

The key points that emerge from the above case studies and discussion of IPAs are the foundational principles of Indigenous control and voluntary participation that underpin the program. The success of these two IPAs has implications beyond the details or even the funding sustainability of the particular conservation model at work, in this case the IPA program.[22] For many remote area Indigenous estate-owning communities in Australia, participation in the conservation sector is one of the only alternatives available to support rural livelihoods. Where the aspirations of local Aboriginal peoples include sustaining their subsistence economy, their participation in the nation's conservation sector generally and the IPA program specifically can provide them with a mechanism to pursue these goals. Arguably, to achieve such success, the principles of the IPA program should underpin all other conservation-oriented programs on Indigenous lands.

It is clear from these examples that to some extent the idea of protected areas in Australia has shifted from a nature-only approach to a concept of protected areas for which the central tenets are natural and cultural resource management regimes governed by local communities in pursuit of environmental security and sustainable economic livelihoods. This trend is also evident globally.

As such, the Australian IPA program offers some critical ideas for the development of community-oriented protected areas elsewhere. Despite cynicism about the nexus of relationships between nation-states, Indigenous and local community struggles, and donor agendas, the niche opened up by the ideology of community-oriented protected areas is significant. If they recognize the relevant political and economic rights and interests of Indigenous peoples and local communities, they can play a role in the maintenance of the biodiversity-related knowledge systems of these groups and, by extension, secure their capacity to control an economically sustainable future through both customary subsistence activities and the negotiated development of their resources within the market economy. Where there is the political and legal will to recognize, support, and engage with Indigenous governance structures in the protection of biodiverse ecosystems, there are potentially myriad positive outcomes for both conservation and sustainable economic and cultural livelihoods.

The success of programs like the IPA program in Australia lies in access to guaranteed land security and the ability of Indigenous people to exercise their own governance structures while accessing the multiplicity of linkages with outside agencies that can assist them to achieve their economic sustainability and land management goals. The IPAs provide a basis whereby Indigenous people can make informed choices about how they exercise their rights and interests in their traditional lifeways and in creating the capacity for a sustainable economic base for their communities within the modern market economy. The IPAs program has resulted, for example, in the establishment or strengthening of land management organizations that have provided the community with employment, increased self-esteem, and an organizational structure that encourages intergenerational dialogue between elders and youth seeking to understand more about their traditional territory[23] and the stories and knowledge of the old people. For instance, when traditional owners are able to involve their children in field trips, they transfer knowledge across generations and strengthen the knowledge of local languages. In some cases, they have been able to reestablish traditional burning practices, maintain waterholes, and reduce feral animal impacts, and they have ensured the maintenance of these traditions by promoting renewed interest among younger generations in "caring for country" (Szabo and Smyth 2003: 155).

An IPA can only be successful in these ways where Indigenous people have exclusive title to their land. Although there have been some projects in which Indigenous groups have been funded to negotiate with state agencies in existing state-owned national parks and reserves, these have generally been less successful for several reasons, including the entrenched power of state conservation agencies, the lack of commitment by states, and the lack of a relationship between Indigenous groups and state conservation agencies from which to pursue any practical engagement.

However, this situation is improving as the necessary interpersonal conservation agency and community relationships start to gain substance. Moreover, as existing IPAs have continued to deliver successful conservation and community development outcomes and with the rapid increase in the number of IPAs in Australia—from eighteen in 2005 to sixty in 2013—they have become increasingly attractive land management models for state and territory conservation agencies. One of the key reasons, along with the success of the Indigenous approach, it must be said, is the federal funding for the plans, which relieves the states and territories of expending their own funds on the significant natural resource management challenges of these now vast areas.

In addition to the need for the legal recognition and protection of Indigenous property and resource rights, it is crucially important that nation-states recognize and respect divergent governance processes, "the practices, mechanisms, techniques and social institutions that influence and regulate conduct" (Nettheim et al. 2002: 377). Indigenous people, particularly those who have maintained a degree of control over their land or sea estates, draw from their own governance structures and decision-making processes and protocols when managing their estates. As the cases discussed in this chapter demonstrate, the recognition of this jurisdiction is of paramount importance in successful land management arrangements for Indigenous peoples. Recognizing the centrality of land security and the ability of Indigenous and local groups to govern their own affairs allows them opportunity to utilize, protect, and enhance their traditional knowledge and customary land management practices according to their own style of governance and economic needs.

Toward a New Paradigm

In contrast to the critiques of community-based conservation now prevalent in the social sciences literature, we argue that community-oriented protected areas are delivering significant benefits to Indigenous peoples in Australia. Such programs are succeeding because they provide access to guaranteed land security and Indigenous people are able to exercise their own governance structures and decision-making authority while drawing on the power of "engaged universals" (Tsing 2005) of nature conservation to create and access multiscalar linkages that can assist them in achieving their livelihood and environmental management goals.

The concepts of sustainable development and biodiversity articulate "a new relation between nature and society on global contexts of science, cultures, and economies" (Escobar 1998: 55). These new understandings of the relationship between nature and society need to also recognize that environmental knowledge is "embodied and practiced" rather than simply "shared and context-free" (Escobar 1998: 62). The traditional biodiversity-related knowledge of Indigenous peoples and local communities is renewed, elaborated, and maintained through continuing practices of subsistence use, land and sea management, and governance of biological resources. Community-oriented protected areas provide the essential territorial spaces that can assist in achieving respect, preservation, and maintenance of their knowledge and innovations and practices in order to promote the conservation and sustainable use of biological diversity.

From the perspective of Indigenous peoples and local communities, for whom basic subsistence activities are either the predominant way of life or a significant part of their economic activities, the maintenance and preservation of their traditional biodiversity-related knowledge traditions and applications are essential to safeguard food security and the provision of other basic economic and cultural needs. Community-oriented protected areas can be used by local communities and Indigenous peoples to aid in securing their territorial base, thus reaffirming cultural identities and guaranteeing some degree of autonomy over the governance of biological resources. They also provide communities with the opportunity to renew and/or continue to support the biodiversity management systems that have underpinned their traditional livelihoods. For these reasons, community-oriented protected areas under the control of the relevant Indigenous and/or local groups are measures that can assist in the preservation and maintenance of traditional knowledge and help the concept of biodiversity conservation to be reenvisioned to include a greater diversity of socio-ecological practices and the legal and political circumstances in which they occur.

Acknowledgments

This chapter is dedicated to the late Mr. N. Manungguritj and the late Mr. Steve Szabo. The authors would like to acknowledge the help of the staff of Dhimurru Land Management Aboriginal Corporation, including Kelvin Leitch and Steve Roeger; Margaret Ayre; Juanita Pope; Bruce Rose; Simon Batterbury; Steve Szabo; and anonymous reviewers. All errors and omissions remain the responsibility of the authors.

Notes

1. An extended version of this chapter was first published as "Community-Oriented Protected Areas for Indigenous Peoples and Local Communities," *Journal of Political Ecology* 12: 23–50 (2005). Since then, the IPA program has expanded considerably.

2. IPAs can now be dedicated over a range of tenures within the customary estate of an Indigenous group and not only over Indigenous-owned land (Bauman et al. 2013).

3. This chapter draws on two research projects: one carried out by Langton and Palmer as part of an Australian Research Council Linkage Project, "Agreements, Treaties and Negotiated Settlements with Indigenous Peoples in Settler States: Their Role and Relevance for Indigenous and Other Australians" (www.atns.net.au), and research carried out by Langton and Ma Rhea that was published as *Traditional Lifestyles and Biodiversity Use Regional Report: Australia, Asia and the Middle East. Composite Report on the Status and Trends Regarding the Knowledge, Innovations and Practices of Indigenous and Local Communities Relevant to the Conservation and Sustainable Use of Biodiversity*, prepared for the Secretariat of the Convention on Biological Diversity, Montreal, UNEP/CBD/WG8J/3/INF/4, September 8, 2003.

4. In Australia's Northern Territory, for example, Aboriginal people own more than 50 percent of the land mass and more than 80 percent of the coastline. The lands and waters that constitute most of this area are not subject to high-density settlement or degradation of natural values by industries such as agriculture, forestry, fishing, pastoralism, and tourism, and they are high-integrity areas both in terms of so-called natural and cultural values. Much of the lands and waters within the Indigenous domain remain subject to Indigenous management systems (see Langton 2003). Indigenous people are also an increasing proportion of rural and remote communities, with a birth rate higher than the rest of the Australian population.

5. *Mabo and Others v. Queensland* (No. 2) (1992) 175 CLR 1.

6. Under Australian law, native title may be recognized in areas of unalienated Crown land where Indigenous people continue to follow their traditional laws and customs and have maintained a link with their traditional territory. These criteria pose severe obstacles for those Indigenous Australians who have in the past been forcibly removed from their lands (see Tehan 2003).

7. In an appeal by Aboriginal activist Marandoo Yanner in relation to his charge under Queensland's Fauna Conservation Act of 1974 for hunting crocodiles; see *Yanner v. Eaton* [1999] *HCA* 53.

8. For example, ongoing commercial purchases by the ILC and Aboriginal land councils. The Australian ILC, which operates under the Native Title Act of 1993 to fund land acquisition and land management activities, has produced the National Indigenous Land Strategy 2001–2006 in relation to Indigenous land and sea management. In land management, the ILC's mandate is to assist Indigenous people to

"manage their lands in a sustainable way providing them with cultural, social, environmental and economic benefits" (ILC 2003: 3). The ILC recognizes the centrality of the Indigenous relationship to land as a defining principle in setting priorities in its land acquisition and management functions. The ILC may undertake land management activities on all Indigenous-held land, including lands it has assisted Indigenous peoples to acquire. For land to be classified as "Indigenous-held land," it must be held by an "Indigenous organization" as defined by the Aboriginal and Torres Strait Islander Commission Act of 1989. Land ownership, and support for the management of that land, is thus legitimized by the administrative category of an "Indigenous organization." These benefits include the employment/training of Indigenous people and Indigenous business development (ILC 1997, 2003; National Native Title Tribunal 2003).

9. A color map is available at http://www.environment.gov.au/indigenous/ipa/map.html (last accessed December 1, 2013).

10. Our analysis here relates only to the cases settled between 1996 and 2005, but we believe our analysis applies also to the additional IPAs established since then. See http://www.environment.gov.au/indigenous/ipa/index.html (accessed September 12, 2013).

11. The fieldwork and archival research carried out in 2004 substantially informs these case studies. Although there has been subsequent fieldwork in the Northern Territory, the original analysis holds.

12. See http://www.environment.gov.au/indigenous/ipa/declared/nantawarrina.html (accessed September 20, 2012).

13. Commenting on the emergence of the IPA program, Muller (2003) noted that while there were nine jointly managed national parks and at least thirty under negotiation in Australia, the experience of Aboriginal peoples in these parks has generally been one fraught with political and management tensions, a zone of contested rather than negotiated management.

14. In 2005, this was the federal Department of Environment and Heritage, now called the Department of Sustainability, Environment, Water, Population and Communities.

15. See http://www.dhimurru.com.au/sea-country.html (accessed September 20, 2012).

16. See http://www.environment.gov.au/indigenous/ipa/declared/dhimurru.html (accessed September 20, 2012).

17. Australian Bureau of Statistics census figures from 2001 indicate that the Indigenous population of Nhulunbuy and surrounding regions was approximately 1650 and the non-Indigenous population was approximately 3600, with the vast majority of these residents in the township itself. The Indigenous population of the township is 7 percent (Australian Bureau of Statistics 2002).

18. See http://www.atns.net.au/agreement.asp?EntityID=880 (accessed September 20, 2012).

19. See http://www.atns.net.au/agreement.asp?EntityID=864 (accessed September 20, 2012).

20. For example, following the death of an elder.

21. For example, tourists climbing to the top of the Uluru monolith is a contentious issue in any case, given that traditional owners have expressly stated that they would

prefer tourists not to climb Uluru at all. However, the joint management situation is such that this is stated only as a preference not as a legally enforceable prohibition.

22. The history of funding for Indigenous land management programs has been fickle, even in cases where the program has been judged to be an outstanding success. For example, the IPA program was preceded by the Contract Employment Program for Aboriginals in Natural and Cultural Resource Management. Beginning in 1987–1988, this program provided environmental employment opportunities for Indigenous people throughout Australia. In 1992–1993, the program was given further impetus, funding, and support following the recommendations of the Royal Commission into Aboriginal Deaths in Custody. It was widely recognized for the contribution it made to environmental management and the social, cultural, and economic objectives (including education participation and outcomes) encompassed in many government initiatives dealing with Indigenous issues (Breckwoldt et al. 1997: 9). However, when the conservative Federal Coalition government came to power in 1996, the program was cut, despite its success. Nevertheless, the legacy of the program has influenced the success and capacity-building capabilities of many of the Indigenous organizations now participating in the IPA program.

23. This concept may also be glossed as *country*, a term that refers in Aboriginal English to the collective identity shared by a group of people, their land (and sea) estate, and all the natural and supranatural phenomena contained within that estate.

CHAPTER FOUR

A Tale of Three Parks

Tlingit Conservation, Representation, and Repatriation in Southeastern Alaska's National Parks

Thomas F. Thornton

Why have Native Americans, in general, and the Tlingit of southeastern Alaska, in particular, enjoyed success in gaining governing authority over cultural resource economies but limited success in gaining comanagement over natural resource economies in the U.S. national park system? Much of the answer to this question lies in how national parks evolved within a particular historical, legal, and cultural context in the United States, wherein the environment became increasingly constructed according to a nature/culture dichotomy in which certain "uninhabited" wilderness landscapes became framed and preserved, fortress-like, as museums of nature and historical landscapes (see Keller and Turek 1998; Spence 1999; West et al. 2006; Dowie 2009). Of course, as many have pointed out, including Theodore Catton (1997: 217) in Alaska, this "romantic impulse to preserve America's past . . . as remnants of a once-continental wilderness," or "vignettes of primitive America," has become increasingly untenable. Wilderness and primitiveness may themselves become fetishes in support of a certain dominant nationalist identity, *topophilia* (love of place; see Tuan 1974), and *historia* (atlas of eternity; see Wallace 2005) to the exclusion of other identities, especially those of Indigenous peoples. Even in countries with legal recognition of multiculturalism, as in Australia and Canada, the state typically requires Indigenous people to authenticate their aboriginality and "connectedness" to land using logics defined by Western law and heritage, thereby strengthening the latter at the expense of Indigenous logics (Povinelli 2002).

Indigenous peoples, including the Tlingit, never accepted the assumptions that underlie the dominant nature/culture paradigm in U.S. national parks and have actively resisted their removal, regulation, and representation by the National Park Service through articulations of their own identities, topophilia, and historia. Recently, Tlingits have begun to enjoy some success in promoting these visions within southeastern Alaska's three national parks. But access to natural resources, such as fish and wildlife, remains stubbornly limited, in part due to conflicting visions of what these resources represent and how and for whom they should be conserved. Here I argue that conflicts over natural resources between park managers and Natives could be reduced if certain natural resources of critical cultural significance were reconceptualized as "inalienable possessions" of cultural patrimony, rather than mere "resources" to be developed or preserved. In this way, the logic of "repatriation," increasingly utilized in the cultural resources realm under such laws as the Native American Graves Protection and Repatriation Act (NAGPRA), could be applied to the natural resource realm to restore Alaska Native relations to critical fish, wildlife, and other features of the land and sea, in national parks and other areas. Such a paradigm shift would help to conserve critical Tlingit cultural landscapes and livelihoods in parks within their homelands, where subsistence and other relations have been severely circumscribed by the establishment of protected area boundaries and regulations.

Tlingits today number more than 16,000, with about 10,000 still dwelling in southeastern Alaska and surrounding regions. They are among the most complex and successful hunting-gathering-fishing peoples of the world, having capitalized on the abundant salmon, halibut, herring, eulachon, seal, shellfish, deer, and other resources in the region through highly effective harvesting and processing methods combined with a flexible, multilayered, and multilocal social structure and dynamic systems of exchange and governance (Thornton 2008). For millennia, Tlingits have dwelled in the coastal Pacific Northwest rainforest ecosystem that is today dominated by the Tongass National Forest, the largest forest in the United States (17 million acres), and other protected areas. Indeed, southeastern Alaska is a patchwork of national forest, monuments (Admiralty Island and Misty Fjords), and parks (Glacier Bay, Klondike Gold Rush, Sitka, and, at the northwestern fringe, Wrangell–St. Elias) that occupy much of

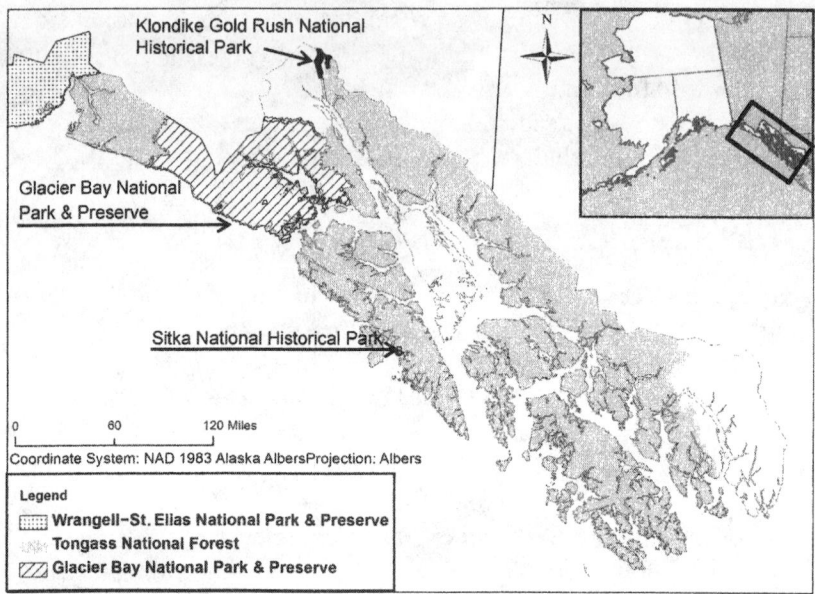

Figure 4.1. National parks in southeastern Alaska.

what is conceived of as Lingít Aaní, Tlingit Country (figure 4.1). Tlingits were granted title to less than 3 percent of their original lands through the Alaska Native Claims Settlement Act of 1971, which also extinguished their aboriginal title and hunting and fishing rights in exchange for limited monetary compensation and subsistence protections.

In Tlingit ideology, the relationship between natural and cultural capital is fused in *at.óow* (valued or sacred possessions). At.óow includes material property, such as land, regalia, and totem poles, as well as nonmaterial cultural artifacts such as personal names, songs, and stories that not only represent feelings toward and relationships with lands and resources but also are born of them (Dauenhauer and Dauenhauer 1994; Thornton 2008). At.óow are a classic example of what Annette Weiner (1985, 1992; building on Marcel Mauss 1967) called "inalienable possessions" (analogous to Māori *taonga* she and Mauss analyzed), and their circulation is tightly constrained by rules governing the maintenance of *shuká* (ancestry) and *shagóon* (heritage-destiny). Production and ceremonial exchange of both alienable and inalienable possessions are critical to maintenance of Tlingit cultural *latseen* (strength and well-being) over time. This point was emphasized by Mauss in his classic analysis of the power of the "gift" as a "total social phenomenon" embodying the very nature of social relations.

As his New Caledonian informant said of the ceremonial gifting of valued foods, "Our feasts are the movement of the needle which sews together the parts of our reed roofs, making of them a single roof, one single world" (Mauss 1967: 19). One reason for this, Mauss observed, is that each precious possession has

> a productive capacity within it. Each, as well as being a sign and surety of life, is also a sign and surety of wealth, a magic-religious guarantee of rank and prosperity. Ceremonial dishes and spoons, decorated and carved with the clan totem or sign of rank, are animate things. They are replicas of the never-ending supply of tools, the creators of food, which the spirits gave to the ancestors. They are supposedly miraculous. Objects are confounded with the spirits who made them, and eating utensils with food. Thus, Kwakiutl dishes and Haida spoons are essential goods with a strict circulation and are carefully shared out between the families and clans of the chiefs (1967: 43).

While the dishes and spoons themselves may be inalienable possessions of the clans, the ceremonial country foods they yield are gifted. But in being given away, country foods retain certain critical and inalienable affinities with their owners as essential sources of identity, place, power, and wealth. As Weiner (1985: 212) stressed, "The affective qualities constituting the giver's social and political identity remain embedded in the objects, so that when given to others, the objects create an emotional lien upon the receivers." As Mauss (1967: 10) put it, "One gives away what is in reality a part of one's nature and substance, while to receive something is to receive a part of someone's spiritual essence." This inalienable valence is what fuels the logic of gift reciprocation and the logic of repatriation of inalienable possessions to their rightful owners.

When relationships with productive places become attenuated, the localized matrilineal clan or house group, the central unit of Tlingit social structure, is correspondingly weakened in its ability to fulfill its reciprocal responsibilities within the socio-ecological circulatory system. This, in turn, weakens not only interclan and interlocal structural bonds and linkages that form the dynamic tapestry of Tlingit society but also the critical substantive and spiritual exchanges with places and their constituent beings that enable these lands to remain productive and sustainable. This weakening of the land's productive capacity is something Mauss and Weiner did not emphasize, but Tlingits do. From a Tlingit perspective, a "protected area" cannot be properly protected or conserved without these critical acts of cultivation, production, and exchange. Such a place will become alienated, inert, and ultimately poor; its productive capacity will be diminished. In short, a land without people ties is just as cursed as a people without land ties. The lives of the people and their sacred places are thus vitally intertwined (Nabokov 2006), as revealed by a closer examination of southeastern Alaska's parks in relation to the logics of inalienable possession and repatriation.

Alaska's National Parks: Old and New

Alaska represents by far the largest segment of the U.S. national park system, containing two-thirds of all park lands. The Alaska National Interest Lands Conservation Act of 1980 (ANILCA), one of the largest land bills in modern U.S. history, enlarged the park system significantly and provided for the creation or expansion of more than a dozen National Park Service "conservation system units," including Denali National Park, Wrangell–St. Elias National Park and Preserve (the nation's largest park), Gates of the Arctic National Park and Preserve, Lake Clark National Park and Preserve, Kobuk Valley National Park, Katmai National Park and Preserve, Glacier Bay National Park and Preserve, Kenai Fjords National Park, Kenai National Wildlife Refuge, Cape Krusenstern National Monument, Aniakchak National Monument and Preserve, Bering Land Bridge National Preserve, Noatak National Preserve, and Yukon–Charley Rivers National Preserve, as well as other properties managed by agencies such as the U.S. Department of Agriculture Forest Service (for example, Admiralty National Monument and Misty Fiords National Monument). Altogether, ANILCA provides for the protection of nearly 80 million acres of Alaska's federal lands, approximately a third of which is designated as "wilderness." With some 57 million acres of wilderness in the state, Alaska comprises the majority of the National Wilderness Preservation System.

In addition to wilderness preservation, another major provision of ANILCA is protection of subsistence uses of wild renewable resources by Alaska's rural residents. The subsistence provisions of ANILCA (Title VIII) constitute a partial restoration of aboriginal hunting and fishing rights extinguished by the 1971 Alaska Native Claims Settlement Act (Berger 1985: 65; Thornton 2007). Although this act presumably settled aboriginal land and resource claims through an award of 44 million acres of land and compensation of $963 million, the congressional conference report for the legislation obliged federal and state governments to provide for the continuing subsistence needs of Alaska Natives. However, ANILCA, despite declaring that continuation of subsistence rights is "essential to Native physical, economic, traditional, and cultural existence," provides only for a rural subsistence preference, not a Native one. Thus, as Berger (1985: 65) argued, "it does not go far enough. More is required if subsistence is to remain a permanent feature of Native life and culture."

What is more, ANILCA's subsistence provisions are unevenly applied to parks and protected areas. Old parks, in existence prior to ANILCA and including all three in southeastern Alaska, are not covered by the subsistence preferences governing the new parks created by the law. Thus, whereas ANILCA represented a "First World settler state . . . hav[ing] at least in some contexts reconsidered earlier wilderness enclosure policies when creating new protected areas in Indigenous peoples homelands" (Stevens 2007), the old parks in the southeast, particularly Glacier Bay, maintained the sharp line between "natural" and "cultural" landscapes, with the National Park Service preserving the former and selectively commemorating the latter.[1] Tlingits, meanwhile, continue to blur this line by actively seeking ways to restore engagements with park landscapes as inalienable sources of natural and cultural capital through the logic of repatriation.

The Native American Graves Protection and Repatriation Act and the Logic of Repatriation

At a contemporary Tlingit potlatch, one is likely to encounter sacred objects of cultural patrimony displayed on tables at the front of the ceremonial house or hall. Some of these may be recirculated items that have been repatriated from museums under the Native American Graves Protection and Repatriation Act (NAGPRA) of 1990, a federal law that mandates return of such possessions from federally funded museums. The process of repatriation is bureaucratic, legalistic, and lengthy, but it has yielded material results for Tlingits and other Native American tribes, which are celebrated. Specifically, 4303 designated sacred objects (defined as "specific ceremonial objects which are needed by traditional Native American religious leaders for the practice of traditional Native American religions by their present day adherents"; 25 USC 3001(3)(C)) and 948 objects of cultural patrimony ("an object having ongoing historical, traditional, or cultural importance central to the Native American group or culture itself, rather than property owned by an individual Native American, and which, therefore, cannot be alienated, appropriated, or conveyed by any individual"; 25 USC 3001(3)(D)) have been repatriated since NAGPRA's inception (National Park Service 2012), along with tens of thousands of human remains and hundreds of thousands of associated and unassociated funerary objects. Moreover, the powerful logic of repatriation can be found in domains far beyond NAGPRA's circumscribed scope.

One of these domains is natural resources, especially Native foods. In the Tlingit potlatch, one also will encounter sacred foods on display. These cultural foods, ideally derived from local ancestral lands, are prepared as gifts to potlatch guests and circulated to living members of the opposite moiety, as well as the hosts' own deceased relatives. Authentic Tlingit food as a sacred possession and ceremonial offering is most powerfully symbolized in the "fire dishes" (*gan s'íx'i*), which are carefully prepared and packaged for deceased matrikin and at the appropriate moment offered up with the phrase [*name of deceased*] *x'éidei* ("into his/her mouth") (see Kan 1989: 184), before being transferred to the deceased through burning or distributed to living relatives. The fire dish rite itself can be viewed as a kind of repatriation ceremony, wherein the fruits of ancestral lands are reunited with the spirits of those departed, who still crave them. Even if the legal framework of NAGPRA does not cover fire dishes or other sacred foods, the cultural logic of repatriation, which is at base a logic of inalienable possessions, does apply, and is the logic by which Tlingits are attempting to reappropriate emplaced food resources that they feel they must possess to be fully Tlingit.

Like sacred objects of cultural patrimony, distributed natural resources, such as ceremonial foods, derive their value through a kind of "keeping while being given away." The fruits of the harvest are shared and circulated through exchanges, but the fundamental exchange, namely the consubstantial relations between emplaced foods and emplaced people, remains inalienable. This relationship is enhanced through ceremonial exchanges, which create "chains of authenticity" (Weiner 1992: 104) and "webs of significance" (Geertz 1973). As products of inalienable wealth, cultural foods become, as Pannell (1994) argued for Australian aborigines (following Myers 1989, 1993), manifestations of "assured identity," which "persist through time and space." Their traceable circulation as gifts from "people of a land" is what gives cultural foods their salience as inalienable markers of identity. By accepting ceremonial gifts of the host presenters, recipient guests must recognize both the status of the producers as "people of the land" and their role in producing exquisite objects of consumption as meaningful (in this context, at least) as those objects of cultural patrimony housed in federally funded museums. Foods of place may be used to "materialize" or make tangible (and edible) connections between deceased ancestors and their lineal territories. The history of these connections may be told as a kind of "atlas of eternity," or historia (Wallace 2005). Thus, the potlatch feasting sustains not only the physical body but also the heritage and destiny (shagóon) or being and becoming of social bodies (matrilineal house groups, clans, moieties) by enacting participants' statuses and roles in relation to each other, ancestors, and their inalienable possessions (at.óow), including land.

Significantly, objects of cultural patrimony that have been returned to Tlingit groups from museums are handled similarly. As clan leader Joe Hotch put it concerning one of his clan's sacred hats that was successfully repatriated, "receiving the Bear Clan hat was more than just the return of an important cultural object; it was like the return of a family member" (Pyrillis 2000: 10). Potlatch-style ceremonies are staged to welcome these at.óow back as sacred possessions rather than mere cultural property (for more on the logic of this distinction, see Welsh 1997; also Glass 2004). Their biographies and lineages are shared with guests to authenticate their status as sacred and inalienable possessions. And, of course, cultural foods are served to celebrate the occasion. Although local museums or other agencies (including national parks) sometimes share conservation responsibilities for these repatriated objects (which, under NAGPRA guidelines, must be cared for according to minimum curatorial standards), there is no rhetoric of "comanagement." Repatriation discourse instead emphasizes reunion and responsibility, both key themes in Tlingit culture. In short, unlike comanagement rhetoric, repatriation follows a Tlingit cultural logic.

The question then becomes: Could repatriation logic be applied to the natural resource economy to facilitate reunions with lands and resources that have been partially or fully alienated from Tlingits, but which they hold to be inalienable possessions? If so, how would it work in practice? In fact, Tlingits are already applying the cultural logic of repatriation to southeastern Alaskan lands, waters, and resources, especially in the region's national parks. This is in spite of having legally settled their land claims nearly forty years ago through the Alaska Native Claims Settlement Act of 1971. Parks, which are national and world heritage museums in a sense, are beginning to respond in kind by supporting some repatriation overtures, especially those concerning symbolic capital, such as "official" representations of time, space, and Indigenous peoples within parks. Repatriations efforts toward material resources, cultural foods in particular, are more contested, however, because of resource management and conservation concerns and because non-Natives assume the logic of inalienable possession does not apply in this sphere. Yet, even here there have been successes, especially when harvests are small and sustainable and can be justified within a sacred or ceremonial context, such as food for a potlatch.

In conducting ethnographic research in all three southeastern Alaskan national parks over the past fifteen years, I have witnessed the cultural logic of repatriation being applied by local Tlingit groups in different ways, with varying degrees of success, in all three settings. It is instructive to compare the three cases to assess the potential for repatriation in the natural resources sphere.

Topophilias and Historias

At heart, most disputes between Native people and non-Native managers and constituents of parks and protected areas stem from strong affective ties to place based on opposing constructions of space and time, or conflicting topophilias (love of places) and historias (atlases of time). To date, much of the literature on Indigenous peoples in parks and protected areas has confined itself to conflicts over material resources, which often elide this more fundamental time–space dimension to Indigenous–state tensions in parks that goes well beyond resource management to notions of progress, ethics, and metaphysics. In his landmark book *Topophilia*, geographer Yi Fu Tuan (1974) defined topophilia broadly "so as to include all emotional connections between physical environment and human beings." Most commonly, the term is translated as "love of place." Tlingit elder Richard Dalton (2000) expressed topophilia succinctly in relation to his clan's homeland within Glacier Bay National Park when he stated: "this is the place we were in love with, because it provided, like an icebox." Of course Glacier Bay is more than just an icebox. The bay and its environs contain dwelling sites (for example, villages, forts, and camps, marked by named places such as Xunaa Káawu Noowú, Hoonah Peoples' Fort), ancestral graves, and, perhaps most potently, ancestral spirits that are still invoked and gifted on visits to the bay. Thus, gazing upon the land, Mr. Dalton elaborated, "I see my grandfathers on that beach, and I see my uncles because this is the place they were in love with." Later, Mr. Dalton remarked wistfully on an abandoned cabin, one of the few visible traces of human dwelling in the park: "If I had my way I would probably be living in that building today; then I could get all the fish I want when I need it." But dwelling is not allowed in Glacier Bay National Park, and, as we shall see, even the harvest of natural resources within the park is at odds with the park management's own topophilic preferences to define Glacier Bay National Park as a wilderness and natural laboratory, which may be traced to its earliest non-Native "discoverer," John Muir.

Defining the homeland and icebox of an Indigenous people as uninhabited wilderness necessarily involves an element of cultural erasure, a cleansing and reenchantment of the landscape as a natural wonder, a national treasure, a biosphere reserve, and even a World Heritage site, as Glacier Bay was named in 1992. For Tlingits this has meant dispossession (cf. Catton 1997). Of course, they are not completely written out. But until quite recently, there was little evidence of them in the park's basic promotional materials. Where Tlingits could be found, they were historicized as part of the precontact, aboriginal past rather than in a living relationship with park lands. "Dead Indians" of the past in dugout canoes were acceptable as images of the "ecologically noble savage," whereas living ones were considered fallen (that is, not traditional), alienated (not "living off the land"), and potential contaminants (invaders) to the wilderness and natural laboratory that has come to define Glacier Bay National Park. This construction of a new atlas of eternity, or historia, defines "a program of collective destiny that the leaders of tribes, nations, and empires [even national parks] use to inspire, to rationalize, to legitimize, and to guide policy" (Wallace 2005: 5–6).

In the hands of the National Park Service at Glacier Bay, historia is the preservation of unspoiled wilderness from the by-products of an ever-expanding and transforming human culture. Wilderness parks are the "then" in the greater American atlas of eternity, the nation's maps of now and then. "Here is an opportunity to see how the physical world shapes the biological," the National Park Service webpage proclaims, "a natural laboratory . . . to study and enjoy through the ages."

Tlingit historia is best encapsulated in the concept of shagóon, which embodies both heritage and destiny (de Laguna 1972; Dauenhauer and Dauenhauer 1994; Thornton 2008), or as one elder put: "what we are now, what we have been since the beginning, and everything that our children must become" (see Thornton 2004a: 370). Tlingit historia does not rely on the classic Western dichotomy between "nature" and "culture" or "now" and "then." As ancestral, birthplace, homeland, icebox, and resonant landscape of being, Glacier Bay lands are Tlingit shagóon in all of its aspects. That is why, despite the cultural erasure, Richard Dalton sees his matrilineal ancestors on the now uninhabitable wilderness beaches of Dundas Bay. It is also why the Hoonah Tlingit have continued to resist the park's exclusionary topophilia and historia and in recent years have made some significant gains toward inclusion as living constituents of the Glacier Bay landscape, which, as a 3.3 million acre World Heritage site (and part of the larger U.S.-Canada 25 million acre World Heritage landscape, among the world's largest protected areas), comprises the bulk of their traditional territory.

The forty-two historical parks within the national park system play a different role than the wilderness parks. For the most part, the historia of these landscapes is not the eternal nature of wilderness, but a way of framing human events and historical landscapes of "then" into a larger narrative of America's inevitable progress toward its ultimate destiny, its "now," as a mighty nation-state. Klondike Gold Rush National Historical Park in Skagway narrates how the wily and fiercely territorial Tlingit were inevitably overcome by the gold feverish stampeders—rugged individualists, perhaps, but aided and abetted by the U.S. military—who transformed the aboriginal trade trails into "golden staircases" and a narrow-gauge railway leading to the Klondike gold fields. In contrast, Sitka National Historical Park, the oldest park in Tlingit Country, commemorates the primal 1804 Battle of Sitka in which the Russians "defeated" the warlike Tlingit, paving the way for colonization and development of "Russian America," Alaska's industrial fur economy, and the territory's eventual sale to the United States in 1867. Tlingits in these communities also have resisted the hegemony of National Park Service historias and topophilias, with varying degrees of success.

I now turn to analysis of some defining events in Tlingit resistance and renegotiation of the dominant topophilias and historias of these historical parks, before returning to Glacier Bay and to the viability of repatriating certain landscapes and natural resources as inalienable possessions.

Gold Rush Centenary as a Terrain for Repatriating the Chilkoot Trail

In 1998, the hundredth anniversary of the gold rush was celebrated at the end of the Chilkoot Trail in Bennett, British Columbia, within the newly created Klondike Gold Rush International Historical Park. It was a time to champion the gold rush as a transformative event, which, though it lasted just a couple of years, brought unprecedented waves of people and wealth to the Alaska and Yukon territories, opening up these remote "frontiers" for development.

In his address for the August 5 dedication of the new international park, Carcross-Tagish First Nation Chief Andy Carvill commented on the nature of the surrounding landscape as a symbol: "As we look back to the time when our two heritages met on the Chilkoot [Trail] a century ago, we must acknowledge that this trail has become a difficult symbol." Elaborating on the conflicting topophilias and historias that inform this landscape, he added, "It is good that we can talk openly here about the hardships and the horrible inequalities that came to this community at the time of the gold rush. By speaking with each other and working together, we can heal the damage to our culture that continues today, with this mis-dedication, the mis-naming of this place as 'the Klondike Gold Rush International Historical Park.' The Carcross/Tagish First Nation looks forward to when this trail will be rededicated as our traditional trade route, in honour of its long-time use by our people" (Carvill 1998).

Indeed, of the three U.S. national park units that have risen on appropriated aboriginal lands in southeastern Alaska and southern Yukon, the Klondike Gold Rush National Historical Park may be the most problematic in terms of its representation and incorporation of Natives because, as Mr. Carvill suggested, it valorizes a colonization event that brought profound stress, change, and loss to local Alaska Native and Canadian First Nation peoples.

Perhaps the most tragic figure in the struggle is the Tlingit leader Lunaat', who claimed inalienable possessory rights over the trail and was killed defending them in the infamous Packer War of 1888. Trying to square his concept of ownership with white notions of common property, he argued that his people had not only the right but also the responsibility to lead people over the trail safely. Lunaat' made his position clear in an 1887 letter to the U.S. government in which he emphasized his clan's right to request permission and compensation for trail use from visitors in part because he had to maintain a "good road" and assume personal responsibility and liability for those who traveled on it. He also emphasized that Tlingit possessory rights do not constitute exclusive or monopolistic property ownership, per se, but are permeable as long as the local tribe's inalienable covenant with its *patria* is acknowledged, preferably through a social tie, or, in the case of strangers, payment or gift. As Lunaat' put it by analogy, "We make our trail for our own use, if others wish to use it should they not compensate us for our labor? The white man builds a wharf and all who lands goods over must pay" (in Thornton 2004b: 131). Unfortunately, his reasoning not only was ignored but the local newspaper railed that the miners using the trails should not have to pay a "dirty thieving, Indian . . . for the privilege of traveling about thirty miles through the woods of Uncle Sam's domain" (*The Alaska Free Press*, May 14, 1887).

While respectful of his tenacity, park representations of Lunaat' do not engage his possessory rights debate, but rather represent him as a tragic figure trying desperately to fend off the inevitable forces of modernity. Interpretive displays immortalize the historical Tlingit traders who carved out the "grease trails" (as the interior trade routes are dubbed due to the seal and fish grease that was traded from the coast for furs and other commodities from the interior), attempted to "monopolize" them, and, once defeated in their territorial designs by the U.S. government and its artillery, were reduced to the status of contract packers for hire by invading whites—valets for the gold rush, if you will. Beyond that, virtually nothing is said of post–gold rush natives. To paraphrase Eric Wolf, the Indians are people with no more history.

Given the park's historia of Tlingit dispossession, demotion, and marginalization in time and space, how can the logic of repatriation apply to reframe the park's history? In fact, this reframing of the Chilkoot Trail historia and historiography has already begun. First, Alaska Natives and Canadian First Nations are insisting that the history of the greater Chilkoot landscape not begin or end with the gold rush. Rather, in Chief Carvill's words, "The gold rush years form a small but painful part of this trail's long history as a Tlingit trade route" (Carvill 1998).

Second, Natives are beginning to remap the landscape to make present their own atlases of time and space. For example, recently the Skagway Traditional Council (with the Bureau of Indian Affairs and National Park Service) led a successful effort to construct a wayside exhibit in Klondike Gold Rush National Historical Park that will feature a Native atlas of time and place. One of the exhibit panels reads, "We are from Skagway. Our grandfathers and grandmothers are our Ancestors who have gone on and we call them *Haa Shagóon*. It is from ages past that they have called this land *Lkóot Aaní* (Chilkoot). That is how we know it today. The names of our land are *Shgagwéi* (Skagway), *Náxk'w* (Naakhu Bay), and *Deiyáa* (Dyea). We who now walk this land seek to learn the ways of our Ancestors, to live in harmony and balance on this land. We have always had respect for each other through our culture. Watch carefully over the land of our grandparents. Thank you so much, our friends and relatives."

The exhibit includes a map with additional Indigenous names for places and these words emphasizing Tlingit shagóon: "These names are rooted into the land. As our culture has been over tens of thousands of years, the language and the land are inseparable. They intertwine like veins and arteries. This is how it has been, and how it shall remain." By restoring Tlingit geographic names to the land in a public display, local Tlingits seek to animate and repossess the park with an ancestral presence that has been historicized and alienated, if not polluted, by the park's neglect, misrepresentation, and reframing of their inalienable homeland.

A third step in the process of repatriation is to reinhabit the park as living Indigenous people. This, too, is happening in private, communal, and intercultural ways. An example of the latter is a Plant Walk that was first sponsored by the Skagway Traditional Council in May 2003 at Dyea. The public walk was led by two elders, Mrs. Jessie Johnnie, a Coastal Tlingit, and Ida Calmegane, a Carcross-Tagish First Nation elder, and involved both narrative representation and material resource consumption. Mrs. Calmegane, a traditional knowledge bearer, trained nurse, and botanical *bricoleur* extraordinaire, was particularly adept at seamlessly mixing storytelling; ethnomedical, culinary, and ecological facts; and select gathering of certain plants within the course of the short walk. In little more than an hour she touched on everything from the best plants for poultice and paint to—upon spotting a boreal toad—the role of this "frog" in healing and enriching her famous forbearer, Skookum Jim Mason, one of the discoverers of the Klondike gold (Smith 1999). At the end of this repatriating walk, there was no question as to patria. We were still in Lingít Aaní, Tlingit Country. And there was a thirst for more engagement with the elders and their ancestral landscape among the many Native and non-Native participants present.

Sitka National Historical Park and Indian Cultural Center as Terrain for Negotiating Historical Agency and Possession

Sitka National Historical Park has its own symbolic problems with Indians. Until recently, the park primarily commemorated two disparate things, both of which local Tlingits found rather distasteful. The first is an odd collection of totem poles, cobbled together by Territorial Governor John Brady for the 1904 World's Fair, which are not local in origin and design (most coming from Haida Country to the south). The second is the 1804 Battle of Sitka in which Sitka Tlingits were temporarily driven from their lands by the Russian colonizers. Unlike Klondike Gold Rush National Historical Park and the vast wilderness in the Glacier Bay National Park, the geographic scope of Sitka National Historical Park is small, about 100 acres, encompassing the battle site and a coastal totem walk and, at a separate site, a restored Russian bishop's house. Yet like the Glacier Bay portrayal, much of the Indian iconography here too has been, at least until recently, dominated by "noble savage" themes. Once vanquished, it seems, the Indian can be appreciated for his traditional artistry and war-making.

But unlike Glacier Bay or Klondike, where local Tlingits essentially have had little or no presence, Sitka Tlingits chose to actively recolonize their little town park by establishing an Indian cultural center within the visitors' center, thereby making their living presence known through local artists and interpreters (see Hope in Dauenhauer and Dauenhauer 1994: 779–84). Significantly, this opportunity to reinhabit the park was provided by a sympathetic superintendent, George Hall, who had collected Tlingit oral histories in both the Sitka and Glacier Bay parks and realized the depth of Indigenous relations to these lands and how poorly the Native people had been treated. According to elder Herman Kitka Sr. (pers. comm., 2007), Hall came to a meeting of the local Alaska Native Brotherhood Camp in the 1960s and asked them specifically, "What can we do to make up for the way you people have been treated by the government?" The group's answer was to establish The Southeast Alaska Indian Cultural Center, opened in 1969, "to impart the cultural values of Southeast Alaska Native Culture to students and visitors" (Sitka National Historical Park 2007a). The *Administrative History of Sitka National Historical Park* provides additional details on the evolution of this unique institution:

> On February 24, 1968, the Board of Indian Arts and Crafts [created by law in 1935 under the U.S. Department of Interior to promote the development of Indian arts and crafts] met at Sitka. At the time, the board operated programs at Sitka [since 1962], at Nome, and at the University of Alaska at Fairbanks. . . . The Tlingit people presented their ideas to the board. They proposed to develop a program that would help the park interpret Tlingit culture and the Tlingit people preserve their traditional art. They asked the board to remove the Eskimo art program from the Sitka center's program. Most appealing to the board members and the park service staff was that Tlingit people would be interpreting their heritage. The Board of Indian Arts and Crafts asked the National Monument staff and representatives of the Tlingits to develop a plan. The board would serve in an advisory capacity and provide funding to set up the program. It was assumed that the park service would take over funding the program after the transition.

...The Alaska Native Brotherhood... submitted its proposal... on April 16, 1968. The proposal revised the agreement between the National Park Service and Board of Indian Arts and Crafts for use of the building... by *Thlinget* cultures for *perpetuation* of such art forms appropriate to historic cultures of *Southeast* Alaska.

...In 1969 the Southeast Alaska Indian Cultural Center opened in the visitor center. The Sitka Alaska Native Brotherhood Camp provided teachers to demonstrate traditional southeast Native arts such as woodcarving, costume [regalia] making, and silverworking to students and visitors. [Sitka Tlingit Elder] A. P. Johnson was the center's director from 1969 to 1971 and also an instructor" (Antonson and Hanable 1987: 144, emphasis in original).

Today, as the park's website notes, "The center achieves this goal by providing a place for local Sitka Tlingits to teach themselves about their own culture, while also helping Park visitors understand the Native people whose history is part of the Park story" (Sitka National Historical Park 2007a). Although housed in the park, the cultural center is an independent, nonprofit Native organization, with its own advisory board. Yet, visitors do not experience it as a separate entity, but rather as an organic, living Native presence in the park. Furthermore, the introduction of local art and artists into the infrastructure and workings of the park has helped reframe the historia and topophilia of the landscape to one inclusive of contemporary Tlingit shagóon and people, thus realizing the center's objective to "sustain and perpetuate the art and culture of Southeast Alaska Indian Tribes in a manner that honors ancestral values" (Sitka National Historical Park 2007c).

Despite its early origins, the Sitka model may be the most successful model of repatriation of Natives into the southeastern parks. A metaphor for this successful accommodation was the raising in 1996 of the Haa Leelk'u Has Kaastaheeni Deiy (Honoring Our Ancestors Who Dwelled along Indian River) totem pole in front of the park's visitor center. Carved by Tlingit artists employed by the Southeast Alaska Indian Cultural Center, the pole memorializes Tlingit clans (Kaagwaantaan, Kiks.ádi, and Coho) who dwelled in Sitka before the Russians arrived. The ceremony marking the installation of the Indian River ancestors' pole was carried out according to Tlingit protocol, with the display and enactment of sacred possessions, such as clan regalia, songs, and dances, and the stories behind them, which define the basis of Tlingit ties to the park. As participants collectively raised the pole, one clearly felt that the park had been reconsecrated as Tlingit land and its historia redefined as a Sitka Tlingit atlas of eternity. In the decade since the pole-raising, this Tlingit historia has begun to infuse the park in other ways, too (cf. Thornton 1998; Sitka National Historical Park 2007b).

Glacier Bay Bird Egg Collecting as an Act of Repatriation

A similar cultural center and tribal house is currently being developed for Glacier Bay National Park to reflect the living heritage of Tlingits as part of Glacier Bay National Park's visitors' center. Hoonah and Yakutat Tlingits are actively remapping and re-inscribing the park and its surrounding environs as Tlingit Aaní. But Hoonah Tlingits have gone a step further in asserting ongoing hunting and gathering prerogatives, which conflict with the park's topophilia and historia.

As has been demonstrated elsewhere, for Hoonah Tlingits it is important to continue harvesting gull eggs and other key cultural foods (for example, harbor seal and mountain goat) from the Glacier Bay National Park (Hunn et al. 2003; Thornton 2008). Because these activities sustain relationships of belonging to inalienable possessions of their homeland and "icebox," they are considered sacred, consubstantial, and constitutive to their identity and being. As one Tlingit interviewed put it:

> This is how we have come to love our country the way our fathers and uncles did. We also felt that we were part of somebody and somebody special when our families took us on these trips [to Glacier Bay to harvest eggs]. We were taught this is who we are and that this is how it's going to be. . . . And the difference between an egg inside Glacier Bay and an egg outside Glacier Bay is Glacier Bay is our traditional homeland. That's where our heart and soul is. That's what ties us to our land. Our food that comes out of there is directly responsible for our strength, our knowledge, our inner peace, as compared to [food] that's outside of the traditional homeland" (quoted in Hunn et al. 2003: S86).

The value of such natural resource areas as a means of conserving physical, social, and Tlingit spiritual relations to country can hardly be overemphasized.

Change in park policy is coming slowly, however. Despite 1999 amendments to the international treaty governing migratory birds permitting

Native egg collecting outside the park and studies showing that egg harvests within the park were sustainable, the park was loathe to approve changes to its own regulations prohibiting the practice. Egging sites outside Glacier Bay National Park have proven unsatisfactory as a substitute for those inside the park, due to their more remote and dangerous (exposed) settings, lower egg productivity, and the fact that they are not as integral to Tlingit shagóon. Finally, in the fall of 2006, the National Park Service undertook a legislative environmental impact statement (Legislative Environmental Impact Statement 2006) proposing to authorize harvest of "glaucous-winged gull (*Larus glaucescens*) eggs by tribal members . . . under a traditional harvest strategy cooperatively produced by [the National Park Service] and [Hoonah Indian Association]." In its 2010 Record of Decision (National Park Service 2010), the park service selected an alternative (no. 3) allowing for two annual harvest visits to five locations in the park. This is promising, but authorizing legislation and management regulations still have to be passed, and there remains in the legislative environmental impact statement the caveat that "monitoring actions . . . would be implemented to ensure that park purposes and values would remain unimpaired" (as required by law), which raises troubling questions of just what is being conserved for whom. Are not park "purposes" and "values," which flow from culturally constructed wilderness topophilias and historias, at odds with those of Hoonah Tlingits? And, if so, is it realistic that they can remain completely "unimpaired" if Tlingit are going to resume some kind of "poetics of dwelling," to borrow a felicitous Heideggerian phrase (see Ingold 2000: 110; Weiner 2001), in Glacier Bay?

Conservation and Reconciliation through Repatriation

The logic of repatriation is being applied by Natives of southeastern Alaska and southern Yukon Territory to area national and international parks in compelling ways to restore their status and roles as stewards of these places, which they consider to be inalienable possessions, deeply constitutive of their being. Should a NAGPRA-type law be extended to include sacred lands and natural resources of cultural patrimony? Some will surely balk at the notion, given that NAGPRA has spawned its own legal and bureaucratic discursive regimes, subcultures, and social dramas (Jacknis 1996), which often seem to constrain Natives to speak in ways just as "uncharacteristic" as traditional ecological knowledge and comanagement regimes have (cf. Cruikshank 1998; Nadasdy 2003). Still, it is certainly worthy of consideration, especially in the United States, where other legal frameworks for protecting sacred landscapes, such as the National Historic Preservation Act and the American Indian Religious Freedom Act, have not proven effective. Ultimately, success will require that sustaining material and symbolic relationships between Indigenous people and their ancestral landscapes be considered as conservation values in themselves. Ideas of "fortress conservation" and "wilderness enclosure" (Stevens 2007; West et al. 2006) will have to give way to more inclusive, bioculturally diverse paradigms of engagement with these landscapes, wherein protecting the land is also conceptualized as a means of protecting and empowering local cultures through collaborative management (see chapter 2; Stevens 1997a; Weitzner and Manseau 2001: 255). There is evidence that this is happening in the case of revisions to gull egg harvesting regulations in Glacier Bay National Park, but progress is slow and piecemeal (rather than a systemic review of all regulations), and management authority is hardly coequal.

Reincorporating Tlingit historias and topophilias into the fabric of southeastern Alaska's national park units is another encouraging step on the trail from "colonization to repatriation" (Cranmer Webster 1992). As Laura Watt (2002: 69) observed, "the tendency of wilderness management—and most natural resource preservation in general—to eliminate human history from the landscape makes for bad public policy. It negates our relationship with the land and creates an unrealistic separation between nature and culture." Similarly, William Cronon (2003) has argued that people actually prefer a "storied" wilderness. The process of repatriating Tlingits into parks is thus mutually beneficial because park history is enriched, while Natives ties and senses of place and time are restored and resources like gull eggs are circulated as gifts born of a covenant with the land, not unlike those distributed at a potlatch.

Failure to acknowledge these gifts amounts to what Kirsch (2006), interpreting the logic of the Yonggom of New Guinea toward non-Indigenous appropriators of their land, terms "unrequited reciprocity." Thus, inclusion of Tlingits is foundational to achieving successful working relationships on a wide range of issues from harvests of natural resources like bird eggs to the representations of history like the gold rush stampede and the 1804 Battle of Sitka. Further, as students of inalienable possession from Lunaat' to Kockleman (2007: 159) assert, responsibilities are just as important as rights and "possession is as much a burden as it is a boon." The National Park Service has acknowledged as much since its 1990 *Keepers of the Treasures* statement (quoted by Tlingits as part of the basis for "Our claim for Glacier Bay"; see Culp et al. 1995: 331) that "Indian tribes must have the opportunity to participate fully in the National Historic Preservation Program, but on terms that respect their cultural values, traditions, and sovereignty."

In his speech at the gold rush centenary, Chief Carvill invoked the logic of repatriation and full participation in national parks through shared stewardship:

> We look forward to when we will have, as promised, an equal partnership as stewards of this place that is so important to both of our histories, and so important to our history together. . . . Our people have much to offer the Yukon Territory, Canada, and the United States. . . . It will be good to repair what has been damaged and to move forward together. It will be good to see this trail and this land cared for in the ways of our tradition. . . . It will be good to see people moving in our land who respect and understand the difficult heritage we share. It will be good to see those people moving in our land with peacefulness, and with hope that we can make such a difficult symbol, the Chilkoot Trail, good for all of us again (Carvill 1998).

To date, this vision has been more fully realized on the Canadian side of the Chilkoot, where "First Nations people still exercise their traditional rights to hunt, fish, and gather wild food on the trail" and the park's international designation inclusively recognizes First Nations (Parks Canada 2007a; see also Neufeld and Norris 1996; Thornton 2004b). Some Canadian parks have gone a step further toward repatriation, such as Gwaii Haanas National Park Reserve and Haida Heritage Site, wherein a Coastal Watchman and Forest Guardian program employs Haidas as protectors and stewards of the land, and an evolving heritage management program seeks to implement a Haida Land Use Vision based on ethnoecological values defined in the aboriginal language (Brennan 2008), even though legal questions of land ownership and rights may remain "unresolved" (Parks Canada 2008). Similarly, a recent article on precarious sites in Canadian Blackfoot territory suggests "repatriation as a model for authentic Blackfoot participation in the care of the remaining sites and the beings who inhabit them" (Chambers and Blood 2009: 253).

The Chilkoot Trail may be a good metaphor for envisioning the path toward repatriation, reconciliation, and respect that must take place in aboriginal–state relations in places like national parks (see Thornton 2004b:

269–72). But the egg maybe an even better one, as a recent addition to the Glacier Bay National Park (2007b) website suggests:

> Imagine that you can hold Glacier Bay in the palm of your hand. It is smooth and round, about the size of a large egg. It is heavy, precious. Slowly you begin to peel back its layers, its meanings. The first layer, world heritage site, comes off. Next, you peel away the layer for the biosphere reserve. You are now looking at the layer for the national park and preserve. Gently you peel that away. Naked and vulnerable, wilderness trembles in your palm. As you marvel at the beauty, the fragility, something catches your eye. You realize that by holding the land up to the light just so, you can see another image distinct yet intangible as the morning mists. This new image reveals the essence of life for a group of people called the Hoonah Tlingits.
>
> To the Hoonah Tlingit, Glacier Bay is not only the place where they once lived, hunted, fished, collected eggs and berries. It is the center from which they gain their identity as people—their spiritual homeland.

In this light and from this perspective (that is, the center), the Tlingit logic of repatriation and inalienable possession would seem difficult to deny. Perhaps the application of such logic will help hatch a new paradigm of conservation based not only on rights (as in the 2007 UN Declaration on the Rights of Indigenous Peoples) but also redress (as in the recent Whakatane Mechanism 2011c) and responsibilities and reciprocity (as in local Indigenous models). Such a paradigm would not simply recognize biocultural diversity, but also engender it in healthy ways that do not artificially dichotomize natural and cultural landscapes or impose a monolithic historia.

Acknowledgments

For advice and support in researching this project, I am grateful to the National Park Service and the cultural resource management personnel in Glacier Bay National Park, especially Wayne Howell and Mary Beth Moss; Klondike Gold Rush National Historical Park, especially Karl Gurcke; and Sitka National Historical Park, especially Ellen Hope Hayes. I would also like to thank the Hoonah, Sitka, and Skagway Tribes and the Carcross-Tagish First Nation for their input and support, especially Ken Grant, Helen Dangel, Lance Twitchell, and Andy and Corrine Carvill.

Most of all, I wish to acknowledge with respect and appreciation the many elders who were interviewed for this project who always cherished these parks as homelands, particularly the late Richard Dalton Sr., Amy Marvin, Pat Mills, Richard Sheakley, Winnie Smith, Lilly White, Al Perkins, Herman Kitka Sr., Nels Lawson, Mark Jacobs Jr., Esther Littlefield, Herb Hope, Ada Haskins, Si Dennis, Paul Wilson, and many others who contributed in innumerable ways to this work.

Notes

1. For more on the social construction and political ecology of this distinction in Alaska, see Stevens (1997, 2007) and Catton (1997), and elsewhere, see Langton et al. (2005) and West et al. (2006). Stevens (2007) noted, "Other First World states . . . have recognized continuing settlement and land use in national parks which have been conceived as cultural landscape heritages and in some cases (Finland, Sweden) depicted or legally designated as 'wilderness.'" In Glacier Bay National Park especially, the prohibitions on Native hunting (for example, of seal, deer, mountain goat, and moose), fishing (limited subsistence fishing only), and gathering (some plant and invertebrate resources, but not bird eggs) have been severe, even though the park constitutes the majority of the Hoonah Tlingits' traditional subsistence territory (cf. Catton 1995; Thornton 2008).

PART II

Complexity and Critiques

CHAPTER FIVE

National Parks in the Canadian North

Comanagement or Colonialism Revisited?

John Sandlos

There is a widespread consensus among wildlife conservationists that parks and protected areas offer the last best hope for preserving biodiversity on a regional scale. Borrowing insights from new scientific subdisciplines such as landscape ecology and conservation biology, environmental advocacy groups have promoted increasingly sophisticated plans for preserving native flora and fauna in networks of protected areas representative of a full range of habitat types within selected regions. In relatively uninhabited areas with an abundance of public lands, such as the Canadian North, efforts to establish protected areas have taken on added urgency as the conservation constituency appeals to governments to "get it right" before the encroachment of industrial development despoils the relatively untouched wilderness character of the region (Conservation of Arctic Flora and Fauna 1994; Peepre and Jickling 1994; Nowlan 2001; Canadian Council on Ecological Areas 2003; Wiersma et al. 2005). The jubilation among conservation groups over victories in northern Canada such as the protection of a broader expanse of the Nahanni River watershed from mining development in August 2007 (Jackson 1998; Langford 2003; Anonymous 2007a: 1; De Souza 2007: 1; Parks Canada 2007b) and the announcement in November 2007 of a new national park surrounding the East Arm of Great Slave Lake (an area that had been subject to intense mineral exploration), suggests that environmentalists still regard the establishment of protected areas as an unmitigated good, the pinnacle of what they can hope reasonably to achieve through their efforts to protect remaining pockets of natural habitat in Canada's hinterland regions (Anonymous 2007b; Struzik 2008).[1]

A broader historical view of parks and protected areas suggests they have not always been the product of the most noble or beneficent motivations of their human creators. Throughout the late nineteenth and early twentieth centuries, the establishment of national parks and other types of protected areas had major social and economic impacts on Indigenous peoples, many of whom were displaced from the environs of the new forest and wildlife preserves in colonized territories in South Asia, Southeast Asia, and Africa (chapters 1, 9, 11; Anderson and Grove 1987; Guha 1989; West and Brechin 1991; Peluso 1992, 1993; Stevens 1997a). Displacement of Indigenous peoples from protected areas was not limited to colonial situations in Africa and Asia, but also occurred in neo-colonial or Fourth World contexts (chapter 1). In North America, Native and non-Native inhabitants of hinterland regions were routinely removed from national parks and other nature preserves, particularly during the late nineteenth-century period of westward expansion in Canada and the United States. The motivations for creating these national parks differed according to national and regional priorities, with protected spaces devoted to disparate goals such as wilderness preservation, tourism development, sport hunting, the conservation of endangered species, and resource extraction. But regardless of the specific purpose behind each park, human communities were often expelled, sometimes violently, from within the boundaries of the new protected areas (chapter 1; Cronon 1986; Catton 1997; Stevens 1997a; Keller and Turek 1998; Spence 1999; Burnham 2000; Sandlos 2005; Binnema and Niemi 2006; Manore 2007). On a broader scale, recent historical scholarship has suggested that the retinue of government fish and wildlife conservation initiatives (for example, parks, hunting regulations, gear restrictions) introduced beginning in the late nineteenth century were one of the primary means by which the state was able to assert control over subsistence-oriented communities inhabiting the hinterland regions of colonized societies (Tober 1981; Warren 1997; Parenteau 1998; Parenteau 2004; Loo 2006).

The conflict between the state and local systems of wildlife management has been central to the politics of the territorial north since the inception of the Canadian government's attempts to regulate the hunting and trapping in the region beginning in the 1890s. The prevailing cultural, demographic, and ecological contexts for conflicts over access to game, however, were fundamentally different in northern Canada than other parts of North America. A harsh climate, limited agricultural opportunities, the presence of a majority Aboriginal population in many areas, the geographically scattered nature of settlement and development, and the overwhelming economic importance of subsistence hunting and trapping to many Aboriginal communities all suggest that northern Canada was not subject to the same processes of wholesale ecological transformation that historians have associated with ecological imperialism farther to the south (Crosby 1972, 2004; Piper and Sandlos 2007). Instead, the history of colonization in northern Canada has more in common with other areas that maintained regional majority populations of Indigenous peoples such as in some African and Asian countries, where the assertion of state bureaucratic control over wildlife, forests, and grazing lands (and not the migration of a white settler population) provided one of the most important administrative vehicles through which the imperial powers attempted to assert authority over subsistence hunters and small-scale agriculturalists in hinterland regions (MacKenzie 1988; Sivaramakrishnan 1999). The historical and contemporary literature on these regions has generally fallen under the rubric of political ecology, a field of inquiry that has devoted a great deal of attention to the environmental, social, and economic injustices associated with wildlife and forest conservation and the establishment of protected areas in the Third World, but that has also engaged with some of these issues in Fourth World contexts, including in the United States, Canada, Sweden, and Australia (chapters 3 and 4; Peluso 1993; Neumann 1998; Nadasdy 1999, 2003a, 2003b, 2005, 2011; Anderson and Nuttall 2003; Beach 2003; Muller 2003; Langton et al. 2005; Neumann 2005; Standlea 2006; Middleton 2010).

The history of wildlife conservation in northern Canada provides a salient opportunity to apply the interpretive framework of political ecology within a Fourth World context in a First World state. Indeed, many of the central themes from the Third and Fourth World literatures, such as Indigenous peoples' exclusion from protected areas, state regulation of resource harvesting activities, the appropriation of wildlife and other resources for the purposes of commercial production, and the dispossession of Indigenous peoples from the local resource base, were similarly tied to the Canadian government's attempts to establish control over the subsistence economies of the region's Aboriginal people (Gottesman 1983;

Calverley 2000; Sandlos 2001; Campbell 2004; Usher 2004; Kulchyski and Tester 2007). The explicit links between the Canadian government's wildlife policies and its sporadic dreams of northward expansion (particularly the long-standing idea that northern big game such as caribou and muskoxen should be saved and propagated as part of a domestic ranching economy that would in turn underpin growth of industry) indicates that conservation initiatives were tied to a broader colonial agenda in the region. Indeed, early northern conservation initiatives sought not just to preserve endangered animals but also to appropriate wildlife to serve expanding commercial interests rather than those of the Dene, Inuit, and Métis who depended on animals for food, clothing, and at times a modest income (Loo 2001, 2006; Sandlos 2002, 2007).

It is tempting to conclude that recent attempts to incorporate northern Aboriginal people and their traditional ecological knowledge into comanagement agreements for specific national parks and wildlife populations have relegated older approaches to wildlife management to the dustbin of historical anachronism, the dimly remembered "bad old days" when conservation and paternalism went hand in hand. Nonetheless, there is increasing evidence that the newer approaches to wildlife management in the region do not represent a clean break from the colonial mentality that dominated conservation initiatives in the past (Stevenson 2004). Recent literature on wildlife and protected area comanagement agreements suggests, for example, that Aboriginal knowledge and political imperatives are still often regarded as marginal and supplementary in importance when contrasted with scientific expertise and bureaucratic priorities emanating from the federal and territorial governments. Sharing power over wildlife does not, according to many commentators, mean that power is distributed equally between government agencies and Aboriginal people. In many respects, the emphasis on apportioning a limited degree of power over wildlife policy rather than simply devolving control to Aboriginal people suggests that federal and territorial wildlife bureaucracies have not faced up to the colonial legacy that has infused the dialogue between the state and Aboriginal people over wildlife issues in the Canadian North. The extent to which contemporary power-sharing agreements tend to marginalize, co-opt, or ignore Aboriginal perspectives on wildlife management—imposing, in essence, managerial solutions on problems that are political in nature—suggests that further policy innovations will be required to fully address the colonial history of state wildlife conservation initiatives in northern Canada.

Colonial Encounters: Wildlife Conservation in the Canadian North

It seems strange at first glance to link early government conservation efforts in northern Canada to broader colonial initiatives in the region. After all, the bureaucratic resources devoted to wildlife conservation in early twentieth-century Canada were extremely limited, occupying hidden corners of the Department of the Interior within administrative bodies such as the Parks Branch, the Department of Agriculture, and the Northwest Territories and Yukon Branch. The few pioneering wildlife bureaucrats who staffed these administrative bodies—men such as Rocky Mountains National Park Superintendent Howard Douglas, Parks Commissioner James Harkin, Dominion Entomologist Gordon Hewitt, Canadian National Museum Zoologist Rudolph M. Anderson, and Chief of the Parks Branch's Animal Division Maxwell Graham—were able to achieve much only through their dedication, their enthusiasm, and their deft employment of political capital derived from strong public support for wildlife conservation in the late nineteenth and early twentieth centuries. Their successes were many: the creation of fifteen new national parks between 1885 and 1929 (figure 5.1), the negotiation of the Migratory Birds Treaty with the United States in 1916, hunting prohibitions on endangered species such as bison and muskoxen, and the positioning of Canada as a world leader in bison conservation (with protected herds in Elk Island and Wood Buffalo National Parks and the now-defunct Buffalo National Park). As with contemporary environmentalists, a primary objective of the early wildlife conservationists was the protection of endangered species and endangered spaces in the Canadian hinterland (Foster 1998; Burnett 2003).

If this policy agenda seems benevolent and public spirited, there is a less savory side to early Canadian wildlife conservation programs. On the most basic level, conservation policies and institutions in northern Canada were imposed with little regard for the material needs and political priorities of Native hunters in the region. In many cases, the government had little scientific evidence to support their claims of wildlife emergencies, but relied instead on highly suspect reports of wasteful and improvident slaughters that filtered down through the popular writing and media reports produced by outside trappers, natural historians, or explorers who briefly passed through the Northwest Territories or harvested wildlife in the region on a seasonal basis (Sandlos 2001, 2007). Perhaps the best historical illustration of the federal government's tendency to impose regulations

Figure 5.1. The national parks of Canada.

on northern Native hunters with little regard for local conditions comes from the Migratory Birds Convention Act of 1917, a piece of legislation that established nationwide open seasons on waterfowl that commenced in the autumn, well after most ducks and geese had migrated from their summer nesting grounds in the Far North (Gottesman 1983). In that same year, the federal government's Northwest Game Act imposed a broad array of unprecedented closed seasons on fur-bearing animals and critical game species such as caribou. Although the statute contained a starvation clause that allowed Native hunters to take big game species when they were suffering from hunger, the government had, to some degree, asserted control over the ability of Aboriginal communities to choose the time of year they could hunt animals on which they depended for their food needs (Government of Canada 1917).

Native hunters in the Northwest Territories also faced restrictions on where they could hunt. When the government created Wood Buffalo National Park in 1922, federal wildlife officials agreed to allow Treaty Indians who had traditionally hunted and trapped in the park to continue their activities (subject to a comprehensive list of wildlife regulations that included an absolute ban on bison hunting). Park officials did, however, summarily expel hunters from the park who were Métis, who were not on the treaty list, or who could not prove that they had maintained a long-standing occupation of the area. In 1927, the federal government took this approach one step farther, expelling all Native and non-Native hunters from the Thelon Game Sanctuary when it was established to protect the dwindling muskoxen herds of the Arctic interior. Those banished from the sanctuary were primarily Chipewyan trappers of small fur-bearers who worked their lines in the southwestern corner of the preserve, well away from the major concentrations of muskoxen at the junction of the Thelon and Hanbury Rivers farther to the north. As with the Migratory Birds Convention, both of these new parks were imposed without consulting Native communities, perhaps the most visible sign of the paternalistic attitude that the government had adopted toward local hunters in the region (Sandlos 2007).

The unilateral imposition of game regulations and the expulsion of hunters from protected areas were only two manifestations of the colonial approach to wildlife conservation in the Northwest Territories. In the early twentieth century, northern dreamers both inside and outside government promoted the "Arctic prairies" as a last frontier for the development of industry and settlement. In order to provide an agriculture base for northward expansion, many boosters recommended the development of a northern ranching industry that could bypass the problem of extreme climate through the domestication of local wildlife, such as muskoxen and caribou, or the importation of hardy northern herd animals, such as European reindeer or Asian yak. Reports from northern explorers, most notably those of Vilhjalmur Stefansson, convinced many federal politicians and wildlife bureaucrats that Canada could extend the reaches of the empire to the farthest corners of the Canadian North if only a stable food base could be provided through the ranching of native wildlife or Old World semi-domesticates (Stefansson and Anderson 1913; Stefansson 1921, 1924; Diubaldo 1998). If Native hunters could be convinced to take up the settled life of the Christian farmer rather than the pagan hunter and trapper, as so many had reportedly done after the introduction of reindeer to Alaska, so much the better it was for the advance of civilization in the region (Porsild 1936; Treude 1968).

The federal government's initial enthusiasm for harnessing the resource potential of northern wildlife is obvious even from the most casual observations of documents from the period. In 1917, the Parks Branch sent its chief of the Animal Division, Maxwell Graham, to investigate the possibility of a mass caribou slaughter near Churchill as a means to ease wartime food shortages (Graham 1918). Two years later the federal government established a Royal Commission, with James Harkin as one of three presiding members, to investigate the economic potential for reindeer and muskox industries (including herds of domesticated caribou) throughout northern territories. It was not until 1935, however, that the federal government established a small reindeer herd in the Mackenzie Delta region after the animals were shepherded on a six-year journey from Kotzebue Sound on the west coast of Alaska (Rutherford et al. 1922). The federal government's enthusiasm for such ventures was dampened with the onset of the Depression and the logistical difficulties with pilot reindeer and muskox projects (not to mention the fraudulent activities of several private reindeer ranching companies). There can be no doubt, however, that the conservation programs implemented during the same period were intended not only to protect species thought to be endangered but also to appropriate wildlife and grazing ranges from local Aboriginal hunters in order to establish a commercial empire in the north (Hewitt 1972).

In the post–World War II era, the big game of the northern territories were once again incorporated into the rhetoric of northern economic development as plans for marketing northern wildlife provided partial justification for a commercial bison slaughter in Wood Buffalo National Park from 1950 to 1967 (Sandlos 2002; Loo 2006). Although commercial considerations faded somewhat in importance due to the perceived scarcities associated with the so-called caribou crisis from the mid-1950s to the late 1960s, the federal government attempted to establish further control over Natives' subsistence practices by instructing field staff (for example, Northern Service Officers, Royal Canadian Mounted Police officers, Indian Agents) to do whatever they could to encourage Native people to shift their harvesting efforts from caribou to alternative food resources. Several fishing projects, such as those at Nueltin Lake in 1950 and Contwoyto Lake in 1959, failed due to poor equipment and a lack of enthusiasm on behalf of the residents (Tester and Kulchyski 1994; Sandlos 2007). Nonetheless, the federal government's efforts to assert control over both the subsistence economy of Native northerners and the wildlife that sustained them suggests that the colonial mentality among federal officials with respect to the northern wildlife conservation programs had survived from its earliest manifestation in the late nineteenth century until the gradual devolution of authority over wildlife to the territorial government in the early 1970s.

Where Past and Present Meet

Over the last four decades, a major paradigm shift in the federal and territorial policy regime governing wildlife management and the creation of protected areas in northern Canada has altered dramatically the relationship between Native hunters and the state in the region. Beginning in the 1970s, increasing political activism among Dene and Inuit groups in response to issues such as the proposed Mackenzie Valley Pipeline and unresolved land claims created a climate whereby Native people were able to assume a more prominent role in the management of wildlife and nature preserves in northern Canada (Watkins 1977; Berger 1988; Sabin 1995). Legal developments, such as the entrenchment of Aboriginal rights in Section 35 of the Canadian Constitution in 1982 and the landmark Supreme Court of Canada's *R v. Sparrow* (1990) decision confirming Aboriginal rights to fish and hunt subject to state regulation only if such conservation measures could be justified, further entrenched the idea that the federal and territorial governments can no longer manage wildlife unilaterally. In addition, the emergence of a vast body of anthropological research on the traditional ecological knowledge of northern Aboriginal people beginning in the 1980s has provided a further impetus for the devolution of a degree of decision-making power over wildlife to Dene and Inuit hunters (Usher 1987; Feit 1988; Freeman and Carbyn 1988: 124; Johnson 1992; Berkes 1994; Fast et al. 1994).

The result has been a plethora of comanagement agreements forged among Aboriginal groups and the state to formalize Aboriginal participation in the wildlife policy process. These comanagement boards are often focused on particular species ranging from the barren-ground caribou to marine animals such as arctic char or narwhal. In addition, several comanagement boards have been established through the comprehensive land claims agreement process (that is, the Wildlife Advisory Committee created through the Inuvialuit Final Agreement in 1984 and the Nunavut Wildlife Management Board that was established as part of the Nunavut Land Claims Agreement in 1993), and these have a broader mandate to advise on the conservation of a range of wildlife species over the extensive settlement area. Aboriginal hunters in northern Canada also participate in a myriad of local forums, from community-based hunters and trappers associations to informal conversations with local game officers, where they can have some influence over wildlife policy and harvesting strategies in their local area (Peepre and Dearden 2002; Berkes et al. 2005). Aboriginal harvesters have clearly become major players in the wildlife policy process in the territorial north, exercising a degree of influence over wildlife management that is often far greater than that of Native hunters and trappers living on reserves in southern Canada.

Perhaps nowhere is the shifting politics of wildlife conservation in the Canadian North more apparent than in changing approaches to the establishment and management of protected areas. Events in southern Canada, particularly protests by families who were expelled from Kouchibouguac or who faced expulsion from the proposed Gros Morne national parks in the 1970s (MacEachern 2001), certainly did have a major influence on Parks Canada's decision to abandon expropriation as the preferred tool for securing park lands. Nonetheless, Aboriginal political activism around the issue of parks has also produced a sea change in attitudes toward local stakeholders within Parks Canada. In the early 1970s, northern Aboriginal groups argued successfully before House of Commons and Senate Committees that the establishment of national parks outside the umbrella of unresolved land claims would amount to an expropriation of Aboriginal title. The three parks established in the north during the 1970s—Kluane, Auyuittuq, and Nahanni—were all created as national park reserves, a new legal designation that did not formally extinguish Aboriginal title to the land base, thus making the parks subject to unresolved comprehensive land claims negotiations processes (Fenge 1993). The Parks Canada Policy of 1979 formalized this new approach by recognizing the existence and importance of Aboriginal rights in potential and existing park locations (Parks Canada 1979), and the 1994 Guiding Principles Operational Policies further emphasized cooperation with local First Nations through dialogue and formal agreements, as well as respect for rights to land and wildlife resources guaranteed through land claims, court decisions, and the Canadian constitution (Parks Canada 1994: 125). Legislative changes to the National Parks Act in 1988 and 2000 permitted Aboriginal hunters to harvest wildlife in select national parks, the vast majority of which are located in northern Canada (Government of Canada 1988, 2000).[2] All of these changes have produced a new model for managing national parks that is specific to northern Canada. No longer is the presence of Aboriginal people—whether in the form of resource harvesting or political activism—regarded as anathema to the preservation mandate of national parks in the region.

As a result, parks and protected areas have become less an object of displacement for Aboriginal hunters and more a valuable tool employed to preserve wildlife habitat and valuable hunting grounds from the encroachment of industrial development. Indeed, Dene and Inuit political organizations have in the past three decades taken the lead on the creation of national parks in the north through the comprehensive land claims process. The completion of the Inuvialuit Final Agreement in 1984, for example, resulted in the creation of Ivvavik National Park on the Yukon North Slope, and the Vuntut Gwitchin Final Agreement established the adjacent Vuntut National Park in 1993, in both cases to protect traditional hunting grounds and the winter range of the Porcupine caribou herd. During negotiations for the Nunavut Land Claims Agreement, Inuit representatives advocated the completion of the parks system in the region (or the setting aside of a national park in each federally designated natural region in Nunavut), but objections from development-oriented federal government departments, particularly the Department of Indian Affairs and Northern Development and Natural Resources Canada, watered down this proposal to a promise for three national parks in Nunavut. Since that time, the federal government has designated Auyuittuq and Quttinirpaaq (formerly Ellesmere Island) National Park Reserves as full national parks and created two new national parks in Nunavut: Sirmilik on north Baffin Island in 1999 and Ukkusiksalik on Wager Bay in 2003. In all of these cases, the land claims process has included impact and benefit agreements with the local communities surrounding the parks and provisions for the joint planning and management through boards and committees with Aboriginal representation (Fenge 1993; Indian and Northern Affairs Canada et al. 1999–2000; Gertsch et al. 2003). Similar advisory committees have been established in older parks such as Wood Buffalo, Kluane, and Auyuittuq through the land claims process or on an ad hoc basis. Aboriginal communities in the Northwest Territories have also taken the lead in designing protected areas strategies in their local region under the umbrella of broader territorial parks planning strategy (PACTeam Canada Inc. 2009).

Obviously such policy innovations represent some degree of progress when compared to the indifferent and at times hostile attitude that Canadian parks and wildlife officials displayed toward northern Aboriginal people in the early twentieth century. But, then again, it is not difficult to demonstrate a positive evolution in northern parks and wildlife policy if one chooses as a historical reference a point in time representing the absolute nadir of the relationship between the state and Aboriginal communities in northern Canada. Choose a different moment in time—for example, the fur trade period from the 1670s to the 1880s, when Aboriginal hunters harvested wildlife to fulfill subsistence and market needs with no interference from state managers—and you change the terms of the debate about the progressive nature of contemporary wildlife and parks policies in the Canadian North. The key question becomes not how much has improved since the "bad old days" (an approach that will inevitably celebrate almost any form of incremental change), but instead how much the governance of wildlife policy has been effectively decolonized to grant Aboriginal hunters something resembling the degree of autonomy and sovereignty they exercised over northern wildlife before the advent of the state management era in the 1890s.

By this measure, the participatory revolution in northern parks and wildlife management remains incomplete. Despite three decades of policies designed to ameliorate the relationship between Parks Canada and northern Natives, the federal government has not surrendered any substantive regulatory powers over wildlife in the parks to Aboriginal groups or comanagement boards in northern areas. On a broad scale, the principles of comanagement and power sharing were not enshrined in the National Parks Act of 2000 as a governing principle for northern protected areas. In parks where Native people enjoy harvesting privileges, the National Parks Act grants park superintendents and/or the federal cabinet a broad range of regulatory powers ranging from harvest limits to permit requirements (Government of Canada 2000). As a result, the powers of the comanagement boards remain largely advisory in nature and subordinate to the final management decisions of park officials or the relevant ministerial authority (Manseau et al. 2005). Even if Aboriginal people are accorded a weak voice at the management table, recent research has suggested that, with the exception of Gwaii Haanas National Park, the traditional environmental knowledge of Native people has not been incorporated significantly into the discussions of any other national park comanagement boards in Canada (Weitzner and Manseau 2001; Doberstein and Devin 2004). In 2006, Parks Canada did take the unprecedented step of establishing an all-Inuit comanagement board at the newly created Torngats National Park. Not only did all parties agree to appoint an Inuit chair but the government also appointed two Inuit as its representatives, with Nunatsiavut (Labrador) and Nunavik (Quebec) Inuit governments each appointing two of their members to the seven-person committee. If the composition of this newest national park comanagement board suggests expanded scope for power sharing between Aboriginal people and Parks Canada, the bias against perceived parochialism endures as board members are mandated to act in the public interest rather than as direct representatives of the Inuit government that appointed them (Canadian Parks Council n.d.). Despite the much-celebrated cooperative approaches to managing parks in northern Canada, it is clear that protected areas and the planning processes that spawn them remain, in part, colonial institutions, symbols of a lack of political will to fully devolve power over landscapes and wildlife populations with the Aboriginal people who have lived in the region for centuries.

The tentative incorporation of Aboriginal people into the decision-making structure surrounding the national parks mirrors many of the problems with species-specific comanagement agreements in the north. While some case studies of comanagement bodies have suggested that Native groups can feel politically empowered through their direct involvement at the management table (Huntington et al. 2002; Gertsch et al. 2003; Feit and Spaeder 2005; Goetze 2005; Parlee and Manseau 2005; Spaeder 2005), there is a large body of literature on comanagement boards (that is, the Nunavut Wildlife Management Board, Beverly and Qamanirjuaq Caribou Management Board, Ruby Range Sheep Steering Committee) in northern Canada suggesting that Aboriginal hunters still occupy a marginal position in relation to government scientists and bureaucratic managers. As with the national parks, many species-specific comanagement boards are empowered only to provide advice to the relevant cabinet minister (Rodon 1998). Often wildlife comanagement meetings and public forums are dominated by technical, scientific, and bureaucratic language and bureaucratic environments (boardrooms, PowerPoint presentations) that are alien to Aboriginal participants (Nadasdy 1999, 2003a; Berkes et al. 2005). In addition, non-Native participants on comanagement boards are often so steeped in Western ideas of what has been termed "imperial ecology" (Worster 1994), a worldview that reduces the non-human world to resources subject to control and management in order to produce a maximum sustained yield, that they fail to incorporate meaningfully Aboriginal knowledge of the natural world unless it can be used as data to support existing scientific premises and conclusions. In cases where the traditional knowledge of Aboriginal people conflicts with scientific studies, or when Aboriginal hunters speak outside the boundaries of rational science and articulate spiritual values or a view of animals as social beings (a worldview that informs the belief of many hunters, for example, that radio-collaring shows a lack of respect for animals), their ideas are often ignored or marginalized (Cruikshank 1998:

211; Nadasdy 1999, 2003a; Spak 2005). Thus, for Aboriginal people to participate in comanagement bodies, they must present their knowledge in a manner that is deemed useful to the scientists and managers with whom they share the boardroom table.

Many critics of comanagement have argued that this tendency to regard Aboriginal traditional ecological knowledge as a supplementary form of scientific data, rather than as a more expansive worldview that challenges some basic assumptions of Western science, has served to co-opt Aboriginal knowledge within a bureaucratic structure of wildlife management, expanding and solidifying state approaches to wildlife management in northern Aboriginal communities (Rodon 1998; Nadasdy 2003a, 2005; Ellis 2005; Kofinas 2005; Mulrennan and Scott 2005). Nadasdy (2005) further argued that many comanagement agreements have failed to incorporate Native participants in a meaningful way because government bureaucrats often do not recognize that wildlife conservation is more than a managerial issue involving only instrumental questions; it is also a contested political terrain that inevitably encompasses issues of power, control, and legitimacy.

The adoption of such an apolitical stance toward comanagement suggests that bureaucratic approaches to wildlife conservation in the Canadian North are still firmly rooted in their colonial past. Although recent attempts to include rather than simply ignore the voices of Aboriginal harvesters are certainly an improvement on past practices, the advent of the new comanagement era in the north has clearly not in many cases resulted in a substantive sharing of political power between Native hunters and the state. To be fair, comanagement can be interpreted as an attempt to build on the respective strengths of local and state perspectives on wildlife, while minimizing the parochial weaknesses inherent to both, but it can also be seen as a means of confirming and legitimizing the presence of the state in a region where local management has historically been the norm. Recall, for a moment, that the comanagement philosophy asks us to accept as a radical innovation the mere inclusion of Aboriginal communities who maintained absolute sovereign control over northern wildlife populations only a generation or two ago. The weak powers accorded to Aboriginal people on many of the wildlife advisory boards offer the state the best of both worlds: maintenance of political authority over wildlife "resources" and the appearance of a consultative and consensus-building approach with Aboriginal hunters.

To take just one example, the federal government's creation of a Wildlife Advisory Board at Wood Buffalo National Park in response to a land claims settlement with the Mikisew Cree in 1986 has failed to alter dramatically the political relationship between the state and local hunters in the region. As its title suggests, the powers of the Wood Buffalo National Park comanagement board are only of an advisory nature; the absolute authority to create game regulations in the park rests with the federal cabinet. Many of the most reviled provisions that accompanied the creation of the park in 1922 remain in place: the absolute ban on hunting bison, the authority granted to the park superintendent to revoke the hunting and trapping permits of those who commit any violation of the game laws, and the implicit exclusion of many local hunters through the restriction of park hunting and trapping permits to 370 (East 1991; Government of Canada 2008). Thus, the existence of the advisory board allows the federal government to claim that it has adopted a participatory approach to managing Wood Buffalo National Park without requiring the surrender of any of its political authority in the region. Moreover, implicit within the advisory nature of the management board is one of the most important principles of past colonial approaches to wildlife conservation: the assumption, inherent by definition to the comanagement philosophy, that local management of natural resources is by itself deficient and that the role of the state is both necessary and at times primary to the formation of wildlife policy in the region.

A more radical approach to wildlife conservation in the Canadian North would include attempts to restore the local management regimes that existed prior to the advent of state management. Such an approach will provoke strong objections from the public and within the state wildlife bureaucracy. Some might adopt the utilitarian argument (used to justify state management since the pioneering efforts of Gifford Pinchot to assert public control over U.S. forests a century ago) that northern wildlife populations and national parks are a public trust that cannot be left subject to the whims and prejudices of local people. Others might object that rapidly changing ecological circumstances (that is, climate change and toxic build-up in the north) and the decline of Aboriginal traditional ecological knowledge due to acculturation render the non-scientific local management of wildlife populations a risky proposition. Still others might argue that the idealization of local Aboriginal wildlife management regimes relies on an overly romantic view of precontact Aboriginal harmony with wildlife populations that cannot be sustained in light of historical evidence (Denevan 1992; Krech 1999). There may be some truth to these criticisms, though all rest on the paternalistic idea that Aboriginal communities are less capable than non-Native outsiders of managing local wildlife populations, and that Western scientific approaches to wildlife conservation are comparatively infallible despite a wealth of historical evidence to the contrary (Worster 1994; Stanley 1995; Bocking 1997, 2004; Grove 1997; Sivaramakrishnan 1999, 2008).

If a complete return to the local management regimes of a previous era seems unlikely, there are some practical steps that could be taken to further decolonize state approaches to wildlife management in the region. Although it is not the intent of this chapter to provide a comprehensive list of proposals, some possibilities for further empowering Aboriginal people within a local management framework have been implicit in the discussion thus far:

- further devolution of power over local wildlife and protected areas in the north through the removal of ministerial overrides from wildlife comanagement and advisory boards;
- integration of wildlife advisory boards into the management structure of national and territorial parks (that is, through a management position meant to represent the views of the board);
- majority representation of Aboriginal harvesters on wildlife comanagement boards;
- adoption of cutting-edge scientific approaches, particularly the "learning by doing" approach associated with adaptive management, which accord well with the practical application of traditional ecological knowledge (Berkes et al. 2000);
- recognition that traditional ecological knowledge is not simply a source of raw data but a worldview that encompasses a wide range of ideas governing the appropriate relationships between humans and non-humans;
- inclusion of scientists on comanagement boards who are not employed by the federal or territorial bureaucracy; and
- creation of several protected areas at the national and/or territorial level that are under the complete managerial control of surrounding Aboriginal communities.

Too often, comanagement has been presented as a catch-all solution—in most cases the only solution—to the strained historical relationship between state and local systems of wildlife management in the Canadian North. A further consideration of local management, or the full devolution of managerial power over specific wildlife populations or protected areas to Aboriginal communities in northern Canada, provides an opportunity to address and reconcile the historical and contemporary imbalances in the distribution of political power between Aboriginal wildlife harvesters and bureaucratic wildlife managers in the region. The politics of mere participation might then give way to a more restorative approach whereby Aboriginal communities are once again able to shape and control their relationships with wildlife populations on which they have depended for generations.

Acknowledgments

An earlier version of this chapter was presented at the Canadian Parks for Tomorrow: Fortieth Anniversary Conference and posted to the University of Calgary's DSpace repository. This edited version of the article is used with the permission of the conference chairs. Final edits were completed with the generous support of a sabbatical fellowship from the Rachel Carson Center for Environment and Society in Munich, Germany.

Notes

1. This chapter is adapted slightly from a paper commissioned for presentation at the Canadian Parks for Tomorrow: Fortieth Anniversary Conference (University of Calgary, Alberta, Canada, May 8–11, 2008). The author wishes to thank the conference organizers for permission to use this material.

2. The National Parks Act allows hunting in Wood Buffalo, Wapusk, Gros Morne, and Mingan Archipelago National Parks and traditional renewable resource harvesting in any park established through a land claim agreement or in any national park established in an area where a Native group has a treaty right to hunt and trap. Traditional resource harvesting occurs under these provisions in Aulavik, Auyyittuq, Gwaii Haanas, Ivvavik, Kluane, Nahanni, Pacific Rim, Pukaskwa, Quttinirpaaq, Sirmilik, Tuktut Nogait, Ukkusiksalik, and Vuntut National Parks. All hunting activities in the national parks are subject to the regulation of the federal cabinet (Government of Canada 2000; Peepre and Dearden 2002).

CHAPTER SIX

State Governmentality or Indigenous Sovereignty?
Protected Area Comanagement in the Ashaninka Communal Reserve in Peru

Emily Caruso

Throughout Peru's history, Amazonia has constituted both an asset and a challenge to the nation-state. Viewed both as a treasure chest of wild and immense riches that would benefit the nation and as an unstable, mysterious, and dangerous frontier, Peruvian Amazonia causes the state a great deal of anxiety. While its chimeric nature eludes the grasp of governance, it also represents "an essential element of the body, but also of the spirit of peruvianity" (Belaunde 2007 [1961]: 55). Since the early twentieth century, the Amazonian region has been at the center of Peruvian ambitions—primarily economic, but also nationalistic.

Twice-president Fernando Belaunde Terry (1963–1968, 1980–1985) was the first to initiate a concerted policy for realizing the Amazonian ambition. The title of his book was *La Conquista del Peru por los Peruanos* (*The Conquest of Peru by the Peruvians*), which was also the name of his project for taming *la selva* (the forest), for rendering it legible, productive, and wholly Peruvian (see Greene 2009). He planned an ambitious road network that would link the lowland jungle to the highland jungle and, more importantly, to the spinal cord of his ambition: the Carretera Marginal. This road slices Peru in its middle, like a long rent through which thousands of Andean peasants (known in Amazonia as *colonos*) have travelled eastward to seek a more prosperous future, while natural resources travel westward toward Lima and foreign countries.

The spirit of this capitalist conquest of Amazonia has been reincarnated by many governments since Belaunde's, the latest being President Alan García's controversial neoliberal program of opening Amazonian territories to large-scale energy-related projects (including petroleum concessions, hydroelectric dams, and extensive biofuel plantations).[1] In addition, conservation initiatives and protected areas, along with the mega-development projects and road construction projects, are increasingly described as one of the prime "administrative vehicles" through which the state rationalizes its expanding control over hinterlands and the populations thriving within them (chapter 1). In Peru, protected areas constitute a large portion of state territory (14 percent of the total surface area). In Peru's Amazonian region, the figure is higher: 20 percent of the region's territory is under state-sanctioned protection.[2] In distant and unruly Amazonia, protected areas are key instruments for the institution of the state's administrative apparatus in the region.

In this chapter, I explore how the comanagement of communal reserves in Peru can be understood as a state tool for the discipline of a marginal space and for bringing Indigenous peoples into the bureaucratic fold. First, I describe how the space of the Ashaninka Communal Reserve (ASCR) is imagined, narrated, and produced as a material place requiring state intervention, and how the disciplining practices of governmental bureaucracy seek to establish state presence in this marginal area. However, over the course of my doctoral fieldwork (2007–2009) among Ashaninka communities, principally in the Ene River valley, I found that Ashaninka people would rarely—if ever—describe themselves as victims or as in the thrall of a greater oppressor; on the contrary, they would rather be presented as "masters of the universe" (Veber 2000: 18).[3] Therefore, the second part of the chapter concentrates on Ashaninka responses: how Ashaninka people relate to the space of the reserve, how they understand the state's involvement in it, and how, in their own perspective, they are in control of the land enclosed within the reserve. I conclude by proposing a rearticulation of the concept of sovereignty in the Indigenous context as an assertion of agency based on Indigenous ontologies.

The Makings of a State Space: Imaginaries, Narratives, and Practices

Communal reserves, according to Peru's Protected Areas Law of 1997, are "areas destined for wildlife conservation for the benefit of neighboring rural populations" (Article 22(g)). The eight current communal reserves are all found in the Amazon region and were mostly established at the request of Indigenous federations. Although Indigenous peoples' ownership of their territories is not explicitly recognized within communal reserves, these federations see communal reserves as tools that ensure state support in protecting ancestral lands and resources that are not contained within the smaller, officially recognized Comunidad Nativa units. Conversely, they are considered part of "national heritage" by the Peruvian state and are incorporated into the National System for Protected Areas in Peru, which is managed by the Servicio Nacional de Areas Naturales Protegidas (SERNANP), which responds directly to the Ministry of Environment. The 2005 Special Regime for the Administration of Communal Reserves (hereafter "Special Regime") establishes the norms for implementation of the category of communal reserve.

The ASCR is located along the Ene, Tambo, and Apurimac River valleys in Peru's central Amazon region, Selva Central, and forms part of the Vilcabamba Conservation Complex (figure 6.1). It covers 184,468 hectares of tropical highland forest, at an elevation of between 300 and 1600 meters above sea level, and remains relatively inaccessible. A number of isolated Ashaninka families still live within the reserve, most of whom have little or no contact with national society. There are twenty-two recognized Native community territories bordering the reserve, of which twenty are populated by Ashaninka, one by Machiguenga, and another by Kakinte communities.

The ASCR was officially established in January 2003, after decades of debate between missionaries, NGOs, and loggers over the fate of the Vilcabamba Mountain Range (see Gagnon 2000; INRENA 2002). A local NGO led the process of creation of the ASCR, and while some local and regional Indigenous federations were actively involved in its establishment, community participation was limited to three workshops (one per valley) attended by community leaders. In 2007, many Ashaninka people living in the reserve's beneficiary communities possessed scant knowledge of it, an indication both of the limited effectiveness of Ashaninka participation and of the degree of disconnection between the loci of decision-making and the affected subjects of those decisions. I now turn to the origins of this disconnection.

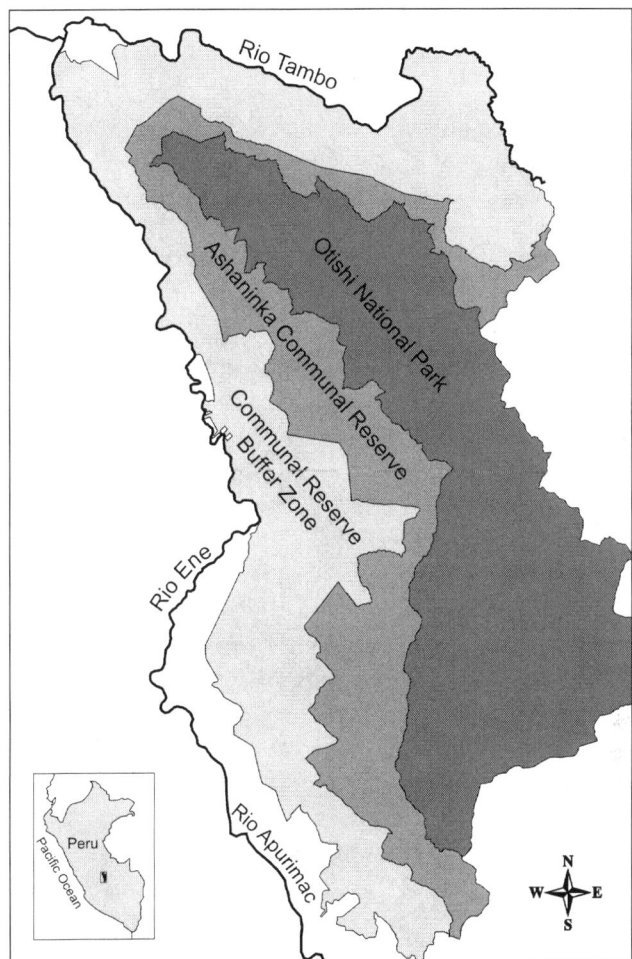

Figure 6.1. The Vilcabamba Conservation Complex is composed of the Otishi National Park, the Ashaninka Communal Reserve, and the Machiguenga Communal Reserve (east of the Otishi National Park; not shown on this map). The Ashaninka Communal Reserve's buffer zone lies to its west and is composed of contiguous Ashaninka community territories.

Imagining the Ashaninka Communal Reserve

Since the 1960s, visits by representatives of National Geographic, the Inter-American Development Bank, the Organization of American States, the Peruvian Franciscan Mission, and other powerful Peruvian individuals all contributed to an account of the Vilcabamba Mountain Range as a site worthy of conservation, given its numerous waterfalls, distinctive geomorphology,[4] and lush vegetation (Castro n.d.). French explorer Jacques-Yves Cousteau visited the area in 1987 and announced that the Vilcabamba Mountain Range was unique in its geology and biodiversity, contributing toward the popular appeal of the bid for its protection (Castro n.d.).

Currently, the most informative website for the ASCR is a dedicated webpage within Parkswatch, a Duke University web-based initiative.[5] According to the Parkswatch document, the ASCR is "one of the most pristine places on the planet," brimming with biodiversity, some which may yet be new to science, found within "extraordinarily" diverse habitats. However, the scientific studies used by Parkswatch to substantiate its claims, and the only research carried out to date on the biology of the Vilcabamba Mountain Range, are Conservation International's 1997 and the Smithsonian Institution's 1998 Rapid Assessment Programmes (RAPs). These research expeditions took the shape of three two-week field excursions to sites that lie within the Otishi National Park and the Machiguenga Communal Reserve, which are many kilometers from the borders of the ASCR (Conservation International and Smithsonian Institution 2001).

Despite no scientist having been to the ASCR, this RAP study has been used in different reports and documents in the process of the reserve's categorization as scientific corroboration for broad statements made about the extraordinary and endemic biodiversity of the ASCR (INRENA 2002; Anonymous n.d.; Castro n.d.). Despite nonexistent data concerning the current state of the reserve's biodiversity, the RAP report, read alongside a couple of aerial photographs taken by the NGO Asociación Cutivireni and the RAP team over ten years ago, has led to the production of the ASCR as a fragile biome and its biodiversity as "under threat." The major threats reported in Parkswatch and the RAP are illegal logging, the construction of roads for timber trafficking, cattle ranching, colonization, unsustainable resource use by a growing Indigenous population, and, most alarmingly in the eyes of the authorities, the presence of remnant groups of Sendero Luminoso[6] and cocaine trafficking, which pose significant challenges to the stability of the Peruvian state in the area. Here, the production, reproduction, and circulation of expert knowledge, disconnected from its original source, yet presented as fact, help to produce the ASCR as requiring not only conservation intervention but also state intervention.

In this way, the ASCR has been socially constructed, or imagined, as a space that requires protection (on the conservation imaginary, see West 2006). The only real place in which the ASCR exists is on the map: it is here that the GIS-defined contours of the reserve establish state presence and ground the abstractions of fragility, purity, endemicity, and diversity in a physical representation. The space of the ASCR, made worthy through its putative "extraordinary" diversity, and materialized through its cartographic representation, is placed in the crosshairs of the state's gaze. This imaginary is then circulated, amplified, and bolstered by the narratives that arise surrounding it.

Narrating the Ashaninka Communal Reserve

Narratives are often used to simplify the disparate realities we encounter in the world around us; they help us to construct a coherent understanding of the world and ourselves within it and organize it into that which is desirable versus that which is objectionable. Conservation narratives are particularly resilient, as they are borne from conservation participants' cultural, emotive, and spiritual life. The basic idea of "conservation" has arisen within a Western perspective, which separates nature from culture and is premised on the notion that the well-being of habitats, species, and humans depends on carrying out the moral duty of setting areas aside for nonintervention (with no habitation or use) or sustainable use (with restricted natural resource use). In the context of the ASCR, the idea of conservation as strict nature protection resonates with the images of untouched, pristine wilderness offered up within the imaginary produced by the articulation of the RAP reports and their circulation.

A principal conservation narrative is that the ASCR beneficiaries must fit into a specific category of indigeneity in order to be worthy of participating in comanagement: they ought to be exclusively traditional, "authentic" Ashaninka people, who hunt with bows and arrows, do not use outboard motors, and wear traditional Ashaninka dress. The narrative of "nontraditional" or "modernized" Indigenous people as a threat to conservation is pervasive: "The Indian with a shotgun is the most effective plunderer of the forest," the head of SERNANP reminded me in early 2008. In light of most Ashaninka community members' lack of unsullied indigeneity, this narrative would have only "noncontacted" people as proper inhabitants of the reserve, while community-based Ashaninka would only access resources sporadically and sparingly.

Conversely, in the belief of SERNANP staff, as well as many non-Ashaninka Peruvians, most contemporary Indigenous people are not ideal conservationists because they "live for the day": lacking an understanding of the future, they are incapable of understanding the concept of sustainability. In this narrative, Ashaninka people are also deemed unfit for the management of the ASCR because they do not have the conservation training (or intellectual capacity) necessary to understand the science of sustainable resource management. Moreover, I was often told by SERNANP and local NGO staff that Ashaninka cannot be trusted to enter into an effective comanagement relationship with the state because they lack the "maturity" to understand the concepts of contracts, policies, and laws; the meaning of signatures, frameworks, schedules, and budgets; and moreover, that they do not understand the "rules of the game." In other words, alongside the narrative that Indigenous people are "not Indigenous enough" to benefit from the reserve, there exists an opposing narrative whereby Ashaninka are "too Indigenous'" to ensure appropriate comanagement.

Furthermore, there is a powerful discourse among SERNANP and some NGO staff that Indigenous peoples erroneously believe that communal reserves ought to be a source of economic benefit, a view the officials assert despite the fundamental legal provision establishing communal reserves "for the benefit of neighboring communities." In effect, these actors often view communal reserves exclusively as strict preservation areas. They have a narrow understanding of how communities ought to benefit from these areas: either only indirectly (enjoying clean air, clean rivers) or for basic, sporadic, and noninterventionist subsistence purposes (such as the collection of medicinal plants or the occasional hunting of game animals). According to them, Ashaninka people are not meant to benefit economically from this space. Moreover, they assert that the ASCR is state territory, not Ashaninka territory, and thus belongs to every Peruvian citizen. Furthermore, because the ASCR has legal status as a protected area of "direct use," the petroleum reserves in its subsoil belong to the state and can—and in their view should—be exploited for the benefit of all Peruvian citizens. As a result, petroleum concession block 108, currently leased to the Argentinian petroleum company PlusPetrol and covering the northern portion of the reserve and the bordering community territories, has become a subject of grave contention between the state and Ene

Ashaninka communities, who vehemently oppose any petroleum development on their lands.

Thus, while there has been no scientific research within the ASCR, and the only conservation actors to have entered its borders are Ashaninka park guards on their periodic field trips,[7] the conservation narratives circulating around the reserve are replete with obstinate definitions of what is "good" and what is "bad" for this territory. These contradictory yet connected narratives provide the rationale for the popular perception of the ASCR as a site requiring intervention. Conservation narratives emerge from and build on imaginaries; together they are "constitutive of reality," a reality that justifies and prescribes certain actions, interventions, and practices (Brosius 1999: 278; West 2006).

Governmentalizing the Ashaninka Communal Reserve

The legal format for comanagement requires the election of an Executor of Administrative Contract, the organization that represents the views of the beneficiary Indigenous populations and acts as partner of the local SERNANP office in matters pertaining to communal reserve comanagement.[8] Once the Executor of Administrative Contract is established, it signs a Contract of Administration with the SERNANP that establishes roles and responsibilities for both parties: from this moment comanagement begins. The Executor of Administrative Contract of the ASCR is named ECO-Ashaninka: its six-person management committee presides over the assembly of forty-four members (two representatives for each beneficiary community), which meets once a year. Moreover, the team of six park guards for the ASCR is selected from members of the reserve's beneficiary communities.

The process of establishing ECO-Ashaninka, obtaining official state recognition for the organization, and signing the contract of administration took four conflictive years to complete. The principal obstacle was a desire on the part of Ashaninka beneficiaries to have their legitimate and representative federations involved in decision-making regarding the communal reserve. SERNANP officials stated that federations have "nothing to do with the reserve" and therefore could not be involved in its decision-making. SERNANP officers' main point of contention was that ECO-Ashaninka was a "technical" and "administrative" organization and ought not be distracted from this mandate by "political pretensions" that could be fomented by the federations. For the first few years, ECO-Ashaninka committee members argued both for federation participation and for a greater voice in the political decisions regarding the communal reserve. However, SERNANP officials took the position that dissent on this topic was not permitted. When the time came to sign the contract of administration, the attempts by ECO-Ashaninka to argue for more balanced roles, responsibilities, and decision-making capabilities were met by veiled threats by SERNANP officials. ECO-Ashaninka leaders were told that if such challenges continued, there might be no contract to sign and no reserve to comanage. After four years of moral, political, and economic struggles to participate effectively in the comanagement process, ECO-Ashaninka management committee members were exhausted and anxious about their own positions, capacities, and legitimacy and the future of the reserve: their resolve began to wane.

Around this time, ECO-Ashaninka's persistent lack of success at gaining control over the comanagement process formed the backdrop to a new intervention. The organization obtained the support of a local NGO that, in addition to providing generous salaries for the management committee, also carried out a series of capacity-building workshops. At the end of the project, the ECO-Ashaninka president observed, "At first we didn't understand our role, but now we have finally understood, thanks to the capacity-building we have received: our role is technical," and, in the context of petroleum, "Our role is not to decide whether the petroleum company is good or bad, not to take sides, but to inform the communities about it." Following further such capacity-building projects, ECO-Ashaninka management committee members began refusing to engage directly with the federations, seeking out their NGO partners instead, and they were seen by some Ashaninka people as having capitulated to the demands of the state as a result of their significant (individual) economic gain from NGO projects and the strictures of their purely administrative role. In this way, they appeared to exemplify the internalization of the regulatory techniques of bureaucracy.

ASCR park guards, who are Ashaninka, represent another element of the administrative apparatus of comanagement. The park guards are chosen from within the beneficiary communities and are required by the local SERNANP office to travel to communities regularly to carry out educational, surveillance, and monitoring activities. They are strongly encouraged by SERNANP staff to use these visits to inform communities of the prohibitions on resource use in the communal reserve and to inform SERNANP of any misdemeanor on the part of community members. On one occasion, park guards reported the presence of a stash of 40,000 square feet of illegally logged timber in the reserve, which belonged to the bordering Ashaninka community. This resulted in a large-scale intervention led by SERNANP, ECO-Ashaninka, and the local police during which the timber was burned.[9] The park guards, therefore, have become instruments of surveillance of their own communities.

Federations and communities have been excluded from the official governance of the reserve because of the divisions created between ECO-Ashaninka and the federations on the one hand and between the park guards and Ashaninka communities on the other. It appears SERNANP has successfully deployed disciplinary procedures of "partitioning and verticality" that seek to divide and control the Ashaninka population (Foucault 1977: 220). However, in order to increase the capacity of ECO-Ashaninka and the park guards to perform their regulatory and disciplining roles, their members were selected from within the very group that the state seeks to control, both creating internal and internalized hierarchies of power and surveillance and multiplying and localizing the sites of state power. Such forms of rule can be fruitfully construed as "governmentality," that is, organizing practices that produce self-disciplined, self-monitored, and responsibilized citizens who fulfill governmental projects (see chapter 1). ECO-Ashaninka and the park guards are the conduits of such techniques of government as members of the population that must be governed: they embody the task of extending governmental rationalities within that population, constituting a conduit for indirect rule of Ashaninka people by SERNANP.

The governmentalizing effects of comanagement are particularly clear in the context of petroleum exploration. Community members and their federation leaders have consistently rejected any petroleum company intrusion into their Comunidad Nativa territories, thus successfully stalling PlusPetrol's activities in concession block 108 for many years. At the time of my research, as the ASCR Master Plan was due to be published, it was feared that ECO-Ashaninka's acquiescent position may pave the way for the company to enter into concession block 108 through the reserve. The sanitized position of ECO-Ashaninka appeared to be making space for the Peruvian state to access lands and resources the Ashaninka consider theirs and have always protected, a supremely political act, which, at least on paper, granted the state much greater control of Ashaninka territory than prior to the establishment of the communal reserve.

In the case of the Amarakaeri Communal Reserve, which is also superimposed by a petroleum concession (block 76) leased by Hunt Oil, this very situation has already transpired (Alvarez 2010). The Master Plan of the Amarakaeri Communal Reserve, carefully crafted by Indigenous leaders from the beneficiary communities with the aim of establishing regulations for strict protection of fragile ecosystems and sacred sites, was summarily dismissed by SERNANP in favor of far more permissive Master Plan regulations, according to which petroleum exploration would be permitted in most of the reserve, including the highly sensitive areas specifically set aside by Indigenous leaders. Alvarez (2010) argued that the participation of Indigenous people in the Amarakaeri Communal Reserve's comanagement was used to legitimize the (illegitimate) presence of the petroleum company in an extremely fragile ecosystem and among a people who actively repudiated petroleum exploration on their lands. State authority trumped Indigenous rights within the comanagement agreement—indeed, trumped them by virtue of the comanagement agreement—in favor of the petroleum concession. Given ECO-Ashaninka's weak position, such a scenario became possible in the ASCR.

Through the creation of depoliticized, technical "Ashaninka" entities (ECO-Ashaninka and park guards) through which SERNANP seeks to control Ashaninka people's intimate relationships with their lands, the ASCR could be seen as a measure for orchestrating and expanding state surveillance and intervention within Ashaninka lives and territory. This situation aligns with Nadasdy's (2003a, 2005) argument that comanagement is an anti-political tool for state expansion into Indigenous lives and territories (see chapters 1, 5, and 12). The creation of a state-manipulated, "Ashaninka" apparatus for comanagement administration promotes state practices of territorial sovereignty, through the domestication of the unruly Ashaninka will, with the objective of capturing Amazonia's marginal and unstable domains and, more importantly, to gain access to its natural resources for commercial development under the guise of conservation.

Ashaninka Space: Histories, Counter-Narratives, and Practices of Self-Determination

Ashaninka people have their own conception of the ASCR, which contrasts sharply with the representations of it by the Peruvian state. This alternative representation, which is grounded in their own histories, cosmovision, and ontologies, constitutes a counter-narrative to the state vision of the ASCR that informs Ashaninka expressions of sovereignty and practices of self-determination.

Ashaninka Histories and Counter-Narratives

The Amazonian landscape is replete with memories, histories, stories, creation narratives, and human agency (see Santos-Granero 2004; Surallés and García Hierro 2005; Alexiades 2009; Hecht and Cockburn 2011). The area encompassed by the borders of the ASCR is a case in point (see figure 6.2). With its high elevation, mountainous landscapes, and rocky outcrops, this space is the home to numerous spirits and mythical beings, places where key Ashaninka narrative histories transpired, as well as sacred and dangerous places, as Jaime from the community of Tsirotiari recounted during an interview in 2010: "There are many stories about what exists in the [area where the reserve is]. I don't know the stories exactly, but you could meet with a water lizard, and if you cook it with chilies then it will transform into a jaguar, and then [the jaguar] can come and eat us. Also in the past there were many who shape-shifted, like the man who shape-shifted into an owl and gouged out the eyes of children. In the reserve I think there are all these things. When you go to the reserve, you will meet [spirits], and if you make a joke or make fun of them, they will do you harm."

The landscape of the reserve is imbued with a powerful nonhuman agency that Ashaninka ignore at their peril. For example, in the Lower Apurimac area, most interviewees speak of "Mamantsiki" (a kinship term), a particular rocky outcrop at the southern end of the reserve that holds special powers. It is forbidden to go to Mamantsiki and to speak its name when there, as people say that terrible things will happen: powerful rains will fall, making one ill with a severe cold, shakes, and fevers followed by death. Many interviewees also speak of the prohibition against burning swidden gardens on mountainsides, which are the homes of many different kinds of spirits and demons, and warn of the spiritual retribution for disobeying this law. With these prohibitions, Ashaninka people have effectively always protected the area now demarcated by the ASCR. They fear that if colonos gain access to these sacred and spirit-filled areas, they will probably behave disrespectfully, causing illness and danger for all Ashaninka living nearby.

Ashaninka people believe that most elements of their territories are the result of sudden transformations, usually of Ashaninka people into plants, animals, and landscape features. One of the most important catalysts of these transformations is Aviréri, the Ashaninka culture hero, who, during his numerous travels, transformed Ashaninka people and the objects he encountered into current lived landscape (Weiss 1975). This landscape,

Figure 6.2. The landscape of the Ashaninka Communal Reserve, as seen from an Ashaninka community.

populated with features that were once Ashaninka people, ghosts of deceased Ashaninka, spirits, and demons, is saturated with Ashaninka identity. Everything Ashaninka people see (or do not see), utilize, consume, and relate to within this land is "Ashaninka."[10] Some of this vast Ashaninka landscape now holds the official denomination of "Ashaninka Communal Reserve."

As a result of NGO, ECO-Ashaninka, and federation-led information and workshops, by 2009 the term *la reserva* (the reserve) was increasingly used by Ashaninka people when talking with outsiders as shorthand for the upland areas lying beyond the borders of the Comunidad Nativa territories. However, while most Ashaninka are fully aware of the location of their mutual Comunidad Nativa borders, they rarely know the precise locations of their communities' borders with the reserve. The highland areas morph into each other, and the official GIS-charted boundary points become meaningless. The boundaries of the reserve are not visibly demarcated; lacking GPS devices, and with only two makeshift park guard cabins in remote locations for the whole reserve, most Ashaninka people enter and exit the reserve without knowing it. So, for them, the ASCR is an abstract concept used when conversing with interested outsiders about an undefined area that is replete with Ashaninka histories. They routinely describe this space, now officially known as la reserva, as an area filled with resources permitting self-sufficiency. It is also regularly narrated as "for the future," a place where generations of Ashaninka to come will be able to move to if lands and resources run out in their Comunidades Nativas: "In the reserve [the land] is generous: if you go there, as soon as you get there you find meat to feed your children. I think it is important that we take care of it for the future of our children, as they will administer it in the future. For example, when the Comunidad Nativa runs out of land, our children will go there to make their *chacras* [swidden gardens]" (Carmen, a community member from Oviri).

This is also a place filled with the animals, plants, and other foods that permit Ashaninka people to live like proper or legitimate Ashaninka (*Ashaninka sanori*). In Ashaninka narratives, it is a place where people go to collect and hunt "as is our custom" and to eat "what is our custom." The space of the reserve incorporates Ashaninka identity, and Ashaninka people embody their territory by working the land, consuming its resources, and sharing substances with the earth.[11] This is a recurrent and mutual relationship: the Ashaninka-ness of the landscape is constantly re-created by the movement of people and animals, and Ashaninka identity is sustained by the consumption of the products of the land and movement within it (see Munn 1996).

Ashaninka also speak of the spiritual "owners" of the animals living in the reserve, keeping game in their corrals in the mountainside, controlling the wealth of the forest. In fact, in recent memory animals have moved far into the highlands, and some people explain that most probably their spiritual owners are keeping them there, held within their rocky corrals, for future release. The reserve is the location of hunting bounty, and the animal owners living there must be treated with respect and caution if they are to provide for Ashaninka in the future. In Ashaninka perspectives, this territory cannot really be owned; it simply has an inherently Ashaninka identity (although this identity is not stable or reified). "La reserva," in this view, is not a thing that is materialized through discourse and practice, as it has been for SERNANP officers. Rather, it represents a series of interconnected and very powerful ideas: the idea of an Ashaninka space, the idea of what it means to live like a proper Ashaninka, the idea of a satisfactory future, the idea of well-being and resource bounty, all ideas that build upon current and historical relationships with this space.

The knowledge that this area exists in the uplands behind the communities and that the state is providing support for its protection has the effect of reassuring many Ashaninka that this is their space, to be used for their future, and for the continued practice of their Ashaninka-ness. The state's involvement is also seen as key to ensuring that the spirits and its sacred spaces are safeguarded from encroachment by colonos and other invaders. Many Ashaninka are in favor of it, so long as it is their version of the reserve, according to which the state is involved in order to help Ashaninka protect these lands and this embodied landscape from intrusion. People have explained to me that the reserve belongs to Ashaninka people, given that its title, conferred by the state, contains the word *Ashaninka*.[12] Thus, for some Ashaninka, the ASCR is now also constituted through their understandings of state projects. What was previously a space that maintained Ashaninka existence and an area that did not require official ownership is now increasingly being claimed as a possession of Ashaninka people through processes of official territorialization that embody formal practices of self-determination.

Ashaninka Practices of Self-Determination

Despite the embodied sense of the reserve being an Ashaninka place, Ashaninka feel increasingly uncertain about what it means for the future of their territory and communities. As a result of intensifying park guard activities and news of the petroleum concession's overlap with the reserve, there is a growing confusion over whether the reserve is really theirs or whether the state has appropriated it. Their questions hover around: "Does it now belong to the state?" "Is the state really going to sell it to the petroleum company?" "Why can we not log in the communal reserve?" and so on. The territory of the ASCR is seen as particularly threatened given that the petroleum concession superimposes its northern half and may be used as an entry point into Comunidades Nativas.[13]

Many Ashaninka do not believe they ought to conserve the ASCR if it may be sold on to third parties by the current government, as relayed in the following statement made by an Ashaninka community leader during a meeting: "Why are we protecting [the communal reserve]? If the government is going to sell it tomorrow, after tomorrow, to the petroleum companies, to the [. . .] logging companies, to the dam companies? We hear [the rumors], we know [what is going on]. When the petroleum company comes, what are we going to eat? Our rivers will be polluted, there will be no more animals. So why should we protect the reserve? We would be protecting it *por gusto* [for nothing]. Instead, we should be taking advantage of the timber before the government sells it all."

The central concern is that, by calling it the ASCR and agreeing to protect it in cooperation with the state, Ashaninka people may have been co-opted into giving up their control over this territory. The fact that the state appears to have commercial interests in the land and its subsoil reinforces a conviction that if the state cannot provide its promised support to their reserve (and, in fact, seems to undermine it), Ashaninka must defend it and use it as they see fit. The state's rules and prohibitions become irrelevant once it has proven itself both useless and a danger to the integrity and protection of the reserve.

Consequently, some Ashaninka households have recently chosen to specifically move to the area of the reserve, although it is strictly forbidden to open new swidden plots within its borders. Most Ashaninka people I have spoken to still use the reserve as they always have, with no reference to rules and regulations the park guards and ECO-Ashaninka have attempted to inculcate during their visits. Others still are profiting from illegal logging within the reserve, the prohibition of which is widely known. It is noteworthy that, generally speaking, the few communities in which the GIS-mapped boundaries of the ASCR's borders are known (at least to the community leaders) are those in which illegal logging inside the reserve is taking place. This suggests that in places where the state's claims to Ashaninka lands are known by Ashaninka, the latter may be self-consciously staking their own claim, ensuring that the reserve is productive for Ashaninka people above all. Ashaninka people are, in these ways, asserting their ownership over these lands, in the face of an expanding disciplinary regime.

This perspective was, ironically, aided by the very institutions established by the SERNANP to ensure appropriate Ashaninka participation in comanagement: ECO-Ashaninka and the park guards. While ECO-Ashaninka representatives travel relatively regularly to the communities, participate in the federation congresses, and are a feature in the Ashaninka political landscape, the organization has no purchase among community members, who consider their federations their most important point of reference. Nor have any ECO-Ashaninka workshops held in communities over the years turned Ashaninka peoples into sanctioned conservationists. On the contrary, with an etiolated ECO-Ashaninka that is unrepresentative of their political aspirations, it has become clear to many leaders in the communities that opportunity for effective participation in the reserve's official management has decreased. Shielded by ECO-Ashaninka's acquiescing presence, the communities actively assert their own forms of control over the ASCR.

The only individuals who can keep Ashaninka behavior in the reserve under surveillance and report back to the authorities are the park guards, and they are a particularly controversial presence in the ASCR. By law, they must be members of the beneficiary Ashaninka communities, and yet their role leads them to work against their kin (in the latter's view). Many Ashaninka community members believe the park guards' role ought to be protecting the reserve from invasion by colonos and unwanted loggers. However, as a consequence of their insistence on rules, prohibitions, and surveillance, they are often negatively received by communities. Occasionally, Ashaninka people will not allow park guards to cross community territories on their way to the reserve, or permission to pass is granted with an accompaniment of threats (particularly in those communities that are involved in logging in the ASCR). Also, during community visits, park guards are sometimes accused of having sold their people out and, as representatives of the state, to be the ones bringing the petroleum company or the dam project[14] to Ashaninka territory. As one ASCR park guard told me: "Sometimes in the communities they don't want [the communal reserve] to be part of the state, they don't want to let us in. At times, they say 'you come here to talk about the reserve, and then you'll go back and sell our territory.'"

The guards themselves find their situation difficult, upsetting, and awkward. Given their presence on the state's payroll, they are not permitted to make statements against the controversial development projects (or any other state imposition) and are constrained by SERNANP into simply informing communities and informing SERNANP about community activities. The park guards' uncomfortable position as Ashaninka community members and state employees provides the communities with ammunition to refuse engagement and to refuse park guard entries, as Ashaninka feel they have more power to reject the impositions of fellow Ashaninka than of powerful outsiders (see Killick 2007).

Park guards have entered a space similar to ECO-Ashaninka: they are viewed as compliant, state-dependent, town-based Ashaninka people. The very presence of these two bureaucratized and state-cooperative Ashaninka entities bolsters the divide between Ashaninka and state. These two entities inadvertently strengthen Ashaninka self-determination by being the principal subjects of state intervention. They are the absorbers of the state's Ashaninka-directed gaze, creating political space and enabling physical space for community-based Ashaninka to pursue their lives as they choose within their territories. Therefore, the creation of a technical "Ashaninka" apparatus of administration and order for communal reserve comanagement has resulted in an even greater separation between Ashaninka communities and the state, rather than an elision of the two as may be expected.

On the side of the federations, a parallel shift took place. In 2009, the Ene Ashaninka Federation (CARE), which represents the largest proportion of beneficiary communities (nine of the twenty-two), established itself as an essential actor in the process of elaborating the ASCR Master Plan by finding funding for and monopolizing the community consultation component of the process (see Caruso 2011). From the perspective of CARE's president, the organization sought to "appropriate the technical" in order to reinject Ashaninka political perspectives into the comanagement process. International legal instruments, provisions of the SERNANP's Special Regime on communal reserves, and Peru's own shifting relationship with Amazonian peoples were all deftly deployed to argue for a major role by CARE in the comanagement process, to the extent that ECO-Ashaninka was nearly supplanted. Through political maneuvering and technical know-how, CARE became a point of reference for the SERNANP office in Lima: any forum of decision-making surrounding the ASCR required the presence of a CARE leader. Moreover, in a strategic move in 2011, the vice-president of CARE was elected to the presidency of ECO-Ashaninka, inaugurating a new era for ECO-Ashaninka–federation–SERNANP relationships. I think of this as anti-anti-politics, or the repoliticization—through the appropriation of governmental techniques—of a process that was depoliticized through state intervention.

These approaches—refusal and anti-anti-politics—do not belong to the realm of resistance, which suffers from certain limiting assumptions that I find irreconcilable with my knowledge of Ashaninka people. Resistance assumes the attribution of either a dominant or subordinate position to the principal actors of a relationship; it assumes that the subordinate actor is self-conscious of subordination and takes actions (of resistance) premised on the existence of a power differential. Ashaninka people elude any ascription of victimhood, disempowerment, or subordination, not because they refuse it, but rather because it is simply not an option for Ashaninka self-conception. Their ego-centric view of the world (Veber 1998; Caruso 2012) empowers Ashaninka to consistently shift their positions in order to remain the protagonists and the ultimate agents of their histories. This perspective permits Ashaninka people to remain in charge of their destiny, while nevertheless aware of the disempowering disciplinary techniques involved in comanagement of the communal reserve.

Rethinking Indigenous Sovereignty in Protected Area Comanagement

In this chapter, I have described how the ASCR is diversely imagined, narrated, and claimed by different actors within the comanagement arrangement. At the intersection of these different practices, the space of the ASCR is produced as an imposing reality and has become a locus of great significance in the struggle between Ashaninka people and the Peruvian state over territory and resources.

Within the comanagement arrangement, the principal actors have adopted different practices for gaining control over the reserve's territory. On the one hand, comanagement has been successfully depoliticized and rendered technical by SERNANP and NGO interventions, particularly through the creation of compliant state-controlled "Ashaninka" institutions: ECO-Ashaninka and the park guards. However, in response, Ashaninka community members and leaders have chosen to contest this depoliticization and the governmentalizing processes by which the state has sought access to Ashaninka lands. Two different approaches have been explored: most community members appear to act as though the state is irrelevant to their relationship with the reserve, using its resources and lands as they see fit, whereas some federation leaders have chosen to capture the tools of the state's technical-administrative apparatus in order to challenge it from within. Naturally, the current state of affairs in the ASCR is not static. Yet there is a growing awareness among Ashaninka people that state presence in their lands is intensifying, with the effect of rendering them even more determined to stake their own claims within their lands. Ashaninka people appear to be challenging state sovereignty within the ASCR, not through open resistance, but through self-conscious acts of sovereignty and self-determination.

Taiaiake Alfred's "politics of resurgence" requires Indigenous peoples to posit the world from within distinctive Indigenous ontological frameworks in order to counter the hegemonic nature of "Empire" (Hardt and Negri 2000).[15] This, I have argued, is precisely what Ashaninka people are doing in the context of the ASCR (and more broadly in the context of the nation-state and transnational interventions on their lands; see Caruso 2012). The Ashaninka ego-centric view of the world does not allow for the presence of another entity or person with more authority than the self over his or her daily activities, choices, and future. Theirs is not a struggle against the oppressor's power from within, but an ontological positioning that does not permit the existence of an oppressor. I propose that Ashaninka are practicing their own form of sovereignty over the lands, resources, and relationships that make up the ASCR, and they do so by thinking, speaking, and acting from within their Ashaninka ontological framework.

Recently, scholars have taken issue with the unquestioned use by Indigenous movements and leaders of the language of Native sovereignty, arguing that it legitimizes European colonizing discourses and perpetuates Western assumptions about how power and control operate (Alfred 1999, 2001; Brown 2007). However, Alfred noted in *Wasáse*, his book aimed at reinvigorating the commitment of Indigenous peoples of the Americas to overcome colonial oppression and find freedom: "If the goal is to obliterate the oppressor's power altogether, any challenge will fail; if we seek instead to initiate a different kind of challenge, in the form of regenerating our own existences in the face of the oppressor's false claims to authority, legitimacy, and sovereignty, we cannot but succeed, and thus, force the state to transform itself" (Alfred 2005: 202).

This mirrors the work of several other Indigenous American scholars who are seeking to reclaim and rearticulate the concept of sovereignty as a source of power and agency emerging from distinctive Indigenous ontologies and epistemologies (Deloria and Lytle 1984; Warrior 1995; Wilkins 1997; Cobb 2005). In this sense, the concept of sovereignty need not be limited to its Euroamerican linguistic, legalistic, and oppressive roots, but can be seen as flexible and reformulated through practice and process. This case study contributes to the discussion on Indigenous sovereignty by showing how Ashaninka people embody their sovereignty over their lands, resources, and futures by standing firmly as the central agents in their ontological and cosmological systems.

Approaching the topic of comanagement from the Ashaninka perspective has prompted me to challenge the view that comanagement is often a colonizing or an anti-political force. This assumes that in many cases Indigenous peoples are disempowered by the state-imposed rules of the game of comanagement, which, as shown in the present example of a state that does not seek to share power and respect rights, appear calculated with the intent of disempowering. However, the situation described here gives voice to Indigenous agency and the Ashaninka people's refusal to be colonized by bureaucratic governmental practices. This research has shown that new paths for inquiry can be explored that take into account Indigenous practices within the framework of comanagement as well as their ontological and cosmological perspectives on the world. These practices and perspectives can destabilize the domination/subordination paradigms in circulation within scholarship on protected area comanagement.

Acknowledgments

This chapter is based on doctoral fieldwork carried out in 2007–2009 with the support of an Economic and Research Social Council CASE Studentship, and it was first presented at the 2009 Annual Meeting of the American Association of Geographers, at a session entitled "Indigenous Peoples and Protected Areas: Conservation through Self-Determination" organized by Stan Stevens. I would like to thank Daniela Peluso for her helpful comments during the drafting of the chapter, Stan Stevens for his comments and edits, and Susannah McCandless for her support as the draft was finalized. Finally, I am forever indebted to my Ashaninka hosts, friends in Satipo, and the communities in the Ene valley in which I carried out my research for their welcome, support, and insights.

Notes

1. See García's editorials in *El Comercio*, Peru's most widely read daily newspaper (García 2007a, 2007b, 2008).
2. See www.sernanp.gob.pe/sernanp/
3. Given the highly dynamic nature of social and political life in the Ene River valley, the analysis in this chapter refers to a particular historical juncture; I therefore write in the past tense.
4. The world's longest natural bridge, known in Ashaninka as *Pavirontsi*, can be found on the border between the ASCR and the Otishi National Park.
5. See www.parkswatch.org.
6. Sendero Luminoso is a Maoist-Leninist insurgent guerrilla organization, led by Abimael Guzmán, that launched a twenty-year internal conflict in Peru. The Ene and Apurimac valleys became the stage of a particularly bloody episode of the war, and many Ashaninka people lost their lives on both sides of the conflict (see Hvalkøf 1994; Espinoza 1995; Truth and Reconciliation Commission 2002).
7. During these six-week field trips, the park guards tend their small subsistence plots that feed them for the duration of the trip, carry out educational workshops with communities, and patrol the borders of the reserve to check for illegal activities.
8. In Caruso (2011), I explored in greater detail the process of bureaucratization and depoliticization of the ASCR's comanagement arrangement.
9. In retaliation, some members of the Ashaninka community burned down some buildings of the neighboring military base of Pichikia, in the lower Ene.
10. The meaning of the term *Ashaninka* is "our relations" or "that which is similar to us."
11. See Caruso (2012).
12. A participant at a community workshop on the ASCR once asked whether it would be possible to "extend the Ashaninka Communal Reserve into the [Otishi

National Park," which borders the reserve, because conferring the name on the park would show it belongs to Ashaninka people.

13. As mentioned above, it is likely that PlusPetrol will choose to begin exploration in the reserve once the zonification of the ASCR Master Plan is completed. According to the law, any zones that are not designated as under "strict protection" or for "wild fauna" are appropriate for petroleum exploration. According to the local SERNANP office, there has been a strong lobby on the part of PlusPetrol to rapidly finish the zonification of the reserve and to ensure that the areas of interest for petroleum exploration are left outside of strict protection zones.

14. In 2008, Alan García's government announced plans for the building of three dams in the Ene–Tambo River system, of which the Pakitsapango dam, a structure of 165 meters to be placed in the lower Ene River, was the flagship project. These dams are part of a nationwide program for the construction of fifteen dams that would produce hydroelectric energy for sale to Brazil. The Central Ashaninka de Rio Ene (http://careashaninka.org/) have developed a robust campaign against the planned dams, which so far has succeeded in stalling the process.

15. I use Hardt and Negri's (2000) term "Empire" to underscore how neoliberal imperialism emerges as a form of global sovereignty in the current political-economic global structure. In this context, when Indigenous peoples claim and appropriate their own forms of sovereignty in the face of neoliberal sovereignty, they are empowered to counter its dominance.

CHAPTER SEVEN

Green Neoliberal Space

The Mesoamerican Biological Corridor

Mary Finley-Brook

Transitions toward transnationalized environmental states and inhabited eco-zones based on ideals of "green" neoliberalism are established as much through economic and political coercion as through staking claim to authoritative environmental knowledge (Goldman 2005). In the Mesoamerican Biological Corridor (MBC), political processes have led to environmental change and the reconfiguration of space and place. Since the 1990s, Central America has been recast and newly promoted as a sustainable development exemplar: from divided and war-torn to transboundary environmental protection, from poverty-stricken to eco-commerce.[1]

My research highlights the spatial attributes of eco-development in poor countries. Maintenance of habitat connectivity is broadly supported in the conservation literature (Miller 2001; Bennett 2003; Ankersen et al. 2006). Since the 1990s, there has been increasing advocacy in international conservation, including IUCN and CBD policy, of ecosystem approaches of landscape-scale conservation beyond the boundaries of protected areas. This includes biological corridors that link protected areas. Conservation landscapes and biological corridors have become an important component of the new paradigm of conservation. However, there has been considerable criticism that many such projects are imposed in top-down fashion and do not sufficiently incorporate rights-based conservation and other new paradigm principles for conservation in Indigenous peoples' territories (Brosius and Russell 2003). Regional-scale land-use and development planning, including corridors, has also become integral to development planning. When a government signs up for debt relief, foreign consultants study every aspect of the economy, including natural resource management, with the purpose of streamlining the state and spurring economic growth. The goal is to transform systems deemed as inefficient, such as the burning of the savanna and forest extraction demonstrated in figures 7.1 and 7.2, into spatially defined, linked, and improved nodes of networked production and communication. In theory, these development clusters, whether for commerce, infrastructure, or resource management, are to be linked by corridors.

There is some concern within the scientific community that the biological corridor concept is in the process of being reconceptualized in development agencies to serve donor agendas in cases such as the MBC (Carr 2004). Ecologist Archie Carr III, one of the original creators of the Paseo Pantera, a precursor corridor proposal to the MBC, proposes that rather than viable biodiversity corridors the MBC represents the "creation of little green enclaves of social justice and opportunity" (Carr 2004: 37). Carr has suggested that Central American parks, the backbone of the MBC, are heading toward becoming "welfare nuclei: designated spaces, perhaps with trees, where the needs of humans would be attended to" (2004: 34). He has proposed that if the MBC continues in the direction it has, there will be the creation of highly uneven spatial development. According to Carr, "inside the protected area, inside the bubble, social welfare would be assured. Outside, it was hell" (2004: 34).

Conservation initiatives in eastern Nicaragua allow for the analysis of Carr's (2004) critique. Nicaragua lies at the heart of the MBC, and an extensive Atlantic Biological Corridor (ABC) covers most of the eastern half of the country. ABC implementation in 1997 coincided with my fieldwork in eastern Nicaragua between 1997 and 2003, which culminated with twenty months living within a proposed corridor segment. At the end of ABC funding in 2006, corridor initiatives only existed in isolated pockets, supporting Carr's claim that the MBC represented scattered green enclaves. Carr's second major critique of the project was that it is donor driven. My analysis of more than 700 proposed ABC subprojects in multi-ethnic villages provides a window to examine attempts to reproduce neoliberal development.

An Eco-efficient, Secure Central America

Development banks and aid agencies are key actors in Central America's shifting ecological and political imaginations. By 2001, the total

Figure 7.1. Annual burning of agricultural fields, Isnawas village, Región Autónoma del Atlántico Norte (North Atlantic Autonomous Region), Nicaragua.

Figure 7.2. Mahogany beams waiting for truck transfer, Alamikangban village, Región Autónoma del Atlántico Norte (North Atlantic Autonomous Region), Nicaragua.

financing for Central American environmental projects like the MBC reached nearly US$1.3 trillion (Minc et al. 2001). Central American eco-development loans from the World Bank and the Inter-American Development Bank alone surpassed US$888 million at this time. In Nicaragua, nearly all environmental project financing from the late 1980s until 2000 came from international sources (Comisión Centroamericana de Ambiente y Desarrollo and Unidad Regional de Asistencia Técnica 2000). Eco-aid critics suggest environmentally friendly projects are largely created as marketing tools to capture donor funds (World Rainforest Movement 2003). Once a project has been brought into the funding pipeline, there is pressure to complete social and ecological assessments and to distribute aid quickly (Goldman 2005). Development banks with a surplus of capital are under pressure to loan, and with ongoing habitat fragmentation in biodiverse areas all over Central America, the potential for corridor proposals is huge.

The MBC is only one leg of a tripartite vision supported by the region's political leaders and the foreign states and donors that back them. The two other initiatives are the Central American Free Trade Agreement (CAFTA), implemented with the United States since 2005, and the Puebla-Panama Plan (PPP)/Mesoamerican Project (MP). The PPP was a scheme put forth in 2001 for transnational infrastructure corridors, such as highways, railroads, and electrical grids, running from southern Mexico to Panama, but the area was later extended to include Colombia. In 2008, Central American leaders decided to change the name of the PPP to the Mesoamerican Project for Integration and Development (herein called the Mesoamerican Project, or MP). Under CAFTA, regional production is increasingly done in massive export processing zones, such as *maquiladoras* and agribusiness plantations linked to PPP/MP railways, shipping canals, ports, electrical grids, and pipelines. These Mesoamerican initiatives have overlapping sponsors and advocates, such as World Bank, Inter-American Development Bank, Central American Bank of Economic Integration, and bilateral aid agencies like the U.S. Agency for International Development.

Opponents of Central American integration are concerned about national sovereignty and local autonomy, as well as ecological degradation from industrialization and infrastructure projects. With its focus on civic participation, poverty reduction, biodiversity protection, and green spaces, the MBC is expected to help diffuse criticisms waged against the other two legs of the MP-MBC-CAFTA triad. The MBC and the MP have been periodically reframed to try to woo support. There was considerable public protest regarding the PPP (Call 2003; MacLeod 2004); by 2003, sponsors repackaged the PPP proposal to highlight environmental programs and strengthen links to the MBC. However, there has been surprisingly little discussion of the intersection of industrial or transportation corridors and their ecological counterparts, despite the fact that the connectivity of the latter is breached by the former when they cross. For example, even under the MP, proposed roads and transoceanic transportation canals in Nicaragua would run east to west, whereas the ABC, at least hypothetically, covers the length of the country from north to south.

While transnational cooperation in the MBC is argued to signify "the construction of a new order" (Miller et al. 2001: 17), the MP-MBC alliance reinforces and extends neoliberalism, an economic and political paradigm that has dominated Central American development programs for more than two decades. Neoliberal policies generally involve trade liberalization, privatization of industries and services, reduction of the public sector, and promotion of market-oriented management practices (Perreault and Martin 2005). With debt relief programs, many state natural resource management responsibilities are either privatized or delegated to NGOs. With shrinking public finance due to structural adjustment programs, Central American leaders search for sources to fund conservation. Opening natural areas to bioprospecting or tourism can help finance programs, as can payments for environmental services. Forests and water, two globally valuable resources historically plentiful in most of Central America, are now experiencing rapid deterioration in quality and quantity. Within the MBC, local communities are given economic incentives to protect watersheds or act as forest guards. Protected resources, however, are not necessarily for local use. Whether outsiders are interested in carbon trade, bioprospecting, or hydroelectric power, local livelihoods are being reoriented to directly assist, or at least not interfere with, resource commerce. Secure and ordered property regimes facilitate market expansion and encourage investment, and so land "regularization" campaigns are often linked to natural resource management initiatives. Packages of proposed loan programs fit together like puzzle pieces and conveniently reinforce donor plans for the expansion of free markets.

Donors encourage state and NGO projects in the region to be focused on market-based solutions. This facilitates export eco-commerce (for example, green lumber products, environmental services, and tree plantations) and limits alternative non-market-based approaches. Project officials have framed the MBC in terms of its ability to simultaneously advance biodiversity protection, Indigenous and rural livelihoods, *and* resource marketing (Central American Commission on Environment and World Bank 2002; MBC 2002). To advance all three goals, while at the same time repaying development loans (with interest), officials need to keep efforts highly synchronized to achieve economies of scale.

There were public demonstrations in many countries in response to CAFTA and PPP negotiations. As a result, the planners behind the initiatives assumed greener language. As McCarthy and Prudham (2004: 279) noted, "incorporations of 'environmentalism' into the heart of neoliberalism's central institutions has done more to smooth the 'roll out' of neoliberalizations than attempts to dismiss or reject concerns outright." This is part of an ongoing process of institutionalizing certain notions of global environmentalism and citizenship while delegitimizing others (Goldman 2005).

Given the massive costs associated with the implementation of the MP, MBC, and CAFTA, initial donors needed additional investors. Accordingly, they had to assure that the historically conflictive region provided a safe investing environment and could protect tourism revenue. As the MBC idea was being promoted, armed groups and drug traffickers were using remote forests, such as protected areas, as exchange nodes. Clandestine air strips for drug trafficking required clearing trees and underbrush. Families were migrating into parks to traffic illicit substances and poach threatened wildlife. The military has sometimes been the only state presence in remote areas of Central America. Ecological projects such as the MBC bolstered the need for armed intervention. Style (2001) referred to this process as "biomilitarization."

Authoritative Eco-spatial Constructs

Many development agencies have spatially and institutionally scaled up their approaches to environmental protection (Chapin 2004). There are perceived benefits from large projects, such as transboundary protected areas. Ecosystem boundaries often extend beyond political jurisdictions and therefore require management cooperation. With shared input from numerous donors, large projects are considered more efficient to administer and less risky due to the sheer number of donors involved. Kaiser (2001) suggested that the NGOs that first promoted a corridor in Central America in the 1990s immediately saw the fundraising potential of the megaproject. Large-scale initiatives reinforce the hegemony of a limited number of conservation organizations and international donors, who contend that they are the only ones with capacity to administer projects of such magnitude (Chapin 2004). Large-scale conservation efforts may privilege transnational institutions at the expense of grassroots groups.

The widening of scale is often accompanied by an increase in environmental managerialism. Megaprojects are frequently based on a poor understanding of local conditions because they use rapid, formalistic impact assessment procedures, leading to blueprint or cookie-cutter solutions. Guided by scientific guidelines, state planners and consultants pinpoint priority biodiversity conservation zones and "appropriate" human development. Local stakeholders are often seen as beneficiaries rather than agents, and their input and activities are tightly controlled.

Large-scale conservation initiatives incorporate vast regions, often without prior local support. State resource management may be extended to areas where it has a poor record of respecting local rights, including communal lands claimed by Indigenous peoples. A landscape-level approach may also be used as an excuse to maintain control of natural resources at higher government levels (Ribot 2004), which runs contrary to the proclaimed processes of decentralization in most MBC member countries. Nevertheless, previously top-down and center-out aid structures are camouflaged so that it seems that there are multiple sites of authority (Goldman 2005). States and donors often work with quangos (that is, quasi-nongovernmental organizations), private agencies, and different hybrid institutions, such as public-private partnerships and advocacy networks. Development agencies promote the idea that they are merely part of decentered partnerships, but they maintain highly asymmetrical positions: actors that lend money have more control than those that borrow or are hired. In environmental programs, as Taylor and Buttel (1992: 406) pointed out, "politics are woven into science at its 'upstream' end." Dominant ecological paradigms then disseminate outward in "epistemic communities" or "knowledge networks" (Goldman 2005).

A framework to analyze international development needs to be able to withstand irregular and potentially rapid shifts among a juxtaposition of agendas and diverse stakeholders. Ongoing relative positioning of multiple actors can be found in Cindi Katz's (2001) topographies of neoliberalism and John Allen's (2004) topographies of power. These authors have provided spatially explicit but fluid conceptual frameworks to analyze the social and material effects produced by the processes associated with such abstractions as globalization, global economic restructuring, and uneven development. These topographies help us to examine the range of social practices through which space and place are created, and they complement Michael Goldman's (2005) insightful critique of the reproduction of green neoliberalism. Multi- and bilateral aid agencies use their power to create authoritative environmental knowledge: eco-commerce thus appears natural and self-evident and donors' priorities neutral or apolitical.

Allen's (2004) analogy of rhizomatic power networks is applicable to the alliance of donors and consultants re-creating Central America. Power can be defined as the capacity that enables the holder to secure particular outcomes or realize certain objectives. Indirect power is "more akin to an all-encompassing rule where things are 'bundled' together—free trade, open markets, human rights, democracy, and freedom—and if you 'buy' one you buy them all" (Allen 2004: 24). Apparently, dispersed or roundabout power has "the potential to flip over into an image of power as so pervasive, so all encompassing in its reach, that it leaves little space for political manoeuvre" (2004: 24). Nevertheless, power networks in capital cities or among donor institutions can become dispersed or weakened in peripheral regions.

Another spatial relationship within the MBC must be highlighted: many biological corridors intersect with Indigenous territories, whether inhabited by Maya, Miskitu (Miskito),[2] Guna, or other groups. Neoliberal economic programs increasingly target Indigenous participation (Rossiter and Wood 2005). They aim to collapse citizenship rights into consumer or client-based models. The "marketization of Indigenous citizenship" follows an economic logic that identifies participation in capitalism as the ultimate sign of equality (Altamirano-Jiménez 2004: 349). The ability to own businesses and compete in the market becomes proof that racial or ethnic inequality has disappeared, particularly when Indigenous peoples are selling eco-efficient goods and services valued in broader markets.

Experimental pilot programs of "free-market" environmentalism (McCarthy and Prudham 2004: 279) promote business ventures that provide employment to add value to natural resource holdings, such as a community woodworking shop in the Indigenous village of Auhya Pihni, one of the initial projects in Nicaragua's ABC. Plans follow a simple economic logic: let the Indigenous peoples and/or protected areas pay for their own development through increased participation in global natural resource markets, whether producing tourism or eco-commodities like shade coffee or Forest Stewardship Council–certified lumber. Aid is granted to groups with historical territorial claims in biodiverse or ecologically important areas to become entrepreneurs in the global economy. However, there is uneven spatial patterning because developers recognize higher economic potential in some Indigenous peoples and natural areas.

The oppressed and poor are supposed to gain freedom through markets, but neoliberal approaches are not designed to address the particular attributes and needs of Indigenous groups (Altamirano-Jiménez 2004; Brook 2005). In Latin America, many Indigenous areas are communally owned. Market-oriented ventures in communal areas that start off as communal risk strengthening the local elite, increasing economic and social inequity, or disrupting collective structures (Mitchell 1996; author's field notes). Insensitive to local practices, donors often require the purchase of outside inputs like agricultural machinery, trucks, and cattle. As they attempt to diffuse desire for foreign goods and a culture of consumption, aid agencies spur rapid and often destabilizing technological shifts in rural areas, which often prove to be unsustainable because they do not complement existing production systems. In rural Central America, neoliberal transformations remain poorly articulated among numerous conflicting agendas.

Patterned Ground: The Mesoamerican Biological Corridor

Containing approximately 40 million inhabitants and 600 protected areas, the Central American corridor took years to be felt on the ground, even in most pilot areas. Starting in the 1980s, northern conservation groups funded by the U.S. government envisioned a natural corridor known as the Path of the Jaguar, or Paseo Pantera. It wasn't until the resolution of civil conflicts in several nations that a transnational project began to develop. The corridor took on the label of "Mesoamerica" when the four southernmost Mexican states joined. Figure 7.3 depicts proposed corridors, but only a small number of those shown on the map were ever created or demarcated on the ground.[3] Boundaries of parks and reserves are contested in many areas.

The MBC uses the slogan *"naturalmente unidos"* ("naturally united") The vision is this: corridors of all sizes will braid across the landscape to connect protected areas. Surrounding buffer zones will host ecologically friendly production, such as agriculture, fishing, and ecotourism. Figure 7.4, from a Nicaraguan corridor brochure, demonstrates the general concept with market terminology of supply and demand.

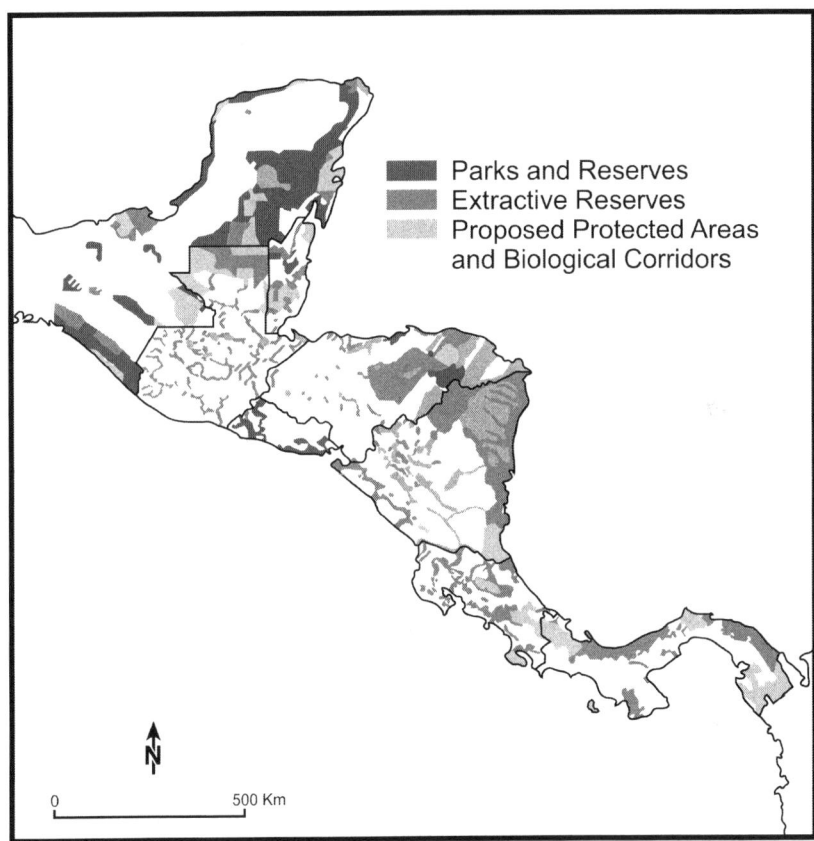

Figure 7.3. Proposed elements of the Mesoamerican Biological Corridor.

There are a large number of major international donors, agencies, and NGOs assisting the MBC (table 7.1). The Central American Commission on Environment and Development (CCAD), made up state authorities from environmental or natural resource ministries, formed in 1989. CCAD sponsored the Central American Alliance for Sustainable Development in 1994. These transnational alliances formed the backbone of the MBC. The United States became an extraregional member of the Central American Alliance for Sustainable Development in 2001. The U.S. National Aeronautics and Space Administration provided MBC offices with technical support and digital imagery. U.S. Agency for International Development funded the Central American Regional Environmental Programs called Proarca (1995–2001) and Proarca II (2001–2006). Proarca programs guided CCAD and thus the MBC.

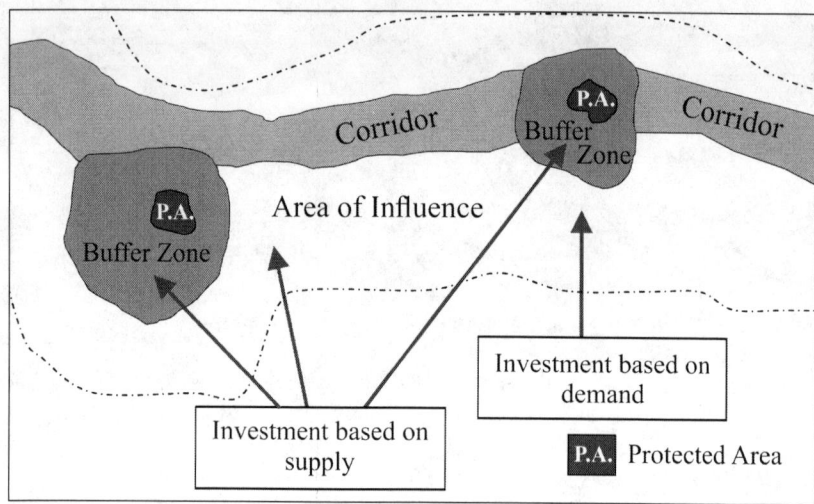

Figure 7.4. Corridor neoliberal structure and finance. The protected areas are shown as regions that are free of supply and demand pressures and economic investment, whereas buffer zones are sources of investment in resource supply. The area of influence experiences both supply and demand pressures and investment. Arrows indicate targets for investment.

Although CCAD is often given credit for the accomplishments of the MBC and has worked diligently to promote the project, ecologist Archie Carr III, one of the original founders of the Paseo Pantera, acknowledged that the MBC appeared "donor-driven" and "CCAD decision-making was being heavily influenced by those able to grant or refuse assistance" (2004: 35). Donors influence projects by distributing funds through major NGO partners, such as the World Wildlife Fund, The Nature Conservancy, and Conservation International. These groups also receive large grants from private firms (Chapin 2004). Not surprisingly, many corridor initiatives include public-private partnerships involving agro-business, forestry, mining, pharmaceutical, and service sector transnationals.

Eco-corridors are linked to the greening of production through the promotion of certified products (for example, lumber, agriculture), environmental services (recreation, carbon sequestration, biodiversity), and the creation of market channels so that Indigenous peoples can "sell under less exploitative conditions" (GEF 1997: 21). Yet, skeptics argue that eco-commerce largely benefits firms. The MBC opens the door for pharmaceutical prospecting by establishing in situ gene banks. It also creates carbon sinks to offset pollution from industrial countries.

Table 7.1. Key players in the Mesoamerican Biological Corridor

State agencies	Donors	NGOs and private agencies
Central American Commission on Environment and Development, national environmental ministries	*Multilateral:* Central American Bank of Economic Integration, International Fund for Agricultural Development, Global Environment Facility, Inter-American Development Bank, United Nations Development Programme, United Nations Environment Programme, World Bank *Bilateral:* Canada, Denmark, England, European Union, Finland, France, Germany, Holland, Japan, Spain, Sweden, Switzerland, United States	Central American Regional Environmental Program, Conservation International, Flora and Fauna International, Ford Foundation, International Tropical Timber Organization, International Union for Conservation of Nature, MacArthur Foundation, The Nature Conservancy, Tropical Agriculture Research and Higher Education Center, Wildlife Conservation Society, World Resources Institute, World Wildlife Fund

Market-oriented conservation is based on the premise of sustainable *use*. The idea of "exploiting forests to protect them" is an argument even found in the Latin American leftist press (for example, Mendoza Vidaurre 2002). There has been a transition in Central America from strictly protected areas to multiple-use zones that highlight the contribution of inhabited landscapes (Carr 2004; Zimmerer et al. 2004), such as shade coffee plantations, to biodiversity conservation. Thus, less land is deemed necessary in access-restricted protected areas.

A MBC goal is to promote "the correct way" of reflecting the value of natural resources leading to more eco-efficient development (Central American Commission on Environment and World Bank 2002: 33). Despite claims of local involvement, the MBC has been criticized for being top-down and garnering narrow public support (Miller et al. 2001). With decades of focus on participation, there is a large body of literature on empowering partnerships. In fact, much has been published by MBC donors. Yet, while there may be local participation in a few exemplary showcase protected areas, or on a small number of MBC-recognized civil society councils, reports from corridor projects suggest they were largely determined by aid agencies, development banks, foreign consultants, corporations, and central governments (Kaiser 2001; Newcomer 2002; World Rainforest Movement 2003; Brook 2005).

National Corridor Projects

Nearly 600 nature reserves exist in the area of the MBC, but unsustainable resource extraction often still occurs even within their cores. According to Franco (2003), half of the reserves created in the Central American region were not staffed, and most were poorly delimited. Only 12 percent had specific management plans. Protected area buffer zones and corridors also generally lack demarcation or monitoring.

The focus of corridors ranges among individual countries. Projects in El Salvador promote biodiversity corridors in shade coffee plantations. This model has been extended to other coffee-producing countries. Costa Rica has the most advanced ecological services program, although other countries hope to follow suit. Its Ecomarkets Program, as the national MBC component is named, includes legally binding contracts for watershed maintenance and forestry plantations for carbon fixation, which is controversial due to disagreement over social and environmental impacts. The debate over plantations increases when genetically modified trees are used. Costa Rica's bioprospecting programs, in place prior to the MBC but extended under corridor initiatives, are also contentious. Critics charge that the exploration of biodiversity for commercially valuable genetic and biochemical resources essentially entails the colonization of the biological and intellectual commons (Toly 2004). This process is sometimes labeled biopiracy due to the charge that Indigenous knowledge is stolen.

Studies of MBC programs often communicate limited participation in corridor planning. In Costa Rica, there was poor awareness of the Path of the Tapir (Newcomer 2002), one of earliest regional corridors. Consultants with The Nature Conservancy, a major international conservation NGO, carried out the initial rapid assessment for its creation. The Nature Conservancy identified the ecological characteristics of the region, relevant environmental and governance institutions, and local perceptions of conservation. Only after deciding priority conservation areas based on these criteria did corridor managers meet with local landowners and begin incorporating them into the process. This initial authoritative decision-making stimulated local distrust. Ankersen et al. (2006: 406) discussed the struggle to move beyond a socio-political landscape charged with the emergence of a "landed conservation gentry."

The corridor project in Honduras was paired with World Bank funding for land administration, as also occurred in Nicaragua (GEF 1997). Within these countries, some initial multi-ethnic support for the corridors was built around promises to pass property laws that would clarify and secure land tenure. However, the land administration offices created were centralized, highly technical, and dominated by private contractors with expertise in digital mapping, aerial photography, and computer technology. Garifuna communities in Honduras with *ejido* (common-property) land holdings were angered when promises to grant titles remained largely unfulfilled (NotiCen 2005). They propose that land administration programs are more about the privatization and transfer of lands to facilitate internationally driven development, including mining, agribusiness, hydrocarbon exploration, bioprospecting, and tourism, than the legitimization or protection of their rights.

Panama, Honduras, and Nicaragua developed a subproject component within national corridor plans. Panama had the earliest and most advanced portfolio of village projects; by 2001, there were seventy-three initiated (ANAM-CBMAP 2001). These projects can be broken down into four categories. The largest number focused on production. Ecological programs were second most popular, followed by infrastructure. There was only one predominately social project. In addition, there was considerable overlap between categories. More than half of the ecological projects could also be listed under production because the species involved (lumber trees, turtles, rabbits, and iguanas) are both economically and ecologically valuable. Subprojects associated with corridors in Nicaragua were similar. Nearly all Nicaraguan subprojects targeted production activities, but there were linkages to environmental activities in approximately 20 percent of the projects, such as sea turtle protection within fishing programs.

Nicaragua's Atlantic Biological Corridor

The U.S.-sponsored conservation projects in Nicaragua that were precursors to the ABC were conflictive. Bernard Nietschmann (1997) recorded the failure of one large marine reserve off the northeastern coast to achieve its goals in the 1990s. Nietschmann (1997: 215) described how after villages had given their permission for the creation of a protected area, U.S. Agency for International Development, in conjunction with the Nicaraguan state environmental agency, the World Wildlife Fund, and the Caribbean Conservation Corp, "changed the project's focus from 'community-based' to 'community participation,' then to 'consultation with communities,' and later to 'on the behalf of the communities.'" Without consulting with the Indigenous peoples, the Nicaraguan government then altered the boundaries and size of the protected area. Nietschmann (1997) suggested that this change was made to create a larger area for commercial fishing, in spite of Indigenous opposition. Riddled with conflict, the conservation initiative eventually fell apart. Failure of such integrated conservation and development projects spurred the search for something new. With considerable international fanfare, Central America's protected areas became integrated into larger plans for "eco-market biological corridors," the new conservation buzzwords.

The context for the initiation of the ABC was politically charged. The project got off to a slow start. There were a series of setbacks related to political conflicts, institutional weaknesses, and Hurricane Mitch. In the late 1980s, Nicaragua created two new autonomous regions, the Región Autónoma del Atlántico Norte (North Atlantic Autonomous Region) and the Región Autónoma del Atlántico Sur (South Atlantic Autonomous Region), which reinforced the power of Indigenous leaders to make decisions regarding resource use on communal land. ABC donors claimed to support decentralized and participatory resource conservation and Indigenous development (GEF 1997). Thus, the corridor should have been compatible with a political regime of multi-ethnic autonomy, but the conservation program was largely implemented in an authoritarian fashion, particularly in the beginning.

From 1997 to 2002, project decisions were handed down from the central government in the capital city of Managua. ABC donors visiting Nicaragua were seldom brought to the actual corridor zone. In 2000, a leader of a nonprofit organization in the North Atlantic Autonomous Region complained that in Managua "they invent a million excuses—there are armed groups and it rains too much—and the donors return home with just the written report" (pers. comm., Spanish).[4]

Representatives in Managua spoke in the name of the communities without consulting with the people of the region. In 2000, a Miskitu activist with experience working with transnational aid agencies stated, "It is a shame that such a big project exists only in name and here at the base, there has been no presence. If there has been any local involvement, it is only with one or two people. Corridor representatives come in for meetings and then leave" (pers. comm., Spanish).

New trucks with the ABC logo were visible in the capital city. A representative of the Indigenous political party Yatama stated in 2000, "Here [in the North Atlantic Autonomous Region] there is no ABC truck or motorboat with the name painted on the side. . . . The biological corridor is not here . . . but in the corridor offices in Managua. They are all rich now" (pers. comm., Spanish). The project appeared to have been co-opted by a state with little commitment to the environment, but eager to access donor funding. In July 2001, a press communiqué from one rebel group from the interior of Nicaragua stated, "Let's not trick ourselves about this biological corridor. This is only one of the many business deals of the president and his gang" (quoted in Centeno 2001; translation by author). There was growing concern that the ABC handed the central government more power over a region struggling to develop autonomy.

Early efforts focused on the large Bosawás Biosphere Reserve, often advertised as "the heart" of the MBC, which had been created in 1991 amid conflict. Indigenous peoples with customary claims were just returning from Honduras, where they had spent the better part of a decade as civil war refugees, when their traditional lands were declared a protected area (Stocks 2003). There has been a decade-long initiative run by The Nature Conservancy to establish comanagement in the Bosawás reserve with the Mayangna and Miskitu peoples, state agencies, and local NGOs. From the beginning, there was a lack of clarity between the core protected area and the buffer zone. There are thousands of Indigenous people living in the core, carrying out agriculture, ranching, forestry, and mining. Mayangna and Miskitu have sought and obtained title to territories that encompass much of the core of the reserve and seek to continue livelihood uses of natural resources that have largely been compatible with forest conservation (chapter 1; Stocks 2003; Stocks et al. 2007; Finley-Brook and Offen 2009). New colonists, meanwhile, have been entering the reserve annually, a trend of great concern to Indigenous peoples and to national and international conservationists. Swidden agriculture and clearing for cattle ranching within and near the reserve deforested large areas. The Bosawás was also a hotspot for illegal big-leaf mahogany extraction and has repeatedly sheltered armed groups. One reporter described park colonists in a national news report as having a chainsaw in one hand and a rifle in the other (Anonymous 1999). Marijuana growing and cocaine trafficking both occurred in the reserve.

After a presidential transition late in 2002, the ABC was reorganized. Many key positions were transferred to the Autonomous Region. However, the output of public information, such as postings on the project website, continued to be administered from Managua. The majority of donor and consultant input also continued to be managed in the capital. Most importantly, financial decisions were not decentralized.

Even without full devolution, there were administrative improvements. The ABC coordinator from the northern Autonomous Region believed that the project was able to achieve more in the first year under its regional structure than it had been able to achieve since 1997 (pers. comm., Spanish). In 2003, project consultants completed diagnostics leading to the proposal of community development subprojects in ninety villages. A predominately technical program became a little more people oriented. However, there were limitations. The large size of the ABC made it difficult to adequately consult with villages, especially given the region's poor communication and transportation infrastructure. The techniques used were rapid and formulaic.

There appeared to be a lack of systemization in the village selection process. National environmental officials and project consultants with the environmental ministry in Managua admitted that personal connections and lobbying on the part of interested parties sometimes weighed in the inclusion of certain villages above others (pers. comm., Spanish). Officials also noted that two individuals were responsible for village choices, and other ABC actors were largely unaware of their selection criteria.

Once villages were chosen, consultations were carried out. An attempt was made to involve different ethnic groups and a spectrum of community members, such as pastors, teachers, elders, and women. The diversity of representation varied between villages as ABC representatives worked quickly and relied on a few local intermediaries to determine who should be invited to meetings. During appraisals, consultants generally spent between one and three days in each village. Development plans were based on this limited fieldwork and a few secondary sources. A regional technical committee later developed and wrote up potential projects based on the most "viable" suggestions from community members (ABC Coordinator, Puerto Cabezas, pers. comm., Spanish).

Cultural and ecosystem descriptions were generalized and repetitious in the project reports created for each village (see Corredor Biológico del Atlántico 2003). The format followed a template, and the differences between proposals were slight. Large parts were cut and pasted from one proposal to the next, which was obvious because consultants sometimes forgot to correct village names in text moved from one proposal to another.

Although the majority of projects were located in Indigenous, black, or multi-ethnic villages, few focused on cultural activities. One exception was a "cultural rescue" project for Garifuna communities. Some other projects encouraged a transition away from traditional practices. For example, housing projects encouraged a change from palm to metal roofing. Eight agricultural projects specifically discussed the introduction of nontraditional crops.

Table 7.2 summarizes proposed ABC subprojects. Less than 7 percent covered environmental activities. Protected areas, environmental education, and regeneration projects were sparse. However, seventeen projects targeting water infrastructure included reforestation along rivers, along with wells, tanks, or water treatment. Even if these projects were reclassified as ecological, proposals in this category would still be less than 10 percent of the total.

The greatest number of proposed Nicaraguan subprojects focused on production. Agricultural intensification was frequently suggested. There were proposals for agroforestry plantations of cacao, coconut, pineapple, and citrus in more than 35 percent of villages. In one village it was openly suggested to replace traditional agricultural crops with cacao plantations. Similar expansion of other niche-market monoculture plantations is widespread throughout Central America.

Table 7.2. Proposed Atlantic Biological Corridor subprojects

Project orientation and type	Number	Percentage
Production: agriculture (75), forestry (53), livestock (49), agroforestry (34), fishing (22), agroforestry with livestock (20), sewing and crafts (14), processing (9), hunting (1)	277	38.9
Infrastructure: transportation (72), water (65), marketplace (40), housing (14), solid waste (9), electricity (7), urban (6)	213	29.9
Social programs: education (83), health (75), land titling (10), sports (5), culture (1), leadership and legal support (1)	175	24.6
Ecological programs: reforestation (27), environmental education (6), restoration (6), conservation (3), fire control (3), ecotourism (2)	47	6.6
Total	712	100

Source: Corredor Biológico del Atlántico. 2003. *Planes de Desarrollo Comunitario*. Managua, Nicaragua: Componente de Planificación y Monitoreo, Proyecto Corredor Biológico del Atlántico

Production projects are likely to contribute to growth in local economies, but there is also potential for negative ecological repercussions, such as deforestation for agroforestry plantations or construction. The intensification of cattle ranching was suggested in more than half of all villages, which could contribute to clearing in broadleaf forests and fire setting in the pine flats to encourage the sprouting of tender grass for herds. New or improved roads, bridges, and docks in forested areas are likely to attract new logging. Infrastructure projects improve opportunities for the marketing of local products, but can also encourage unsustainable extraction and production. Many projects also required the use of fossil fuels, such as with rice thrashers, electrical plants, trucks, and boats. Machinery requires a steady investment in fuel, which has proven difficult for villagers to maintain in previous development projects in the region (author's field notes).

Land tenure remained unprotected in the majority of ABC villages. In spite of donor claims to support the resolution of tenure (GEF 1997), demarcation and titling was directly targeted in less than 2 percent of subproject proposals, although it was sometimes listed as a proposed activity under resource extraction in order to clarify the ownership of resources for marketing. If Indigenous or ethnic rights were a priority, land tenure disputes would be resolved in every village. Following Nicaraguan law, the lack of formal titles facilitates state control over land use; all untitled areas are considered state property by default. Because the budget of the environmental ministry is insufficient, conservation policymakers use military enforcement. The U.S. Department of Defense has encouraged Central American militaries to become involved in the MBC, but Hartmann (2004) is concerned that the use of armed forces may increase coercion in order to protect state and donor resource interests.

Nicaragua's Atlantic Biological Corridor: Donor-Driven Development

Although Nicaraguans in various positions made decisions related to the ABC, there was a high degree of foreign influence in the creation of the project and in the direction that it took. Technological transfer encourages the replication of favored global project models. Nicaraguan universities, where the ABC consultants who wrote the village plans were trained, teach international techniques. State institutions, universities, and NGOs are inundated with internationally sponsored conferences, workshops, trainings, and meetings where technical information is communicated. These events are generally oriented around eco-efficient production and the marketing of natural resources. In Nicaragua, these "talkshops" even occur at the village level. I have observed numerous meetings, many within proposed ABC corridor segments, where experts funded by transnational aid organizations or environmental groups teach local communities about improved seeds, green product certification, or community firms.

Of the more than 700 Nicaraguan subprojects proposed, over 60 percent suggested a potential future collaboration with multi- or bilateral aid agencies or the state institutions they funnel money through (Corredor Biológico del Atlántico 2003). My review of proposed projects demonstrates that ABC was highly successful in terms of the replication of development planning according to global agendas, although implementation of these plans was largely ineffective. Donors and consultants defined what would be studied during ABC development. Research results were later used to justify donor involvement. Official project studies covered marine resources, mining, forestry, transportation and infrastructure, tourism, and rural economies. Corridor donors, such as the World Bank and the Inter-American Development Bank, are believed to have a comparative advantage in many of these areas. Thus, the development planning that these donors funded would stimulate growth in their financial portfolios. Similarly, in the 1990s, a criticism of the Tropical Forestry Action Plans, a massive international environmental campaign pressed on developing countries, was that they were being used to advance future lending. Many of the same actors that created the action plans, such as the World Bank and the UN Development Programme, are behind the MBC.

Proposals suggest the ABC would cover nearly the entire eastern half of Nicaragua. Donors planned to use Indigenous peoples to promote biodiversity conservation. According to the 1997 ABC proposal: "One key element of the [Government of Nicaragua's] strategy for the Atlantic is to minimize access to high biodiversity areas. One mechanism for achieving this is by strengthening and enforcing land and natural resource rights of indigenous communities" (GEF 1997: 7). Tension is currently increasing between Indigenous peoples and *mestizo* colonists. Competition for lands for logging and cattle ranching in the interior of the country has already led to violence (Brook 2005).

During the consolidation of the ABC, the Nicaraguan state did not enforce Indigenous land claims as donors originally proposed. A World Bank–financed study on eastern Nicaraguan land tenure, done by the

Central American and Caribbean Research Council, was highly unpopular with the central government, which tried to bury the findings (Gordon et al. 2003). In the late 1990s, Gordon and his colleagues collected ethnographic data that supported Indigenous land claims covering a large uninterrupted portion of Nicaragua's Caribbean region. The contradictory positioning of the World Bank as Indigenous peoples' advocate, environmental protector, and money lender created a window of opportunity for an activist-oriented group, in this case the Central American and Caribbean Research Council, to advance multi-ethnic rights and communal resource governance in spite of an entrenched state position. This is an example of the complexity and texture of transnational development, with its multiplicity of interloping agendas.

Nicaragua's ABC received World Bank financing for eight years (1997–2005). Nearing the end of this funding cycle, donors made future commitments to the corridor segments that they prioritized, which most often pertained to individual protected areas. The portioning of biodiversity hotspots among major donors is common around the globe (Sundberg 2003). The disproportionate focus on hotspots makes for patchy environmental program coverage. In spite of claims to prioritize connectivity (MBC 2002), select MBC areas received high levels of attention, while the majority of the region continued to be deforested. For example, after 2006 there was an extension of the largest reserve in Nicaragua, the Bosawás Biosphere Reserve, into the Corazón Transboundary Biosphere Reserve in cooperation with Honduras. World Bank funding for the Corazón project was approved for six years, in spite of concern in Nicaragua's North Atlantic Autonomous Region that once again the regional government was left out of this decision-making process. The project was handed down from the central government and donors without sufficient consultation with the impacted Indigenous peoples, suggesting that many of the errors committed under the ABC are being repeated at a smaller, but still transnational, scale.

The central MBC office, located in Managua, closed at the end of 2006 as donor support phased out. Any remnants of corridors created in the eight partner countries over the past decade are now largely the responsibility of the CCAD. The millions of dollars spent to consolidate the MBC had limited results, although some corridors continue in countries where programs were more advanced, such as Panama. While the implementation of physical biological corridors was expected to expand across Central America (Miller et al. 2001), natural habitat outside of protected areas is increasingly fragmented. Under technical development plans, the future of the region appears to involve sporadic Indigenous reserves and biodiverse pockets surrounded by cattle ranches, resource concessions, agroforestry plantations, industry, and tourist resorts.

MBC initiatives in some countries today appear to reflect postneoliberal "free-market environmentalism" processes rather than the initial neoliberal framing. Free-market environmentalism goes beyond neoliberalism when it contradicts the notion of the retreat of the state (Bakker 2010). Nicaragua, for example, is now an economically hybridized country in that it has returned to socialist state institutional structures while maintaining capitalist trade relations. In eastern Nicaragua, this has been associated with increased state involvement in Indigenous livelihoods, as demonstrated with collective land titling since 2010, which was in part a response to the Inter-American Human Rights Court's decision in 2001 that charged the Nicaraguan state with violating the rights of the Sumu-Mayangna village of Awas Tingni as the result of a foreign timber concession; the court demanded resolution to land tenure insecurity in Awas Tingni and other collectively held Indigenous territories. Beyond the actions brought about by this court case, over time, Nicaraguan socialism has become increasingly market oriented and involves a carrot-and-stick approach of providing support for approved types of production, while developing the state apparatus to control extractive activities in remote areas such as Indigenous territories and protected areas. However, few ABC pilot projects got off the ground and marketing prospects were seldom successful, although expectations for the marketing of resources often continue to be strong.

The assumption of aid agencies that green markets would unite a shared vision for development has proven to have been unrealistic. Like many development projects, the MBC has generated significant local variation. Subnational development projects, like those discussed in eastern Nicaragua, generated a scalar mismatch because they drew attention and resources away from the broader goal of protecting regional ecosystems. A World Bank–sponsored review of the MBC suggests that donors were not able to maintain control over national processes, and fractionalization of regional efforts occurred (Independent Evaluation Group of the World Bank 2011). Meanwhile, biodiversity in the MBC area remains highly threatened. The other two legs of the MP-MBC-CAFTA triad have consolidated more quickly, suggesting that transnational actors have maintained control over national efforts in these spheres, and free trade and infrastructure are greater priorities to those with political power in the region. The MP, CAFTA, and the MBC share an asymmetric spatial reach where particular areas or clusters of high biodiversity are prioritized and peoples and places are valued unevenly.

Contradictory and Exclusionary Green Space

The MBC suffered from a series of internal contradictions. First, it was framed as a solution to local poverty, yet the majority of initial activities targeted governments, corporations, and international consulting agencies. Second, the creation of actual biological corridors, supposedly the backbone of the MBC, advanced slowly or in many locations did not advance at all. Meanwhile, proposed industrial corridors and resource trade have placed biodiversity and natural habitat at further risk. Lastly, technical planning across a massive spatial scale contradicted local decision-making. Participation was largely limited to rapid appraisals involving a small segment of the population. In Nicaragua most decisions were made by a few ABC representatives, such as technical consultants.

The greatest impact from the ABC has been the reproduction of "green science" (sensu Goldman 2005) and advanced training in the art of writing development studies and project proposals within state environmental bureaucracies and a few NGOs and universities. MBC activities were also exclusive, because only a handful of participants represented each country's concerns. Meanwhile, policies and plans often solidified at donor meetings in locations such as Paris and Stockholm. While publicly advertising poverty reduction in marginal areas of Central America, the MBC advanced the political and economic positions of an elite global network.

In many locations, the ABC has become yet another forgotten development project that had no visible impact on the ground. It was merely another foreign-sponsored initiative in the name of Indigenous peoples and the environment that created little benefit for either. The fact that the ABC project achieved few tangible results should not be surprising. Developers often face challenges to implement actual projects, especially when proposals are based on rapid assessments and brief consultations. ABC maps suggested a dense network of parks, corridors, and buffer zones should cover most of Nicaragua's Autonomous Region. The creation of these digital maps within national offices demonstrated that planning activities and mapping techniques were vastly improved. However, technical programs, training, and consultant salaries took time and resources away from other conservation and development efforts. There was little assistance to the vast territory shown in the maps. The project had little success in improving biodiversity conservation, and nearly all the project initiatives fell apart after donor funding ended. Attention in recent years has retreated from trying to protect whole corridors to focusing on biodiversity hotspots and the remaining areas of rich biodiversity where habitats have not yet been highly degraded.

In spite of contradictions and tensions, the material and discursive recreation of Mesoamerica moves forward. Central government agencies, transnational NGOs, private firms, and aid agencies worked in conjunction to advance market mechanisms, while assuring people that this (and this alone) will bring both ecological sustainability and social justice. Initial project assessments helped development banks and donors determine how to frame additional proposals, but national and subnational efforts were later limited so that global agendas, including free trade and strategic infrastructure development, remained at the forefront.

The MBC was defined among powerful allies with shared political and economic agendas, carefully packaged, and then transmitted to a whole region as highly essential development planning. Central America was to be spatially repatterned to contribute more fully to global free trade and regional economic integration while protecting the environment. The unwieldy megaproject could not meet many of its proposed poverty reduction and ecological conservation objectives and appears likely to magnify rather than reverse historical patterns of uneven development between eastern and western Nicaragua. Indigenous peoples in the eastern zone remain largely marginalized and exploited, testifying to a fundamental contradiction or failure in the design and implementation of state- and donor-sponsored regional projects like the MBC and the ABC created in the name of eastern Nicaraguan Indigenous peoples. Rhetoric promoting participation and benefit sharing with Indigenous peoples never materialized into policies or practices that would reverse or address historical mistreatment. As a result, when seeking a way forward, local groups such as the Miskitu Indigenous Council of Elders today choose to promote ties to the greater Caribbean region, rather than seeking deeper integration into national and Mesoamerican structures such as the ABC and MBC. Future efforts to integrate conservation and sustainable local and regional development programs through the implementation of biological corridors would benefit from a more grassroots-driven, more fully and effectively participatory approach that affirms the principles and standards of the new conservation paradigm, including recognition of Indigenous peoples' collective tenure of territories, lands, and waters; rights-based conservation; and equitable sharing of benefits. Such new paradigm standards must be promoted not only in protected areas, but also in Indigenous peoples' territories outside of protected areas within larger conservation landscapes and biological corridors.

Acknowledgments

Fulbright-Hays, the National Science Foundation, the Lincoln Institute of Land Policy, the Homer Lindsay Bruce Fellowship, and the University of Richmond financed the author's Nicaraguan fieldwork (2002–2003 and 2006–2007) that contributed to this analysis. Thanks to Greg Knapp, Ken Young, Stan Stevens, and anonymous reviewers for helpful comments during the revision of drafts of this chapter.

Notes

1. This chapter is adapted from my 2007 article "Green Neoliberal Space: The Mesoamerican Biological Corridor," *Journal of Latin American Geography* 6(1): 101–24.

2. This chapter refers to the Miskitu people, as this is the name by which they refer to themselves in their language. Chapter 8 refers to the Miskito people, the version of the name that is standard in Honduras.

3. For a color version of this map, see Camacho et al. (n.d.: 17).

4. Quotations in this subsection from personal communications from Indigenous people and from NGO staff are anonymous to protect the confidentiality of interviewees as promised in agreed research protocols. These quotations express views that I found to be widespread during my fieldwork. I emphasize Indigenous peoples' perspectives in this subsection, rather than those of state officials, international conservationists, and other MBC proponents whose contrasting views are clearly stated in the documents cited in the chapter. These Indigenous peoples' perspectives are particularly relevant to evaluating the MBC and the ABC from the standpoint of the standards of the new paradigm.

CHAPTER EIGHT

"Bargaining with Patriarchy"
Miskito Struggles over Family Land in the Honduran Río Plátano Biosphere Reserve

Sharlene Mollett

The establishment and consolidation of protected areas in Latin America, referred to recently as the conservation "boom," has become a growing subject of geographic inquiry (Zimmerer and Carter 2002; Sundberg 2006). This so-called boom is often understood as the diffusion of global conservation principles at the national level, often viewed favorably by environmental organizations as "one of the best indicators of the region's contribution to global conservation" (Valente 2007: 1). Today, after moving away from "fortress conservation" (sensu Brockington 2002), a protected area model that relied on the exclusion of humans from inside protected area space, international efforts acknowledge the existence of people inside protected areas, a move that suggests that conservation practices have become more "humanized" (Colchester 2004; Stevens 2005).

The Honduran Río Plátano Biosphere Reserve (RPBR) seemingly exemplifies such a move. Sponsored under the United Nations Educational, Scientific, and Cultural Organization's (UNESCO's) Man and the Biosphere Program in 1980 and recognized as a United Nation's World Heritage site since 1982, international and national priorities for the reserve purport not only the goals of biological diversity but also the protection of cultural diversity through community conservation and comanagement initiatives (AFE-COHDEFOR 2000; IUCN 2007). Financed by the German government under the auspices of the State Forestry Administration,[1] the RPBR encompasses 815,000 hectares and is located in the northeastern Mosquitia region, also known as the department of Gracias a Dios. Spatially, the RPBR is divided into three primary zones (figure 8.1). The Miskito, the reserve's largest Indigenous group (20,000 members) inhabit much of the cultural zone, along with small communities of Garifuna, Tawahka, Pech, and native *ladinos*.[2] The buffer zone is predominantly ladino farmers, who have migrated to the Mosquitia over the last twenty-five years.[3] The nucleus zone, while once used by Indigenous people and native ladinos alike, is now a place where human activity is prohibited. Together, indigenous and non-Indigenous peoples number over 40,000 and reside inside the reserve's cultural and buffer zones, respectively (AFE-COHDEFOR 2000). However, recent *ladino colono* migration into the cultural zone, from both outside the RPBR and from within the buffer zone, has spurred conflict over access to and control of land and natural resources between the Miskito and ladino colonos. At the same time, Miskito leaders are engaged in heated debate with the Honduran state over conservation policies that support the presence of ladino colonos inside Miskito territories.

This chapter examines the way in which the Honduran state's El Proyecto de Catastro y Regularización (Cadastral and Land Regularization Project), launched by the state in the name of biodiversity protection and sustainable development, has specific consequences for Indigenous women. To do so, I reflect on aspects of Kandiyoti's (1988) well-known notion of "bargaining with patriarchy" to examine the way patriarchal bargains shape Miskito women's subjectivity in the face of a racialized land project and rising Miskito tenure anxieties inside the RPBR.

This research draws from a larger project conducted in 2003 on the northern coast of the RPBR, with subsequent research visits in 2005 (two months) and 2007 (two months) for a total of sixteen months (see Mollett 2006a). My analysis draws upon ethnographic participant observation, semistructured and open-ended interviews, oral histories, focus groups, an agricultural and livelihood survey, and archival data collection in the Miskito village of Belen (population 900) and ladino colono settlements inside Belen Miskito agricultural regions. My research also benefits from interviews and archival data collection with a variety of environment-development organizations inside the RPBR and in the cities of La Ceiba and Tegucigalpa.[4]

After outlining the literature on community conservation and Indigenous natural resource struggles, I introduce the Proyecto de Catastro y Regularización and interrogate the multiple ways in which the state seeks to consolidate reserve boundaries and require residents to individualize

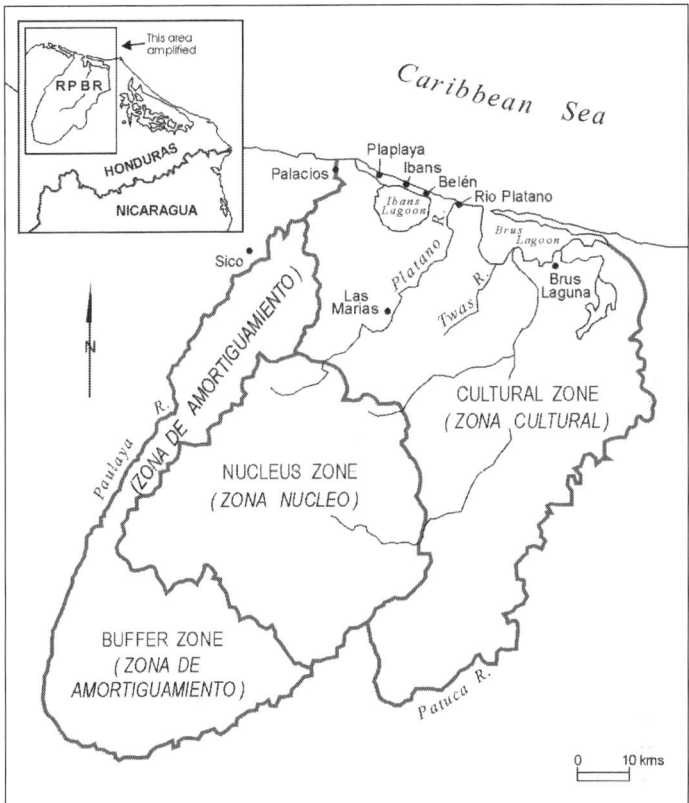

Figure 8.1. The Río Plátano Biosphere Reserve and select coastal villages.

customary and collective Miskito family land. Drawing from ethnographic research in Belen, I then examine how matrilocal residential and matrilineal inheritance patterns are contradicted by a racialized land project and male dominance, which together spur struggles over family land. Through these land tensions, Miskito women simultaneously challenge and acquiesce to male dominance in the village. Thus, underlying the purported goals of conservation and sustainable development exist racialized and patriarchal norms that devalue Miskito customary collective tenure arrangements in favor of individuation, and as a result, intensify gender struggles over family land. Miskito customary rights are not static, but are actively negotiated and evolve and amalgamate around state initiatives currently conducted in the name of protected area conservation. Ultimately, I argue, such strategic bargaining underpins the abilities of Miskito women to actively contest their invisibility as farmers and to claim long-standing rights to family lands.

Community Conservation and Indigenous Natural Resource Struggles

The move from fortress conservation to community-based conservation strategies has gained traction among conservation organizations (chapters 2 and 12; Stevens 2005). These strategies work to advance the development opportunities for local people as a means for improving nature protection (Brechin et al. 2002; Tsing et al. 2005) and to open a space for local community participation in protected area decision-making (Herlihy 2001). By calling for collaboration, it is assumed that conflicts over natural resources will be abated. But conservation practices, community based or otherwise, are often impeded by salient differences given to land and natural resource use priorities distinctly held by officials and local people (Chapin 2004; Norgrove and Hulme 2006; Sundberg 2006).

Policy discourse at the IUCN and UNESCO's Man and the Biosphere Program encourages Indigenous peoples' inclusion within protected area design. Yet, the recognition of protected areas as inhabited spaces has not contributed to the protection of Indigenous geographies and land tenure arrangements. As conservation institutions continuously seek authority by collaborating with national governments, critics argue that these alliances tend to affirm extant tensions between Indigenous people and the state by legitimizing state rule (Colchester 2003, 2004; Chapin 2004; Neumann 2004; Sundberg 2006; McElhinny 2007). For example, in Latin America, Indigenous peoples' tenure arrangements are shaped by protected area policies, where almost 90 percent of protected areas overlap with Indigenous peoples' territories (Negi and Nautiyal 2003; Colchester 2004). With this overlap and despite the fact that many Latin American states are signatories of the International Labour Organization's Convention 169 Concerning Indigenous and Tribal Peoples in Independent Countries (ILO 169), a treaty that grants concrete legal support for the formalization of Indigenous land and territorial claims (Seider 2002), state-led conservation initiatives are wary of legally titling lands to Indigenous peoples.

International conservation imaginaries continue to construct Indigenous peoples and their land uses into static subjectivities often idealized around subsistence production and noncapitalist accumulation. Moreover, any use that falls beyond such imaginaries is deemed inappropriate for biodiversity and environmentally transgressive (Daniels 2002; Heatherington 2005). In a similar way, collective land claims by Indigenous peoples inside protected areas are also challenged (Griffith 2001; Plant and Hvalkøf 2001). For many Indigenous groups, collective rights to land, which disallow the notion of land simply as a means of production, embrace the concept of territory that is embedded with multiple cultural and political meanings (Offen 2003). Yet, conventional modes of land tenure favored by states focus on individual holdings and posit Indigenous collective land tenure systems as "backward" and "inefficient." Such tensions are reinforced among states, conservation agencies, and Indigenous communities (Colchester 2003).

Although disruptions to Indigenous customary tenure arrangements via conservation regulations have received increased attention in recent years by geographers and political ecologists (Neumann 1997, 2004; Nietschmann 1997; Chapin 2004; Colchester 2004; Stevens 2005; Brook 2005; Rinne 2007), much less attention has been given to the specific ways conservation and protected area management shape access to natural resources for Indigenous women (for an exception, see Sundberg 2004). Illustrated via a diversity of case studies, feminist political ecology scholarship demonstrates how gender—a social category that interacts with race, class, ethnicity, and other social markers—shapes natural resource access, distribution, control, and knowledge about the environment for women (Carney 1996; Rocheleau et al. 1996; Jarosz 2001). Indeed women, due to their gendered roles, experience conservation regulations differently from their male counterparts (Ogra 2008).

Certainly, since the late 1980s, land redistribution policies have favored neoliberal market-assisted land reforms and bolstered state involvement in land markets (de Janvry et al. 2001). At the same time, increased attention to gender was mandated to provide new opportunities for improved land access and property for women (Deere and Leon 2001). Yet, few of these benefits reached many Indigenous women. In fact, while feminist scholars indicate that the inclusion of women beneficiaries in market-based land titling projects in Latin America have improved substantially since the 1970s (Deere and Leon 2001), many of these projects have only formalized individualized family holdings (Jansen 1998; Jacobs 2002). For women who rely on customary access to collective lands, individualized land titling at the household level has revealed how women are "structurally disadvantaged" in comparison to the men in their families and communities (Jacobs 2002; Brondo 2007). Prevailing gender hierarchies present restrictions for women's participation in land titling programs, and when codified in national policies, gender ideologies ignore women's contributions and roles as farmers and producers. Instead, women are seen to "help" their husbands in agriculture at different periods of the year (Jacobs 2002; Deere and Leon 2003; Brondo 2007). Such ideologies are strengthened by the powerful overlap of state and local patriarchal pressure that restrict women's access to and control over land (Agarwal 1994; Rocheleau et al. 1996; Jarosz 2001).

The Honduran Mosquitia: Matrifocality and Family Lands

The Mosquitia region extends along the Caribbean shore from eastern Honduras to southern Nicaragua and stretches inland to the interior highlands of both countries. The Miskito Indians, formerly known as the Zambo-Miskito, possess a shared ancestry of Amerindian, European, and African mixture and were often described as a "contact" culture (Floyd 1967; Helms 1971). Remarkably, the Miskito were resilient throughout British and Spanish colonial rule, as demonstrated by Miskito territorial expansion and population growth (Offen 1999; Thompson 2001; McSweeney 2004). Long considered a bastion of natural resources (sea, land, and forests), the Honduran Mosquitia region was controlled by the British until 1859. Miskito alliances with the British furnished the Miskito with territorial authority over other Indigenous groups and at times bolstered Miskito resistance against Spanish settlements in the Mosquitia (Floyd 1967; Offen 1999). Such territorial control remains embedded in the collective memories of the Miskito peoples (Mollett 2006b).[5]

On the northern coast of the RPBR located between the Caribbean Sea and Ibans Lagoon, the Miskito village of Belen was founded in 1947. Belen's founders arrived in search of land to grow food because Cocobila, once praised for the abundance of coconut trees, was a narrow sandy strip overcrowded by homes with little fertile land for cultivation.[6] In present-day Belen, Miskito land tenure arrangements are organized through separate familial social units or matrilocal residential groups, which, for the purpose of this article, I will refer to as "family land."[7] Miskito family lands constitute a series of economic obligations among kin and are the active social and economic entity that assigns privileges to family members (Helms 1971; Perez Chiriboga 2002: 81). For example, when a couple weds, access to land for cultivation and a place to build a house is provided by the mother of the bride. The proliferation of Miskito residential arrangements is sustained by an enduring practice of matrilocal residence patterns or matrilocality, in which a couple (along with the bride's female siblings and their families) lives in close proximity to the mother of the bride, and often her siblings and families share kitchens, water pumps, boat docks, food, and child care. However, many men (approximately a third) also remain with their parents inside the original family settlement, receiving wives from Belen or other villages to share in family lands.[8] Within family land settlements and often between them, a system of *pana pana* (one another) or reciprocity also shapes access to natural resources. This local cooperative work system involves different kin groups who call upon each other to assist primarily in agricultural activities and food exchanges.

Men and women share in a variety of tasks in household maintenance and land use both up river and on the coast. In Belen, 70 percent of households cultivate house or kitchen gardens close to residences. These gardens are most often tended by women, and villagers plant fruit trees; small to medium areas of yucca, plantain, *malanga* (taro), sweet potatoes; and a variety of herbs, spices, and medicinal plants. Women accompany each other throughout the day while conducting such chores as laundry, hauling water, child care, cooking, selling food, and collecting firewood. Although families spend much of the year on the coast, family land also includes agricultural lands referred to as *kiamps* (secondary settlements). As swidden agriculturalists,[9] the majority of Miskito cultivation occurs in kiamps across the lagoon, an up-river region often referred to as *el otro lado* (the other side). In many kiamps, entire Miskito families will live for weeks at a time, from the January planting season to harvest season in July.

In general, men tend to clear up-river agricultural plots together, and travel back and forth from the coast to monitor crops and collect timber and *leña* (firewood). While up river, men and women often plant together as the men prepare the soil and the women plant the seeds. Farming is also supplemented by fishing (shrimp and crab), an activity shared by Miskito men, women, and children. Both men and women envision the forests and rivers as prime spaces for Miskito cultural reproduction provided through the abundance of such things as medicinal herbs, food production, fresh water, wildlife, and a place to feel connected to ancestors and with God.

Matrilocal residence patterns often translate into matrilineal inheritance. This, however, does not mean that Miskito women always control family land. For instance, in Belen the majority (63 percent) of Miskito households contend that coastal family land and kiamp lands are inherited predominantly on the maternal side. Nonetheless, it is important to note that villagers have also inherited lands from their father's line (12 percent), and even more (25 percent) have cleared new lands for themselves, often augmenting the lands handed down from parents and other relatives. Rules of descent, based heavily on the biological ties to one's ancestors, bind Miskito people to a particular place. A man who moves to his wife's family lands still retains his social identity with his kin group and in the village of his birth "both in his opinion and the opinion of others" (Helms 1971: 53).

However, patriarchy also has a long history in the Mosquitia. Helms (1971) and Hobson Herlihy (2002) argued that Miskito society has been shaped by a history of patriarchal institutions such as the state and the Moravian Church, who encouraged nuclear families, male heads of households, and patrilineal inheritance of names and property. The institutionalization of male power in the Mosquitia was also facilitated through external employment opportunities (via transnational corporations in extractive economies) that until recently were only available to men (Dennis 2004).[10] Although Helms (1971) and Hobson Herlihy (2002) analyzed patriarchy as a foreign import emphasized in times of "bust" and de-emphasized in times of "boom" when men migrated from villages for work, Offen reported that within Miskitu society, "there has always been a leadership model featuring male positions of authority organized hierarchically over space" (1999: 169). Contemporaneously, male dominance is bolstered as Miskito men enjoy a greater exposure to Westernized languages (particularly Spanish and English), cultures, and foreign economies than do women.

Patriarchal norms in Belen complicate matrifocality, particularly with regard to matrilineal inheritance of land. Theoretically, Miskito women hand down family land to their daughters upon marriage (Hobson Herlihy 2007). Yet, in practice, land is overwhelmingly bequeathed by the father (or brother, uncle) to the son-in-law. Indeed, because men often control land through their labor (clearing, planting, harvesting, and herding animals), the nuances of matrilineal customary land inheritance tend to resemble the transfer of land from the maternal side to the husband. Similarly, for single women (female-headed households), or women with husbands who do not farm, fathers and brothers often maintain control of the family's agricultural lands as their labor is often called upon to clear secondary growth from fallow lands.

Access to and control of family land is especially important to Miskito women given the limited income-generating opportunities on the coast. Commonly, women earn money through domestic work, such as housekeeping and laundry services in the homes of wealthier Miskito and native ladinos. A small number of women own modest grocery stores and sell a variety of foodstuffs. Women are the primary managers of small guest house operations, and in recent years the sale of second-hand clothing is a growing activity. According to Miskito women attendees of a 2003 focus group in Belen, the sale of agricultural surpluses also provides some income, but as most villagers sell their products at the same time, local markets become oversaturated and incomes from their sale remain low. Despite such opportunities, rarely do women claim to earn more than the monthly average income of 1000 lempira (approximately US$60).

In contrast, Miskito men have many more opportunities for earning money. The major economic activity in Belen is the Bay Island lobster industry. Men enjoy access to such occupations as *buzos* (lobster divers), *cayuceros* (canoe men), teachers, small grocers, motorboat drivers, drivers, carpenters, and pastors. Of 134 households, in 28 percent a member of the household is a buzo and in 38 percent a cayucero. In 8 percent of households there is a member who works as a tank monitor, a cook, or a sailor. Indeed, 74 percent of households have a male member engaged in the lobster industry, primarily as wage workers in a variety of occupations. Due to the risk and skill associated with diving, buzos are the highest-paid laborers in the industry and earn between 10,000 to 15,000 lempira (about US$500–800) per trip (fifteen days) for a season of eight months. Cayuceros, usually the buzos' kin, a younger sibling or child, make 20 percent of the buzo's salary. All others earn a percentage from the sale of the boat's catch. From a very young age, boys aspire to become buzos because large salaries facilitate their roles as providers and gifters, a role that fits well into Miskito society where men give food, material, and money as an act of generosity to wives, girlfriends, and family. These salaries far exceed the income-generating opportunities available to Miskito women, and, in fact, many women depend on these salaries via their husbands.

Additionally, teachers in Belen, most of whom are men, are among the highest-paid teachers in the country, as they earn more than twice the salaries (15,000 lempira or US$800 per month) offered elsewhere in Honduras. Sources of income for Miskito men include work as field laborers, mechanics, canoe builders, and pastors. While male economic dominance in Belen alone does not disrupt Miskito women's customary access to land, Miskito men's enhanced power positions, as proposed under the land regularization project, El Catastro, directly menace women's long-standing land security under customary tenure arrangements upon which many women rely, particularly with fewer economic opportunities available to them in the village.

The Río Plátano Biosphere Reserve and Catastro y Regularización

In recent years, state consolidation and ownership of the RPBR boundaries has produced much Miskito critique. In 1997, the Honduran State Forestry Administration (AFE-COHDEFOR) became the legal owner of RPBR lands. Specifically, state ownership prohibits the formalization of Miskito land ownership and restricts land use to subsistence production in the cultural zone. Additionally, the growing influx of *colonos* inside the cultural zone has incited Miskito leaders to seek the removal of colonos due to "destructive land uses." However, previous state promises to remove colonos from the cultural zone do not only remain unfulfilled, but since 2000, colonos who arrived before 1997 are now also legally recognized as residents (AFE-COHDEFOR 2000).

In 2003, state reserve officials announced El Proyecto de Catastro y Regularización (Cadastral and Land Regularization Project). As a key element of natural resource management, this land legalization project is to award formal land rights as "use" rights to Indigenous and non-Indigenous residents. Through these efforts, the state aims to secure the commitment of RPBR populations to sustainable natural resource practices. For colonos migrating from arid agricultural regions and experiencing cyclical exclusion from land in favor of large-scale commercial farming, this was welcomed. For the Miskito Indians, Catastro y Regularización misses the opportunity to grant "ownership" rights that will allow Indigenous groups to control ancestral lands inside the reserve. Instead, the promise of formal land designation—a goal for both Miskito and colono residents alike—has raised Miskito tenure anxieties as state conditions for formalization seek to reorder Miskito customary tenure arrangements.

Financed with 1.5 million Euros from the German government, reserve officials contend that Catastro y Regularización will provide a functioning cadastral survey and legal framework to ensure long-term conservation goals and sustainable natural resource practices in the buffer and cultural zones (AFE-COHDEFOR 2002). Moreover, the state seeks "to *change* the systems of production towards sustainable systems, to develop a consumption market and to provide a base for an efficient and transparent taxation and territorial legislation" (AFE-COHDEFOR 2002: 8, emphasis mine). Although on paper the project offers Indigenous residents the choice between collective and individual land contracts, in practice, state and municipal officials insist that collective arrangements are "impractical" and "unnecessary." They further argue that individual titles facilitate tax collection, a potentially important source of revenue for a system of municipal administration that often lacks the necessary resources to develop and provide services to its communities. As such, formal land rights will be awarded in the form of *contractos de usufructo* (usufruct contracts) as a means to augment land tenure security that, according to the state, is central to "long-term conservation and sustainable use of natural resources" (AFE-COHDEFOR 2002: 8). As an aim of conservation, RPBR land is to remain inalienable.

Yet, since the project was launched, Belen and other coastal Miskito communities have questioned state plans to implement formal land rights as designed under Catastro y Regularización. Miskito leaders, under the auspices of local land defense organizations RAYAKA (life) and TASBA (land), argue that contractos de usufructo only grant use rights or *dominio útil* and not *dominio pleno* (full ownership). Furthermore, the individuation of collective family land enacts a significant obstacle to Miskito demands for collective territorial legislation. The project's design offends common Miskito sensibilities. Customarily, the value in land is traditionally derived from the work that is required to make a plot productive. For instance, an elderly Miskito woman noted that it is her "work" (that is, planting trees and/or crops) that is valuable to her, and she hopes that after she died her children will be able to continue to draw food from her land.

TASBA leadership insists that the dismissal of Miskito customary values on work and the commodification of Miskito land through taxation embedded in the project's design is "hegemonic." Indeed, Miskito leaders are wary that individual plots and taxation reflect ladino colono land tenure arrangements, as seen both in the reserve and elsewhere in the country. According to a well-known Miskito leader from the municipal capital of Brus Laguna, the pressure to individuate family lands, especially without dominio pleno, sparked TASBA and RAYAKA members to reject negotiations with the state. Suspended in 2004, the project has not reconvened inside the cultural zone, but renewed promises of Miskito territorialization are circulating at the time of writing in 2014.

In Belen, land disputes occur in the context of racial and gender hierarchies in Honduras. Such hierarchies are persistently constructed through the legacy of norms and discourses of *El Mestizaje* (Wade 1997; Whitten and Torres 1998; Bonnett 2000). In Latin America, el Mestizaje, a nineteenth-century discourse of racial mixture, refers to the commingling of blood and cultural practices and was designed, socially and ideologically, to construct a new identity through the miscegenation of Amerindian peoples and Europeans. Throughout the nineteenth-century independence era, elites aspired for a decolonized society and culture and sought the maintenance of European values through the concept of *blanquiamiento* (whitening). Europeanness, as a sign of modernity, was central to Latin American independence and subsequent nation-building around a fictitious notion of a homogeneous *mestizo* population, idealized as an "advanced" race (Bonnett 2000; Barahona 2002; Tilley 2005).[11]

While the discourses of el Mestizaje pushed Indigenous peoples to the nation's peripheries, Indigenous women occupied a contradictory position in Latin American nation-building. More than Indigenous men, Indigenous women's bodies as microgeographies represented the sites of reproduction of Indigenous cultures and bodies. Thus, through sexual relations with European and mestizo men (both by force and by consent) and as the bearers of Indigenous culture, Indigenous women embodied the site and processes of el Mestizaje. At the same time, due to their proximity to land and natural resources and the remote locations of their communities, Indigenous women also embodied the emblems of indigeneity, rurality, and inferiority, imagined as barriers to nation-building and advancement (Radcliffe and Westwood 1996; Smith 1997; Nelson 1999; Safa 2005).

Presently, the Honduran state aims to reorder Miskito tenure arrangements under Catastro y Regularización. This reordering resembles a specific history of state whitening projects designed to transform the racial and cultural composition of the Mosquitia region (Mollett 2006a). Since the Wyke-Cruz treaty of 1859, the Honduran state has sought to integrate the Mosquitia's natural resources into the nation. Integration required the transformation of Miskito systems of production, namely nomadic farming and hunting and gathering, to resemble sedentary systems practiced by ladinos outside the Mosquitia (Barahona 1998; Thompson 2001). As the state coveted the Mosquitia's natural environment, concessions were granted to foreigners as a means to develop extraction and agricultural exportation and bolster the national economy. The state required, however, that all concessionaries be from "white nations" and their colonists also be from "the white race" (Rivas 1938). Like elsewhere in Latin America, "the importance of foreign (white) immigrants [was] rooted in a presupposed practical knowledge and taken for granted ancestral virtue of order, thrift, and hard work" (Clark 1998: 387), qualities that state officials presumed Indigenous populations lacked.

Contemporaneously, the legacy of racial discrimination in Latin America has required that Indigenous land movements show racial and ethnic solidarity. However, this has meant that Indigenous women's interests in land formalization are often subsumed by collective demands (Deere and Leon 2001; Nash 2001; Safa 2005). Although some Indigenous women's voices are acknowledged in land movements (Hernandez Castillo 2005), in Honduras, Miskito women are only beginning to publically challenge male authorities over land and natural resources.

Gendered Land Access: The Menace of Individualized Property Arrangements

Gendered power relations significantly shape Miskito women's access to formal natural resource rights. As feminist political ecology scholarship has noted, formalized land tenure programs often exclude women from ownership opportunities despite the fact that women carry a disproportionate share of household and community responsibilities (Carney 1996; Rocheleau et al. 1996; Jarosz 2001). Such ongoing exclusion of women from land titling programs obliges interrogation of the processes of formalization and a critical examination of who benefits from titling and registration (Grigsby 2004).

In Belen, Miskito women are conscious of male dominance in the village. In 2003, during a focus group of fifteen Miskito women from Belen and follow-up interviews with some of the same women in 2007, a positive awareness was expressed that Miskito men have defied a history of "outsiders" trying to steal Miskito lands. Miskito women also articulated that the state, and more recently ladinos, "do not respect Indigenous peoples" as they consider the Miskito to be *"zambos tontos."*[12] For Miskito women, the movement is as much about securing land as it is about disrupting representations of the Miskito as "lazy" and thus unworthy of property rights.

Furthermore, Miskito women did not openly problematize the greater wage labor opportunities enjoyed by Miskito men. Instead, women often express gender relationships to reflect a notion of complementarity in which Miskito culture dictates that "both men and women have their role . . . that is how the community functions." Like communities of Indigenous women in Mexico and the Andes, gender relations are often explained by such complementarity whereby "women are not just like men, they are different; but it is precisely their difference that legitimizes their capabilities and establishes their rights to the same opportunities as men" (Cervone 2002: 190). Until recently, this guaranteed Miskito women's customary access to land and farming, essential to their culturally specific roles as "good mothers" and "smart wives." Patriarchal norms that granted male dominance in the land movement and economic opportunities were balanced by women's sustained access to family land, because "women have *always* worked in the forests both alone and with [their] husbands" (Miskito woman farmer, interview, 2007). After the launch of Catastro y Regularización, Miskito women expressed that some Miskito men had increasingly begun to disrupt notions of complementarity and placed women's long-standing access to collective forests and family lands in jeopardy.

Inside the RPBR, Miskito women privately acknowledge that the imperative to register land individually threatens to favor men at the expense of the solidarity of family lands. Indeed, under the proposed land project, Miskito men stand to consolidate a disproportionate number of parcels through registration, as land contracts will be assigned in the names of the head of the household. According to the state's census in 1997/1998, "household heads" were always considered to be men, unless a woman did not have a husband. In Belen, for example, the state considers that only 25 percent of households are female-headed. Making matters worse, the number of women farmers in Belen, according to the state, is less than 10 percent (AFE-COHDEFOR 1998).[13] Under Catastro y Regularización, women's participation in the multiple sites of Miskito production is ignored by state plans for individuation.

In Belen, the lack of state recognition granted to women as producers simultaneously occurs as the value of land seemingly increases. For instance, Arnold (1997) noted that customary law in an Aymara community in Bolivia changed with increased population pressures. With a similar logic, De la Cadena (1995) noted that in the Quechua communities of Cuzco, Peru, the more land loses its value as a source of income and power, the more women are able to acquire and control more land. As the speculative value of land increases in the context of Catastro y Regularización in Belen, male attempts to redistribute family land challenges a history of land security enjoyed by many Miskito women. Yet, Miskito women frequently participate in these relations to guarantee their material security (see also Rankin 2003), even when women critique how "men are more important in this family" (Mina, interview, Belen, Gracias a Dios, 2003). As tenure anxieties grow, women's ability to exercise their customary claims become increasingly subject to approval by the male family head or other Miskito men in the village.[14]

Rumors of land registration and subsequent individuation have provided new sources of power for male appropriation of land in Belen. For some, aspirations of wealth, once considered to taint Miskito systems of reciprocity, are intensifying and, at times, supersede village customs that favor women's customary access to family land. But the exclusion of women as beneficiaries of land registration also reflects the way state practice is infused by a history of ladino patriarchy, underscored by the model of the male-headed households and of men as primary economic providers, despite national property codes. Women, on the other hand, are continually consigned to the role of the "dependent housewife" as a legacy of the moral and sexual norms of el Mestizaje, despite being active and central to household production through agricultural tasks and informal exchanges. Such national imaginings are codified and recorded in census figures.

Access and control of land for Miskito women is also threatened by the way the state treats protected areas as, to use Gregory's (2004) phrase, "spaces of exception." In the RPBR, project designs ignore constitutional rights that allow Indigenous peoples communal titles in dominio pleno (Republica de Honduras 1992). This is significant because under Catastro y Regularización the state only offers dominio útil, a right that does not challenge state ownership of RPBR lands. State practices also ignore Honduras's commitment as a signatory of ILO 169, which obliges signatory states to permit collective ownership of ancestral lands for Indigenous peoples and to protect these lands from encroachment from non-Indigenous peoples. More specifically for Miskito women, Catastro y Regularización ignores constitutional reforms that grant Honduran single women the right to own land and married women (at their request) the right to own land jointly with their husbands (Republica de Honduras 1992). Because constitutional rights are not acknowledged inside the reserve, Miskito women are making patriarchal bargains to strategically resist the erasure of their customary land rights under the proposed land project. In Belen, family members secure power at a variety of scales whereby family membership rights are not always guaranteed, but are contingent on the way external circumstances, such as Catastro y Regularización, shape village tenure relations.

Toward Gendering Land Titling Inside Indigenous Space

Intra-Miskito struggles reveal varying images of land and custom that are deployed by villagers to win disputes in the context of Catastro y Regularización. My ethnographic research in Belen suggests that the practice of conservation posited under the proposed land project has particular consequences for Miskito women. Greater wage labor opportunities and customary male dominance in Miskito society and the nation alike make it possible that both Miskito men and wealthy villagers (mainly men) will disproportionately benefit under Catastro y Regularización, particularly if villagers are denied collective registration. Although proposed land individuation may deepen Miskito women's reliance on Miskito men, such reliance is at times key to women's own projects of resistance against exclusion from family land. Such patriarchal bargains are visible in the way individual women acquiesce to and contest Miskito women's subjectivity in Belen (for three case studies, see Mollett 2010).

Although there is a renewed rhetoric of state commitment to title Miskito lands inside the reserve, at the time of writing in 2014, the Catastro y Regularización project has not demarcated lands in the cultural zone. While Miskito men at TASBA and RAYAKA renew debate with the state, Miskito women face the delicate predicament of balancing their loyalty to the land movement while simultaneously working to secure access to family land. Such positioning illustrates the entanglements of reciprocity, duty, and power granted through customary access to Miskito space in the reserve. State consolidation of protected area boundaries via Catastro y Regularización fashions racialized and gendered struggles over land and territorial rights. The Miskito (and particularly Miskito women) contest the ways in which paradigms for national development and notions of national progress continuously devalue Indigenous tenure arrangements and land-use systems, erasing Miskito women and their work as farmers from the land systems in the RPBR. For development geographers and policymakers concerned with the increasing conflicts inside protected areas, the awareness of how conventional land legislation may erase Indigenous women and their customary rights from rural areas may assist in reducing some of the adverse and "unintended consequences" of conservation practices (Zimmerer 2006a: 69), particularly inside the overlapping homelands of Indigenous peoples.

Acknowledgments

I would like to thank the Miskito village of Belen and neighboring communities inside the RPBR for participating in this research project. I also thank the Social Science and Humanities Research Council of Canada; the International Development Resource Center; and the Department of Geography, University of Toronto, for supporting this research. Also, I am deeply grateful to Stan Stevens for inviting me to participate in this publication and for his continuous support and mentoring throughout the years. Finally, I thank Taylor and Francis for granting permission to reprint parts of the original article: Mollett, S. 2010. "*Esta Listo* (Are You Ready)? Gender, Race and Land Registration in the Río Plátano Biosphere Reserve," *Gender, Place and Culture* 17(3): 357–75.

Notes

1. AFE-COHDEFOR was renamed the National Institute for Conservation, Forest Development, Protected Areas and Wildlife Refuges in 2008.

2. In part, the cultural zone refers to the UNESCO's Biosphere Reserve model that seeks to understand the linkages between cultural and biological diversity and to recognize the cultural landscape of this area, home to predominantly Indigenous groups.

3. Native *ladinos* and *ladino colonos* are two distinct groups. Native ladinos refer to ladinos (the dominant ethnic group in Honduras) whose families have resided in the Mosquitia for more than fifty years. Colonos refer to those colonists who arrived inside the cultural zone since the 1990s, who tend to live in separate settlements up-river from Miskito villages, and who are overwhelmingly seen by Indigenous groups to be present in the reserve illegally.

4. In all, for this larger project, multiyear qualitative interviews (separate from everyday ethnographic conversations) number approximately 120.

5. While contemporary research on the Honduran Mosquitia builds upon Nicaraguan case studies, scholars of the Honduran Mosquitia caution against blindly applying Nicaraguan circumstances to Honduran Miskito phenomena, regardless of the apparent similarities (Offen 1999; Perez Chiriboga 2002; Hobson Herlihy 2002).

6. In Miskito, Cocobila was formerly known as Kukubila, "full of coconuts."

7. These territorial units of family land are sometimes called *razas* in Belen and elsewhere in the Mosquitia. However, the word *raza* has multiple meanings based on language and geographic location. To avoid confusion, I have chosen to refer to these territorial units as "family" land.

8. My findings differ from those of Hobson Herlihy (2007), who noted that in Kuri, a Miskito village located approximately 3 kilometers west of Belen, men were absent from the village throughout her fieldwork period in the late 1990s.

9. Swidden agriculture, also synonymous with shifting cultivation or slash-and-burn agriculture, is exemplified by clearing and burning naturally extant vegetation to establish a field plot. Plots are rotated so that a small parcel of land is actively planted and harvested while a larger parcel of previously harvested land lies fallow (Dodds 1994: 241–90).

10. Nonetheless, I must qualify that since 2003, some women have left the village to study in the capital (to become teachers primarily) and work as domestics and cooks in tourist venues in La Ceiba and the Bay Islands.

11. Honduran-born historian Dario Euraque (1998) explained that during the colonial period, the "ladino" label referred to anyone who spoke Spanish and adopted aspects of Spanish culture, despite their race or racial mixture. The term *mestizo* refers to more than racial mixture or miscegenation between a Spanish (European) person and an Indian person. Ladino, however, has become synonymous with mestizo in Honduras. In fact, the definition also includes individuals with multiple racial origins, as long as they speak Spanish.

12. *Zambo* refers to the offspring of an Indian and black union. Previously a colonial term, it is now considered a pejorative way to refer to a Miskito person. *Tonto* means "stupid."

13. It seems likely that at least 75 percent of the land will be registered under the men's names. In the up-river agricultural village (Belen-kin) of Banaka, 97 percent of households are classified as male headed and 3 percent are women headed, and in Paru 88 percent are male headed and 12 percent are women headed (AFE-COHDEFOR 1998: 1).

14. The full version of this paper includes field note excerpts that detail how Miskito women's strategic bargains over family land unfold.

PART III

Moving Forward

Opportunities, Constraints, and Negotiations

CHAPTER NINE

Mutual Gains and Distributive Ideologies in South Africa

Theorizing Negotiations between Communities and Protected Areas

Derick A. Fay

With the rise of joint management of protected areas, representatives of adjoining communities are increasingly involved in formal negotiation processes with state officials, NGOs, and other actors. With a few exceptions (Glavovic 1996; MacDonald 1997; Steenkamp 2001), the literature on community–protected area relations has seldom deployed theoretical work on negotiation from psychology and management studies. Insights from this literature, which I refer to here as "negotiation theory," can provide tools both to analyze negotiations over protected areas and to maximize the benefits to local communities in these negotiations. I focus here on representations of the "negotiation game," that is, the ways in which actors involved in formal negotiations over resources view these negotiations. Negotiation theory draws attention to the relationships between actors' structural position and the ideologies that they bring to negotiations, and it suggests ways in which the tendency of NGOs, policy-makers, and others to frame negotiations as win-win situations from the outset may work to the disadvantage of community representatives in negotiations.

I use this analytic approach to examine two land claims on protected areas in South Africa: the Makuleke community's claim on the Pafuri Triangle, a portion of Kruger National Park, and the adjoining communities' claim on Dwesa-Cwebe Nature Reserve, on the coast of the former

Transkei. These cases were two of the earliest land claims on protected areas to be resolved under South Africa's postapartheid land restitution program. While the Restitution of Land Rights Act of 1994 provided a framework for the claim process, these claims were initiated in the mid-1990s, when there were no clear national or provincial laws or policies regarding land claims in protected areas; the negotiation processes themselves determined the allocation of land rights. In both of the cases considered, the eventual settlements resolved the land claims while maintaining the protected status of the land. Since their inception, at least twenty-six land claims have been filed for other protected areas, and roughly forty claims have been filed for different parts of Kruger National Park alone (Kepe 2008; Robins and van der Waal 2008: 67).

In both the Dwesa-Cwebe and Makuleke cases, a community and a conservation agency were involved in the negotiations, contending over rights to a piece of land (see table 9.1). In common with most claims on conservation areas, many other parties were also involved (cf. Wynberg and Kepe 1999). Some of these entered with the stated aim of mediating the relationship between the communities and conservation agencies, whereas others entered with their own interests. In each, two constellations of NGOs entered the fray. In addition, other branches of government had various roles, occasionally conflicting or unclear in the wake of the recent political transition. Finally, in each case, tourism interests were involved, whether concerned with existing facilities or future development.

Drawing upon the literature on these claims,[1] as well as unpublished sources and ethnographic fieldwork on the Dwesa-Cwebe claim, I analyze the negotiation processes involved in the early stages of each. I show how and why, in both of these cases, NGOs that attempted to mediate between the communities and conservation agencies and framed the negotiations as a win-win scenario instead came to be perceived as collaborating with the conservation agencies. This was not a result of deliberate collusion, but because of the way these NGOs' representations contradicted the pressures on community representatives. As negotiation theory would suggest, community representatives instead inclined toward a view of the negotiations as an antagonistic, distributive process and allied with a second set of explicitly advocatory NGOs.

Mutual Gains and Distributive Negotiation Ideologies

Rubin's invaluable literature review identified two models of negotiation: a "mutual gains" model and a "distributive" or "concession-convergence"

Table 9.1. External parties involved in the Dwesa-Cwebe and Makuleke claims

Parties	Dwesa-Cwebe	Makuleke
Conservation body	Eastern Cape Nature Conservation (ECNC)	National Parks Board (NBP), later reconstituted as South African National Parks (SANP)
Advocacy NGOs	The Village Planner (TVP) and the Transkei Land Service Organization (Tralso)	Friends of Makuleke and the Legal Resources Centre at Makuleke
Mediatory NGOs	Rhodes University Institute of Social and Economic Research's Dwebe Project	GtZ-funded Training and Support for Resource Management (Transform) project at Makuleke
Other government agencies	Department of Land Affairs (DLA), Land Claims Commission (LCC), Department of Water Affairs and Forestry, Department of Economic Affairs and Tourism, and Wild Coast Spatial Development Initiative (WCSDI)	Restitution and Public Land Management directorates of the DLA and the LCC
Tourism interests	Haven Hotel, Transdev, owners of private cottages inside Cwebe Nature Reserve, and the WCSDI	Private-sector tourism operators and consultants

model (Rubin 1994: 1).[2] The former, made famous in Fisher and Ury's best-selling *Getting to Yes* (1981), focuses on finding outcomes that all sides find acceptable and that are mutually beneficial. Rather than regard conflict as a "zero-sum" or "fixed-pie" game, the mutual gains approach espouses "creating value" and finding "win-win solutions" (Rubin 1994: 2). When negotiations are conceived according to a mutual gains model, negotiators are imagined as partners, working toward an optimum solution for both. Harmony is valued, while confrontation is seen as disruptive or antisocial.

The distributive or concession-convergence model, on the other hand, represents negotiation as an agonistic, competitive process. It is termed *distributive* in the sense that each side is aiming to get as large a piece as possible of a fixed pie. It can be envisioned as analogous to bargaining in a marketplace, where each side names a price and negotiators, through concessions, gradually converge on an acceptable medium. Negotiators are imagined as fundamentally opposed, aiming to cut their losses and maximize their gains. Conflict is part and parcel of the process, as each party works toward its own interests.

I refer to both of these approaches as ideologies because each encompasses an implicit and sometimes explicit morality (Rubin 1994: 2); once a negotiation game is defined by one set of terms or the other, certain courses of action are no longer seen as legitimate. Controlling these definitions is itself a political act, which circumscribes the possible options of one's opponents; the imposition of a particular definition of the negotiation game can serve to legitimate or delegitimate strategies and thereby open up or close off options for negotiators.

Rubin described the morality associated with the mutual gains ideology: "The possibility that everyone wins is not only appealing. It carries with it a sense of moral rectitude and fairness that many of us want to believe in" (Rubin 1994: 2). Actions that create consensus, uncover shared interests, or are "constructive" are positively valued, whereas dissent, concealment, and self-interested action are negatively valued. Herein is the power of the definition of the game: once a negotiation situation is defined as a mutual gains scenario, actions that may be sensible and advantageous in terms of the interests of one party can be represented as immoral and uncooperative. When negotiations are viewed as a distributive contest, on the other hand, the behavior and tactics that may be considered appropriate or legitimate are quite different: self-interested, confrontational, antagonistic, deceptive, and/or adversarial behavior aimed at maximizing gains and minimizing losses.

The mutual gains ideology permeated discussions of land reform and conservation in South Africa in the period discussed, as exemplified by the title of Wynberg and Kepe's *Land Reform and Conservation Areas in South Africa: Towards a Mutually Beneficial Approach* (1999; see also Glavovic 1996: 496). A mutual gains approach to negotiation, however, is not always the best one for all involved, for a situation that preserves the appearance of harmony can nevertheless have clear winners and losers (Rose 1991).

Despite the appeal of the mutual gains ideology, Rubin identified certain circumstances under which a distributive approach may be more likely, appropriate, and/or successful. As I will show, many of the circumstances that Rubin identified characterize the positions of community representatives involved in negotiations over conservation areas. First, a distributive approach is likely because the strategic approaches that parties take are determined by their experiences with other parties in the negotiations (cf. Wynberg and Kepe 1999: 42; Bazerman et al. 2000). These relationships have typically been negative for communities in and around protected areas in South Africa, frequently involving dispossession and displacement. Given such histories, it is unlikely that they would immediately embrace a proposal to build on common interests with their past antagonists.

Second, distributive approaches are advantageous when negotiations are being carried out by representatives, because of the tensions created by the expectation that representatives will be accountable. This approach "lends itself better to [reporting back] than the more convoluted mutual gains approach. Each concession I manage to ratchet from you is another success story worthy of report" (Rubin 1994: 4), whereas lengthy analysis of interests to determine potential mutual gains may give representatives few concrete accomplishments on which to report. The pressures of representation are particularly acute for leaders who represent family and neighbors, with whom they have multistranded social ties.[3]

Finally, distributive approaches give a particular advantage to parties who have threats available (for example, occupation of the protected area, fence-cutting). As noted by Rubin (1994: 3–4), "negotiators may find that threats can be used to force the other side to yield, as when one side threatens to walk away from the table unless a concession is made."[4] In a mutual gains scenario, however, "threat would make little sense, since the shared objective is to solve the problem" (Rubin 1994: 3–4).

In the Makuleke and Dwesa-Cwebe claims, the tensions between the mutual gains and distributive ideologies appear clearly in the practices and statements of the NGOs and community leaders involved. In each case, community leaders' preferences for a distributive approach led to the involvement of two NGOs, one explicitly linked with the communities and committed to a distributive approach and another perceived as allied with the conservation authority and committed to a mutual gains approach.

The Makuleke Claim

My primary sources on the Makuleke claim are the writings of Conrad Steenkamp, an anthropologist and consultant directly involved in the Makuleke negotiations, concentrating here on the period from roughly 1994 to the resolution of the land claim in mid-1998. Steenkamp's own analysis of negotiators' strategies made use of the distinction between mutual gains and distributive approaches to negotiation (for example, 2001:

172–74). I aim to build on this analysis by drawing on Rubin's explication of the relationships between social position and negotiation strategies.

The Makuleke claim focused on an area known as the Pafuri Triangle, in the northernmost corner of the Kruger National Park, bordering Zimbabwe and Mozambique (figure 9.1). Bounded by the Limpopo River in the north and the Levhuvu River in the south, the area contains up to 75 percent of Kruger National Park's biodiversity (Steenkamp and Uhr 2000: 2). Prior to being evicted in 1969, the Makuleke community and their ancestors drew on a range of resources: cultivating maize and sorghum on the rivers' floodplains, grazing their livestock in diverse ecozones, hunting, fishing, and foraging (Steenkamp 2001: 31–32). Grazing forage in the area was particularly rich and drought resistant (Steenkamp 2001: 34).

The area was originally demarcated as a protected area in 1904 under the British colonial regime, but was degazetted in 1913 as conservation regulations proved unenforceable (Steenkamp 2001: 38). When Kruger National Park was created in 1926, it did not include the Pafuri Triangle, but by 1931 the park management began to seek to acquire the Pafuri Triangle, eventually convincing the Transvaal provincial government to proclaim it a Provincial Game Reserve. After several decades of uncertain tenure and increasing restrictions on subsistence activities (Steenkamp 2001: 39–44), the Makuleke were finally forcibly removed from the Pafuri Triangle in 1969 to an area 60 kilometers south.

The Makuleke community began organizing a land claim in the early 1990s. The land claim did not include demands for the residential or subsistence rights the community had lost in 1969 and prior years (Steenkamp 2001: 111ff.). Instead, from the outset, the claim was tied to aspirations for economic development through an ecotourism initiative: "In 1994 . . . a private sector game lodge operator approached the Makuleke with a proposal for a joint venture in the Pafuri Triangle. The basic idea was [to use the] land claim as leverage to gain consent from the National Parks Board . . . for access to the land" (Steenkamp and Uhr 2000: 5). The land claimed also encompassed the Madimbo corridor, an area then being prospected for diamonds by a private firm (Steenkamp 2001: 110–31). No tourism facilities existed at the time of the claim, although its location adjoining Kruger National Park made it a high-potential site for such activities.

With the support of the NGO the Group for Environmental Monitoring and the minister of land affairs, the planning and training components of the game lodge proposal received funding in 1995 from the German development agency Deutsche Gesellschaft für Technische Zusammenarbeit

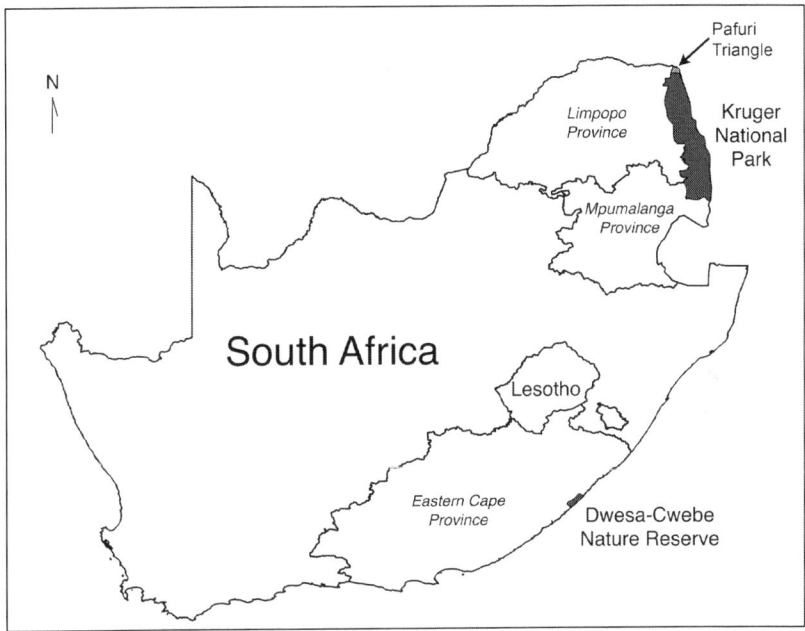

Figure 9.1. Dwesa-Cwebe Nature Reserve and Kruger National Park.

(Society for Technical Cooperation; hereafter GtZ), as the Makuleke Ecotourism Project, under the auspices of its Transform project. At this stage, Transform was conceived as a land restitution support program.

While planning and training began to move forward, the land subject to the claim and investment proposal was still under the control of the National Parks Board (NPB). The NPB had initially appeared tentatively receptive to the game lodge proposal, but in early 1995 the NPB adopted a more "hard-line position on the Makuleke" (Steenkamp and Uhr 2000: 11). The NPB wanted to: (1) "settle the claim without setting a precedent"; (2) maintain NPB control over the Pafuri Triangle because of its high conservation value and strategic location; and (3) restrict community interests and commercial development to the periphery of the Kruger National Park, preferably to buffer zones, and to maintain the Pafuri Triangle as a "wilderness area" (quotations from interviews with KNP in Steenkamp and Uhr 2000: 8).

Over the course of 1995 and early 1996, the GtZ became wary of involvement in potential conflicts over the game lodge and hesitant over its support. The Department of Land Affairs (DLA) Restitution Research directorate also released a report that suggested that the Makuleke land claim would be unsuccessful if brought before the Land Claims Court (Steenkamp 2001: 132–33). These concerns led to a major shift: "In 1996, one year after the launching of the project, the nature of Transform's support to the Makuleke project changed dramatically" (Steenkamp, unpublished manuscript: 6), from a focus on supporting land restitution to a focus on facilitating negotiations.

This reorientation enabled the NPB to engage with Transform. The GtZ embraced the NPB's involvement, taking an explicitly mutual gains view of the situation, favoring dialogue and participation over the representation of community interests. In March 1996, Transform undertook a planning process that, for the first time, incorporated the NPB as a "stakeholder" (Steenkamp and Uhr 2000: 13). "In what was described as a 'positive move' by the GtZ project manager, the NPB became part of the Transform steering committee" (Steenkamp, unpublished manuscript: 6). Rather than advocating for the Makuleke, Transform invited all parties to participate as "stakeholders." This commitment to incorporating the perspectives of all parties meant that Transform was ill-positioned to take an advocacy role for any one party (cf. deKoninck 2007).[5]

The NPB began to use its engagement with Transform to press for its own interests, proposing the creation of a "buffer zone" along the western edge of Kruger National Park. As Steenkamp explained, "the issue of the buffer zone, now on the development agenda at Makuleke, clearly reflected the KNP's interests . . . and was repeatedly rejected by the Makuleke" (Steenkamp, unpublished manuscript: 6).

These changes affected the Makuleke leadership's positions. Transform's funding for the ecotourism project and the associated training were to be shelved "until after the land claim," which Transform now viewed as "uncertain" (Steenkamp and Uhr 2000: 13). This shift threatened the Makuleke community representatives, because it could compromise their position with respect to their constituents. Faced with a situation in which they were expected to report back on tangible gains (cf. Rubin 1994: 4), the delays and changes in the agenda compromised the position of the Makuleke leadership. Steenkamp and Uhr cite Gibson Maluleke's description of his frustration at a meeting with the GtZ in April 1996: "Minister Hanekom told the people he wants to see the ecotourism project ready in November this year. . . . Now . . . there are delays with the ecotourism project. . . . It seems we will keep on talking for centuries. . . . When the people begin to doubt the leadership they lose confidence" (Steenkamp and Uhr 2000: 15). Under pressure to proceed with securing benefits, the prospect of protracted negotiations with an old enemy was not appealing to the Makuleke leadership, for it had the potential to undermine leaders' standing in their communities.

Transform, on the other hand, represented the changes in the process as a success, invoking a mutual gains ideology. Recounting a November 1996 planning workshop, the GtZ project manager wrote that "a lot of mistrust existed between the different stakeholders, especially the communities and the people from the conservation agencies.... Now they are all considered as partners and are sitting around the same table" (Steenkamp and Uhr 2000: 14).

This positive assessment ignores actions that were taking place outside the Transform-facilitated process. As Steenkamp explained, even as Transform and the GtZ were encouraging the NPB and the Makuleke to approach the land conflict from a mutual gains perspective, the NPB was taking a distributive approach to the land issue: they were setting specific positions from which they refused to back down, rather than presenting their interests in an open-ended process. In the same week as the planning workshop discussed in the previous paragraph, the NPB made a submission to the National Land Claims Commission opposing the land claim and recommending that the Makuleke be granted commercial rights on the periphery of the claimed area, not in the Pafuri Triangle itself.

While Transform tried to represent the negotiations as a win-win situation, the NPB's actions reflected a distributive strategy. Given this approach on the part of the NPB, Steenkamp argued that the Makuleke's early concession, a commitment to maintaining the conservation status of the land even if the land claim were successful, may have been a mistake. In effect, this move swung the balance of the distributive game in NPB's favor: "given the fact that the NPB was following a distributive bargaining strategy, it was inappropriate of the Makuleke negotiation team to concede immediately on the conservation status of the land"; instead, concealing their ultimate objectives would have been more appropriate for a distributive strategy (Steenkamp and Uhr 2000: 15). As the negotiations went on, "in spite of the Makuleke's initial concession on the conservation status of the land, the NPB negotiators were unwilling to budge on key issues such as land ownership" (Steenkamp and Uhr 2000: 16).

For a period after the shift in Transform's approach, the Makuleke leadership continued to participate in Transform activities, hopeful that Transform might still deliver some benefits. Eventually, however, they requested that Transform no longer play a role in the land claim process, feeling that Transform constituted a threat to the claim. As Steenkamp and Uhr explained, by rejecting Transform's role in planning, the Makuleke leadership opted against a process that was being represented as a technical exercise to find a solution that satisfied all parties in favor of an approach that would allow "for the give and take of a distributive bargaining process" (Steenkamp and Uhr 2000: 16).

Rather than deny or attempt to minimize the conflicts that had become evident from the actions of the NPB, the Makuleke leadership instead turned to a harder strategy and to another set of NGOs: the Friends of Makuleke, a consortium of consultants who had worked at Makuleke in various capacities, and the Legal Resources Centre, the country's leading public interest legal NGO. These NGOs, together with the Land Claims Commission, came to be the primary sources of support to the Makuleke land claim. Two aspects of these NGOs' approach fit with the concerns and experience of the Makuleke: (1) they explicitly made resolution of the land claim a central priority; and (2) they recognized the existence of conflicts between the NPB and the Makuleke community and were willing to treat the NPB as antagonists.

The process that followed, leading up to the agreement signed on May 30, 1998, has been characterized as "18 eighteen months of tough distributive bargaining" (Steenkamp unpublished manuscript: 3). The eventual outcome was an agreement on land restitution and the joint management of the Pafuri Triangle area as conservation land, stipulating that "the land will be used solely for conservation and related commercial activities," with no mining, agriculture, or residences allowed, and it grants South African National Parks (SANP), the institutional successor to the NPB, right of first refusal in the event that the land is ever offered for sale. Although diamond prospecting had proven fruitless in 1996, the Makuleke had requested mining rights. This was dropped in the final agreement, creating the appearance of a concession (Steenkamp 2001: 186). Under the agreement, the land is managed jointly by SANP and Makuleke representatives as a contractual national park (de Villiers 1999: 60–61; cf. Reid 2001).

Although my analysis has focused on the period up to the 1998 agreement, tensions have continued between SANP and the Makuleke. Steenkamp and Grossman (2001: 7) argued that SANP's approach has remained focused on controlling development in Pafuri as much as possible and that representing the situation as mutually beneficial is unrealistic. Assertions of "harmony," rather than recognition of conflict, they argue, "hark back to the semi-feudal patron and client . . . predemocracy people and park relations" (Steenkamp and Grossman 2001: 8). The ideology of mutual gains, they suggested, continues to be invoked to mask ongoing conflicts and attempts by SANP to continue to restrict the rights of the landowners. More recently, Makuleke leaders have complained that the conservation authorities fail to acknowledge their status: "Makuleke are not always treated as 'landlords' by [SANP], but are often positioned as simply one of the many 'neighboring communities,'" while "participation [in conservation management] is often perceived to be largely rhetorical" (Robins and van der Waal 2008: 67). They have also not been included in the management structure for the newly created Great Limpopo Transfrontier Conservation Area, which would incorporate Makuleke territory (Spierenburg et al. 2008: 93).[6] Meanwhile, SANP has rejected the replication of the Makuleke model, with its provisions for transfer of land and ecotourism, reflecting a hardening of their overall position on restitution of protected areas (Spierenburg et al. 2008: 93).[7]

The Dwesa-Cwebe Claim

Dwesa and Cwebe Forests are situated on opposite sides of the Mbhashe River, on the southeastern coast of South Africa (figure 9.2). The forests span approximately 18 kilometers of coastline and extend inward for 3 to 5 kilometers, encompassing more than 5700 hectares. They were first demarcated in the early 1890s, and between the 1890s and 1930s the Forest Department forcibly removed the African residents of the forests and brought an end to cultivation of crops in the grasslands at the margins of the demarcated forest (figure 9.3). During the same period, the administration allowed whites to establish the Haven Hotel and holiday cottages in the same areas (Fay et al. 2002).

The removed people settled in the grasslands outside the forests, and until the 1970s they retained restricted access to forest products, marine resources, and grazing within the reserve boundaries. In 1978, however, the Transkei homeland[8] government formally established the Dwesa-Cwebe Nature Reserve and subsequently fenced the forests and eliminated all local resource access. The Haven Hotel continued to operate, although it has often run at a loss, relying primarily on seasonal domestic tourism, while the holiday cottages remained under private control.

The land claim at Dwesa-Cwebe began in the early 1990s with a locally initiated process explicitly aimed at extracting concessions from the conservation authority. Leaders from two villages on opposite sides of the river were introduced through an NGO, the Transkei Land Service Organization (Tralso). Tralso and the Village Planner (TVP), an NGO established

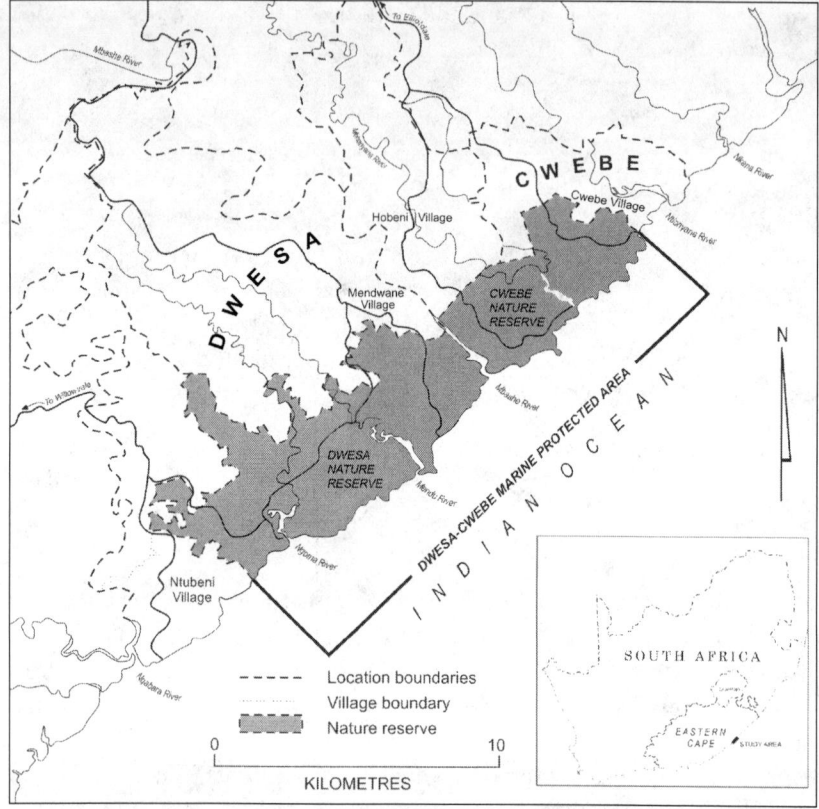

Figure 9.2. Dwesa-Cwebe Nature Reserve.

by former Tralso staff member André Terblanche, provided ongoing support to the land claim over the following years.

Other initiatives went on without NGO support. In keeping with a distributive strategy (Rubin 1994: 3–4), threat was part of Cwebe residents' strategy from the outset, most notably in the form of a training camp for Umkhonto WeSizwe (the African National Congress's military wing), where cadres drilled with automatic weapons a few hundred meters from one of the Cwebe Nature Reserve gates.

The situation never came to violence. Residents of the Cwebe and Dwesa communities launched a coordinated mass protest inside the reserve in the midst of a severe drought in 1993–1994, aiming both to directly extract forest resources and to extract concessions from the conservation authority. Immediately afterward, following a visit by Eastern Cape

Figure 9.3. Cwebe leaders point out the sites of their ancestors' homesteads in Dwesa-Cwebe Nature Reserve.

Minister of Agriculture Tertius Delport, the reserve management opened negotiations with locally elected Village Conservation Committees.

These negotiations defused the situation, as the conservation authority made several critical but temporary concessions: establishing a permit system for use of forest products and making the grasslands within the reserves available for grazing until drought conditions abated. Relations also improved in September 1995, when responsibility for the reserve was transferred from the Mthatha office of the Eastern Cape Nature Conservation (ECNC) to its East London office, increasing its logistical and managerial capacity[9] and resulting in the replacement of most reserve staff, thus "eliminating personal antagonisms that had existed between some managers and community leaders" (Palmer et al. 2002a: 116).

Over the same period, local leaders invited Tralso to return, in order to prepare to submit a formal land claim, a process spearheaded by TVP. The Tralso/TVP project documentation clearly anticipated a distributive negotiation process and placed these NGOs unequivocally on the side of the claimants. Its stated aims included "to assist the affected communities in *maximizing restitution possibilities*, within the framework of the land claims court processes" (Tralso 1995: 5, emphasis mine) and "the preparation of land use management plans to challenge official and other views of externally planned use of the land" (Transkei Land Service Organization 1995: 6). The text reveals an implicit understanding of the process as potentially conflictual and antagonistic.

In the meantime, plans were underway for a second NGO intervention. Christo Fabricius, then ECNC's head of scientific services and "an early champion of community involvement in conservation" (Palmer et al. 2002b: 15), organized a workshop with the sponsorship of World Wide Fund for Nature–South Africa to develop a project for cooperative management of the reserves. This initiative eventually led in early 1996 to the Dwebe Project, based out of Rhodes University's Institute for Social and Economic Research.

In the view of Gerry Pienaar of ECNC, the Dwebe Project was "precisely aimed at building a platform for proper negotiation between ECNC and local villagers."[10] In the months that followed, however, it became clear that community leaders were more skeptical. As Terblanche explained, "ECNC viewed the Dwebe Project as its (credible and independent) vehicle for effecting negotiations . . . [but] the communities will very clearly not permit the Dwebe Project such a role."[11] There were various reasons for the Dwesa-Cwebe leadership's mistrust, including some negative experiences with Dwebe fieldworkers and the perception that Dwebe was drawing leaders' efforts away from the land claim.

The situation was complicated by the fact that ECNC was unable to take a firm position on the land claim. Given the fluid state of provincial conservation policy, Pienaar commented that "we do not now have a mandate to negotiate final agreements on policy issues." He also expressed concern that "national stakeholders will demand that we strongly contest any land claim, expending considerable energy and cost on this issue rather than on constructive development."[12] Community leaders, on the other hand, wanted a tangible gain and stronger negotiation position. In February 1996, they took the position that resolution of the land claim was a precondition to further negotiations over such issues as joint management of the reserves.[13]

While community representatives were insecure of their victory in the land claim, Dwebe was trying to invite them into a win-win mutual gains process, in which they would face pressures to cooperate in the name of development rather than concentrate on succeeding in the land claim. In the early months of 1996, the Dwebe project organized a series of meetings with the aim of drafting an interim constitution for a joint management committee. Uncertainty over the status of the land claim, however, led the community leadership to withdraw from participation in April 1996.

The morality of the mutual gains ideology is evident in Dwebe staff's reply to the communities' withdrawal. The Dwebe Project team reiterated their support for the claim and then articulated the role they envisioned for the project: "to encourage the upgrading of the existing reserves so as to ensure their contribution to the local economy." The final paragraph of this letter both represents the claim as a "problem" and upholds a collaborative model of the process: "we hope that problems like the land claim will be resolved so that we can put our minds to the economic development of your communities."[14] This quotation recalls the morality of the mutual gains ideology: it problematizes attempts by one party to extract concessions and maximize gains, while upholding a collaborative vision of working in everyone's "best interests."

When the community leaders withdrew from Dwebe's negotiation process, ECNC found themselves in a bind, as they lacked the "jurisdiction and authority" to respond to the land claim.[15] The challenge facing ECNC was, in effect, how to concede the claim (and thereby allow negotiations to go forward) without putting the conservation status of the land at risk. They eventually agreed not to challenge the claim provided that the reserves continued to remain a jointly managed protected area. In a position paper of April 24, 1996, ECNC stated that it recognized and "accept[ed] the *moral* grounds for a restitution claim" (emphasis in original) and accepted that some form of restitution was appropriate, with the content of this restitution to be negotiated among "all the stakeholders."[16]

By nominally conceding the claim (even while leaving the *content* of restitution open), ECNC made a move that implied the hope of a mutual gains–type negotiating process. They expressed the hope that rather than putting forward competing positions, "all the stakeholders" would now sit down and figure out what exactly had been conceded.

At the same time, like SANP in the previous case, even as they aimed to participate in a collaborative process, ECNC maintained a fallback position. The ECNC statement did not deny the legal validity of the claim, but it maintained an implicit threat that its representatives would reiterate, noting that "our understanding of the documented evidence is that a strictly legal restitution claim could be difficult to substantiate."[17]

The ECNC statement was prepared for a negotiating meeting held on the following days (April 25–26, 1996). At this meeting, the community leadership concurred that the land would continue to be used as a nature reserve, and agreed to resume its participation in the joint management negotiations.[18]

Nevertheless, as negotiations went on toward a Deed of Settlement for the land claim, TVP and the Dwesa-Cwebe leadership clearly continued to anticipate a distributive negotiating process. In strategic planning meetings prior to the claim, Terblanche enumerated a set of "extreme" positions that might be conceded over the course of the negotiations.[19] These recommendations included: (1) setting twenty-one years as the upper limit for the duration of ECNC's lease; (2) providing for compensation if the lease is terminated; (3) providing training and education; (4) management capacity building; (5) formalizing a "50/50 basis" for joint management; (6) fixing a time frame for the resolution of land- and resource-use questions; (7) granting residential rights in the reserve to descendants of families that were removed; (8) investigating the possibility of removing the fence and extending the conservation zone to include adjoining residential areas; and (9) giving priority to local people in employment.

This style of negotiation gave rise to the perception that Terblanche was extreme in his demands; as one observer put it, "André won't be happy until he sees cows swimming in the ocean."[20] Over subsequent months, points 2, 7, and 8 were dropped. Regardless of whether they were ever serious proposals, this approach gave a strong position from which the claimants could appear to be making concessions.

The claimants' strategy was clearly based on a distributive model of the negotiations. Terblanche provided both the communities' fallback position and relayed an implicit threat: "In our experience, economic restitution, as opposed to the restoration of full land property rights, would not under any conditions be acceptable to the claimants. . . . The claimants recognize that the only authority that they presently bring to the . . . structure to jointly regulate and control the reserves, is the power to disrupt."[21]

A preliminary Deed of Settlement was finally signed in June 1996, making the transfer of land contingent on the continued conservation status of the land under joint management, although this was not the end of the land claim process.

Under the terms of this agreement, joint management planning resumed under the auspices of the Dwebe Project in October 1996. Dwebe contracted a facilitator previously employed by GtZ/Transform (the project discussed above in the Makuleke case) to conduct a LogFrame analysis.[22] The comments of then-Dwebe fieldworker Herman Timmermans give a sense of the tension between the community leadership's focus on tangible benefits and Dwebe's focus on the LogFrame process. A follow-up evaluation meeting "revealed frustration on the part of community participants. . . . [C]ommunity representatives would have preferred to grapple in detail with issues rather than simply rearrange and organise them . . . [and] did not . . . share the project team's enthusiasm regarding the performance of the professional facilitators. . . . Some people felt that little progress had been made as old outstanding issues had been raised and listed but not actually dealt with" (Timmermans 1997: 11).

While Dwebe was pushing for a recognizable "participatory process," anticipating an implicit audience of donors and development professionals (cf. Mosse 2001: 28) and aiming to show progress through the creation of a forum for mutually beneficial negotiations, community leaders were more concerned with the demands of their local constituents for material concessions.

Joint management planning went ahead under the understanding that the land claim would not be part of the joint management process and would be addressed by the communities in partnership with Tralso/TVP. For various reasons, including the question of whether ECNC actually was in a legal position to negotiate regarding the land claim and uncertainty about the legal validity of the claim, the DLA did not respond to community leaders' queries in late 1996 and early 1997.

Given this lack of response and the resulting uncertainty about the state of the land claim, early in 1997 the community leadership again withdrew from the joint management committee negotiation and the Dwebe Project. In March of that year, the Dwesa-Cwebe leadership issued a memorandum calling for: (1) immediate enforcement of existing agreements between the communities, DLA, and ECNC; (2) referral of the land claim deed of settlement to the Land Claims Court; (3) suspension of joint management committee meetings until final settlement of the land claim and statutory recognition of the joint management committee; (4) an urgent meeting between community leaders and senior government officials; and (5) the immediate suspension of the Dwebe Project's activities.[23]

This tactic led to plans for a meeting (eventually held in August 1997) with Minister of Land Affairs Derek Hanekom to clarify the status of the claim. In a preparatory statement for this meeting, Terblanche reiterated two of the circumstances that Rubin argues make a distributive strategy appropriate: the position of the leaders as *representatives* and their possession of *threat* as one of their major bargaining chips: "The existence of signed but unhonoured agreements, and the failure of tangible changes to materialise threatens the long-term credibility of existing leadership structures. It is highly improbable that such good agreements will ever again be negotiated, should present negotiations collapse" (Terblanche 1997: 7).

The situation was resolved, for the time being, by Hanekom's visit in August 1997. During this visit, he assured the claimants that he supported their claim and that the state intended to transfer land either through the Restitution Act or the State Land Disposal Act (which bypass the restitution process), subject to the agreement of cabinet colleagues, the creation of necessary legal entities, and clear guarantees for future conservation (Palmer et al. 2002a). The claimants' bargaining position was strengthened substantially as a result: if ECNC or other parties challenged the legal validity of the claim, they could turn to the minister's pledge to use the State Land Disposal Act.

Since Hanekom's visit and the Land Claims Court's decision that restitution would be contingent upon continued conservation at Dwesa-Cwebe, joint management returned to the local policy agenda, with ECNC drafting management plans for the reserves. Intergovernmental discussions over land tenure and jurisdiction, the future of the Haven Hotel and holiday cottages, and a tourism development initiative that ultimately failed to attract investors all contributed to delays in the eventual resolution of the claim (in July 2001).

The ongoing story of Dwesa-Cwebe is told elsewhere (Palmer et al. 2002b, 2006; Ntshona et al. 2010). The reserve management has continued to play a distributive game. After the resolution of the land claim in 2001, the reserve management (eventually transferred from ECNC to the newly constituted Eastern Cape Parks and Tourism Authority) unilaterally—and in violation of on-the-ground agreements that were unfortunately not incorporated into the legal Settlement Agreement—cancelled all local harvesting rights, leading to ongoing discontent and conflict; access was only partially restored in 2009.[24] Likewise, the representation of local government and communities as "partners" in development has worked to communities' disadvantage. Local government spent substantial funds from the restitution award on meetings and planning consultants without the consent of the landowning trust and failed to implement

Figure 9.4. Dwesa-Cwebe residents meet with NGO supporters regarding strategies to restore customary fishing rights.

a 2003 Development Plan for the area. The Settlement Agreement and related documents failed to provide measures to hold local government accountable (Palmer et al. 2006), and (as of 2012), Dwesa-Cwebe leaders were seeking the assistance of the Legal Resources Centre regarding legal strategies to get conservation authorities and local government to uphold the Settlement Agreement (figure 9.4). As at Makuleke, the formal resolution of the claim has been only one step in a process requiring ongoing vigilance and advocacy to defend community interests.

Toward a Critical Understanding of Community–Protected Area Negotiations

In this chapter, I have argued that explicit attention to mutual gains and distributive negotiation ideologies can illuminate the statements and actions of the parties involved in negotiations over protected areas at Makuleke and Dwesa-Cwebe. Negotiation theory can be a fruitful resource for the ethnographic analysis of community–protected area relations.

In the Makuleke case, community leaders, hoping for a cooperative response from the NPB, extended a major concession: that the land would continue to be used for conservation purposes. Their position changed after the NPB came to participate in Transform's stakeholder-based negotiation process, using this mechanism to shape the terms of debate in their favor while also maintaining a hard-line fallback position. The Makuleke leadership and their allies, seeing the NPB's change in strategy, came to question the appropriateness of the mutual gains definition of the situation implicit in Transform's approach. Eventually, they withdrew from Transform in favor of support provided by Friends of Makuleke and the Legal Resources Centre, NGOs that took an explicitly distributive view of the situation.

At Dwesa-Cwebe, the sequence was reversed. Community leaders began with the support of NGOs that took an explicitly distributive perspective (Tralso/TVP), and an antagonistic relationship with the conservation authority. When an NGO entered the area and attempted to promote a cooperative, mutual gains process, it faced difficulties securing local support in the face of suspicions and concerns to secure victory in the land claim, as community leaders were reluctant to accept a mutual gains framing when they were uncertain about their primary goal of securing land rights.

Examining these two processes suggests some tentative conclusions about conflicts between local populations and protected areas. First, one should not expect a single NGO to do it all. Recognizing this from the outset is likely to lead to less tension and potential conflict. Rather, the participation of multiple NGOs may be both common and desirable, provided that their roles are clearly defined, with one unequivocally supporting locally articulated community interests and another taking a mediatory role. To expect a single organization to play both these roles seems unrealistic and likely to breed distrust and/or organizational schisms.

The implicit moralities of the mutual gains and distributive ideologies also suggest that criticisms of NGOs may take predictable forms. In each of these cases, observers and other NGO participants suggested that the advocatory NGOs (Friends of Makuleke and TVP) were prolonging the process to serve their own interests. These accusations of vested interests contrary to the claimants likely reflect a frustration with the perceived "immorality" of distributive negotiation approaches, as if the claimants would share the mutual gains perspective if they were not being manipulated by outsiders. Likewise, the mediatory NGOs that suggested community demands were not "constructive" were accused of focusing on public and donor relations rather than community interests and colluding with conservation authorities.

Second, these cases suggest that a mutual gains scenario, while appealing to many, may not be appropriate at the outset of claims, given the pressures that incline community representatives to a distributive view. An NGO that prematurely promotes a win-win scenario is likely to see its initiative backfire, leading to mistrust and the loss of community support.

More importantly, a mutual gains approach may undermine the bargaining position of communities. This point can be illustrated by examining Wynberg and Kepe's (1999) framework for addressing land claims on protected areas, which explicitly promotes a "mutual gains" view of these situations, and considering whether the Wynberg and Kepe framework is likely to maximize the benefits to the claimants. Their first two proposals, that communities "1) organize themselves and put forward unified positions; [and] 2) seek advice on the actions required to proceed with the claim" (Wynberg and Kepe 1999: 32–33), are clearly well taken. The first is likely to reduce complexity and internal conflicts, though it may be problematic where definitions of "community" and "claimant" groups are contested.[25] The second point is also appropriate. As I have suggested, this step is likely to lead to the involvement of an explicitly advocatory NGO presence.

The third and fourth points, that communities "3) have clear visions of intentions, and minimize the changes in their positions (though it is acknowledged that some change may be necessary); [and] 4) provide as much information as possible" (Wynberg and Kepe 1999: 32–33), are more problematic, in the sense that they ask communities from the outset to commit to a mutual gains process that may not work to their advantage. Asking communities to minimize changes in their positions conflicts with the adoption of a distributive approach; as in the examples of the Dwesa-Cwebe leadership's call for residential rights within the nature reserve and the removal of the fence, and the Makuleke leadership's early interest in diamond mining, it is to the advantage of a negotiator in a distributive process to have extreme positions from which one can back down.

Likewise, Wynberg and Kepe's third recommendation assumes that all parties will start openly and honestly as they would under an ideal mutual gains situation. As in the Makuleke case, however, opening with this position may be a mistake: the Makuleke conceded the continued protected status of their land at the outset, and rather than responding constructively to this concession, the NPB countered with a set of hard-line positions.

The fourth point, that communities should openly share information, potentially conflicts with strategies appropriate for a distributive process, in which concealment of one's ultimate objectives may be an effective strategy for maximizing concessions from one's opponents. In effect, this recommendation effectively asks communities to give up several potential bargaining chips before they enter the game. This may ultimately weaken the community's position, for, as Rubin put it, "judicious misrepresentation may be required and expected if effective agreements are to be obtained through concession-convergence" (Rubin 1994: 3).

Many readers (and indeed, this author) may find themselves dimly hoping that a win-win scenario might be possible for these and other cases involving claims on conservation land. I should be clear that I am not arguing against win-win scenarios, but aiming to be cautious about who wins and by how much, and asking what strategies will allow communities to maximize their benefits through negotiations.

To this point, I have emphasized the factors that incline community representatives toward a distributive approach, suggesting that this may be nearly inevitable, given the historical and structural circumstances underlying these negotiation processes. The trust that can emerge through interpersonal interaction in the negotiating process is one countervailing force. Likewise, both sides may recognize that they will be engaged with their fellow negotiators over the long term.[26] A mutual gains approach is recognized in the negotiation literature as more likely where there is a long-term relationship between the negotiating parties (Rubin 1994: 4).

Nevertheless, as I have argued here, expecting communities to prematurely adopt a mutual gains view of negotiations with protected area management and conservation agencies is naïve. More importantly, it is threatening to the interests of communities because such an ideological framing of the negotiation game both undermines some of the most effective strategies available to communities (for example, threat, concealment, and concession) and places community leaders in a position where their legitimacy may be threatened by the delays inherent in a mutual gains approach.

Acknowledgments

This research was funded by the Research Institute for the Study of Man in 1998 and the Wenner-Gren Foundation for Anthropological Research (grant no. 6329) in 1999. Thanks are especially due to the Dwesa-Cwebe Land Trust and the residents of the Dwesa-Cwebe communities. Full acknowledgments appear in Fay (2007).

Notes

1. Wynberg and Kepe (1999) and Kepe et al. (2003) provided overviews of issues around land claims on protected areas. On Dwesa-Cwebe, see Terblanche and Kraai (1996) and Palmer et al. (1997, 2002b, 2006). Palmer et al. (2002b) and Tropp (2006) discussed the history of forestry and conservation in the region in more detail. Timmermans (2004) and Fay (2005, 2011) discussed some dynamics responsible for the demand for building materials. On the challenges of comanagement in the region, see Kepe (2008). On Makuleke, see de Villiers (1999), Steenkamp and Uhr (2000), Reid (2001), Steenkamp (2001), Steenkamp and Grossman (2001), Turner (2002), and Robins and van der Waal (2008), and more recent literature reviewed therein. Harries (1987) provided historical background on the Makuleke community, and Carruthers (1995) described the history of conservation in the northern Transvaal and the establishment of Kruger National Park. Walker (2008) and Nustad (2011) discussed the St. Lucia wetlands claim.

2. Pagination in Rubin (1994) refers to the electronic version.

3. Insofar as a distributive approach helps community representatives in their relations with their constituents, it may also work to maintain the viability of the negotiations. If community representatives come to be perceived as "sell-outs" or ineffective, leaders who step up to take their place are likely to be more extreme in their demands and/or to reject negotiations altogether. Such was the case at Dwesa-Cwebe in late 2004 (after the period considered in this paper): frustrated by their representatives' inability to win concessions from the reserve management, a group of local residents took matters into their own hands by cutting the reserve fence and harvesting wood and shellfish.

4. Such threats have proven effective at a number of points in the Dwesa-Cwebe negotiations, before and after the period covered in this paper (Palmer et al. 2002a: 139–41).

5. deKoninck (2007: 85) provided a valuable set of critiques of the deployment of the notion of "stakeholder" in community–protected area negotiations in Australia, concluding that the "stakeholder approach serves to legitimate certain outside interests while making Aboriginal claims to seemingly extraordinary rights illegitimate."

6. Both of these authors also discuss recent tensions between the Makuleke Communal Property Association and traditional authorities.

7. Emergent national policies around land claims on protected areas reflect this more hard-line stance. In May 2007, "the Minister of Agriculture and Land Affairs and the Minister of Environmental Affairs and Tourism . . . the two relevant government departments on the land claims in conservation areas issue came to a formal, legally binding agreement to use comanagement as the only strategy to reconcile land reform in protected areas" (Kepe 2008: 312), allowing for transfer of title only where it was feasible (Walker 2008: 110). More recently, the Directors General of the Departments of Environmental Affairs and Tourism and the DLA eventually secured cabinet approval to offer "equitable redress" as the only option for resolving claims, that is, awarding financial compensation and/or alternative land, "possibly coupled with other benefits [such as] introduction of a 'community levy' . . . on all visitors to be channeled into a Community Trust Fund to fund future community development projects;

broad-based [black economic empowerment] opportunities and equity in commercial concessions," while preserving both state ownership and the conservation status of the claimed land (GCIS 2009).

8. "Homelands" were political entities created by the South African government to defuse criticism of apartheid; the Transkei homeland was granted "self-government" in 1963 and "independence" in 1976, but Pretoria maintained tight control over its budgets and policies.

9. Gerry Pienaar, ECNC fax to André Terblanche of April 11, 1996. Files held by André Terblanche, Ncise, Mthatha (hereafter AT files).

10. G. Pienaar fax to Dwesa-Cwebe villages of November 27, 1995, cited by A. Terblanche in fax to G. Pienaar, January 30, 1996. AT files.

11. A. Terblanche fax of January 30, 1996 to G. Pienaar. AT files.

12. G. Pienaar letter to A. Terblanche of February 13, 1996. AT files. Nevertheless, Pienaar was concurrently cooperating with the DLA, providing feedback to the DLA via TVP on land tenure arrangements that might be employed if the claim succeeded. G. Pienaar to A. Terblanche fax of March 8, 1996.

13. AT fax to G. Pienaar of February 15, 1996.

14. H. Timmermans, K. Ralo, R. Kingwill, P. McAllister fax of April 16, 1996, to Dwesa-Cwebe conservation committees. AT files.

15. G. Pienaar fax to A. Terblanche of April 16, 1996. AT files.

16. "Land Claim against the Dwesa and Cwebe Nature Reserves: Position Statement by [ECNC], April 24, 1996." In Land Claims Commission binder II-AA.

17. "Land Claim against the Dwesa and Cwebe Nature Reserves: Position Statement by Eastern Cape Nature Conservation," April 24, 1996. Land Claims Commission files.

18. Minutes of negotiation meeting, Dwesa-Cwebe Land Claim, April 25–26, 1996. In Land Claims Commission binder II:K.

19. A. Terblanche fax of May 20, 1996, to Tralso/Dwesa-Cwebe leadership. AT files.

20. Duncan Peltason, pers. comm., 1998.

21. A. Terblanche fax of May 27, 1996, to H. Winkler, DLA. Files held by Kuzile Juza, Hobeni Communal Property Association.

22. LogFrame analysis involves collecting lists of potential project objectives, ranking them, and identifying "killer assumptions" that may lead to project failure.

23. March 18, 1997, handwritten note by A. Terblanche, signed by Dwesa-Cwebe community leaders. AT files.

24. Analyses of the quantities and uses of material removed under the permit system can be found in Lieberman (1997) and Timmermans (2002, 2004). The analysis leading to current recommendations appears in Fearon (2010).

25. The problem of defining community is nearly ubiquitous. For discussions pertaining to these cases, see Robins and van der Waal (2008) on Makuleke and Palmer et al. (2002b) on Dwesa-Cwebe.

26. Conversely, discontinuity in negotiating personnel can damage hard-won trust, as in the transition from ECNC to the Eastern Cape Parks and Tourism Authority at Dwesa-Cwebe.

CHAPTER TEN

Conservation and Maya Autonomy in Guatemala's Western Highlands

The Case of Totonicapán

Brian W. Conz

Contemporary efforts to implement new paradigm approaches to conservation may help to redress the legacies of fortress conservation (Brockington 2002) and the Yellowstone model (Stevens 1986, 1997a), but they face social, political, and ecological complexities at multiple scales. In many countries, national protected areas policy is changing to reflect progressive global discourses on best practices for more inclusive conservation programs, but the place-specific conditions, in which policy is transformed into lived experience, present perhaps the greatest challenge. The situation is particularly acute when, as has often been the case, policy-makers have "gotten it wrong" in the first instance, creating feelings of resentment for conservation agencies and NGOs at the local level, and, in some cases, damaging existing conservation institutions (chapter 1; Stevens 1997a; Brockington et al. 2008). However, in the process of contesting policies that are imposed on Indigenous communities by national and international conservation entities, new opportunities for the shift toward rights-based conservation may also emerge (Campese et al. 2009; Stevens 2010).

In this chapter, I discuss some of the challenges and consequences of protected area creation in the Guatemalan community of Totonicapán, with special attention to changes in local politics, forest-dependent livelihoods, and forest ecology. I conclude that, while the implications of protected area creation in Totonicapán remain contested and ambiguous, the contestation and negotiation of conservation policies has been a key context through which Maya autonomy, cultural identity, and traditions of environmental stewardship were articulated. Conservation policies and environmentalism more broadly have created a space through which these goals have been furthered, even as they were resisted in their various imposed manifestations.

Regional Context and Methodology

In their recent survey of changing forest tenure and community rights to natural resources across the global South, Larson et al. (2010: 24) discussed three themes that have helped to foster formal recognition of customary "bundles of rights" to forests and territories for communities: (1) Indigenous rights, (2) biodiversity conservation, and (3) the decentralization of natural resource management. Latin America has been especially prominent in this process over the past twenty years, witnessing powerful Indigenous rights movements as well as investments in biodiversity conservation, making it an important region for monitoring the implementation of the new paradigm. Yet, the performance of a variety of approaches—from Indigenous territories and extractive reserves to community forest concessions and comanaged parks—has been mixed in terms of the ability of these policy tools to support cultural and social goals, improve livelihoods, and respect Indigenous autonomy (Cisneros and McBreen 2010; Pacheco et al. 2012).

Among Latin American countries, Guatemala is noteworthy for its large Indigenous population as well as for its significant biodiversity. The country's highland region is a densely populated patchwork of semi-autonomous homelands of Indigenous Maya peoples where policy-makers and Indigenous leaders alike face the challenge of instituting forest conservation programs that reinforce local management institutions, build on existing conservation practices, and ensure access to the cultural resources and livelihood benefits that forests provide (Elias et al. 2009). In the 1990s, Guatemala's protected area network expanded dramatically, and numerous protected areas were created in the southwestern highlands, a rugged and mountainous area of agricultural landscapes and pine-oak forest patches. Historically the setting of extremely tight land markets, property conflicts, and intensive land use, the highlands are also the region that has seen the most significant survival of communal governance and communal forest tenure among the area's Maya communities. The expansion of protected areas there has been underwritten by concerns over threatened biodiversity and the diminishing ecosystem services—especially hydrological resources—provided by forested watersheds and driven by international funding and enthusiasm for addressing these concerns through protected areas (Elias and Wittman 2005). Perhaps not surprisingly, given the historical preponderance of land conflicts in the region, protected area projects and other conservation programs have proven to be highly charged politically, creating new contexts for old disputes between local communities and local authorities and between local authorities and the state natural resource agencies.

The regional municipal park (RMP) Los Altos de San Miguel in Totonicapán, the largest of its kind in the highlands, illustrates the complexities of creating externally defined protected areas in the region. The park was created in 1997 in the K'iche' Maya department of Totonicapán and contains forests and grazing lands held under forms of communal ownership that are often overlapping and contested. Although there was initially optimism that the protected area designation could reinforce communal tenure, the outcomes of RMP status and other related conservation programs have been ambiguous. From the perspective of the park's creators, which included NGOs, government agencies, municipal politicians, and various local leaders, the park's creation involved both the consent and participation of local people. From a more critical perspective, however, the park was hastily declared and was part of a larger trend throughout the highlands whereby authority over communal forests was concentrated in the hands of municipal authorities, the official comanagement entity, along with the Protected Areas Council (CONAP; Elias and Wittman 2005; Wittman and Geisler 2005).

In some senses the case of Totonicapán can be read as a textbook example of the pitfalls that await attempts to overlay customary arrangements with state-sponsored, internationally defined park designations, especially in the context of historically antagonistic relationships between the state and Indigenous peoples. Viewed from another perspective, however, the controversies and conflict the park's creation sparked also helped to define and reinvigorate the local tradition of Indigenous political autonomy and resource governance.

This local case study has broader implications for Indigenous activists working at the regional and national levels. The possibility of designating regional autonomous areas for the Maya peoples of Guatemala was taken off the table during the mid-1990s peace negotiations (Diaz-Polanco

1999), whereas protected areas expanded dramatically. During the same period el Movimiento Maya (pan-Maya Movement), a multifaceted social movement for Indigenous rights in Guatemala, has gained ground, pushing for greater awareness of Maya issues and institutions (Arias 2008; Warren 2008). The management of Maya communal lands and other natural resources has become a forum for continued discussions of autonomy, local power, and governance, so the Indigenous management of some of the larger-scale communal properties-cum-protected areas like that of Totonicapán is especially important to examine.

The information and analysis presented here is based on ongoing geographic fieldwork that began in 2003. The methodology has included multiple site visits to communities and forest and grazing commons; participant observation of forest-based livelihood activities; ethnographic observations; and ethnographic interviews with villagers, Indigenous leaders, NGO personnel, and government agency staff. In 2006, I carried out an extensive series of semistructured individual and focus-group interviews in two mountain villages, one located on the edges of the park polygon and the other located within it. Access to these communities was acquired through field-season volunteer work with local NGOs and through consultation with community councils.

The K'iche' Maya and the Forests of Totonicapán: A Tradition of Conservation

The relative stability of forest cover of the Sierra Madre in the *municipio* (county) of Totonicapán[1] (figure 10.1), in the southeast of the department of the same name, has been remarked upon for many decades (Veblen 1975; Elias 1997). The montane forests contain considerable floral diversity including species of oak, pine, and alder as well as the regionally endemic fir *Abies guatemalensis*, known locally as the *pinabete*. By some estimates the fir's largest extant stands exist in the mountains, which are surrounded on all sides by areas that have suffered considerable degradation and deforestation. The forests of Totonicapán, although used intensively by generations of Maya K'iche' carpenters, gatherers of nontimber forest products, and sheep herders, continue to provide refuge for wildlife species while protecting watersheds and hydrological resources for hundreds of thousands of people.

The most comprehensive exploration of the forest conservation dynamic was undertaken by biogeographer Thomas Veblen during the early

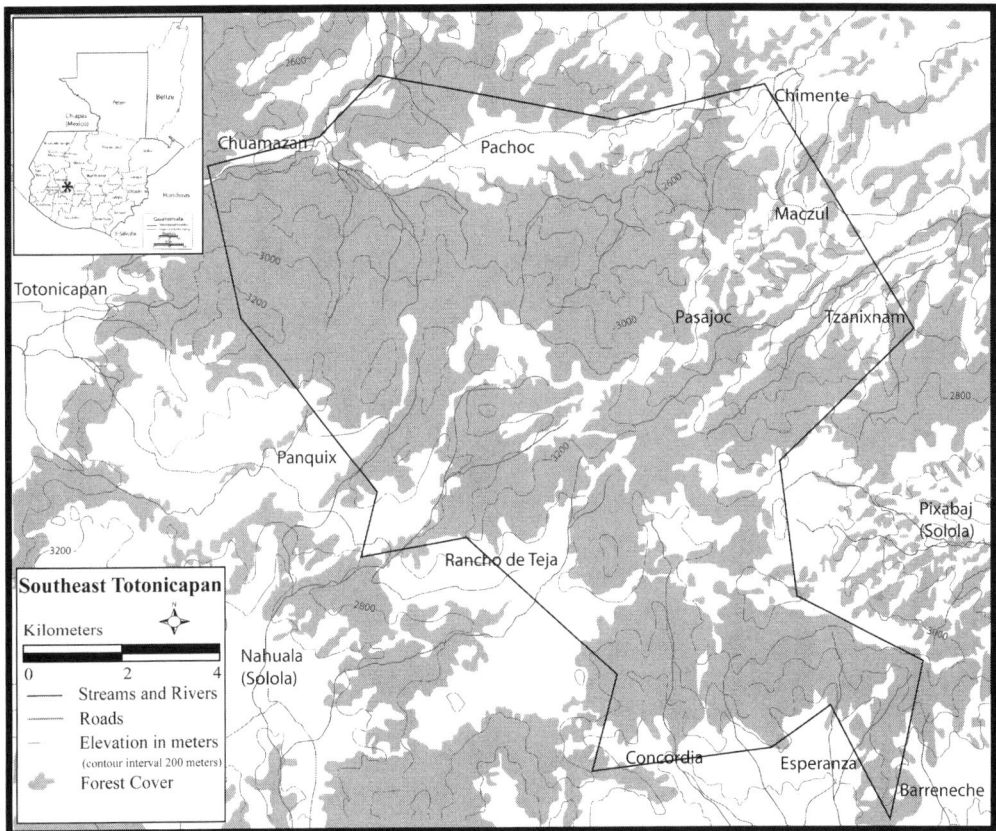

Figure 10.1. Southeast Totonicapán and Los Altos de San Miguel Regional Municipal Park.

1970s. Veblen (1975, 1978) highlighted the resilience of pine species in the face of centuries of human use, the economic importance of the forests for local communities, and the cultural attitudes and forest vigilance traditions of the K'iche' of Totonicapán. Subsequent studies corroborated many of Veblen's findings, although important changes were also documented (Utting 1993; Elias 1997). Beginning in the early 1980s, a constellation of social, political, and ecological factors transformed the forest conservation dynamic in the area, leading to an increase in forest degradation and a process of renegotiation in forest governance (Utting 1993).

In addition to its reputation for forest conservation, Totonicapán is also one of the best-known examples of Indian self-governance and political power in Guatemala. Over 90 percent of the population of the county of Totonicapán are K'iche' ethnicity, and as in many other majority Indian locations in the highlands, governance has historically involved an arrangement of parallel political institutions, one representative of the state (the county government) and one representative of Indian communities. Political representation of Indian communities has traditionally taken place through a council of elders known as the Principals and through the village-level Alcaldes Auxiliares (communal mayors) (Arias 1990; Grandin 2000). These customary councils include several offices responsible for village administrative tasks, such as the recording of births and deaths, as well as the management of natural and cultural resources, such as forests, sacred sites, boundaries, and water sources. Today, the Indigenous/non-Indigenous dichotomy is less clear, as Totonicapán typically elects Indigenous officials to its local government posts, but the institutions remain distinct.

Although the Principals lost influence in many communities throughout the highlands in the 1970s (Falla 2001), in Totonicapán they appear to have maintained considerable influence into the early 1980s, especially regarding issues of forest governance. By 1988, however, this group of elders was increasingly seen by some county residents as being a corrupt gerontocracy biased toward the city of Totonicapán to the exclusion of the more rural communities. The waning influence of the Principals as forest governors coincided with the poverty and aftermath of Guatemala's internal conflict, the ascendancy and increasing influence of national political parties, as well as a more than doubling of the population since the 1970s (Ekern 2001, 2006; Tiu and Garcia 2003). The combination of these factors led to a wave of forest degradation and resource piracy involving an increase in the harvesting of timber resources, firewood extraction, and the destructive collection of the inner bark of a pine species (*Pinus ayacahuite*) for use in the tanning industry. Studies by Guatemalan researchers revealed that declines in forest cover in Totonicapán reached as much as 15 percent between 1972 and the late 1980s, with 40 percent forest loss in select locations (Utting 1993: 60). This human-induced forest degradation has been exacerbated by periodic outbreaks of the round-headed pine beetle (*Dendroctonus adjunctus*) and associated forest fires.

Concern over forest degradation and associated threats to water resources led, in 1994, to the formation of a council of micro-watershed organizations who took the lead in filling the void in forest vigilance. The watershed organizations grew out of a combination of the traditional village-level work crews and the new demands of water infrastructure of the 1980s, when cistern and PVC piping technologies became available through development projects, bringing water from mountainside springs into household compounds. The work crews that installed this infrastructure also became involved in patrolling the water sources and the forests surrounding them, supplanting, in some areas, the traditional institution of the village-designated forest guard. The union of the watershed organizations into the Committee for the Conservation of the Communal Forests of Totonicapán initially involved twenty-three village organizations, expanding to sixty-three member committees by 1995. The process had been encouraged by remnant elements of the Principals concerned with the vacuum in forest governance.

"A Forest with Many Fathers": Los Altos de San Miguel Regional Municipal Park, 1997–2004

The grassroots response to the problem of forest degradation in Totonicapán drew the attention of internationally linked conservation organizations working in Guatemala, most notably Greenpeace Central America and the Swiss NGO Helvetas. Seeking to reinforce the mission of the watershed committee, these organizations provided technical, financial, and advisory assistance and helped to give rise to the Maya K'iche' environmental organization Ulew Che' Ja' (UCJ), a Maya name meaning Earth, Trees, and Water.

Helvetas's work in Totonicapán was linked to its ProBosques program and part of its broader efforts toward decentralizing forest management and reinforcing local forest governance throughout the western highlands through the creation of RMPs. Working with CONAP, Helvetas secured RMP status for several communal and municipal forests in the western highlands. The RMP was seen as an appropriate designation for the highland communal forests because it incorporates a degree of flexibility regarding use rights and lends itself well to a comanagement arrangement. Los Altos de San Miguel RMP encompasses part or all of nine major towns and several smaller settlements that surround the extensive forest of the Sierra Madre, most of which are located above 2500 meters and whose combined population is more than 20,000 people. Other important RMPs of the region include Zunil, Quetzaltenango, and Cantel, but Los Altos de San Miguel is by far the largest. At more than 16,000 hectares it is nearly three times the size of nearby Quetzaltenango RMP, the next largest in the highlands RMP network. In addition to the large population in and around the park, issues regarding land and forest tenure there are among the most complex in Guatemala's system of protected areas, making Los Altos de San Miguel an especially complicated situation.

Planning for this park was by some accounts participatory and involved the spectrum of stakeholders in the county (Greenpeace 1998; Aguilar and Skarwan 2000). In the years leading up to the park declaration, Greenpeace and Helvetas sponsored a number of workshops on watershed and protected area management to which community representatives were invited. An inventory of the more than 1000 springs in the mountains was also conducted. Their highly visible Campaign to Save the Pinabete received local and national attention. Radio campaigns to publicize the protected area were mounted as well. The ProBosques program expended considerable resources to sponsor technical studies, including a comprehensive biodiversity survey and a draft management plan for the park, which included discussion of a spectrum of resource-use regimes within the park polygon. According to Guatemalan conservationist Estuardo Secaira (pers. comm., October 2006), the Los Altos de San Miguel RMP could be considered Guatemala's first experience with consultation. As Greenpeace asserted in their book *Los Bosques de Totonicapán* (1998: 46), "the communities decided to declare the communal forest a protected area, since they recognized that this would be the best way to preserve their natural heritage."

In retrospect, however, there appears to have been a key group of stakeholders that was marginalized in the process. In the wake of the fall of the Principals, the general assembly of communal mayors itself was in a state of transition. Without their official link to the county government and without, for a period, an official meeting place, it appeared to some as if the Indigenous polity was being displaced altogether by the county government and UCJ. In Zone 2 of Totonicapán's urban center, during the mid-1990s several years passed with no one stepping forward to take on the role of communal mayor. During the late 1990s, however, the assembly reconvened with renewed vigor, implementing an election process for the governing council (in contrast to the selection process used for the Principals) and harnessing the strength of a new generation of educated K'iche's (Ekern 2001, 2006).

Thus, the creation of the park and the rise of UCJ were paralleled by a reorganization of the customary Indigenous governing body. The mayors reinvented themselves in the process, a fact that is reflected in their choice of a new name. Historically the mayors have been referred to as Alcaldes Auxiliares, in reference to their role of reporting deaths and births and other business to county officials representative of the central government.

In the late 1990s, the mayors began to refer to themselves by the arguably more autonomous term Alcaldes Comunales de los 48 Cantones (the Communal Mayors of the 48 Towns; hereafter AC48).

These changes occurred in the context of an increasingly powerful and assertive county government that is well funded and, through the comanagement agreement with CONAP and UCJ, with an apparently popular mandate to protect the forests. The non-Indigenous county mayor became a key promoter of the park. In 2000, however, a scandal in UCJ involving the embezzlement of several thousand dollars by the NGO's secretary led to rumors that the forest was being turned into a national park, that local people would lose access, and that it had been sold to foreigners. The AC48 stepped in, calling for communities to disassociate themselves and their water committees from UCJ (Ekern 2001, 2006), and in August 2003, a special envoy of communal mayors traveled to the CONAP office in Guatemala to ask that the protected area be dissolved.

UCJ managed to survive this controversy. It continued to attract foreign donors, shifting its strategy from patrolling the forest to reforestation while, for a time at least, recasting itself as a branch of the AC48.[2] The AC48 meanwhile continued to assert its role in the governance of the county as the legitimate representative of the Pueblo Indigena, the Indigenous population of Totonicapán. Its election processes came to be major public events, drawing thousands and filling auditoriums.

Implementation of the protected area, as it was conceived of in 1997, was essentially abandoned after the scandal, although its legal status was not lifted despite the 2003 request. The rivalry between the AC48, UCJ, the county government, and an increasingly assertive state forestry agency reached a new apogee with negotiations over the management of a major round-headed pine beetle outbreak that gained national attention in 2004. I discuss this new round of contestation after addressing some of the impacts on mountain villages and their forest-dependent livelihoods resulting from the park designation.

Los Altos de San Miguel Regional Municipal Park: Impacts on Livelihoods

The polygon used to delimit the area of the RMP in Totonicapán suggests a degree of spatial unity that is not reflected in the landscape or in the lived experiences on the ground. In terms of forest tenure, the park and its buffer zone (that was never fully defined) is a patchwork of often contested holdings used and policed by village-level polities and patrilineal clans, interspersed with areas of communal forest shared by the people of the county of Totonicapán as a whole. Numerous disputes over forest commons continue to occur and involve user groups seeking greater decision-making power in managing the forests that surround them.

The contemporary use of the forest is also a complex issue and one that the protected area planners did not adequately take into account. A variety of subsistence and commercial uses continue to sustain mountain communities, including both timber and nontimber forest products and livestock grazing (principally sheep). Most prominent among these activities is the collection and sale of firewood and the harvest of large trees for lumber and furniture-making. In general, the firewood trade is focused in the western portion of the Sierra Madre, where several towns located along the main roads into the city of Totonicapán are able to take advantage of the demands of city and suburban areas, including the near-industrial-scale demands of bakeries, for which firewood is the primary source of cooking fuel. Historically, the impacts of the trade in firewood have been mediated by the low-tech nature of extraction, and many of those who gain supplemental income from the sale of firewood continue to use horses, mules, and their own backs to haul their product into town. In the past decade or so, however, greater access to pick-up trucks and chainsaws has enabled many mountain villagers to specialize in firewood sales, and the thinning of nearby forests has become apparent.

Distant from the city environs, especially in the southeast of the Sierra Madre in the vicinity of towns such as Tzanixnam and Barreneche, forest-based livelihoods continue to involve the harvest of mature timber resources for the production and sale of lumber and furniture. The consequences of this are evident in the map of forest cover in the county (see figure 10.1). The eastern portion of the Sierra Madre shows considerably more fragmentation than the western areas, a testament to several generations of cutting and carpentry and the persistence of relatively large sheep herds.[3] Extensive and in some cases badly eroded grazing lands dominate significant portions of the Sierra Madre.

My findings suggest that the creation of the RMP influenced this contemporary pattern in several ways. According to interviews in the northwestern Sierra Madre village of Chuamazan, in response to the increased vigilance of the forests and the subsequent declaration of the RMP, many villagers shifted from carpentry and furniture-making to the more lucrative and, perhaps, more easily concealed activity of firewood collection and sale. Many in Chuamazan and other villages also liquidated their extensive sheep herds in response to warnings from UCJ and supporters of the park.

In the eastern village of Pasajoc, distant from the city of Totonicapán, the livelihood staples of the area remain intact. This generally poorer and more remote community continues to be a place of woodcutting for carpentry and furniture-making by men and boys, and several households maintain sheep herds often in excess of thirty head, shepherded by women and children in the mountains. These activities, intensified in recent decades as village populations have grown and changing consumption patterns have created demand for more cash income, have transformed the forests surrounding the village in terms of cover and composition, leading to erosion and slope instability. Important conservation measures in Pasajoc remain in place, including forest patrols and a chainsaw ban (trees are felled with axes and boards and beams are ripped from logs using hand saws, rather than chainsaws as in other nearby areas) enforced by local forest guards, but the depletion of large trees, principally white pine (*Pinus ayacahuite*) and Guatemalan fir (*Abies guatemalensis*), continues.

The RMP declaration cannot be said to have had no effect on forest management and forest-dependent livelihoods in Totonicapán. In important ways it appears to have changed the livelihood practices of certain villages by discouraging dependence on timber resources for small carpentry enterprises and reducing sheep herds. Its effects were uneven, however, impacting those closer to the city and thus more easily policed, while allowing those distant from the city center to continue as before. The creation of the protected area, although it may be said to have helped raise popular consciousness regarding the importance of the forests, never addressed the livelihood concerns of those dependent on the forest and grazing commons or the related issue of deteriorating forest health.

Some scholars critical of the designation of the protected area have suggested that the degree of restrictions on livelihood activities have had an inverse relationship with protection. The case of the pinabete tree protection efforts of the 1980s is an example where outright prohibition of cutting the tree led to the abandonment of community norms of moderate use and increases in illegal harvest (Tiu and Garcia 2003: 222; Elias and Wittman 2005). This suggests that the issue of forest use rights, including those with commercial values associated with them, must be addressed by Totonicapán's leadership in the interests of healthy forests and communities, a point I return to in the next section.

Land, Trees, and Water: New Contexts for Debate, 2004–2006

While inhabitants of the mountain villages have struggled to ensure the economic vitality of their communities, the broader questions of large-scale forest management have been debated since the early 2000s by several stakeholders, including the AC48, UCJ, an absentee protected areas agency (CONAP), and the Guatemalan National Forestry Agency (INAB). Events in recent years have heightened the sense of urgency regarding issues of forest and watershed health, management, and access. Arguably the most significant of the recent events—which also include the perceived threat of water privatization and a mining concession—from the standpoint of my discussions here was the social, ecological, and political fallout from a serious pine beetle outbreak. The handling of this outbreak helped further reconfigure resource governance in Totonicapán.

The most serious consequence of forest pressures generated by forest-dependent livelihoods is a cascading effect at the landscape scale involving the relationship between forest degradation, round-headed pine beetle outbreaks, and forest fires (Billings et al. 2004). The round-headed pine beetle has a historic presence in Totonicapán and may play an important role in creating low-level disturbance of the forest ecosystem and perpetuating the existence of pine forests that might otherwise give way to more shade-tolerant species (Veblen 1975). Yet, outbreaks may also be symptomatic of a forest ecosystem under stress. The preference of woodcutters producing lumber for sale in the furniture industry or elsewhere is for white pine and fir, because these are less resinous and have a finer grain. When these species are removed, *Pinus rudis*, the other important pine species above 3000 meters and the preferred host of the pine beetle, is left to predominate. Thus, portions of the Sierra Madre have become vulnerable to beetle outbreaks such as the one that occurred in 2004, affecting an estimated 45 hectares (figure 10.2).

The 2004 beetle outbreak and the question of forest management was perhaps the first time since the collapse of the park agreement that the AC48, UCJ, and state agencies found reason to begin serious discussions of collaborative forest management. State response to the outbreak, which is said to have been precipitated by a devastating fire in 1998, was slow at best and may have been unwelcome given historic attempts to use beetle outbreaks to do salvage logging, often taking more timber than that actually affected by the pest (Reddy 2002). Indeed, in 2004–2005, INAB sought to

Figure 10.2. Forest impacts in Totonicapán's Sierra Madre from the round-headed pine beetle outbreak of 2004 and subsequent removal of diseased trees.

intervene and do salvage logging operations that would also have involved extensive clear-cuts. In spite of a shared sense of the need for action on the part of some local people, the plan was rejected by the AC48 and UCJ. The dominance of INAB and the near-complete absence of CONAP in the course of the deliberations highlighted the ambiguous nature of the state's role in managing the protected area and perhaps also its desire to influence forest management in the direction of commercial forestry.

Arguably the most significant outcome of the conflict surrounding the beetle outbreak was the marginalization and effective dissolution of the once prominent Indigenous NGO UCJ. Since the corruption scandal involving UCJ in 2000, the NGO had been on shaky ground relative to its constituency, but it continued to attract the financial and technical support of international donors because, as a legally incorporated NGO, the group served easily as a conduit for funds. Most of these funds went toward reforestation efforts, especially the cultivation of native tree seedlings in a tree nursery just north of the urban center. The promise of tree seedlings to plant around village water sources and micro-watersheds continued to

Figure 10.3. A communal mayor of the AC48's *junta directiva* holds aloft the *barra*, symbol of Indigenous office, at a public gathering.

draw village work crews to volunteer at the nursery, but the operation was increasingly eyed with a degree of resentment by the AC48. Though the AC48 found common cause with UCJ, sharing the stage at public events became an uncomfortable affair, with both *junta directivas* (leadership councils) carrying their own *barras*, the staffs of office that the AC48 consider a near sacred symbol of their community authority (figure 10.3).

In 2006, the leadership of UCJ publicly opposed a new cutting plan intended to address the pine beetle problem, which, the organization alleged, was approved by the AC48. The AC48 responded swiftly and decisively to the opposition, making it clear in a memo addressed to the People of Totonicapán and UCJ that they had not approved the plan and that, regardless, any decision on the management of the pine beetle threat would be the result of a consultation process directed exclusively by them. The AC48 followed the memo with action, evicting UCJ from their office in the communal meeting hall and taking over the tree nursery, which sits on communal land. These actions had the effect of further delegitimizing UCJ in the eyes of the people and its donor agencies.

Lessons and Directions for the Future of the Communal Forests of Totonicapán

Several key questions have arisen in the wake of the declaration of the Los Altos de San Miguel RMP in 1997. What did the process of the declaration look like and to what extent did it involve those who should be recognized as the rights-holders? What were the implications for those who depend most directly on the forest for their livelihoods? What have been the consequences for Totonicapán's forest management institutions and semi-autonomous Indigenous governance structure? Finally, what hope is there that forest and rangeland degradation will be arrested, especially in the interest of forest and hydrological resources, but also in the interest of the Sierra Madre's rich biodiversity? The answers to each of these questions are complex and at times contradictory, as I have suggested. The outcome of the declaration of the protected area was certainly not what was intended by the NGO and CONAP staff that pushed the implementation, but it has had several unintended consequences, not the least of which was to help strengthen and restore, through a process of resistance and reinvention, the historically important council of Indigenous communal mayors that I have referred to here as the AC48.

Arturo Escobar described the contemporary constellation of territory, ecology, and culture as a historical moment resulting from the "irruption of the biological as a global problem, on the one hand; and the irruption of the cultural and the ethnic on the other" (Escobar 1998: 63). The experiences in Totonicapán and in Guatemala generally are a fine illustration of this. The attempts to expand protected areas in the southwestern highlands were informed by international discourses on the importance of biodiversity conservation, including, to a certain extent, the emerging discussion of local and Indigenous participation in planning and implementation. National policy had not come so far by 1997 to fully account for the second component of Escobar's historical moment, in this case the pan-Maya movement for cultural rights and recognition, including control over communal territories and the potent local manifestations of the movement that is Totonicapán (Ekern 2006). Although throughout the initial process of protected area designation the local people of the county were certainly seen as important stakeholders, recognizing them as "rights-holders" did not happen.

But could it have happened? As I have described, the AC48 had not consolidated its current status within the county, had not yet recovered from its fractured relationship to the Principals in the late 1980s, and certainly had not been recognized nationally for its cultural importance in what has come to be known as *la juridica Maya*, customary Mayan law. In the absence of an authoritative body to recognize as the representatives of the "rights-holders," a local NGO was created, given legal standing as such, and propped up as the authority over forests. This provided perhaps the final inspiration for those interested in preserving the traditional council of mayors to step up and declare their own primacy in matters pertaining to the forests. So, although the representation that the crisis was used by municipal officials to make their own bid for control over the forests is important, it should also be clear that the foreign NGO/local NGO (UCJ) alliance was one born of necessity, created with the legitimate desire to protect forests in a time of vulnerability. With its near-complete dissolution, however, there is a least one fewer "father" of the forest to contend with as other interested parties, including the state agencies CONAP and INAB, as well as the county government deal more directly with the legitimate representatives of the Pueblo Indigena in the important and difficult work of balancing the conservation and development goals of the area. In conclusion, I identify some of the promising directions this work may take, as well as some caveats.

First, the growing enthusiasm for nationally and internationally recognized Indigenous Peoples' and Community Conserved Territories and Areas (ICCAs) (chapters 2, 3, 11, and 12) may hold some promise for the communal territories of Totonicapán.[4] It would seem entirely appropriate that Totonicapán's well-known case of Indigenous conservation—arguably the best known in all of Guatemala if not Central America—should be recognized in a special category acknowledging the historical role played by local K'iche' communities. This course of action was recommended over a decade ago by the Nature Conservancy's Estuardo Secaira in his important work on conservation, the pan-Maya Movement, and Maya spirituality in Guatemala (Secaira 2000). However, relegating the municipal government to a secondary role in governance would be politically untenable and also historically inconsistent, because the municipal forest office has for over a century played at least some role in forest vigilance, hiring forest guards, firefighters, and nursery extensionists with its government budget.

Alternatively, smaller scale ICCAs might be declared within the larger protected area. These could, for example, encompass important sacred sites as well as community forests. Such a move to recognize Indigenous peoples' governance of sacred natural sites in the protected area would dovetail with a current effort for a law on the protection of sacred natural sites in Guatemala being spearheaded by Oxlajuj Ajpop, an organization of Mayan spiritual leaders that is a member organization of the ICCA Consortium (chapter 12), with support from the Nature Conservancy, the IUCN's Cultural and Spiritual Values of Protected Areas specialist group, and the Netherlands-based NGO COMPAS (Gomez 2010). Several sites in the mountains might be said to lend themselves to such a special category, such as the dense forests that surround the complex of altars and religious gathering sites in the far west of the Sierra Madre. This could contribute to greater awareness of the historical and cultural significance of the mountains of Totonicapán, while also furthering the goal of recognizing ICCAs throughout Guatemala. However, considerable difficulty in creating such ICCAs would be encountered in the mapping process. Defining boundaries has often been a hazardous endeavor in the highlands in general and in Totonicapán in particular, with several recent examples of tense standoffs over communal property boundaries.

There is also the prospect for a refined shared governance arrangement for the communal forest. Conceivably, a new designation could be implemented that establishes a formal comanagement agreement between the county government and its forestry office (now increasingly populated with Maya K'iche' professionals) and the AC48 with its representative council of community mayors. This is, indeed, the de facto reality on the ground, and it can now be said that a considerable degree of communal ownership by the Pueblo Indigena has been recognized by the municipal government. There is an AC48 forestry office staffed by a university-trained forester who acts on behalf of the AC48 and is presumably more capable of working directly with the communities in their efforts to secure both livelihoods and forest health. This situation maintains the status quo with regard to de jure forest ownership (with the municipal government as owner/manager of the park), but it could translate into a greater degree of local decision-making power; financial and technical support for mountain communities; and more effective, adaptive, and sustainable management strategies.

However, if the AC48 is able to continue the successful reestablishment of its authority over communal resources, and if the municipal forest office seeks to better establish its legitimacy as a comanager of these, both will have to respond to the livelihood needs of those dependent on the forest and grazing commons, primarily the mountain communities. An important step toward addressing these concerns is to better understand the contemporary spatial patterns and social dynamics of forest use. Past studies (for example, Utting 1993) were undertaken prior to contemporary issues of transnational migration and new consumption patterns, whereas more contemporary studies (for example, Tiu and Garcia 2003) have tended to emphasize a unidirectional loss of culture and generation change. A more promising direction for research is suggested by scholars who have looked at the effects of transnational migration on forests and communities in Latin America, where financial remittances are being used to fortify and sustain rural households, in some cases encouraging reforestation and forest regeneration through land abandonment (Bebbington 2000; Klooster 2003). Hecht (2004) has shown that contemporary forest regeneration in El Salvador can be attributed in part to environmental activism, with local and international NGOs' reforestation work suggesting the power of grassroots environmentalism to address forest degradation.

Finally, there is a great deal of interest in financial incentive programs that can provide funds to local people for implementing sustainable management practices, including reforestation on private and communal holdings. So far the implementation of these programs has been limited, due in part to the sometimes complicated burden of demonstrating unquestionable ownership over the property. Several projects under the Forest Incentives Program nonetheless have been initiated in Totonicapán as of this writing. Another incipient actor on the forest landscape in Guatemala, and indeed throughout the global South, is the REDD+ program of the United Nations Food and Agriculture Organization, a program that has already proven controversial among Indigenous peoples concerned that it could herald in a new era of land-grabbing similar to those initiated by international conservation or biofuels (Larson et al. 2010: 218–21). The ability of the AC48 and the municipal forest office to navigate these waters, facilitating the flow of benefits into the hands of forest-dependent communities while buffering them from the predations of transnational capital, will be an important indicator of their effectiveness as contemporary land managers.

There are concerns, however, that the AC48 will increasingly become a stepping stone for leaders seeking to get involved in national level politics, thereby diminishing the significance of the institution and inviting a degree of political favoritism and clientelism that will taint the spirit of *k'ax kol*, the "suffering for community" that service in traditional offices embodies (Ekern 2006). This is certainly not a situation unique to Totonicapán, as traditional and customary governance and resource management institutions throughout the global South are transformed by greater interaction with national and international politics, markets, and ideologies (Li 2004). The increased politicization of the forests—that is, the leveraging of their cultural and economic significance for political ends—will continue to present the Pueblo Indigena of Totonicapán with challenges to the integrity of their local governance and management traditions.

The negotiations and discussions surrounding the forest, grazing, and water commons management in the Sierra Madre of Totonicapán have entered a new era. The experiences of the 1980s and 1990s, including grassroots mobilization to head off forest degradation, the declaration of a nationally recognized protected area, the rise and fall of an Indigenous NGO, and the reemergence of an Indigenous governing body, have potentially left the population and its leadership with a set of lessons that may be applied to current and future scenarios. A measure of Indigenous political autonomy has been consolidated even as the county government has also grown in influence. Conservation policies in Totonicapán may be said to be coming of age in a period of greater awareness of rights-based approaches to conservation, with considerable effort in the directions of "conservation through cultural survival" (Stevens 1997a) and conservation through self-determination (Nietschmann 1992a, 1997). The struggles to deal with the rapidly changing political and social landscapes of the 1980s and 1990s may be said to have yielded a certain degree of stability at the close of the first decade of the twenty-first century, although the enduring social and ecological challenges of resource management remain, and the questions of whether natural resource management and conservation will take the form of a formally designated protected area, what form of protected area governance will be implemented, and whether or not ICCAs will be recognized may well reemerge.

Acknowledgments

I would like to thank Stan Stevens for his work on this volume and for his guidance and inspiration in all stages of this research project. I thank also the Department of Geosciences at the University of Massachusetts Amherst, and the Fulbright-Hays program for its financial support of the fieldwork. Finally, I thank the people of Totonicapán, especially Alejandro Alvarado, Agustín Par, the communities of Chuamazan and Pasajoc, and Pablo Poncio of Pastoral de la Tierra for their assistance, insights, and friendship.

Notes

1. Totonicapán is the name of one of Guatemala's twenty-two departments. It is also the name of the *municipio* (translated here as county) of Totonicapán, which is the host of the departmental capital, a city of roughly 10,000, also called Totonicapán. Here I refer to the county of Totonicapán when using the name, unless otherwise specified.

2. The shared space of forest vigilance includes both the forest and the meeting hall, which the two organizations shared until UCJ was evicted in 2008.

3. It should also be noted that forest fragmentation in the eastern Sierra was likely increased by the social impacts of the internal conflict of the 1980s, due to the area's proximity to the borders with the departments of Sololá and Quiché.

4. The potential for ICCA recognition in Totonicapán was highlighted by its hosting of the ICCA Consortium's first regional meeting in Mesoamerica, in March 2013.

CHAPTER ELEVEN

Indigenous Peoples' and Community Conserved Territories and Areas in the High Himalaya

Recognition and Rights in Nepal's National Parks

Stan Stevens

In Nepal, as in many other parts of the world, Indigenous peoples continue to protect sacred natural sites, collectively manage forest and grazing commons, and maintain sustainable land-use practices even after their territories have been expropriated and made state-administered protected areas. As in many other countries—and notwithstanding international treaty obligations and guidance from the IUCN and CBD—these customary practices are often ignored or suppressed by state authorities despite their cultural, livelihood, and conservation significance. This violates Indigenous peoples' rights to territory, culture, self-governance, and access to and management of lands, waters, and resources, while diminishing protected areas' conservation effectiveness and potential.

This chapter examines the conservation and human rights dynamics created by the overlap in the high Himalayan region of Nepal of national parks and Indigenous peoples' territories, institutions, and practices that meet IUCN criteria for Indigenous Peoples' and Community Conserved Territories and Areas (ICCAs). Here a set of inhabited protected areas has been established in the customary territories of Indigenous peoples in a Fourth World social and political context. Although many of their institutions and practices have been officially ignored or supplanted, Indigenous peoples continue to uphold values and maintain customary land-use and management systems that make important contributions to conservation. In some cases, they have adapted or expanded these to address new conservation challenges and goals. In this chapter I examine the status of Indigenous peoples' ICCAs and rights in four large, inhabited high Himalayan national parks, particularly Sagarmatha (Mount Everest/Chomolungma) National Park and World Heritage Site (SNP).[1]

Nepal's National Political and Social Context

The country of Nepal, a Hindu kingdom from the establishment of the state in the late eighteenth century until 2008, has an ethnically diverse population of 26 million that includes fifty-nine state-recognized Indigenous peoples who together constitute 37 percent (2001) or more of the total population. The 2002 National Foundation for Development of Indigenous Nationalities Act defines *Adivasi janajati* as those ethnic groups or communities that "have their own mother tongue and traditional customs, distinct cultural identity, distinct social structure and written or oral history of their own." A traditional homeland or geographic area is also often considered to be an important characteristic (LAHURNIP n.d.). The customary territories of these peoples, while not yet mapped, appear to compose the majority of Nepal's total land area and almost all the high Himalayan region. None of Nepal's Indigenous peoples, however, have legally recognized territories or reserves. Current national law does not recognize customary territories, collectively owned land, customary law, Indigenous peoples' governance systems, or customary land-use and management practices.

These Indigenous peoples' territories, along with scores of formerly independent states, were incorporated into the kingdom of Nepal by conquest. Since the unification of Nepal, a Hindu high-caste ethnic elite has dominated national society, politics, and the state bureaucracy. For Indigenous peoples, the result has been generations of discrimination and oppression. From the perspective of the Nepal Indigenous peoples movement, Nepali-speaking upper Hindu castes are a dominant national ethnic elite that has socially, politically, and economically excluded and marginalized Nepal's diverse Indigenous peoples for two centuries. This ethnic elite is said to have used control of the Nepal state to expropriate Indigenous peoples' customary territories (forcibly annexing many of them into the Nepal empire in the late eighteenth and early nineteenth centuries through military conquest), nationalize Indigenous peoples' collectively owned lands in the 1950s and 1960s, impose new governance institutions, and attempt to coercively assimilate Indigenous peoples to create a single national culture based on their own religion, language, and customs (Battachan 2000, n.d.; Lawotri 2001; Gurung 2003; Tamang 2003; Upreti and Adhikari 2006; Anaya 2009b; Gurung 2009; Stevens 2014; Limbu n.d.). Most of the Maoist revolutionary forces that fought in the 1996–2006 People's War that led to the end of the monarchy and to the declaration of a federal republic were Indigenous people. The interim government's 2007 agreement to ratify the International Labour Organization Convention 169 Concerning Indigenous and Tribal Peoples in Independent Countries (ILO 169)—the first country in Asia to do so—and vote in the UN General Assembly in favor of the United Nations Declaration on the Rights of Indigenous Peoples (UNDRIP) ended a prolonged national strike and other agitation for Indigenous rights. Lack of implementation of ILO 169 thus far, however, has led to concern that the ethnic elite and the political parties they control do not intend to honor the rights affirmed in ILO 169 and UNDRIP or to create Indigenous peoples' autonomous states or administrative areas within the federal republic. This has been a major factor in recent national political discord and insecurity (Gurung 2009; for more details, see Stevens 2013, 2014).

Himalayan National Parks and Indigenous Rights

Since the early 1970s, Nepal has established an extensive national network of thirty-two protected areas. These include ten national parks, six conservation areas, three wildlife reserves, one hunting reserve, and twelve national park or wildlife reserve buffer zones.[2] More than 23 percent of the total area of the country is now in protected areas.

Among Nepal's protected areas, the Himalayan protected areas are particularly extensive. The nineteen Himalayan protected areas, which constitute about 19 percent of the total area of Nepal, account for 83 percent of the total area in protected areas, including 77 percent of the area in national parks, 99 percent of the land in conservation areas, and 61 percent of the area in buffer zones. Seven of Nepal's ten national parks are in the Himalaya. Four of these Himalayan national parks are located in the high Himalaya and include substantial regions above 3500 meters (figure 11.1).

Figure 11.1. High Himalayan national parks of Nepal.

These high Himalayan national parks—SNP, Makalu-Barun (M-BNP), Langtang (LNP), and Shey-Phoksundo (S-PNP)—are the only Nepalese national parks larger than 1000 square kilometers. Together they constitute 73 percent of the total area in Nepal's national park system. All are in the customary territories and continuing homelands of Indigenous peoples.

The Himalayan region of Nepal is the homeland of at least thirty-seven of Nepal's fifty-nine state-recognized Indigenous peoples. It is a magnificent cultural landscape shaped by centuries of their settlement, land use, expressions of faith, care for sacred sites, and conservation stewardship through ICCAs. The four high Himalayan national parks are within the traditional territories of the Sharwa (Sherpa),[3] Dolpo-pa, Yolmo, Tamang, Lhomi, and Rai[4] peoples, most of whom continue to maintain their traditional socio-ecological systems (sometimes with significant recent modifications, such as participation in tourism development), including their permanent and seasonal settlements, seasonal transhumance patterns, customary land-use and collective land management practices, and custodianship and protection of sacred natural sites within what are now national parks. None of these national parks were established with the consent of Indigenous peoples and other resident communities. Indeed, SNP, LNP, and M-BNP were all established over the strong objections of resident Indigenous peoples (Stevens 1993; Battachan 2000). James Anaya (2009b), the

United Nations Special Rapporteur on the Rights of Indigenous Peoples, noted in his country report on the status of Indigenous peoples in Nepal that "in the Himalayas, most of the land areas of the six existing national parks cover Adivasi Janajati traditional lands. The National Parks and Wildlife Conservation Act provides no recognition of indigenous peoples' right to consultation or to access their traditional lands and resources, while giving quasi-judicial powers to the park chief wardens."

Although the establishment of these national parks has adversely affected Indigenous peoples' customary land-use and management systems and undermined their self-governance and rights, resident peoples were not displaced altogether as they were in lowland national parks and wildlife reserves (Brown 1997; McLean 1999; Müller-Böker 1999; Battachan 2000; McLean and Straede 2003).[5] They retained individual title to their houses and fields and continued to inhabit and use them as enclaves of private lands within the parks. Their collectively owned and managed forests and grazing lands, however, were nationalized and placed under national park administration (and today constitute most or all of the area of these parks). Moreover, Indigenous peoples lost legally recognized self-governance over their territories when new state policies, regulations, and enforcement mechanisms superseded and replaced customary village authority and institutional arrangements for collectively managing forests, grazing lands, cultural sites, and other areas.[6] This did not mean, however, that all villages simply abandoned responsibility for commons and sacred sites. Instead, despite lack of legal status, some villages have maintained some or all of their institutions and practices. This means that these national parks have been superimposed over what can be considered to have been, in effect, preexisting—and in some cases still maintained —ICCAs.

The high Himalayan national parks have been sharply criticized by resident Indigenous peoples for undermining their livelihoods, welfare, development, cultural integrity, and self-governance. Strict restrictions imposed on their hunting, forest use, swidden agriculture, and other land-use and management practices (Stevens 1993; Battachan 2000; Tamang 2003; Campbell 2005; Armbrecht 2009) and lack of respect for their custodianship of sacred natural sites has economically, culturally, socially, and politically dispossessed and disadvantaged them. Indigenous peoples' control of their territory and lives; their customary relationships with their lands, each other, and their spirits and gods; and their use and management of their forests, pastures, and cultural sites have all been undermined (Tamang 2003; Stevens 2009, 2010, 2013, 2014). Because national park policies and practices thus ignore Indigenous peoples' customary law and institutions, they violate multiple rights associated with cultural and social integrity, livelihoods, control of territory, self-governance and self-determination, and development (chapter 1; Stevens 2010, 2013, 2014). The widespread violation of Indigenous peoples' rights to territory, self-governance, use and management of natural resources, and cultural integrity in Nepal's national parks has attracted the concern of James Anaya (2009b), the UN Special Rapporteur on the Rights of Indigenous Peoples. He recommended that the Nepal Office of the UN High Commissioner on Human Rights investigate the situation and called for revision of Nepal's national park laws and policies to facilitate greater participation by Indigenous peoples in protected area management, guarantee their access to natural resources for subsistence use and an equitable share of protected area benefits, and provide redress for past loss of land and access to natural resources. Anaya suggested that remedy and redress should include "where possible, restoration of indigenous peoples' access to resources or a return of their land." Unfortunately, there has been no reply from the government of Nepal to these observations and recommendations. New national legislation will be required to bring the country's national parks into compliance with international protected area and Indigenous rights standards.

Himalayan National Park Regulations and Rights

The high Himalayan national parks are administered under the Himalayan National Park Regulations (1979). These are sometimes said to recognize the rights of residents to subsistence use of natural resources (Stevens 1997b; Ministry of Forests and Soil Conservation 2007), but they establish procedures for national park wardens to authorize conditional natural resource use privileges rather than acknowledging inalienable rights that the state has the responsibility to honor. At the discretion of park wardens, Indigenous peoples are allowed to continue to graze, cut wild grass for fodder, collect deadwood for use as fuel, fell trees and quarry stone for house construction, and gather some wild foods and medicines from their former village lands and commons. Access to these resources, however, is usually authorized on a scale far below former customary uses. Other customary use is banned altogether, including hunting, fishing, swidden (rotational forest farming), and the burning of forest floors or grasslands to improve grazing conditions. These bans and use restrictions ignore the importance of customary land use and management to Indigenous peoples' cultures and livelihoods and their roles in maintaining cultural landscapes and ecosystems (Stevens 1993, 1997b; Campbell 2005). There is no acknowledgement that land use in national parks should be subject to customary law, values, and practices. Neither natural resource management nor the protection and care of sacred places has been legally delegated to Indigenous peoples in any national park (despite a provision in the national park act for management by users groups).

There is also no recognition that Indigenous peoples should participate in protected area governance and management. The national parks instead are administered solely by the Department of National Parks and Wildlife Conservation (DNPWC). Unlike some of Nepal's other protected areas (conservation areas and buffer zones), none of the national parks are governed by Indigenous people or with them in shared governance arrangements. There are no national park advisory committees. No current national park wardens or senior DNPWC staff members are Indigenous people, and very few Indigenous peoples are employed as staff by the various Himalayan national parks. National park management plans are written and authorized in Kathmandu by the DNPWC and its consultants and authorized by the Ministry of Forests and Soil Conservation. Although in some cases Indigenous peoples have been consulted in the development of the laws, administrative rules, and management plans that affect them, Indigenous leaders often contend that they have not fully and effectively participated in their development. Certainly, Indigenous peoples cannot be said to have approved and authorized them through their free, prior, and informed consent, as required by UNDRIP.

Far from recognizing that Nepal now legally acknowledges Indigenous peoples and rights, the Nepal government avoids use of the term "Indigenous peoples" in protected area laws, administrative rules and regulations, and management plans. Indigenous peoples are instead referred to as "local inhabitants," "local people," "local residents," or "stakeholders." Alcorn and Royo (2007) identified this practice as one of several "red flags" that signal lack of respect for Indigenous rights.

Himalayan National Parks and Indigenous Peoples' and Community Conserved Territories and Areas

Indigenous peoples' conservation of territories and areas through their institutions and practices are not officially recognized in Nepal as ICCAs (chapter 2).[7] ICCAs are not recognized either as an appropriate form of governance for protected areas or as self-governing, culturally based systems within or outside of government-declared protected areas (Stevens 2008a, 2010, 2013, 2014; Jana and Paudel 2010).[8] As a result, the significant conservation contributions made by Indigenous peoples and local communities through their cultures and customary institutions go unacknowledged and unsupported. This is an important issue both because it fails to recognize Indigenous rights and because it threatens to undermine long-standing conservation achievements. As Jana and Paudel (2010: 29–30) observed, "State actions that favour centralized management of natural resources have largely hindered the continuity and growth of ICCAs in Nepal. . . . Yet, there are customary ICCAs with *de facto* status predating the establishment of official PAs [protected areas] that still coexist with the PAs and help maintain significant biodiversity."

The four high Himalayan national parks are all situated within Indigenous peoples' customary territories (see figure 11.2 for the overlap of SNP and the park's buffer zone and the Sharwa territories of Khumbu and Pharak). All were superimposed on diverse, preexisting Indigenous systems of collectively managed community forests, rangelands, and sacred places. This overlap persists today where Indigenous peoples continue to self-manage their lands and land use rather than simply to accept national park governance of them. The Sharwa, for example, have maintained many of their village-based land management practices and their region-wide cultural protection of wildlife within what is now SNP. Indeed, since the establishment of the national park, the Sharwa have created new conservation institutions on their own initiative, and some villages have adopted new institutions and regulations that have significantly strengthened conservation of community-managed commons. In some parts of their territory, Sharwa now impose on themselves and self-enforce conservation measures that are stricter than national park regulations. They do so even in some areas of the national park where state authorities have little or no on-the-ground administrative presence.[9]

Since 2008, when they attended an IUCN workshop on protected area governance, Sharwa leaders and some leaders of Indigenous peoples in several other high Himalayan protected areas have been referring to their conservation of their territory and local areas within it as "ICCAs." They find this to be a convenient umbrella term that usefully encompasses their conservation of their territory and particular areas through diverse institutions and practices, and hope that their use of it as an "engaged universal" (chapter 3; Tsing 2005) will give them increased national and

Indigenous and Community Conserved Territories in the Himalaya • 269

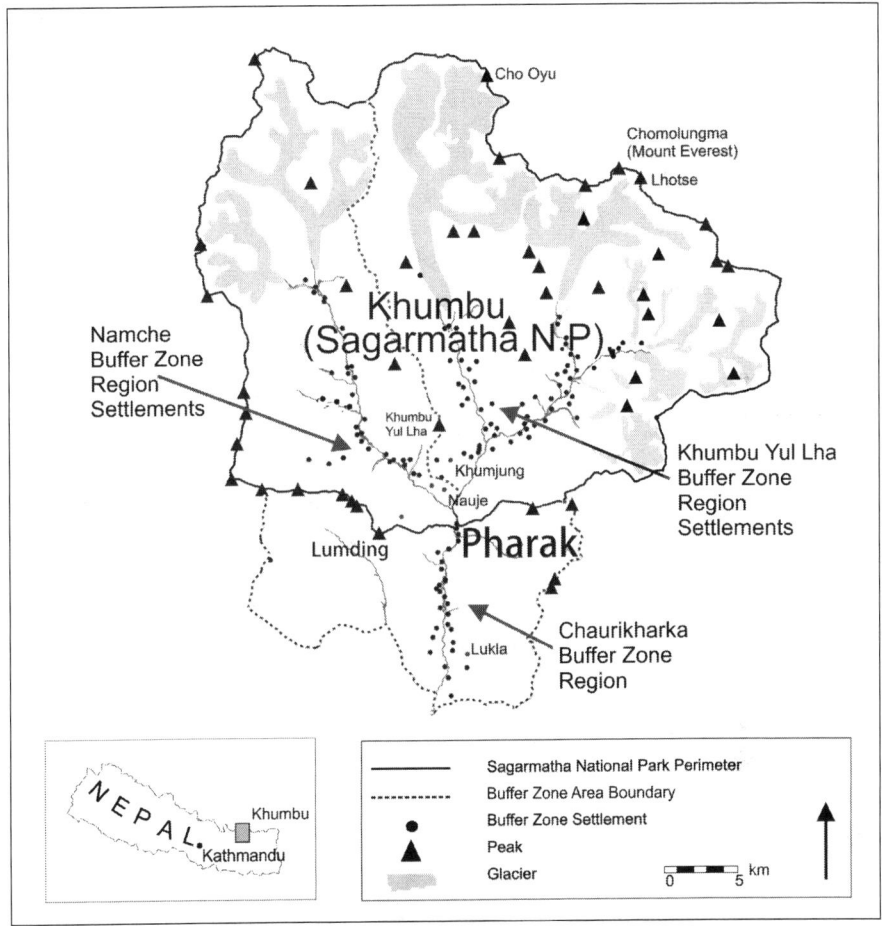

Figure 11.2. The Sharwa territories of Khumbu and Pharak and Sagarmatha (Mount Everest) National Park and Buffer Zone. Not all Sharwa settlements are shown. Notice the many settlements within the perimeter of the national park, all of which, along with all of Pharak, are legally part of the buffer zone. According to current Sharwa interpretation, the Khumbu *beyul* encompasses all of Khumbu; some Sharwa believe it also includes all or most of Pharak.

international legitimacy and help mobilize greater international assistance. Some leaders now use the concept of "ICCA" in regional, national, and international meetings and in interactions with the Nepal state, referring to "our ICCAs" in these contexts rather than using the many emic terms for their institutions and practices such as the Sharwa terms *kyak shing* (closed wood), *lami nati* (lama's forest), or *beyul* (hidden valley) or alternative etic concepts such as "community forest" or "sacred natural site." They hope that by thus framing their institutions and practices in current international conservation and rights discourse that they can better mobilize international recognition and support that may be critical in successfully convincing DNPWC officials of the importance of their conservation contributions and the need to better recognize and respect their self-governance and land management.

In some cases, Sharwa and other Indigenous peoples continue to maintain customary management practices even though these are not considered legitimate by the Nepal state and have no legal standing. Some maintain village governance of village lands, for example, even though the state does not recognize the existence of village assemblies, village law, or village lands. Sharwa and Dolpo-pa maintain customary systems of collective management of grazing, and Sharwa maintain some of their community forests even though the state has revoked their authority and replaced community forest management with new state-designed institutions that have different goals, institutional arrangements, and rules (see figure 2.4). And Sharwa and other peoples continue to protect sacred forests even though the state claims ownership and sole governance authority for them and does not acknowledge that they are sacred. In effect, Indigenous peoples maintain some aspects of customary self-governance and de facto stewardship of their territories, cultural sites, and natural resources despite state administrative pressures to abandon and deny them. This persistence reflects a sense of responsibility, a desire to continue to affirm their identities and valued ways of life, and conviction that these institutions and practices are important to culture, livelihood security, social cohesion, and environmental quality and sustainability.

The areas involved can be large. Sharwa cultural and conservation leaders maintain that their ICCAs not only include areas and sites within SNP but also encompass its entire area. They understand all of Khumbu to be a sacred site and to be conserved through their way of life, values, and land-use and management practices. From this perspective all of Khumbu can be regarded as an Indigenous Conservation Territory (see chapter 2), a large ICCA grounded in Sharwas' conception of territory, relationships with the world, and sense of self-responsibility.

Spiritual beliefs contribute significantly to conservation in the high Himalayan national parks. One remarkable aspect of this is the beyuls, sacred Himalayan hidden valleys and Buddhist sanctuaries believed to have been consecrated in the eighth century by the adept Padmasambhava (figure

Figure 11.3. Eastern Khumbu within the Sagarmatha (Mount Everest) National Park and Buffer Zone. The lower slope of the sacred mountain Khumbila, the abode of the regional guardian god Khumbu Yul Lha, is at the left, with Chomolungma (Mount Everest/Sagarmatha), the abode of the goddess Jomo Miyolangsangma, on the left skyline. The Sharwa village of Khumjung with its temple forest, in the foreground, is in the buffer zone. All other forest in the photo is part of the national park as well as being administered by Khumjung and Khunde villages as protected community forest. Grazing throughout the area shown is within the national park but is governed by the Khumjung and Khunde village assemblies.

11.3). Three of these national parks, SNP (Beyul Khumbu), M-BNP (Beyul Khenpalung), and LNP (Beyul Dagam Namgo in Langtang Valley, Beyul Yolmo Kangra in Yolmo), are encompassed by or include beyuls. For believers these are among the most important sacred natural sites in the Himalaya and Tibet (Diemberger 1997; Sherpa 2003; Baker 2004; Spoon and Sherpa 2008; Lim 2008).[10] The fourth high Himalayan national park, S-PNP, also has a sacred valley, the valley of Kunasa, in which there are multiple sites sacred to Dolpo-pa, who follow the Bonpo religion (Aumeeruddy-Thomas et al. 2004).[11] In the Khumbu case, Sharwa maintain a strong cultural proscription against killing that they seek to apply in the beyul to ban hunting, animal sacrifice, and the slaughter of livestock not only by Sharwa but also by others.

The high Himalayan national parks once had many locally managed and conserved areas that meet IUCN and CBD conceptions of ICCAs, and some of these continue to be maintained. These include community-managed forests, community-managed rotational grazing systems, and many sacred natural sites (mountains, forests, trees, lakes, springs, caves, and rock formations). Some villages within the parks continue to manage livelihood commons through village law and enforcement mechanisms.[12] Most of SNP's temperate and subalpine forests and grasslands and its extensive alpine areas (figure 11.3), for example, are managed by village assemblies (villages in Khumbu's western valley have abandoned customary management since the mid-1980s). Today the village assemblies of the central and eastern Khumbu Sharwa villages continue to regulate grazing and forest use through customary village law (*yul thim*) enforced by community-chosen officials (*nawa*). The regulations impose restrictions on forest use and create rotational zoning systems for regulating grazing, wild grass cutting, harvesting crops and hayfields, and collecting deadwood (Stevens 1993, 2008b). Indeed, some community forests now have stricter regulations than the national park requires, adopted over the past decade in response to increasing use pressures from tourism development and migrants. Many sacred places and cultural sites, moreover, are cared for and respected in ways that have enormous conservation significance. This is very evident in SNP, where extensive temple and lama's forests constitute the region's most intact old forests (figure 11.4). Protected from all tree felling, the lopping of branches, and even in most cases from the gathering of deadwood, these forests provide key habitat for endangered musk deer and other wildlife (Stevens 2008b).

Sharwa have also established new conservation institutions at their own initiative. Residents of the largest village in SNP, Khumjung, created a new kind of conservation area in 2005. The Lakyok Bird Conservation Area is located on the slope of the sacred mountain Khumbila (Khumbu Yul Lha) and is protected by Khumjung village against firewood collection and stone quarrying to prevent disturbance of ground-nesting pheasants and other birds. Sharwa leaders persisted in seeking its recognition despite the SNP warden's reluctance to authorize it, arguing that the area deserved stricter protection than it had under SNP regulations.

On a larger scale, since 2002 Sharwa have expanded their community management of forests far beyond their customary boundaries and regulations to create a regional firewood collection management system that may be unique in Nepal's Himalayan national parks. Villagers have

Figure 11.4. Pangboche village and temple in eastern Khumbu and the sacred Yarin lama's forest on the slope in the background. According to oral traditions, this forest, now within Sagarmatha (Mount Everest) National Park, has been strictly protected under village customary law for 400 years.

chosen for the first time, through decisions of their village assemblies and/or local buffer zone institutions, to self-impose ceilings on household collection of deadwood. They have adopted regulations that restrict firewood collection to two or fewer periods per year, each of no more than two weeks in length. Households are further limited to gathering no more than two loads (about 60 kilograms total) of firewood per day. These new regulations have reduced firewood collection in SNP considerably. Household firewood use has decreased regionally by two-thirds or more. The reduction in firewood use by the region's many family-operated hotels and restaurants, which formerly consumed large amounts, has been even more dramatic because all families are held to the same firewood collection limits regardless of whether they operate tourist businesses. Alternative energy (electricity from hydroelectricity and solar power as well as propane, kerosene, and dried dung) has surpassed fuelwood as a regional energy source. Moreover, villages now also decide which forested areas they want to open to firewood collection and for how long. This has enabled Pangboche, Khumjung, and Khunde villages to close some customarily used forests in order to allow them to recover from heavy past use. Through this new firewood collection management system, Khumbu Sharwa have begun to address recent pressures on their forests from population growth and tourism development, in the process extending village management far beyond its earlier extent to encompass all Khumbu forests.[13] Sherpa leaders continue to seek recognition from the DNPWC of their legal and moral responsibility for forest management and consider this vital to the effectiveness and sustainability of their forest ICCAs.[14]

In-depth documentation of the conservation significance of Indigenous peoples' land-use and management institutions and practices in the national parks has not yet been carried out. This will be a priority as Indigenous peoples continue to strive for their recognition and respect, substantiating Indigenous peoples' contentions that forest cover, rangeland, and biodiversity have been maintained in large areas of the national parks not because of national park regulations but because of the character of their land use, their efforts to address new adverse impacts from tourism and other development, and their collective management. Although there are certainly sites where recent impacts are visible, there is indeed evidence that Indigenous peoples' institutions and practices have contributed to conservation, including some of the best-conserved areas and sites. The existence and condition of their community and sacred forests, for example, and the overall diversity and numbers of wildlife in some of their territories often contrast sharply with conditions in other areas. Those Indigenous peoples who do not kill wildlife because of their religious beliefs (or who kill only those animals that prey on their livestock) argue that this has strongly contributed to biodiversity and animal numbers in their territories, including the survival of endangered and rare species that have been regionally extirpated in nearby regions and other ecologically similar areas of the Himalaya (among them snow leopard, common leopard, wolf, jackal, fox, wild dog, musk deer, Himalayan tahr, blue sheep, jharal, serow, barking deer, red panda, and langur monkeys). Sharwa observe that wildlife in all of SNP and large areas of M-BNP is protected because of their Buddhist beliefs and values, and that wildlife protection would be much more difficult if these areas were the territories of peoples with hunting traditions.

The high Himalayan national parks are understaffed, and there is little on-the-ground park administration in large parts of the parks. Sharwa and Dolpo-pa point out that as a result wildlife, forest, and alpine conservation in the vast areas beyond the immediate surrounds of park headquarters almost entirely depends on their cultural values and land management.

Some Sharwa leaders claim that the Sharwa are responsible for 80 percent or more of conservation in SNP, and they resent some SNP wardens' misrepresentation of them as a conservation problem rather than a key asset.

Struggling for Recognition, Respect, and Rights

In Nepal, continuing stewardship by high Himalayan Indigenous peoples of their territories and resources often coexists uneasily with national parks governed by the state under different assumptions and principles. There have been no understandings about shared jurisdictions or nested, coordinated ones through which Indigenous peoples' values and institutions can be acknowledged and respected. These are made difficult because of the state's annexation of Indigenous peoples' territories, the DNPWC's sole legal authority for national park governance, the degree of management discretion given to park wardens, lack of state recognition of customary institutions and law, and the poor status of Indigenous rights recognition.[15] Due to this lack of formal recognition, wardens, who vary greatly in their respect for Indigenous peoples' cultures and their land-use and management practices, have often been unaware of, ignored, or weakened ICCAs.[16] In some cases wardens have known about and given tacit approval to customary land management institutions and practices (such as community grazing management in SNP; see Stevens 1993, 1997b). In other cases they have ignored customary institutions and practices, and some wardens have pressured Indigenous peoples to use their customary collective land management institutions to enforce national park regulations rather than customary law (Stevens 1993, 1997b). Conflicts occur when national park management ignores the existence of customary Indigenous authority and practices or fails to respect them. Lack of respect can take many forms. Some wardens, for example, have authorized natural resource use that would not be allowed under customary law (such as felling trees in a sacred forest or in violation of village regulations for community forest use) and have overridden community efforts to enforce their conservation regulations. In one recent case in SNP, a community was ordered to apologize for seeking to have members of the park's army protection unit honor community forest regulations. Another common form of disrespect results from state imposition (often at the initiative or with the assistance of conservation NGOs) of new local conservation institutions and programs without Indigenous peoples' free, prior, and informed consent or concern for whether they duplicate, undermine, or conflict with existing Indigenous ones.

Indigenous peoples have begun organizing to seek greater recognition and respect for their conservation institutions and practices within the national parks. In 2009, Indigenous leaders from SNP, S-PNP, and Annapurna Conservation Area were among the founders and initial officers of Nepal's first organization to promote ICCA recognition, the ICCA Network Nepal. A series of national dialogue meetings have been held, but thus far efforts to educate Ministry of Forests and Soil Conservation and DNPWC officials and raise recognition and rights issues have had little impact. Indeed, Indigenous peoples' concerns have often been ignored or dismissed with false accusations that they are being manipulated by international organizations for their own self-serving purposes.

Sharwa leaders in SNP encountered similar entrenched attitudes and experienced a powerful backlash when they began to refer to their conservation practices as ICCAs and sought recognition for them from the DNPWC and SNP in 2008. Sharwa leaders were attacked in the national press and subjected to a DNPWC investigation after they issued a resolution in 2008 that affirmed that they consider Khumbu to be an ICCA and the importance of their values, institutions, and practices for conservation in SNP (see Stevens 2008b, 2009). Sharwa leaders were informed by the SNP warden (incorrectly) that their resolution was illegal and were ordered to both retract it and apologize. While a preeminent Sharwa leader subsequently issued a retraction, he refused to apologize and instead joined seventeen other regional leaders, including leaders of virtually all major Sharwa community organizations, in sending a joint letter to the director-general of the DNPWC protesting misrepresentations of their actions and intentions. The national controversy died down without any positive steps being taken. Sharwa efforts to bring their ICCAs to the attention of the prime minister of Nepal the following year also failed. Sharwa leaders petitioned the prime minister to recognize Khumbu as an ICCA on the occasion of his first visit to their territory (and the convening there of the first cabinet meeting outside of the capital), but received no response.

In retrospect some Sharwa leaders see the 2008 confrontation with the DNPWC and SNP as the result of their not having effectively raised officials' awareness and understanding of their intentions, international ICCA policies, and Sharwa institutions and practices. Others believe, in part based on conversations with DNPWC officials and staff, that the conflict stemmed primarily from officials' determination not to share power, recognize rights, or set a precedent in SNP that might lead to demands for ICCA recognition in other high Himalayan national parks.

Recognizing and Respecting Indigenous Peoples' and Community-Conserved Territories and Areas in Protected Areas

The IUCN and CBD have both noted that state protected areas often overlap with ICCAs and can undermine their integrity and effectiveness. Recent IUCN publications have reported that "many [ICCAs] have been subsumed within government protected areas without acknowledgment of their preexistence as independently governed ICCAs" (Borrini-Feyerabend 2010: 3) and that "it is likely that much of the related knowledge, institutions and practices have suffered as a result" (Borrini-Feyerabend et al. 2010: 38). The CBD's 2012 technical report on ICCAs similarly noted this strong overlap of ICCAs and state-governed protected areas and cautioned that "the establishment, expansion, and management of state and private protected areas often conflict or overlap with the customary territories, areas and practices of indigenous peoples and local communities and this tends to undermine traditional land and resource management within ICCAs" (Kothari et al. 2012: 64). In light of such concerns, the IUCN (2012d) adopted a policy in 2012 on overlap situations as part of the IUCN WCC 2012 Resolution 5.094, Respecting, Recognizing and Supporting Indigenous Peoples' and Community Conserved Territories and Areas. This resolution includes a call for states, conservation organizations, and IUCN leaders and institutions to "recognize and support ICCAs in situations where they overlap with protected area or other designations." It does not, however, elaborate on what appropriate recognition and support may mean in such situations.

Further IUCN policy development is likely to follow, given that appropriate recognition of ICCAs in these situations is essential to achieving the goals of the new paradigm, implementing UNDRIP and other international law, and rectifying past injustices and ongoing human rights violations (Stevens 2010, 2013, 2014).[17] Among the rights associated with ICCAs are Indigenous peoples' rights to recognition of their ownership and control of customary territories, collectively owned lands, and natural resources; self-governance; self-determination; maintaining cultural integrity and participating in the cultural life of their peoples; maintaining and revitalizing culture, customary institutions and practices, and spiritual relationships with territories; use and management of lands and natural resources; custodianship and care of sacred places; free, prior, and informed consent; participation in decisions affecting themselves and their lands, including development decisions; rights to life, food, and shelter; the right not to be coercively displaced from their territories; and the right to not be subjected to coercive assimilation.[18] Appropriately recognizing and respecting ICCAs and rights in situations in which state-established and state-governed protected areas overlap with ICCAs will require establishing procedures for such ICCAs to be recognized as protected areas or as areas governed by Indigenous peoples within protected areas with shared governance or other governance arrangements acceptable to them. Such recognition will require reform of the governance arrangements and management of a vast number of protected areas worldwide.

Greater awareness in Nepal of the existence and value of ICCAs, including customary ICCAs, may lead to recognition and respect for them both within and beyond Nepal's current national parks and protected area system. Achieving greater appreciation of ICCAs, however, will be difficult. Although government officials are increasingly well informed about international protected area standards and international human rights law, and some acknowledge that national law and administrative regulations related to the national parks require amendment, the DNPWC has not yet developed new paradigm policies or pilot programs (Paudel et al. 2012). Many officials, wardens, and staff remain opposed to recognition of ICCAs as protected areas or within the national parks. There seems to be particular resistance to the recognition of customary ICCAs that are grounded in Indigenous peoples' cultures and rights. Nepal civil society, including national offices of international NGOs that work closely with Nepal government ministries and departments, also continues to be unsupportive. Many of these conservation NGOs avoid using the term ICCA, continue to fail to support customary land management institutions, and instead promote new institutions they have designed themselves. Often these new institutions preclude or conflict with customary ones. They are seldom flexible enough in design for Indigenous peoples and local communities to integrate them with customary institutions and practices.

In Nepal, as in many other states, opposition to ICCAs occurs in a larger political ecological context of discourses, relationships, institutions, and practices that creates barriers to respect for Indigenous peoples and rights. Refusal to acknowledge the value of ICCAs often reflects not only lack of appreciation of Indigenous knowledge and practices by government officials, national conservation NGOs, and conservation and natural resource management "experts," but also the marginal social and political status of Indigenous peoples, lack of legal recognition of Indigenous rights, and reluctance to honor international commitments and national law that affirm those rights. Current protected area relationships and practices in Nepal are entrenched in a tremendous power differential between DNPWC officials and Indigenous peoples, officials' attitudes and discourses that demonstrate disagreement with new protected area paradigm principles, a lack of interest in sharing power, and a refusal to acknowledge that the "local inhabitants" of the Himalayan national parks are Indigenous peoples with Indigenous rights. It will be a challenge to change these attitudes and relationships. Inclusion of Indigenous rights provisions in the new constitution that is now in development—if this should indeed be done—may create legal and judicial support for new paradigm reforms. It seems likely, however, that securing appropriate ICCA recognition and respect will even then require a protracted struggle and possible recourse to national and international courts, rights monitoring, and dispute resolution mechanisms.

Given the political ecologies of conservation in Nepal, it seems quite possible that ICCA recognition will continue to be problematic. The Nepal government may well continue to fail to recognize Indigenous peoples' collective land tenure, customary law, and customary institutions for natural resource management even though it has an obligation to do so as a ratifier of ILO 169. Government officials may continue to insist that ICCAs cannot be recognized within national parks or may modify that position reluctantly and only after increased awareness and capacity building, greater national and international monitoring and encouragement, and heightened political pressure from Indigenous peoples and civil society. There is also the strong possibility that if the Nepal government does eventually recognize ICCAs, it will only do so for government-designed, standardized institutions such as those Nepal has already created for buffer zones, conservation areas, and community forests. Requiring adoption of standardized structures, procedures, and practices, however, may prevent Indigenous peoples and local communities from continuing to maintain customary ICCAs and violates multiple human and Indigenous rights.

Despite these considerable challenges, the ICCAs within the high Himalayan national parks may yet become the site of new conservation collaborations between Indigenous peoples, government agencies, and international and national conservationists and conservation organizations. Unlike Nepal's lowland national parks, Indigenous peoples are still in place in the high Himalaya and continue to maintain customary ICCAs and to create new ICCAs to respond to new conditions. Many peoples may welcome a new relationship with the DNPWC based on recognition of their status and rights as Indigenous peoples. Much can be done by progressive officials to use their authority, initiative, and spaces within current law and regulations to remake relationships and interactions with Indigenous peoples and to recognize and coordinate with their ICCAs. Greater appreciation and respect for ICCAs and for rights may yet lead to national park governance and management that fully support Indigenous peoples' cultures, self-governance, and conservation stewardship of their lands.

Acknowledgments

I appreciate the friendship and support of the many Sharwa who have made me welcome in Khumbu, as well as the opportunities they have given me to work with them on research and community projects over more than thirty years. I am particularly grateful to Sonam Hishi Sherpa, Tenzing Tashi Sherpa, Sonam Gyalzen Sherpa, Ngawang Tenzin Zangbu, and the late Konchok Chombi Sherpa for sharing their knowledge and insights. I thank two anonymous reviewers for their encouragement, suggestions, and copyediting assistance, and Piper R. Gaubatz for her cartographic work. This chapter benefited also from the encouragement and editorial assistance that Holly Jonas, Ashish Kothari, Phil Camill, Hetal Hariya, and several anonymous reviewers provided for earlier publications on which this chapter is partly based. My thanks to Natural Justice and United Nations University–Institute of Advanced Studies (UNU-IAS) for permission to use material that previously appeared in the book *The Right to Responsibility: Resisting and Engaging Development, Conservation, and the Law in Asia*. I appreciate also that *Conservation and Society* is an open-access journal, with all content licensed under the Creative Commons Attribution license.

Notes

1. Parts of this chapter were originally published as "Defending and Strengthening Sharwa (Sherpa) Rights and ICCAs in Sagarmatha (Mount Everest) National Park, Nepal," in *The Right to Responsibility: Resisting and Engaging Development, Conservation, and the Law in Asia*, edited by Harry Jonas, Holly Jonas, and Suneetha M. Subramanian (Kota Kinabalu, Malaysia: Natural Justice and United Nations University–Institute of Advanced Studies, 2014, 71–98) and in *Conservation and Society* as "National Parks and ICCAs in the High Himalayan Region of Nepal: Challenges and Opportunities" (doi: 10.4103/0972-4923.110946), part of a special section titled "Policy and Practice of Community-based Conservation" edited by Philip Camill, Jessica Brown, and Ashish Kothari. This journal is open access, and content is licensed under the Creative Commons Attribution license.

2. In Nepal, conservation areas are a legally designated type of protected area. The government of Nepal also considers buffer zones to be part of the protected area system and reports them as protected areas to UNEP's World Database on Protected Areas. The goals, policies, and governance of these different types of protected areas vary considerably (Stevens 1997b; Heinen and Mehta 1999, 2000; Heinen and Shrestha 2006). Policies also differ strikingly between the lowland and Himalayan national parks, with much greater authorization of land use under the DNPWC's Himalayan National Parks Regulations of 1979 (Stevens 1997b).

3. The Indigenous people of the Mount Everest region refer to themselves as "Sharwa," but during the twentieth century became nationally and internationally renowned as "Sherpas."

4. The Nepal government refers collectively to more than twenty peoples in eastern Nepal as the "Rai" despite many of them seeking recognition as distinct peoples.

5. Indigenous peoples and local communities were also displaced from one of the mountain national parks, Rara National Park. No Indigenous peoples or local communities have been relocated from Nepal's six conservation areas or the twelve buffer zones.

6. None of this changed when the enclave settlements in all four national parks were later declared to be part of park buffer zones (see Stevens 2013, 2014).

7. See Stevens (2008a) and Jana and Paudel (2010) for discussion of ICCAs in Nepal more generally.

8. Nepal has one protected area, Kanchengjunga Conservation Area, that is an ICCA in that governance authority was handed over by the government of Nepal in 2006 to a management committee composed of representatives of regional organizations. This is not regarded, however, as a precedent or foundation for further transfers of administrative authority.

9. The generalizations presented in this chapter about Sharwa and other Indigenous peoples' institutions and practices do not convey regional variation, complex local dynamics, or intracommunity controversies over land management and conservation. Decision-making in Khumbu Sharwa villages, for example, reflects ongoing interactions among community members who vary considerably in economic and social situations, power, influence, views, aspirations, and concerns. For more in-depth discussion of an earlier era, see Stevens (1993).

10. The connection between culture and conservation is especially enhanced by the high Himalayan Indigenous peoples' religious beliefs. Several of the peoples of the high Himalaya self-identify as followers of Buddhism or Bon and consider this to be central to their ethnic identities, cultures, and livelihood practices. Sharwa, for example, consider their adherence to a particular Buddhist school, the Nyingmapa, essential to their identity as Sharwa. Nyingmapa are noted for their reverence for nature spirits, including guardian mountain gods (*yul lha*) and tree and water spirits (*lu*). As followers of Padmasambhava (Guru Rinpoche), Nyingmapa, in contrast to some other Buddhist schools, believe in Guru Rinpoche's consecration of beyuls (hidden valleys).

11. Two of Nepal's high Himalayan conservation areas, Gaurishankar Conservation Area and Manaslu Conservation Area, also include beyuls. Both are the customary territories of Indigenous peoples; Sharwa inhabit Beyul Rolwaling in Gaurishankar Conservation Area and the Tsumba and Ghale inhabit Beyul Kyomolung in the Tsum and Nubri valleys of Manaslu Conservation Area.

12. Although the work of documenting and assessing the current status of these institutions and practices has only just begun, for SNP, see Stevens (1993, 2008b) and Sherpa (2003); for S-PNP, Ghimire and Parajuli (2001), Aumeeruddy-Thomas et al. (2004), and Bauer (2004); for LNP, Fox et al. (1996), Baker (2005), and Campbell (2005); and for M-BNP, Diemberger (1997).

13. Sharwa leaders consider the firewood collection management system to be a Sharwa conservation practice because it is a Sharwa idea and because it is administered by Sharwa buffer zone institutions on the advice of village assemblies. Such a system likely would have been politically impossible for SNP administrators to propose and implement, because it would have been strongly resisted as a violation of customary use rights. Some recent national park superintendents have expressed appreciation for the system and sought to support it, including by directing staff to assist in monitoring firewood collection in some parts of Khumbu. This has raised concern, however, that SNP administrators may try to intervene in and co-opt the system. Another issue is that, although the system was developed by Sharwa leaders and adopted in regional meetings, it remains controversial because some people do not have easy access to alternative energy or cannot afford it.

14. The firewood collection management system is included in the recently negotiated *Sagarmatha National Park Internal Working Procedures* (Sagarmatha National Park and Buffer Zone Management Committee 2011). This document was developed by the SNP warden and buffer zone representatives to clarify existing practices and procedures. Sharwa hope that it will ensure that future SNP wardens do not undermine existing Sharwa institutions and practices. However, although the document acknowledges the importance of Sharwa conservation contributions to SNP, discusses the role of buffer zone institutions and nawa in village forest management, and outlines some aspects of the regional firewood collection management system, it does not mention the central role of the village assemblies and village law (yul thim) in forest management and represents the role of the buffer zone institutions simply as providing advice to the national park warden. Nothing is said, moreover, about customary Sharwa collective governance of agropastoralism through decisions of the village assemblies or Sharwa custodianship of sacred natural sites. Sharwa rights as an Indigenous people are not mentioned.

15. The informal understandings about some aspects of forest management in the 2011 *Sagarmatha National Park Internal Working Procedures* may be a step toward formal recognition.

16. Sharwa often remark that "each warden makes his own law."

17. Appropriate recognition and respect is a key requirement. Recognition that fails to affirm the rights articulated in UNDRIP clearly is inappropriate. Requiring that Indigenous peoples declare ICCAs in their territories and that they be integrated into a national protected area system, requiring that ICCAs be nationally standardized (and thus undermining customary institutions), or co-opting self-governance (and hence turning ICCAs into shared governance or state institutions), for example, all violate the rights of Indigenous peoples. It is critical that Indigenous peoples participate in the design of any state mechanisms for recognizing ICCAs and that ICCAs are only recognized with their free, prior, and informed consent.

18. For more detailed discussion of ICCAs and rights, see Stevens (2010, 2013, 2014).

CHAPTER TWELVE

Advancing the New Paradigm

Implementation, Challenges, and Potential

Stan Stevens

The new protected area paradigm embraces Indigenous peoples' conservation achievements and capacity and considers them vital to creating, sustaining, and restoring global biocultural diversity. It envisions global conservation as being strengthened, legitimated, and made more sustainable by validating Indigenous peoples' control over their territories and supporting their self-governance, cultures, livelihoods, and rights. Such protected areas offer conservationists and states a means to repudiate past misunderstandings and mistakes and to build new relationships based on respect and rights. This can make possible protected areas enriched by Indigenous peoples' knowledge, commitments to territory and culture, and collective institutions and practices and transform protected areas into key sites of restitution and reconciliation worldwide rather than a nexus of dispossession, human rights violations, and conflict.

Yet while the conservation and social justice potential of these new kinds of protected areas is vast, effectively realizing principles such as those shown in sidebar 12.1 on the ground will be difficult. Drawing in part on this book's case studies, this final chapter discusses experiences with implementation thus far and suggests ways forward.

Sidebar 12.1. Principles for Fostering the New Paradigm

- Recognize Indigenous peoples as peoples in accordance with international understanding and law (and not simply as ethnic minorities, local populations, or local communities). Indigenous peoples should be recognized as rights-holders and not merely stakeholders with regard to conservation and development in their territories, including the establishment, governance, and management of protected areas.
- Restore ownership of territory that has been incorporated in protected areas without Indigenous peoples' free, prior, and informed consent.
- Appropriately recognize Indigenous peoples' ownership and control of their territories and their individual and collective land and marine tenure in accordance with their wishes and their customary law, institutions, and practices.
- Avoid coercive displacement or marginalization (physical, economic, political, and cultural) of Indigenous peoples from protected areas and facilitate remedy and redress for past injustices.
- Ensure that protected areas affirm and support Indigenous peoples' livelihood security and sustainable use of natural resources, including both customary uses and endogenous development grounded in culture and self-determination.
- Ensure that protected areas equitably share benefits and responsibilities with Indigenous peoples in ways that take into account their status as territorial owners or custodians, their rights, and their self-affirmed responsibilities to their territory and peoples.
- Include Indigenous peoples' territories and ICCAs in national protected area systems only with their free, prior, and informed consent.
- Ensure that governance of all protected areas in Indigenous peoples' customary territories is carried out by them or in shared governance arrangements developed with their full and effective participation.
- Ensure that all shared governance arrangements secure Indigenous peoples' full and effective participation in governance; are based on their free, prior, and informed consent; and respect their knowledge, values, decision-making processes, and human and Indigenous rights.
- Recognize and respect Indigenous peoples' self-governance in all protected areas, including through their customary governance institutions and law. Respect Indigenous peoples' right to adapt and change their customary institutions and practices in accordance with their rights to self-governance and self-determination.
- Appropriately recognize ICCAs in accordance with Indigenous peoples' wishes as protected areas, as components of national protected area systems, as self-governing areas or zones within larger protected areas, or outside of protected areas as "other effective area-based conservation measures" (Conference of the Parties to the CBD 2010).

From Paradigm Shift to Standard Practice

The policies adopted by the IUCN since 2003 and CBD decisions since 2004 provide detailed guidance for how protected areas can be reformed to contribute to the IUCN's vision of "a just world that values and conserves nature." The articulation and adoption of these principles and policies is itself a major achievement, and their application in increasing numbers of protected areas worldwide demonstrates that they can be realized. Yet reform has been slower than many had hoped: it is proving to have been easier to conceive a paradigm shift and to gain endorsement for it from the IUCN and the CBD than to implement it on the ground worldwide.

Old paradigm assumptions continue to be strongly held by many international conservationists, government officials and bureaucrats, and donors, despite decades of discussion, international policy development, and experience with new approaches. These attitudes still dominate much international conservation planning and many programs. Many organizations and donors continue to emphasize old paradigm approaches and fail to prioritize and support new paradigm ones; this is evident in gap analyses, protected area planning, and investment in improving national and global protected area coverage and effectiveness. In many countries, the old paradigm appears to be even more strongly entrenched among officials and protected area agency bureaucrats. The slow pace of implementation has disappointed advocates, although it is not surprising given the degree of change that the new paradigm requires in conservation thinking, present social and political relationships, and the current political economy of conservation funding that channels relatively little funding directly to Indigenous peoples. Members of the International Indigenous Forum on Biodiversity, which represents Indigenous peoples in the CBD, for example, noted in a 2008 CBD meeting that "we had high hopes when the Program of Work was adopted in 2004, but in reality, the continued establishment of protected areas in indigenous land and territories still violates the human rights and collective rights of Indigenous Peoples, including [the] right to free prior informed consent." They charged that "the establishment of protected areas continues to result in the expropriation of our lands, territories, resources and the loss of our cultures and livelihoods" and declared: "We are profoundly disappointed that neither this decision [VII/28 on protected areas] nor Element 2 of the Programme of Work on Governance, Equity, Participation and Benefit Sharing are being effectively addressed and implemented" (International Indigenous Forum on Biodiversity 2008a).

That same year Marcus Colchester of Forest Peoples Programme observed that "as far as indigenous peoples are concerned, the 'new paradigm' still exists more on paper than in practice" (Colchester et al. 2008: 13). On the basis of early reporting on protected area situations in several countries in Southeast Asia and Africa, Forest Peoples Programme concluded that what "we have found is that despite adopting new policies and despite some encouraging examples of progress, which show that conservation through securing indigenous rights is possible, in practice conservationists have hardly changed their ways. Protected areas are still being run in top down ways that exclude indigenous peoples and deny their rights" (Forest Peoples Programme 2008).

Concern has also been voiced within the CBD and IUCN. The Executive Secretary to the CBD (2010: 2) noted that the implementation of the governance and equity goals of Element 2 of PoWPA "was limited and way behind in achieving the targets." Disappointment in the slow pace of implementation of Element 2 has been voiced as well in decisions by the Parties to the CBD (2008), including COP 9 Decision IX/18 (section A, par. 4(c)). The IUCN has urged the CBD to do more to implement PoWPA, which has greater weight than IUCN recommendations and resolutions because it is associated with an international treaty. The IUCN has informed the Conference of the Parties of the CBD that it feels Element 2 is "crucial and yet [is] among the least effectively advanced" elements of the PoWPA (IUCN 2008a). The IUCN made action on Element 2 a priority for COP 10 in Nagoya, stressing as its top recommendation in a position paper (IUCN 2010a: 1) on "Enhancing the Contribution of Protected Areas to Biodiversity Conservation" that the "IUCN calls on COP 10 to urge Parties to expedite efforts towards the effective implementation of Programme Element 2 of the Programme of Work on Protected Areas (PoWPA), particularly to enhance the quality of Governance in PAs [protected areas], and to ensure full and meaningful involvement of indigenous and local communities in PA management and governance structures in ways that promote improved livelihoods, access to natural resources as well as equitable sharing of benefits derived from PAs."

The same document (2010a: 3) highlights Element 2 in additional recommendations in which

> IUCN urges Parties to:
> Expedite efforts towards the full and effective implementation and monitoring of Programme Element 2, noting that the review of PoWPA

noted that this is the element, despite its importance where least progress has been achieved.

Fully consider the implementation of Programme Element 2 to existing and new PAs [protected areas] and expanded national PAs systems, including MPAs [marine protected areas], as required to meet CBD target 11.

IUCN invites Parties to:

In promoting the implementation of Programme Element 2, utilize the full range of tools and methodologies such as those developed by IUCN . . . [including through] ICCAs . . . and Social Assessment of Protected Areas.

Where implementation has occurred, it has often been incomplete and inconsistent. Diverse countries have created protected areas governed and/or managed by or with Indigenous peoples, including states in both the global North and South (among them Australia, Canada, South Africa, the United States, Indonesia, Peru, Bolivia, Colombia, and the Philippines). Often, however, this has come about because of court decisions, comprehensive land claim settlements, strong social movements, or international pressure associated with individual protected areas. As a result, these protected areas often embody principles that are not yet national law, policy, and standard practice. In some countries, some forms of protected areas (but not others, such as national parks) have been reformed, or new paradigm principles are incorporated only in newly declared protected areas and not also existing ones. There are also other troubling patterns. Many more countries, for example, have recognized shared governance of protected areas than have recognized ICCAs. Moreover, ICCAs, including customary local ones, often are not appropriately recognized and respected in situations where state-governed protected areas overlap with them. It also is disturbing that there have been relatively few cases of restitution, that few countries have adopted national laws strongly affirming the rights of Indigenous peoples within protected areas, and that there is no sign yet of an international Truth and Reconciliation Commission on Protected Areas and Indigenous Peoples or of similar institutions at the national level.[1]

Criticisms of the pace and unevenness of new paradigm adoption highlight the urgency of reform and frustration with progress thus far. It is nonetheless of enormous significance that the critical first steps for transforming protected area–based conservation, namely the conceptualization of the new paradigm and its effective integration into international conservation policy, have been taken. Certainly in many countries the challenge of realizing such a major course change in societal relations, governance, and conservation will be enormous. Yet the slow early pace is not grounds for despair or for a call to abandon the new paradigm. Important implementation efforts are now underway and are discussed in the next section.

Ongoing Initiatives

Significant initiatives are underway to advance new paradigm implementation through awareness raising, capacity building, assessment and evaluation, mediation, and jurisprudence. Implementing the new paradigm has become a major focus of efforts by the IUCN, the CBD, and some conservation and social justice organizations, including Forest Peoples Programme and the ICCA Consortium. Some donors (most notably the Global Environment Facility's Small Grant Programme) are emphasizing funding of new paradigm approaches, including ICCAs. The UN human rights monitoring mechanisms and international courts are also becoming involved through recommendations and decisions by the UN Special Rapporteur on the Rights of Indigenous Peoples, the Inter-American Commission on Human Rights, the Inter-American Court on Human Rights, and the African Commission on Human and Peoples' Rights.

The CBD has begun to place increased emphasis on implementing Articles 8(j) and 10(c) of the Convention, as well as meeting the goals and targets of PoWPA. A major aspect of this has been efforts to increase the participation of Indigenous peoples in decision-making, planning, and assessment and evaluation, including in national planning for protected areas. Decisions of the Conference of the Parties of the CBD and the efforts of the Secretariat of the CBD continue to emphasize governance, including the inclusion of ICCAs and protected areas with shared governance in national protected area systems. Detailed discussion of these diverse efforts is beyond the scope of this chapter. The following brief overview of recent IUCN initiatives is intended only to suggest some of the types of initiatives now underway.

The International Union for Conservation of Nature and New Paradigm Implementation

Governance and rights recognition are now key concerns for the IUCN. The current IUCN Programme 2013–2016 (IUCN 2012a), approved at the World Conservation Congress (WCC) 2012, highlights "effective and equitable governance of nature's use" as one of its three pillars with emphasis on natural resource use and management by Indigenous peoples and local communities. Moreover, IUCN leaders agreed at a high-level meeting with Indigenous peoples and NGOs in 2011 to a set of actions known as the Whakatane Mechanism that committed the IUCN to evaluation and improvement of the application of its policies on Indigenous peoples, rights, and protected areas; advancing realization of UNDRIP; drafting an IUCN Policy on Conservation and Human Rights; establishing the Whakatane Assessment process on Indigenous peoples and protected areas; and regularly reporting on its efforts to the UN Permanent Forum on Indigenous Issues and the UN Expert Mechanism on the Rights of Indigenous Peoples (Forest Peoples Programme 2011a, 2011b, 2011c).

Several of the IUCN's many component units, including three of its six commissions, are also engaged with the new paradigm. The World Commission on Protected Areas (WCPA), for example, declared fostering "governance, equity, and livelihoods" to be one of five strategic directions and priorities in its Strategic Plan 2005–2012 (IUCN WCPA 2010) and continues to support recognition of ICCAs and protected areas with shared governance. The WCPA publication *Guidelines for Applying Protected Area Management Categories* (Dudley 2008) highlighted new paradigm thinking, and its journal, *Parks*, has promoted the new paradigm in a series of special issues. The latest IUCN best practice guidelines, *Governance of Protected Areas: From Understanding to Action* (Borrini-Feyerabend et al. 2013), which were produced by a partnership that included WCPA; the Secretariat of the CBD; IUCN's Commission on Environmental, Economic, and Social Policy (CEESP); and the ICCA Consortium, emphasize good governance, rights affirmation, assessment and monitoring that includes governance quality and rights, and appropriate recognition of ICCAs and shared governance of protected areas. Protected areas of all governance types are now included in the World Database on Protected Areas maintained by the WCPA and UNEP World Conservation Monitoring Centre. Efforts are being made to improve the listing of ICCAs in the World Database on Protected Areas and to develop a global ICCA registry. Governance also figures in the WCPA's discussion of creation of a new

"Green List of Well-Managed Protected Areas" and its efforts to include social indicators in evaluations of protected area governance and management effectiveness (Borrini-Feyerabend et al. 2013). This will be advanced by 2012 WCC Resolution 5.042 (IUCN 2012b) that calls for strengthening the role in protected area assessment and certification of rights-based conservation, with particular attention to the rights of Indigenous peoples and traditional local communities. The WCPA also has made governance one of the core areas of concern for the next IUCN World Parks Congress (WPC) in Sydney, Australia, in 2014. "Enhancing the diversity and quality of governance" will be one of the eight thematic streams of the WPC.

The CEESP has strongly promoted the IUCN's adoption of a new conservation ethic, including a proposed natural resources governance framework, and has developed strong relationships with the global Indigenous peoples movement leaders and institutions. It also has greatly advanced discussion of rights-based conservation and protected area governance through its journal *Policy Matters* and a series of briefing notes. Recently the CEESP also has begun to play a more activist role by using IUCN expertise and influence to help mediate disputes between Indigenous peoples and states and to make exemplary cases of new paradigm approaches better known and emulated. This process, known as the Whakatane Assessments, seeks to bring parties into a dialogue, conduct a participatory field assessment, and facilitate reforms that reflect the IUCN's new paradigm standards. The process involves representatives from the IUCN (CEESP, WCPA, and regional and national IUCN offices), Indigenous peoples' organizations, Forest Peoples Programme and other NGOs, and concerned government agencies. Pilot assessments were carried out with the Ogiek people for Mount Elgon National Park, Kenya, and the Karen people for Ob Luang National Park, Thailand, in 2011 and 2012, and further development and application of the Whakatane Assessments were an important subject of discussion at the Vth WCC in 2012 (Forest Peoples Programme 2011a, 2011b, 2011c; IUCN CEESP 2011, 2012; IUCN and Forest Peoples Programme 2012).

The Commission on Environmental Law has also become involved in protected area governance and rights issues with its *Guidelines for Protected Areas Legislation* (Lausche and Burhenne 2011). Moreover, together with the CEESP, in 2011 it established a new intercommission Specialist Group on Indigenous Peoples, Customary and Environmental Laws and Human Rights. This group's goals include improving policy, monitoring implementation of WCC resolutions, and assisting in implementing the Whakatane Mechanism.

Other IUCN groups that have been actively promoting the new paradigm are the Global Protected Areas Programme; the intercommission (WCPA/CEESP) thematic group TILCEPA (now also known as the Theme/Strategic Direction on Governance, Communities, Equity and Livelihood Rights in Relation to Protected Areas); the CEESP thematic group Theme on Governance, Equity, and Rights; and the IUCN Environmental Law Centre.

Several of these different IUCN commissions and groups have been involved since 2008 in the Conservation Initiative on Human Rights, an effort by IUCN and seven other international conservation organizations to enhance conservation through greater attention to human rights in conservation policy and practice. The members agreed on a set of common principles and to individually develop and uphold their own policies (Springer et al. 2010).[2] While this is an important step, there remain questions about the members' degree of commitment to rights-based conservation, whether they will strongly promote the realization of UNDRIP within and around protected areas, and how effective internal, voluntary ethics codes and complaint mechanisms will be. Although the initiative has certainly raised awareness of rights among the largest conservation organizations, the initial *Conservation and Human Rights Framework* (Conservation Initiative on Human Rights n.d.) affirmed commitment to uphold the standards of the Universal Declaration on Human Rights (1948), which emphasizes individuals' rights, but did not mention UNDRIP or ILO 169. IUCN has gone much further with its strong emphasis on upholding UNDRIP, which figures prominently in several 2012 and 2014 WCC resolutions and in the IUCN Policy on Conservation and Human Rights for Sustainable Development adopted by the 2012 WCC (IUCN 2012e). The ongoing development of the Conservation Initiative on Human Rights and its members' implementation of rights-based conservation will be closely watched. Whether major conservation organizations can embrace a larger view of rights-based conservation remains to be seen. Certainly the major transnational conservation organizations can be a considerable force for protected area reform if they choose to be.

Protected Areas and the New Paradigm: Experience

An increasing number of protected areas in diverse countries already embody new paradigm principles or are regarded in national or international circles as doing so. In-depth, fieldwork-based analyses of protected areas such as those provided in this book, however, caution that many protected areas that have been represented as "participatory" and "community-based" fall significantly short of new paradigm standards. Two aspects of the new paradigm that are proving particularly problematic are the challenge of gaining recognition for Indigenous peoples' control over territory, including restitution of lands incorporated in protected areas without consent or compensation, and securing their full and effective participation in protected area governance.

Restitution and Recognition: Territory, Tenure, and Protected Areas

Despite the IUCN's advocacy, few Indigenous peoples have regained ownership of lands or waters that were incorporated without their consent in protected areas. Restitution outcomes have often been disappointing and in some cases have fallen short of securing Indigenous peoples' rights. The cases of South Africa's Kruger National Park, Dwesa-Cwebe Nature Reserve, and Kalahari Gemsbok National Park (chapter 9; Magome and Murombedzi 2003; Ellis 2010; Kepe 2010), the Río Plátano Biosphere Reserve in Honduras (chapter 8), the Bosawás Biosphere Reserve in Nicaragua (chapter 7; see also Stocks 2003; Finley-Brook and Offen 2009), Australia's Uluru-Kata Tjuta and Kakadu National Parks (Weaver 1991; De Lacy and Lawson 1997; Ross et al. 2011), and Death Valley National Park in the United States (Haberfeld 2000; Catton 2009), as well as the lack of implementation as of early 2014 of the 2010 African Commission on Human and Peoples' Rights's decision on the Endorois and Lake Bogoria National Reserve in Kenya, all testify that restitution has been partial and problematic even in some of the most widely celebrated cases.[3] Restitution often has only restored ownership of part of the expropriated territory and then often only with significant conditions attached to it (see sidebar 12.2).

When restitution does take place, it often fails to recognize Indigenous peoples' land tenure in culturally appropriate ways. Customary institutions and law are typically ignored, even in situations in which land tenure rights have been recognized, land titling had been initiated, and the requirement to affirm customary tenure is clearly set out in guiding court decisions and national law (chapters 7 and 8). Both the Nicaraguan and Honduran cases highlight how difficult it will often be to achieve recognition of Indigenous peoples' customary tenure, despite states' obligations to international rights treaties and decisions by regional courts, because of national law, jurisprudence, and practices that reflect the ethnocentrism and prejudices of non-Indigenous national ethnic elites (see also Stocks 2003; Finley-Brook and Offen 2009). Many states will continue to balk at legal recognition of collective and customary tenure and may attempt to prevent the use of oral traditions and participatory mapping in establishing legally recognized tenure.[4]

The new paradigm demands more than restitution beset with conditions that violate rights; ignore Indigenous peoples' knowledge, institutions, aspirations, and concerns; and continue to prevent their full and effective participation in protected area governance and management. It envisions restitution not only as a remedy and redress for past injustices but also as the basis for a new relationship between the state and Indigenous peoples.

Sidebar 12.2. Restitution: Common Limitations and Shortcomings

- Ownership may be restored for only a small part of the lands and waters now within a particular protected area.
- Collective tenure may not be recognized.
- Customary tenure institutions and practices often are not recognized.
- Usufruct rights may not be recognized.
- Overlapping use rights by multiple Indigenous peoples and local communities may not be recognized.
- Continuing designation of the restored territory as a protected area may be required as a condition of restitution, even when Indigenous peoples may not wish this.
- The protected area management goals, policies, and regulations for the restituted areas may not be revised in accordance with Indigenous peoples' goals, values, and wishes.
- Restored lands and waters may be required to have shared governance even when Indigenous peoples would prefer to govern them, and decision-making processes may be instituted that have insufficient regard for Indigenous peoples' knowledge, values, and rights.
- Restitution may not include the right to return for displaced peoples and may be conditional on their agreement not to resettle.
- Restitution of land and sea tenure may not include restitution of use rights and may be conditional on agreement not to use these areas in customary ways.

continued

- Specific future use and development of restored areas may be prohibited or all future use may be required to conform to existing protected area goals and regulations as a condition of restitution.
- Collective land and sea management (ICCAs) under customary institutions may not be recognized as a right and may not be respected.
- Care and protection of sacred places may not be entrusted to their custodians.
- Concerns about secrecy, appropriate access, privacy, and the ecological and spiritual integrity of cultural sites may not be respected.
- Restitution may take place on a specific case basis only, with the proviso that no precedents are set.

Governance: Challenges to Recognizing Sovereignty and to Sharing Power

Both the IUCN and CBD affirm that Indigenous peoples have a right to participate fully and effectively in protected area governance and have called on states to recognize ICCAs and protected areas with shared governance (chapters 1 and 2). Experience thus far with these forms of protected area governance provides insight into critical contexts and conditions, best practices, and problematic approaches.

INDIGENOUS PEOPLES' AND COMMUNITY CONSERVED TERRITORIES AND AREAS

Many Indigenous peoples seek to govern their own protected areas or gain recognition and respect for their conservation practices in situations where state-governed protected areas now overlap with their territories. There are very few examples, however, of states that have followed IUCN and CBD advice to facilitate the inclusion of ICCAs in national protected area systems when Indigenous peoples so wish.[5] The Indigenous Protected Areas (IPA) in Australia (chapter 3) are outstanding examples of Indigenous peoples' self-declared and self-governed protected areas being recognized and included in a national protected area system at their request.[6] The communal conservancies of Namibia are another important example.

Lack of appropriate recognition and respect for ICCAs in situations where state-governed protected areas overlap with them is an issue that affects a vast number of existing protected areas. This will prove difficult to address in many states where there are severe obstacles to recognition of Indigenous rights due to overarching Fourth World social and political relations, problematic legal and policy contexts, and obstructive administrative culture and social attitudes in government agencies concerned with protected areas. The IUCN's recent call to "appropriately recognize and support ICCAs in situations where they overlap with protected area or other designations" (IUCN 2012d) may nonetheless spark further discussion of appropriate policies and procedures, including at the IUCN WPC 2014 in Sydney, Australia. It will be important to develop more detailed IUCN and CBD guidance and safeguard policies for ICCA–protected area overlap situations, to include the status of ICCAs within protected areas in evaluations of protected area governance and management effectiveness, and to develop conflict management and resolution mechanisms.

The IUCN and CBD emphasize the issue of *appropriate* recognition and respect for ICCAs. There is great concern that increased international policy and funding emphasis on ICCAs may spark action by states and NGOs that may co-opt, undermine, or destroy ICCAs by inappropriately recognizing them. WCC Resolution 5.094 (preambular par. 7) (IUCN 2012d) observed that not only "lack of respect" but also "inadequate or inappropriate recognition and support for ICCAs by governments, conservation organizations and donors" can "undermine their integrity and conservation effectiveness and violate a range of procedural and substantive rights." Particular problems are anticipated with recognition that requires culturally insensitive (and rights-violating) standardization; ignores customary arrangements, law, and values; creates onerous bureaucratic requirements; or intervenes in ICCA operations through authorization, oversight, or financial mechanisms. Other concerns are that inappropriate recognition may threaten the integrity and effectiveness of ICCAs by seeking to replace them with shared governance practices or with new local institutions designed and imposed by state agencies or NGOs. Appropriate recognition will be particularly difficult in cases where state-governed protected areas overlap with ICCAs. In these cases, respect for ICCAs may require securing Indigenous peoples' land and marine tenure; national law and policy affirming the rights of Indigenous peoples in protected areas and the delegation of governance authority to them; and the recognition of ICCAs as protected areas or zones and governance jurisdictions within larger protected areas governed by states or through shared governance arrangements. It will often also be necessary to negotiate legally binding agreements that guarantee Indigenous peoples' governance authority and responsibilities for their ICCAs and to clarify specifics in memoranda of understanding and management plans for individual protected areas.

Key aspects of appropriate and inappropriate recognition are discussed in several IUCN, CBD, and ICCA Consortium publications. Recognition must be attentive to rights and responsibilities, including the right to give or to withhold free, prior, and informed consent and rights to territory, self-governance, and culture. WCC Resolution 5.094 places particular stress on recognizing the rights of Indigenous peoples, including their "governance of and rights to the lands, territories and resources which they have traditionally owned, occupied or otherwise used or acquired," recognizing and engaging with "customary laws, institutions, protocols and decision-making processes," and upholding the "intrinsic natural and cultural values present in ICCAs" (IUCN 2012d). Sidebar 12.3 identifies a number of best practices (see also Borrini-Feyerabend et al. 2010, 2013; Jonas et al. 2012; Kothari et al. 2012). States with social and political structures that discriminate against and marginalize Indigenous peoples can be expected to resist appropriate recognition of ICCAs. Many states may seek to ignore ICCAs, recognize them only on paper, or recognize them in ways that fall far short of the spirit of the new paradigm.

Sidebar 12.3. Key Best Practices for Appropriate Recognition and Respect of Indigenous Peoples' and Community Conserved Territories and Areas

1. Legally recognize Indigenous peoples' ownership of their territories and establish mechanisms to review past injustices, including treaty issues. Procedures for the restitution of nationalized land should be developed with the full and effective participation of Indigenous peoples.
2. Legally recognize Indigenous peoples' collective land and sea tenures and customary law with provisions for this to be done with full and effective participation by Indigenous peoples.
3. Legally recognize Indigenous peoples' customary self-governance institutions, including ICCAs, with provisions for this to be done with full and effective participation by Indigenous peoples.
4. Adopt ILO 169 and incorporate UNDRIP and ILO 169 in national law with Indigenous peoples' full and effective participation.
5. Legally recognize ICCAs with specific legislation developed with Indigenous peoples' full and effective participation. Provisions should:
    A. acknowledge the importance of Indigenous peoples' cultures for global cultural diversity, biocultural diversity, and for conservation and sustainability;

B. recognize that ICCAs require self-governance, and that this must not be undermined or compromised by inappropriate recognition, oversight, or financial mechanisms;
C. ensure that legal recognition of ICCAs provides for flexibility in governance arrangements, processes, and goals so as not to infringe on or undermine the customary character of ICCAs or Indigenous peoples' ability to adapt them and to innovate;
D. recognize that ICCAs often meet international definitions of protected areas and make provision for Indigenous peoples to include their ICCAs in national protected area systems or other national area–based conservation systems when they so wish;
E. ensure that certification of ICCAs or their inclusion in national protected area systems does not impose standardized institutional structures, regulations, or management plans and does not otherwise compromise or undermine them;
F. provide for secure financing and other support when ICCAs are recognized as part of national protected area systems or other area-based conservation systems;
G. provide funding for Indigenous peoples to document, plan, evaluate, and certify their ICCAs; and
H. recognize in national law that ICCAs should be appropriately recognized and respected in situations where state-declared and state-governed protected areas, private protected areas, or cogoverned protected areas overlap with them, including through measures such as:
   a. delegation of protected area governance authority to Indigenous peoples;
   b. protected area specific laws and administrative rules and regulations concerning recognition and respect for ICCAs as protected areas, as well as within protected areas;
   c. legally binding memoranda of understanding and conservation contracts to recognize and respect ICCAs;
   d. recognition and respect of ICCAs in protected area management plans;
   e. designation of ICCAs as zones within protected areas;
   f. devolution to ICCAs of governance jurisdictions for activities such as forest use, grazing, hunting, fishing, and plant collection;
   g. provisions for self-assessment and evaluation of ICCAs by Indigenous peoples; and
   h. development of effective conflict management and resolution mechanisms with Indigenous peoples' full and effective participation.

SHARED GOVERNANCE OF PROTECTED AREAS

Shared governance arrangements are likely to become increasingly common. Very often this will be at the insistence of states that are reluctant to recognize Indigenous peoples' full ownership and authority over their territories, self-governance, or governance of protected areas. In other cases it may be at the urging of Indigenous peoples who hope that shared governance will remedy exclusion from decision-making and rights violations. Some Indigenous peoples may seek such collaborations with states or with conservation organizations for immediate ends and strategic purposes, including to defend their territories against imminent threats or to gain access to financial and logistical support. Others may prefer not to share governance of protected areas, but find this preferable to alternatives and may participate in shared governance as an interim arrangement, a "strategic compromise" (Tofa 2007) that gives them time and opportunities to (re)build their self-governance and management capacity before seeking to self-govern protected areas in their territories.

Shared governance of protected areas can become a means for Indigenous peoples to gain greater authority over their territories and lives, secure rights, and develop new relationships with the state and non-Indigenous people (see sidebar 12.4, p. 300, for principles of effective shared governance). It is important to learn from positive experiences, develop best practices, and continue to regard shared governance of protected areas as a possible means to effective conservation, rights recognition, and social reconciliation. However, although shared governance continues to be extolled in international circles and there are exemplary cases such as Gwaii Haanas National Park Reserve and Haida Heritage Sites (shared governance by the Haida Nation and the government of Canada), experience in diverse countries cautions that in practice it often falls short of new paradigm goals (on Canada and Peru, see chapters 5 and 6).[7] This reflects many factors. Problematic protected area governance arrangements and decision-making processes are primary factors, but these are often shaped by underlying social and political structures and dynamics. Contexts of territorial control, power dynamics, rights recognition, respect for difference, and other aspects of interethnic and interracial relations are often crucial. Among the common failings of shared governance arrangement are:

- inadequate scope: participation limited to certain aspects of governance and management, such as hunting regulation;
- inadequate authority: participation limited to consultation or advice;

- arrangements that promote unequal power relationships, voice, and authority;[8]
- arrangements that fail to respect Indigenous peoples as rights-holders and reduce them to one among many stakeholders;
- arrangements that undermine, replace, or conflict with Indigenous peoples' own systems of governance and representation;
- processes of decision-making based on cultural and social conventions that disadvantage and marginalize Indigenous people and conflict with their decision-making protocols; and
- processes of decision-making that ignore or denigrate Indigenous knowledge, values, and customary practices.

There is no single optimal institutional structure for securing Indigenous peoples' effective participation in shared governance while upholding cultural integrity and rights. Particular arrangements may be deemed more or less culturally, socially, and politically appropriate by different Indigenous peoples in specific contexts and situations and over time. One common approach (including in Australia and Canada) has been to establish management committees in which representatives of Indigenous peoples constitute half or more of the total members. Indigenous peoples may consider it important to ensure that the chair is an Indigenous person, that an Indigenous person is a cochair, or that the chair rotates between Indigenous and non-Indigenous partners. In the case of Gwaii Haanas National Park and Haida Heritage Site, where Haida hold half the seats and cochair the Archipelago Management Board, an additional key factor has been the agreement that all decisions are made on the basis of consensus (Borrini-Feyerabend et al. 2013; Archipelago Management Board n.d.). Neither the composition of a committee nor its leadership, however, guarantees Indigenous peoples' full and effective participation in governance; much depends on purview and authority, procedural practices, epistemological issues, interpersonal dynamics, and legal safeguards for their rights and responsibilities.

Decision-making procedures can be crucial and often disadvantage Indigenous peoples. Key issues for their full and effective participation in management committees, for example, include meeting times, length, and sites; language(s) and interpretation; whether meetings are open or closed; who sets the agenda, how long in advance it is decided, and how flexible it is; who chairs or facilitates the meeting and how; and what procedures are followed for discussion and decision-making (including not only whether decisions are reached by consensus or vote but also whether attention is given to how cultural issues may influence participation and decision-making). Processes often seem to replicate the customs of state agencies and NGOs, ignoring Indigenous protocols. This forces Indigenous peoples to take on the burden (and assimilative pressures) of participating in non-native languages and through culturally alien bureaucratic and managerial forms and procedures (chapter 5; Nadasdy 1999, 2003a, 2005; Lawrence 2000; Stevenson 2004, 2006; Haynes 2009, 2013; Ross et al. 2011).

Because of the likelihood that shared governance will continue to be important, and indeed may become more common than it now is, it is worth looking more closely at some key structural and epistemological barriers (Ross et al. 2011) or challenges to Indigenous peoples' full and effective participation in these governance arrangements.

> **Sidebar 12.4. Principles of Effective Shared Governance of Protected Areas**
>
> - Recognize Indigenous peoples' status as Indigenous peoples and their human and Indigenous rights and responsibilities.
> - Recognize Indigenous peoples' territories, collective land and sea tenure, self-determination, self-governance, and customary law or agree to differ on issues such as territorial ownership while dispute resolution processes proceed.
> - Only undertake shared governance with the free, prior, and informed consent of Indigenous peoples.
> - Provide for periodic review and renegotiation of shared governance arrangements.
> - Provide, when agreed to by all parties, for shared governance to be an interim arrangement to facilitate transition to Indigenous peoples' self-governance of protected areas in their customary territories.
> - Establish formal, clear, legally binding agreements on shared governance that include institutional arrangements, decision-making processes, dispute resolution mechanisms, protected area goals and management categories, and key policies and regulations.
> - Ensure that Indigenous peoples have at least equal decision-making power and authority in shared governance arrangements.
> - Develop decision-making processes with Indigenous peoples' full and effective participation that respect their own decision-making protocols.

- Ensure that when management boards are established these are not merely advisory and define their purview to include policy-making, planning, assessment and evaluation, oversight of day-to-day management, fiscal responsibility, and accountability.
- Ensure that Indigenous peoples approve the means by which management board members are selected.
- Ensure that Indigenous peoples have at least equal representation and leadership on management boards.
- Provide capacity building for all involved, including for improving cross-cultural communication, relationships, and interactions.
- Foster trust and a strong shared commitment to working together.
- Carry out joint work and training, the shared experience of which can foster better interpersonal relationships, mutual understanding, and respect.
- Strive for decisions that reflect respect for Indigenous peoples' values and knowledge as well as non-Indigenous peoples' concerns and knowledge.
- Recognize ICCAs that overlap with or are contained within these protected areas.
- Provide legal authority for Indigenous rangers, guardians, and others designated by Indigenous peoples to enforce customary law and protected area regulations.

STRUCTURAL FAILURES OF SHARED GOVERNANCE

Many institutional arrangements and practices that are represented as "shared governance" perpetuate existing disparities in power and authority and fail to secure and promote rights. Indeed, protected area governance arrangements that ostensibly "share power" and facilitate new collaborations among partners can instead further the disempowerment and assimilation of Indigenous peoples. In some cases, institutional arrangements and practices seem designed to fail to meet the spirit of sharing power and the principles of the new paradigm by preventing Indigenous peoples' full and effective participation in decision-making and ensuring inadequate recognition and respect for their cultural identities and integrity, ownership and control of territories, self-governance, and self-determination. In these cases "shared governance" may be constructed to be a means of overt state territorialization or more subtle "environmentality." In other cases, problematic structural arrangements may reflect interethnic, often racialized prejudices that permeate the institutional cultures of state agencies and non-Indigenous NGO partners and shape power relationships, decision-making processes, and decisions. Such naturalized values and assumptions can indeed even distort well-intentioned (although paternalistic) efforts to design and implement inclusive institutional arrangements, making shared governance a form of "deep colonising" (Rose 1996; see chapter 2).[9] Asymmetrical power relations and decision-making dynamics can obstruct Indigenous peoples' full and effective participation in shared governance even when they are acknowledged as the owners or custodians of the territories in which protected areas have been established (see, for example, Lawrence 2000; Magome and Murombedzi 2003; Haynes 2009, 2013).

The IUCN and CBD urge that Indigenous peoples participate fully and effectively in protected area governance in accordance with their rights. But "participation" can be conceived in diverse ways (Pimbert and Pretty 1995; Cooke and Kothari 2001), many of which do not meet the standards of the new paradigm. Consultation alone—advice without authority—is insufficient (Weaver 1991; Sneed 1997; Stevens 1997a). Shared governance must mean more than an opportunity to volunteer advice that may have little or no influence on policy or planning or to participate in decision-making only on specific issues such as wildlife or forest management and not in the governance of the protected area itself (chapter 5; Stevens 1997a). Participation also has to mean more than the opportunity to contribute time and labor to programs that have been designed by others. Indigenous peoples are not simply a resource whose participation can be "framed as a social tool for achieving objectives already decided by conservation scientists, rather than as a human right" (Jeanrenaud 2002: 26).

There is a danger that participation in these various narrow terms may be taken to constitute consent, and hence to legitimate policies and practice that Indigenous peoples have not, in fact, authorized or had the opportunity to help shape. Such participation may constitute co-optation rather than collaboration. Berkes (2008:41) has referred to this "potential for the co-optation of indigenous knowledge and coercing people to work within Western-style governance that is foreign to their thinking" as "the dark side of co-management." As Jeanrenaud (2002: 28) noted, conservation in this way risks the "danger that such words as 'community' and 'participation' can become rhetorical devices or confer an aura of authority on conservation organizations [and state agencies], which is then used to legitimate access to and control of resources, with little relation to local interests or goals."[10]

One way that this can come about is through encouraging (or inducing or coercing) Indigenous peoples to participate in state- or NGO-designed and -promoted institutions that endeavor to foster new conservation values and "subjectivities," what Agrawal (2005) called "environmentality" and others have called "green governmentality" (Luke 1997; Rutherford 2007). As a form of governmentality (Foucault 1991, 2010), this may be intended to promote the internalization of new values and consequent self-regulation.[11] Rights are violated when environmentality represents coercive or induced assimilation and the undermining of customary values and governance institutions. Environmentality can contribute to state territorialization by increasing legibility and state control under the guise of sharing power, a "Trojan horse"–like ruse (Blaikie 2005) that is a "pretext to co-opt community-based management and extend the power of the state" (Berkes 2009a: 1693). This has conservation as well as social justice costs. By fostering the exclusion (and loss) of Indigenous knowledge and institutions, these forms of governmentality can undermine Indigenous peoples' existing conservation contributions, preclude the development of new synergies, and threaten biocultural diversity and the realization of protected area conservation goals and standards.[12]

EPISTEMOLOGICAL ISSUES AND SHARED GOVERNANCE

Shared governance can be epistemologically problematic when it fails to honor and respect Indigenous peoples' knowledge and worldviews. Decision-making can privilege Western science and science-based technomanagerialism and ignore, trivialize, or distort Indigenous peoples' science, knowledge, and expertise (chapter 5; Nadasdy 1999, 2003a, 2003b, 2005; McGregor 2004; Stevenson 2004, 2006; Spak 2005; Sandlos 2008; Ross et al. 2011). Shared governance participants trained in Western science have often been reluctant to accept the legitimacy of other types of knowledge or have valued only those components of it that they can mine for useful data and readily incorporate into their existing assumptions, methods, and analyses. Coproduction of knowledge is possible, but it requires that all involved acknowledge the validity of multiple epistemologies and work together with respect, humility, and appreciation of difference (Berkes 2009b). Shared governance may require "not a synthesis of the two kinds of knowledge, but an ability to develop mutual respect and trust, a task that can easily take a decade . . . and does not always succeed" (Berkes 2009a: 1699). It will be important to draw on perspectives from both Indigenous knowledge and Western science to address conservation challenges, and to consider, as Berkes (2009b: 154) advised, whether "the two kinds of knowledge should not be blended or synthesized," but rather that each "should retain its own integrity."

Epistemological conflicts are often severe and can overwhelm institutional arrangements intended to share power, such as management boards in which Indigenous peoples have an equal or majority number of seats. By silencing difference and obstructing dialogue and negotiation, these inequalities and biases create major barriers to Indigenous peoples' effective participation in governance; make it likely that decisions will not reflect their values, concerns, and aspirations; and increase the risk that governance will violate rights. They are aggravated by lack of capacity. State and NGO participants may have inadequate understanding of Indigenous peoples' languages, cultures, and protocols and may be unaware of historical and political contexts or of international law and standards concerning Indigenous rights and rights-based conservation (Haynes 2009, 2013; Ross et al. 2011). They also may have poor skills in cross-cultural interaction, negotiation, and dispute resolution. State agency and NGO participants may be unconscious of or unconcerned about such significant capacity shortcomings on their own part, while assuming that evidence that any cross-cultural challenges that Indigenous peoples may have with language, techno-scientific management and legal terminology, or bureaucratic protocol justify their lesser voice in decision-making. Although it will often be difficult to change the epistemological biases in protected area decision-making, measures that may help include providing capacity-building opportunities for all involved, ensuring availability of interpreters so that all participants can speak in the language each prefers, working together on projects, and making funds available for Indigenous peoples to hire their own staff and consultants, including their own legal counsel, scientists, and technical specialists.

Epistemological problems are all the more formidable because they are typically strongly embedded in unequal interethnic and racialized relationships that are fundamental to the social and political plight of Indigenous peoples in many countries. This political dimension is often ignored by techno-managers and authorities who believe that decision-making can and should be technical, supposedly objective, and apolitical. This "anti-politics machine" (chapter 6; Ferguson 1994; Nadasdy 2005) position (or posturing) insists that effective protected area management can only be achieved through the application of Western science and techno-managerialism. It fails to consider whether legitimating only certain knowledge and expertise is not itself an application of power. By denying the highly political nature of protected areas, it creates a distorted, self-interested representation of the contexts of governance and management, choosing to ignore that decisions about access to resources are entwined with interethnic, racial, and local/national issues of sovereignty, self-determination, ownership and control of territory, power relations, and the proper role and character of the state in multi-ethnic societies, as well as Indigenous, minority, civil, and human rights. Empowering anti-politics as a foundation for protected area governance politicizes the framing not only of management "problems" and "solutions" but also of governance itself. In effect, anti-politics defines who makes decisions by limiting what can and cannot be said and which voices are taken seriously. This ensures that decisions—from goals and regulations to allocation of resources and responsibilities and recognition of rights and privileges—are made in ways that privilege knowledge and values held by particular people and interests and silence and exclude others. This corrodes the mutual respect, trust, and parameters of fairness that should ground shared governance, promotes autocracy and paternalism, and violates diverse rights.[13]

Securing Biocultural Diversity, Conservation, and Justice

Protected areas embodying the new paradigm can become a powerful means of securing biocultural diversity, strengthening biodiversity conservation, and promoting justice across the vast areas of the planet that are the customary territories of Indigenous peoples.[14] The new paradigm offers an opportunity to reform what have often been appallingly unjust social, political, economic, and ecological relationships and to create protected areas that simultaneously sustain the life of the planet, the cultural heritage, well-being, and livelihoods of thousands of distinct peoples, and Indigenous and human rights. It makes possible protected areas that foster dignity, self-governance, and self-determination. It creates opportunities for protected areas that benefit from Indigenous peoples' knowledge, values, and stewardship instead of being a means and justification for separating them from their homelands, undermining their identities and relationship with the world, denigrating their cultures and knowledge, and destroying their livelihoods and development aspirations. Such new kinds of protected areas can help create new interethnic, interracial, intercultural, and governmental understandings and relationships. This can make protected areas a central site of reconciliation between Indigenous peoples and other members of national societies rather than a primary source of conflict.

The new paradigm imagines different ways of understanding political ecologies of conservation, sustainability, and associated social and environmental movements. It envisions specific institutional arrangements, policies, and practices through which new conceptualizations of "conservation" and conservation institutions and new shared understandings of ecology, biocultural diversity, and human rights can advance environmental justice. In doing so, the new paradigm makes possible protected areas that are at once both biologically rich homelands and places of restitution, return, reinhabitation, and cultural rediscovery and rejuvenation for those who have been displaced and dispossessed by past protected area policies. It creates sites of secured livelihoods and of self-directed, culturally and ecologically appropriate development. And it restores territorial integrity, self-governance, and self-determination to peoples long disempowered. Such protected areas can be an important means of decolonization and indeed of remaking the Fourth World.[15]

The policies already developed by the IUCN and CBD can point the way, but in many countries, realizing the new paradigm likely will require not only raising the awareness of lawmakers, bureaucrats, conservationists and conservation organizations, and the general public but also intensifying pressure for change. Constitutional and legislative reform, increased accountability to national and international judicial systems, and active national and international human rights monitoring mechanisms will be important. So, too, will be further initiatives by the IUCN, the CBD, international and national conservation organizations, donors, and social justice and conservation organizations. In addition, continuing vigilance, commitment, and action by Indigenous peoples and local communities will be crucial to negotiate and secure reforms and to hold state agencies and conservation organizations accountable for rights and conservation commitments and honoring the spirit of national and international law, obligations, and standards. Protected area reform may often be achieved and secured only through strong, sustained direct actions, media campaigns, and lobbying at local, national, and international scales. In many cases Indigenous peoples may need to wage campaigns and sustained movements that draw on resources and strategies that make adroit use of national, regional, and international networks, federations, and alliances.

Although many proponents of the new paradigm find the pace of national implementation thus far disappointing, there have been developments in many parts of the world that would have been nearly unimaginable a few years ago. Momentum is likely to build. The mainstreaming of UNDRIP in the UN system and beyond, together with regional court decisions, is likely to give added impetus to Indigenous peoples' efforts to gain recognition of territory, restitution of lands, stronger participation in protected area governance, and respect for the conservation significance of their institutions and practices. The IUCN, the CBD, human rights organizations, UN and national human rights monitoring institutions, and international courts are likely to become increasingly engaged in rectifying protected area injustices and advancing new paradigm reforms. International conservationists and conservation organizations may develop greater appreciation of the importance of Indigenous peoples' territories and contributions to conservation and the value of long-term alliances with them. More conservation organizations may adopt rights-based codes of ethics guided by UNDRIP, and the creation of an independent inspection panel could increase compliance incentive (Alcorn 2010). Such an institution could be linked, as Alcorn (2010) suggested, to a new international institution that also engages with states, such as the international Truth and Reconciliation Commission for Indigenous Peoples and Protected Areas envisioned at the Vth WPC in 2003 (WPC Recommendation V.24). This could involve, among other institutions, the IUCN, the UN Special Rapporteur on the Rights of Indigenous Peoples, the UN Permanent Forum on Indigenous Issues, the UN Expert Mechanism on the Rights of Indigenous Peoples, and regional and national human rights monitoring organizations. Intergovernmental agencies and other donors also are expected to increase their commitments to improving the quality of protected area governance and management, including attention to rights recognition and the participation of Indigenous peoples in protected area governance. They will also be asked to provide more conservation funds directly to Indigenous peoples, in contrast to the present situation (Alcorn 2010).[16] Efforts will continue to hold states accountable for their obligations under international law. This could include the development of certification programs for protected areas that require strong recognition of rights, including restitution of Indigenous peoples' territories and their full and effective participation in governance.

Protected area reform will be accelerated when states reform their national constitutions and laws to respect Indigenous rights and responsibilities, including Indigenous peoples' ownership of their territories and their maintenance of customary forms of individual and collective land tenure, self-governance, and law. Constitutional and national law reform—in some cases encouraged by court decisions—can ensure that civil, human, and Indigenous rights apply in protected areas as they do everywhere else, and that state agencies charged with implementing national environmental law also are held accountable for upholding human and Indigenous rights enshrined in national and international law and treaties. In this context, state protected area agencies may experience legal and governmental pressure to adhere to new paradigm principles and standards at the same time that they are encouraged and assisted to do so by the IUCN, the CBD, and donors.

In much of the world, however, it will be a long and difficult struggle to move from internationally affirmed principles to transformation of national policy and practice. Realizing the new paradigm requires overcoming the prejudices, privileges, vested interests, and agendas of powerful actors and redressing legacies of continuing injustice and suffering. It requires envisioning and promoting both very different approaches to conservation and fundamentally different social relationships. It links concern with the global condition of ecosystems and species with securing Indigenous peoples' realization of the rights, freedoms, and responsibilities articulated in UNDRIP.

This is not only a challenge to conservationists and conservation organizations (Chapin 2004). It is a challenge to states and to international institutions concerned with conservation, sustainable development, and justice. It is a challenge not only to reenvision international conservation and development but also to remake attitudes and relationships that continue to exclude, dispossess, and oppress Indigenous peoples. The implementation of the new protected area paradigm will thus be as difficult as the other great struggles it is entwined with: the global struggles to defend biodiversity, Indigenous peoples' territories and cultures, and human and Indigenous rights. In many countries and societies it is likely to be a multigenerational struggle. Yet wherever it succeeds—even partially and unevenly—the realization of the new paradigm will build new ways of working and living together, contributing to remaking both conservation and the place of Indigenous peoples in national societies by securing biocultural diversity and rights. The new paradigm thus reenvisions protected areas as geographies of hope,[17] not only for the human spirit, as Wallace Stegner (1997) famously observed in his 1960 letter advocating protection of wilderness areas but also for the diversity and richness of nature and the entwined, mutually constitutive futures of Indigenous peoples and life on earth.

Notes

1. Rights-based approaches to forest governance and management, including for forest tenure reform, also have been slowly and only partially implemented (Sikor and Stahl 2011).

2. The members of the Conservation Initiative on Human Rights are the IUCN, Conservation International, World Wide Fund for Nature, The Nature Conservancy, Wildlife Conservation Society, Birdlife International, Fauna and Flora International, and Wetlands International.

3. The outcome of a landmark precedent for restitution, the 2010 decision by the African Commission on Human and Peoples' Rights and the African Union against Kenya, is notable in this respect. This decision required restitution as part of the remedy and redress for the government of Kenya's violation of six articles of the African Charter on Human and Peoples' Rights in its 1970s eviction of the Endorois from what is today Lake Bogoria National Reserve (Morel 2010). The government of Kenya, however, has thus far failed to take any action to implement this decision, or even to meet with the Endorois (Minority Rights 2012). Government officials did not attend a 2013 workshop to discuss implementation with members of the Endorois, the African Commission on Human and Peoples' Rights' Working Group on Indigenous Populations/Communities, the Kenya National Commission on Human Rights, representatives of the UN Office of the High Commissioner for Human Rights, and the UN Special Rapporteur on the Rights of Indigenous Peoples (African Commission on Human and Peoples' Rights 2013). In 2011, moreover, Kenya inscribed the Lake Bogoria National Reserve on the World Heritage site list as part of the Kenya Lake System World Heritage Site without the free, prior, and informed consent of the Endorois. The African Commission on Human and Peoples' Rights and IUCN have both protested this action as failing to meet the principles of UNDRIP. IUCN WCC Resolution 5.047 called for the government of Kenya to implement the African Commission's Endorois decision and to ensure the full and effective participation by the Endorois in the World Heritage site's management and decision making (IUCN 2012c). Restitution in South Africa's Kruger National Park has also been problematic. The famous case of restitution of land to the Makuleke has been criticized for the conditions attached to it and for the comanagement arrangements that were subsequently implemented (chapter 9; Magome and Murombedzi 2003). Moreover, a 2009 cabinet decision halted processing of other restitution claims in Kruger National Park that collectively encompassed nearly half the park's total area, offering financial compensation but not the restoration of land ownership (Whande 2010).

4. Participatory mapping (including three-dimensional modeling and participatory GIS) has become a key tool being used by many Indigenous peoples in efforts to gain title to their customary territories, including in situations when protected areas have been superimposed on them (Herlihy 1997; Nietschmann 1997; Zingapan and De Vera 1999; Eghenter 2000; Stocks 2003; Oyono et al. 2010).

5. Indigenous peoples may also often be reluctant to accept state recognition of their ICCAs, fearing that this will lead to co-optation, marginalization, and loss of self-governance that will threaten their ability to maintain stewardship over their territories in accordance with their cultural values and responsibilities.

6. IPAs are not gazetted as protected areas, but state recognition of them as part of the national reserve system requires that they conform to several requirements, including that they devise a management plan and gain state approval of it before their IPAs are recognized and receive funding. Meeting state management planning expectations or qualifying for and accepting state funding does not seem to have undermined Indigenous peoples' ability to set their own goals and policies. Whether this continues to be the case merits careful ongoing monitoring.

7. It should be remembered, however, that many of these shared governance arrangements are recently instituted and are not necessarily permanently locked into existing relationships and practices. The experience of working together, increased understanding of Indigenous peoples' conservation contributions and of their territories' ecosystems, broader social change, and lessons learned from early experience may all contribute to improving relationships, Indigenous peoples' participation in decision-making, and respect for their rights and responsibilities.

8. States and conservation NGOs often refuse to engage with Indigenous peoples as equal partners. Inequity is also an issue when customary institutions and practices foster elite domination of decision-making and marginalize other community members, often including women and young people.

9. Deep colonizing occurs, for example, when comanagement arrangements are created without recognizing Indigenous peoples' territorial ownership or rights and when they co-opt their authority, create new institutional arrangements that undermine customary leadership, or establish decision-making processes that exclude their knowledge, values, and customary law.

10. Jeanrenaud did not conclude, however, that all such recent "paradigm translation" by conservation organizations is "strictly technocratic and insidious" and found honest efforts by practitioners to reform old paradigm approaches in ways that have created spaces and opportunities for new mutual understanding and for collaborations based on shared interests (Jeanrenaud 2002: 47).

11. As Bryant (2002: 287, emphasis in original) observed in a related context: "Empowerment is thus apparently bought at a price. The very practices that enable the downtrodden—usually with NGO help—to sometimes 'see off' the forces of [state, autocratic] *sovereignty* are also an irresistible invitation for processes of *governmentality* to intrude ever more systematically into the lives of marginalized peoples."

12. The introduction of new institutions by state agencies and outside NGOs, however, does not necessarily result in simple hegemonic environmentality even when this is intended. The degree to which Indigenous peoples forsake their existing cosmovision, institutions, and practices when participating in new institutions can easily be misunderstood. Indigenous peoples' resiliency may be underestimated, including their ability to adapt and integrate new ideas, terminology, and institutions with preexisting ones and their strategic use of new language and institutional arrangements to promote their own values and agendas in ways that "creatively respond to project interventions and even capture them for their own ends" (Jeanrenaud 2002: 26; also see Acciaioli 2008).

13. However, it is also important to recognize, as Emily Caruso discusses in chapter 6, that characterizing these kinds of "shared" governance simply as a "colonizing or anti-political force" may not adequately recognize Indigenous peoples' enduring agency and own perspectives on their sovereignty and relationships with the state.

Indigenous peoples may continue to affirm their identities and live their lives in ways that embody their distinctive cosmovisions and relationships with their territories without being co-opted or assimilated into new ways of thinking and acting as a result of the establishment of protected areas. Nonetheless, the outcome of "shared" governance that does not reflect their values and rights can be management plans and decisions that legitimize unwelcome interventions in their territories and lives and foster state territorialization.

14. The new paradigm can also transform protected areas in vast additional areas that comprise the customary territories, lands, waters, and resources of local communities.

15. In this sense, the new paradigm envisions (post)colonial, decolonizing protected areas (Stevens 2006, 2007).

16. The Conference to the Parties of the Convention on Biological Diversity (2012), for example, in COP 11 Decision XI/14 (section A, par. 8 and 9) called on states to include in their requests to GEF and other donors funding to support Indigenous peoples to develop their own community conservation plans and to document, map, and register their ICCAs, as well as support to states to strengthen their recognition of ICCAs.

17. The phrase "geography of hope" was first used in association with protected areas by Wallace Stegner, who coined it to advocate for the importance of wilderness preservation for the human spirit in his famous 1960 "Wilderness Letter." For Stegner (1969: 153), preserving wilderness was a "means of reassuring ourselves of our sanity as creatures, a part of the geography of hope." Many have used the phrase since in other contexts. Geographer Julianne Hazlewood (2012), for example, recently applied the phrase to encompass the practices and networks through which Indigenous peoples in Ecuador maintain identity and livelihoods amid deforestation and oil palm plantation development. I have been using the phrase (Stevens 2007) to contrast with Stegner's perspective, envisioning protected areas based on the new paradigm as part of a larger geography of hope for both global biodiversity and Indigenous peoples.

References

Aboriginal Management Board. n.d. "Gwaii Haanas National Park Reserve and Haida Heritage Site: Management Plan for the Terrestrial Area." http://www.pc.gc.ca/eng/pn-np/bc/gwaiihaanas/plan/plan1.aspx. Last accessed on February 19, 2014.

Acciaioli, Greg. 2008. "Environmentality Reconsidered: Indigenous To Lindu Conservation Strategies and the Reclaiming of the Commons in Central Sulawesi, Indonesia." In *People, Protected Areas and Global Change: Participatory Conservation in Latin America, Africa, Asia and Europe*, Perspectives of the Swiss National Centre of Competence in Research (NCCR) North-South, University of Bern, Vol. 3, edited by Marc Galvin and Tobias Haller, 401–30. Bern: Geographica Bernensia.

Adams, William M., and Jon Hutton. 2007. "People, Parks and Poverty: Political Ecology and Biodiversity Conservation." *Conservation and Society* 5(2): 147–83.

Adams, William M., and Martin Mulligan, eds. 2003. *Decolonizing Nature: Strategies for Conservation in a Post-Colonial Era*. London: Earthscan.

Adams, William M., Ros Aveling, Dan Brockington, Barney Dickson, Jo Elliott, Jon Hutton, Dilys Roe, Bhaskar Vira, and William Wolmer. 2004. "Biodiversity Conservation and the Eradication of Poverty." *Science* 306(5699): 1146–9.

AFE-COHDEFOR. 1998. *Censo Poblacional 1997/98*. Tegucigalpa, Honduras: Proyecto Manejo y Protección de la Biosfera Río Plátano.

———. 2000. *Plan de Manejo, Reserva del Hombre y La Biosfera del Río Plátano*. Tegucigalpa, Honduras: Proyecto Manejo y Protección de la Biosfera Río Plátano.

———. 2002. *Informe Estudio de Factibilidad. Proyecto Reserva del Hombre y la Biosfera del Río Plátano, Componente Catastro y Titilación*. Tegucigalpa, Honduras: Proyecto Manejo y Protección de la Biosfera Río Plátano.

African Commission on Human and Peoples' Rights (ACHPR). 2005. *Report of the African Commission's Working Group on Indigenous Populations/Communities*. DOC/OS (XXXIV)/345. Copenhagen: ACHPR and International Work Group for Indigenous Affairs.

———. 2013. "Final Communique of the Workshop on the Status of the Implementation of the Endorois Decision of the African Commission on Human and Peoples' Rights." http://www.achpr.org/news/2013/10/d96/. Last accessed on February 22, 2014.

Agarwal, Bina. 1994. *A Field of One's Own: Gender and Land Rights in South Asia*. Cambridge, UK: Cambridge University Press.

Agius, P., J. Davies, R. Howitt, S. Jarvis, and R. Williams, 2004. "Comprehensive Native Title Negotiations in South Australia." In *Honour Among Nations? Treaties and Agreements with Indigenous People*, edited by M. Langton, M. Tehan, L. Palmer, and K. Shain, 203–19. Melbourne: Melbourne University Press.

Agrawal, Arun. 2002. "Common Resources and Institutional Sustainability." In *The Drama of the Commons*, edited by Elinor Ostrom, Thomas Dietz, Nives Dolšak, Paul C. Stern, Susan Stonich, and Elke U. Weber, 41–85. Washington, DC: National Academy Press.

———. 2005. *Environmentality: Technologies of Government and the Making of Subjects*. Durham, NC: Duke University Press.

Agrawal, Arun, and A. Ashwini Chhatre. 2006. "Explaining Success on the Commons: Community Forest Governance in the Indian Himalaya." *World Development* 34: 149–66.

Agrawal, Arun, and Clark C. Gibson. 1999. "Enchantment and Disenchantment: The Role of Community in Natural Resource Conservation." *World Development* 27(4): 629–49.

———, eds. 2001a. *Communities and the Environment: Ethnicity, Gender, and the State in Community-Based Conservation*. New Brunswick, NJ: Rutgers University Press.

———. 2001b. "The Role of Community in Natural Resource Conservation." In *Communities and the Environment: Ethnicity, Gender, and the State in Community-Based Conservation*, edited by Arun Agrawal and Clark C. Gibson, 1–31. New Brunswick, NJ: Rutgers University Press.

Agrawal, Arun, and Kent Redford. 2005. "Poverty Alleviation and Biodiversity Conservation: Shooting in the Dark." University of Michigan, SNRE and Wildlife Conservation Society. http://polisci.ucsd.edu/calendar/kent-arunpaperdraft6a.pdf. Last accessed September 6, 2005.

———. 2009. "Conservation and Displacement: An Overview." *Conservation and Society* 7(1): 1–10.

Agrawal, Arun, and Jesse C. Ribot. 2000. *Accountability in Decentralization: A Framework with South Asian and West African Cases*. Washington, DC: World Resources Institute.

Aguilar, F., and D. Skarwan. 2000. "Semillas Para el Desarrollo Forestal: Conflictos, Consensos y Negociacion entre Actores." Quetzaltenango, Guatemala: Helvetas ProBosques.

Alcorn, Janis B. 1994. "Noble Savage or Noble State? Northern Myths and Southern Realities in Biodiversity Conservation." *Ethnoecológica* 1: 7–19.

———. 2005. "Dances around the Fire: Conservation Organizations and Community-Based Natural Resource Management." In *Communities and Conservation: Histories and Politics of Community-Based National Resource Management*, edited by J. Peter Brosius, Anna Lowenhaupt Tsing, and Charles Zerner, 37–68. Walnut Creek, CA: Rowman and Littlefield.

———. 2010. "Indigenous Peoples and Conservation." White paper prepared for the MacArthur Foundation. http://production.macfound.org/media/files/CSD_Indigenous_Peoples_White_Paper.pdf. Last accessed September 23, 2013.

Alcorn, Janis B., and Antoinette Royo. 2007. "Conservation's Engagement with Human Rights: 'Traction,' 'Slippage,' or Avoidance?" *Policy Matters* 15: 115–39.

Alexiades, Miguel N. 2009. "Mobility and Migration in Indigenous Amazonia: Contemporary Ethnoecological Perspectives—an Introduction." In *Mobility and Migration in Indigenous Amazonia: Contemporary Ethnoecological Perspectives*, edited by Migue N. Alexiades, 1–46. Oxford, UK: Berghahn.

Alfred, Taiaiake. 1999. *Peace, Power, Righteousness: An Indigenous Manifesto*. New York: Oxford University Press.

———. 2001. "From Sovereignty to Freedom: Towards an Indigenous Political Discourse." *Indigenous Affairs* 3: 22–34.

———. 2005. *Wasáse: Indigenous Pathways of Action and Freedom*. Peterborough, Ontario: Broadview Press.

Allen, John. 2004. "The Whereabouts of Power: Politics, Government and Space." *Geografiska Annaler: Series B, Human Geography* 86(1): 19–32.

Altamirano-Jiménez, I. 2004. "North American First Peoples: Slipping up into Market Citizenship." *Citizenship Studies* 8(4): 349–65.

Altman, J. 1987. *Hunter-Gatherers Today: An Aboriginal Economy in North Australia*. Canberra: Australian Institute of Aboriginal Studies.

———. 2003. "People on Country, Healthy Landscapes and Sustainable Indigenous Economic Futures: The Arnhem Land Case." *The Drawing Board: An Australian Review of Public Affairs* 4(2): 65–82.

Alvarez del Castillo, Alex. 2010. "Conservación Participativa en la Reserva Comunal Amarakaeri, Perú." *Revista Latinoamericana de Conservación* 1(1): 18–37.

Amend, Stephen, and Thora Amend, eds. 1995. *National Parks Without People? The South American Experience*. Gland, Switzerland: IUCN.

Amend, Thora, Ruth Petra, Stephanie Eissing, and Stephen Amend. 2008. "Land Rights Are Human Rights: Win-Win Strategies for Sustainable Nature Conservation, Contributions from South Africa." In *Sustainability Has Many Faces*, No. 4. Deutsche Gesellschaft für Technische Zusammenarbeit (GtZ). Heidelberg, Germany: Kasparek Verlag.

Anaya, James S. 2004. *Indigenous Peoples in International Law*. Oxford, UK: Oxford University Press.

———. 2009a. *International Human Rights and Indigenous Peoples*. Austin, Texas: Wolters Kluwer.

———. 2009b. "Promotion and Protection of All Human Rights, Civil, Political, Economic, Social and Cultural Rights, Including the Right to Development: Report by the Special Rapporteur on the Situation of Human Rights and Fundamental Freedoms of Indigenous People, James Anaya, Addendum: Report on the Situation of Indigenous Peoples in Nepal." A/HRC/12/34/Add.3, July 20, 2009. http://www2.0hchr.org/english/bodies/hrcouncil/docs/12session/A-HRC-12-34-Add3_E.pdf.

Anderson, David, and Richard H. Grove. 1987. *Conservation in Africa: Peoples, Policies and Practice*. Cambridge, UK: Cambridge University Press.

Anderson, D. G., and M. Nuttall, eds. 2003. *Cultivating Arctic Landscapes: Knowing and Managing Animals in the Circumpolar North*. New York: Berghahn Books.

Anderson, M. Kat. 2006. *Tending the Wild: Native American Knowledge and the Management of California's Natural Resources*. Berkeley: University of California Press.

Anderson, M. Kat, and Michael G. Barbour. 2003. "Simulated Indigenous Management: A New Model for Ecological Restoration in National Parks." *Ecological Restoration* 12(4): 269–77.

Ankersen, T. T., K. E. Regan, and S. A. Mack. 2006. "Towards a Bioregional Approach to Tropical Forest Conservation: Costa Rica's Greater Osa Bioregion." *Futures* 38: 406–31.

Anonymous. 1999. "Mafia Forestal Amenaza Bosawás." *El Nuevo Diario* (Managua, Nicaragua). February 18. http://archivo.elnuevodiario.com.ni/1999/febrero/18-febrero-1999/nacional/nacional11.html. Last accessed February 18, 2014.

———. 2007a. "Canadian Boreal Initiative Applauds Federal Government for Advancing Expansion of Nahanni National Park Reserve." *Canada News Wire* (Aug 8). http://proquest.umi.com/pqdweb?did=1316762571&Fmt=7&clientId=65345&RQT=309&VName=PQD. Last accessed March 7, 2008.

———. 2007b. "One Step Closer to East Arm National Park." *Up Here* 23(1): 16.

———. n.d. "Ashaninka C.R. Management Plan." Background document used during the process of categorization of the Vilcabamba Conservation Complex.

Antonson, Joan M., and William S. Hanable. 1987. *Administrative History of Sitka National Historical Park*. Anchorage, AK: National Park Service.

Arias, A. 1990. "Changing Indian Identity: Guatemala's Violent Transition to Modernity." In *Guatemalan Indians and the State: 1540 to 1988*, edited by C. A. Smith, 230–57. Austin: University of Texas Press.

———. 2008. "The Maya Movement: Postcolonialism and Cultural Agency." In *Coloniality at Large: Latin America and the Postcolonial Debate*, edited by M. Morana, E. Dussel, and C. A. Jaragui, 519–38. Durham, NC: Duke University Press.

Armbrecht, Ann. 2009. *Thin Places: A Pilgrimage Home*. New York: Columbia University Press.

Armitage, Derek, Fikret Berkes, and Nancy Doubleday, eds. 2007. *Adaptive Co-management: Collaboration, Learning, and Multi-Level Governance*. Vancouver: University of British Columbia Press.

Asian NGO Coalition for Agrarian Reform and Rural Development. n.d. "3-D Mapping: A Tool for Community Empowerment." http://www.angoc.org/portal/wp-content/uploads/2010/07/19/ideas-in-action-for-land-rights-advocacy/14-3-D-Mapping-Tool-for-Community-Empowerment.pdf. Last accessed July 5, 2013.

Aumeeruddy-Thomas, Yildiz, Yeshi Choden Lama, and Suresh Ghimire. 2004. "Medicinal Plants within the Context of Pastoral Life in the Village of Pungmo, Dolpo, Nepal." In *Strategic Innovations for Improving Livelihoods in the Hindu Kush-Himalayan Highlands*, Vol. II, edited by C. Richard and K. Hoffman, 107–28. Kathmandu, Nepal: ICIMOD.

Australian Bureau of Statistics. 2002. "Population Distribution: Aboriginal and Torres Strait Islander Australians. 2001." ABS Catalogue no. 4705.0. http://www.abs.gov.au/AUSSTATS/abs@.nsf/allprimarymainfeatures/2315409AD11513DFCA2573370013F824?opendocument. Last accessed February 20, 2014.

Australian Government Department of the Environment. 2012. "CAPAD [Collaborative Australian Protected Area Database] 2012 National Summary." http://www.environment.gov.au/node/34737. Last accessed on February 22, 2014.

———. n.d. "Indigenous Protected Areas," http://www.environment.gov.au/indigenous/ipa/. Sustainability, Environment, Water, Population and Communities. Last accessed February 10, 2014.

Autoridad Nacional del Ambiente-Corredor Biológico Mesoamericano del Atlántico Panameño (ANAM-CBMAP). 2001. "Subproyectos Aprobados y en Ejecución al 30 de Noviembre de 2001." http://www.cbmap.org/cbmap_subproyectos.php. Last accessed May 5, 2005.

Ayre, M. 2002. "Yolngu Places and People: Taking Aboriginal Understandings Seriously in Land and Sea." Ph.D. dissertation, University of Melbourne.

Baker, Ian. 2004. *The Heart of the World: A Journey to the Last Secret Place*. New York: Penguin.

Bakker, K. 2010. "The Limits of 'Neoliberal Natures': Debating Green Neoliberalism." *Progress in Human Geography* 34(6): 715–35.

Barahona, Marvin. 1998. "Introducción, Imagen y Percepción de los Pueblos Indígenas en Honduras." In *Rompiendo el Espejo. Visiones sobre los Pueblos Indígenas y Negros en Honduras*, edited by Marvin Barahona and Ramón Rivas, 17–41. Tegucigalpa, Honduras: Servicio Holandés de Cooperación al Desarrollo y Editorial Guaymuras.

———. 2002. *Evolución Histórica de la Identidad Nacional*, 2nd ed. Tegucigalpa, Honduras: Editorial Guaymuras.

Battachan, Krishna. 2005. "Dominant Groups [Only] Have Right to Live?" *Dauligiri* 1: 42–66.

———. n.d. "Indigenous Peoples and Minorities in Nepal." http://www.nefin.org.np/articles/dr-krishna-b-bhattachan. Last accessed September 6, 2013.

Bauer, Kenneth. 2004. *High Frontiers: Dolpo and the Changing World of Himalayan Pastoralists*. New York: Columbia University Press.

Bauman, T., C. Haynes, and G. Lauder. 2013. "Pathways to the Co-management of Protected Areas and Native Title in Australia." Research Discussion Paper no. 32. Canberra: Australian Institute of Aboriginal and Torres Strait Islander Studies.

Bazerman, Max, Jared Curhan, Don Moore, and Kathleen Valley. 2000. "Negotiation." *Annual Review of Psychology* 51: 279–314.

Beach, Hugh. 2003. "Political Ecology in Swedish Saamiland." In *Cultivating Arctic Landscapes: Knowing and Managing Animals in the Circumpolar North*, edited by D. G. Anderson and M. Nutall, 110–23. New York: Berghahn Books.

Bebbington, Anthony. 2000. "Re-encountering Development: Livelihood Transitions and Place Transformations in the Andes." *Annals of the Association of American Geographers* 90(3): 495–520.

Belaunde, Victor A. 2007 [1961]. "La Amazonía y la Peruanidad." In *Antología de la Amazonía del Peru, 1539 1960*, edited by E. Rivera Martinez, xxxix–xlv. Lima: Fundación Manuel J. Bustamante de la Fuente.

Belaunde, Terry F. 1994 [1959]. *La Conquista del Peru por los Peruanos*. Lima: Minerva.

Bennett, A. F. 2003. *Linkages in the Landscape: The Role of Corridors and Connectivity in Wildlife Conservation*. Gland, Switzerland: IUCN.

Berger, Thomas. 1985. *Village Journey: The Report of the Alaska Native Review Commission*. New York: Hill and Wang.

———. 1988. *Northern Frontier, Northern Homeland: The Report of the Mackenzie Valley Pipeline Inquiry*. Vancouver, BC: Douglas and McIntyre.

Berkes, Fikret. 1994. "Co-managing: Bridging the Two Solitudes." *Northern Perspectives* 22(2–3): 18–20.

———. 2004. "Rethinking Community-Based Conservation." *Conservation Biology* 18(3): 621–30.

———. 2008. *Sacred Ecology*, rev. 2nd ed. New York: Routledge.

———. 2009a. "Evolution of Co-management: Role of Knowledge Generation, Bridging Organizations and Social Learning." *Journal of Environmental Management* 90: 1692–1702.

———. 2009b. "Indigenous Ways of Knowing and the Study of Environmental Change." *Journal of the Royal Society of New Zealand* 39(4): 151–6.

Berkes, Fikret, Nigel Bankes, Melissa Marschke, Derek Armitage, and Douglas Clark. 2005. "Cross-Scale Institutions and Building Resistance in the Canadian North." In *Breaking Ice: Renewable Resource and Ocean Management in the Canadian North*, edited by Fikret Berkes, Rob Huebert, Helen Fast, Micheline Manseau, and Alan Diduick, 225–48. Calgary: University of Calgary Press.

Berkes, Fikret, Johan Colding, and Carl Folke. 2000. "Rediscovery of Traditional Ecological Knowledge as Adaptive Management." *Ecological Applications* 10(5): 1251–62.

Bertzky, Bastian, Colleen Corrigan, James Kemsey, Siobhan Kenney, Corinna Ravilious, Charles Besançon, and Neil Burgess. 2012. *Protected Planet Report 2012: Tracking Progress towards Global Targets for Protected Areas*. Gland, Switzerland and Cambridge, UK: IUCN and UNEP-WCMC.

Billings, R. F., S. R. Clarke, V. Espino Mendoza, P. Cordón Cabrera, B. Meléndez Figueroa, J. Ramón Campos, and G. Baeza. 2004. "Bark Beetle Outbreaks and Fire: A Devastating Combination for Central America's Pine Forests." *Unasylva* 217(75): 15–21.

Binnema, Theodore, and Melanie Niemi. 2006. "'Let the Line Be Drawn Now': Wilderness, Conservation, and the Exclusion of Aboriginal People from Banff National Park in Canada." *Environmental History* 11(4): 724–50.

Blaikie, Piers. 2005. "Is Small Really Beautiful? Community-Based Natural Resource Management in Malawi and Botswana." *World Development* 34(11): 1942–57.

Blaikie, Piers, and Harold Brookfield. 1987. "Common Property Resources and Degradation Worldwide." In *Land Degradation and Society*, edited by Piers Blaikie and Harold Brookfield, 186–96. New York: Methuen.

Blaikie, Piers, and Sally Jeanrenaud. 1997. "Biodiversity and Human Welfare." In *Social Change and Conservation: Environmental Politics and Impacts of National Parks and Protected Areas*, edited by Krishna B. Ghimire and Michel P. Pimbert, 46–70. London: Earthscan.

Blasar, Mario, Harvey A. Feit, and Glenn McRae. 2004. *In the Way of Development: Indigenous Peoples, Life Projects, and Globalization*. New York: Zed Books.

Boast, Richard. 2008. *Buying the Land, Selling the Land: Governments and Maori Land in the North Island, 1865–1921*. Melbourne, Australia: Victoria University Press.

Bocking, Stephen. 1997. *Ecologists and Environmental Politics: A History of Contemporary Ecology*. New Haven, CT: Yale University Press.

———. 2004. *Nature's Experts: Science, Politics, and the Environment*. New Brunswick, NJ: Rutgers University Press.

Bodley, John. 2008. *Victims of Progress*, rev. 5th ed. Lanham, MD: AltaMira Press.

Bonnett, Alistair. 2000. *White Identities: Historical and International Perspectives*. New York: Prentice Hall.

Borrini-Feyerabend, Grazia. 2008. *Governance as Key for Effective and Equitable Protected Area Systems*. IUCN CEESP Briefing Note 8. Gland, Switzerland: IUCN.

———. 2010. *Strengthening What Works: Recognising and Supporting the Conservation Achievements of Indigenous Peoples and Local Communities*. IUCN CEESP Briefing Note 10. Gland, Switzerland: IUCN.

Borrini-Feyerabend, Grazia, Nigel Dudley, Barbara Lassen, Neema Pathak, and Trevor Sandwith, eds. 2013. *Governance of Protected Areas: From Understanding to Action*. Gland, Switzerland: IUCN.

Borrini-Feyerabend, Grazia, Jim Johnston, and Diane Pansky. 2006. "Governance of Protected Areas." In *Managing Protected Areas: A Global Guide*, edited by Michael Lockwood, Graeme L. Worboys, and Ashish Kothari, 116–45. London: Earthscan.

Borrini-Feyerabend, Grazia, and Ashish Kothari. 2008. *Recognizing and Supporting Indigenous and Community Conservation: Ideas and Experiences from the Grassroots*. IUCN CEESP Briefing Note 9. Gland, Switzerland: IUCN.

Borrini-Feyerabend, Grazia, Ashish Kothari, and Gonzalo Oviedo. 2004a. *Indigenous and Local Communities and Protected Areas: Towards Equality and Enhanced Conservation*. Gland, Switzerland: IUCN.

Borrini-Feyerabend, Grazia, Barbara Lassen, Stan Stevens, Gary Martin, Juan Carlos Riascos de la Peña, Ernesto F. Ráez-Luna, and Taghi Farvar. 2010. *Bio-Cultural Diversity Conserved by Indigenous Peoples and Local Communities: Examples and Analysis*. Tehran: ICCA Consortium and Cenesta for GEF SGP, GTZ, IIED, and IUCN/CEESP.

Borrini-Feyerabend, Grazia, Michel Pimbert, M. Taghi Farvar, Ashish Kothari, and Yves Renard. 2004b. *Sharing Power: A Global Guide to Collaborative Management of Natural Resources*. London: Earthscan.

Bourdieu, Pierre. 1977. *Outline of a Theory of Practice*. Translated by R. Nice. Cambridge, UK: Cambridge University Press.

Bowler, Diana, Lisette Buyung-Ali, John R. Healey, Julia P. G. Jones, Teri Knight, and Andrew S. Pullin. 2010. *The Evidence Base for Community Forest Management as a Mechanism for Supplying Global Environmental Benefits and Improving Local Welfare*. Advisory document prepared on behalf of the Scientific and Technical Advisory Panel of the Global Environment Facility. http://www.thegef.org/gef/pubs/STAP_CFM. Last accessed on February 15, 2014.

Bray, David Barton, Elvira Duran, Victor H. Romas, Jean-François Mas, Alejandro Velazquez, Roan B. McNab, Deborah Barry, and Jeremy Radachowsky. 2008. "Tropical Deforestation, Community Forests, and Protected Areas in the Maya Forest." *Ecology and Society* 13(2), Article 56 [online]. http://www.ecologyandsociety.org/vol13/iss2/. Last accessed March 3, 2014.

Bray, David Barton, Leticia Merino-Perez, and Deborah Barry. 2005. *The Community Forests of Mexico: Managing for Sustainable Landscapes*. Austin: University of Texas Press.

Brechin, Stephen, Peter R. Wilshusen, Crystal L. Fortwangler, and Patrick C. West. 2002. "Beyond the Square Wheel: Toward a More Comprehensive Understanding of Biodiversity Conservation as Social and Political Process." *Society and Natural Resources* 15(1): 41–64.

———, eds. 2003. *Contested Nature: Promoting International Biodiversity Conservation with Social Justice in the Twenty-First Century*. Albany: State University of New York Press.

Breckwoldt, R., R. Boden, and R. Williams. 1997. *Contract Employment Program for Aboriginals in Natural and Cultural Resource Management*. Evaluation Biodiversity Group, Environment Australia. Canberra: Environment Australia.

Brennan, Sean. 2008. *Haida Gwaii Yah'Guudang*. http://www.coastalguardian watchmen.ca. Last accessed June 30, 2008.

Brockington, Dan D. 2002. *Fortress Conservation: The Preservation of the Mkomazi Game Reserve, Tanzania*. Oxford, UK: James Currey.

Brockington, Dan D., and James Igoe. 2006. "Eviction for Conservation: A Global Overview." *Conservation and Society* 4(3): 424–70.

Brockington, Dan D., Rosaleen Duffy, and Jim Igoe. 2008. *Nature Unbound: Conservation, Capitalism and the Future of Protected Areas*. London: Earthscan.

Brondo, Keri V. 2007. "Land Loss and Garifuna Women Activism on Honduras's North Coast." *Journal of International Women's Studies* 9(1): 99–116.

Brook, Mary M. 2005. "Re-scaling the Commons: Miskitu Indians, Forest Commodities, and Transnational Development Networks." Ph.D. dissertation, University of Texas at Austin.

Broome, Neema Pathak. 2009. *Community Conserved Areas in India: A Directory*. Delhi: Kalpavriksh.

Brosius, J. Peter. 1999. "Analyses and Interventions: Anthropological Engagements with Environmentalism." *Current Anthropology* 40(3): 277–309.

———. 2004. "Indigenous Peoples and Protected Areas at the World Parks Congress." *Conservation Biology* 18(3): 619–20.

Brosius, J. Peter, and Diane Russell. 2003. "Conservation from Above: An Anthropological Perspective on Transboundary Protected Areas and Ecoregional Planning." *Journal of Sustainable Forestry* 17(1/2): 39–65.

Brosius, J. Peter, Anna Lowenhaupt Tsing, and Charles Zerner, eds. 2005. *Communities and Conservation: Histories and Politics of Community-Based National Resource Management*. Walnut Creek, CA: Rowman and Littlefield.

Brown, Katrina. 1997. "Plain Tales from the Grasslands: Extraction, Value and Utilization of Biomass in Royal Bardia National Park, Nepal." *Biodiversity and Conservation* 6: 59–74.

Brown, Michael. 2007. "Sovereignty's Betrayals." In *Indigenous Experience Today*, edited by Marisol de la Cadena and Orin Starn, 171–94. Oxford, UK: Berg.

Bryant, Raymond. 2002. "Non-governmental Organizations and Governmentality: 'Consuming' Biodiversity and Indigenous People in the Philippines." *Political Studies* 50(2): 268–92.

Bryant, Raymond, and Sinead Bailey. 1997. *Third World Political Ecology*. New York: Routledge.

Burnett, J. A. 2003. *A Passion for Wildlife: The History of the Canadian Wildlife Service*. Vancouver: University of British Columbia Press.

Burnham, Philip. 2000. *Indian Country, God's Country: Native Americans and the National Parks*. Washington, DC: Island Press.

Call, W. 2003. "Mexicans and Central Americans 'Can't Take Any More.'" *NACLA* 36(5): 9–13.

Calverley, David. 2000. "Who Controls the Hunt? Ontario's 'Game Act,' the Canadian Government and the Ojibwa." Ph.D. dissertation, University of Ottawa.

Camacho, Isabel, Carlos del Campo, and Gary Martin. n.d. "Community Conserved Areas in Northern Mesoamerica: A Review of Status and Needs." http://cms

data.iucn.org/downloads/mesoamerica_cca_study.pdf. Last accessed February 22, 2014.
Campbell, Ben. 2005. "Nature's Discontents in Nepal." *Conservation and Society* 3(2): 323–53.
Campbell, Craig. 2004. "A Genealogy of the Concept of 'Wanton Slaughter' in Canadian Wildlife Biology." In *Cultivating Arctic Landscapes: Knowing and Managing Animals in the Circumpolar North*, edited by David G. Anderson and Mark Nutall, 154–71. New York: Berghahn Books.
Campese, Jessica, and Grazia Borrini-Feyerabend, eds. 2007. "Conservation and Human Rights." *Policy Matters* 15.
Campese, Jessica, Terry Sunderland, Thomas Greiber, and Gonzalo Oviedo, eds. 2009. *Rights-Based Approaches: Exploring Issues and Opportunities for Conservation*. Bogor, Indonesia: Center for International Forestry.
Canadian Council on Ecological Areas. 2003. *Designing Protected Areas: Wild Places for Wildlife*. Proceedings Summary of the 2003 Canadian Council on Ecological Areas and Circumpolar Areas Network Workshop, September 9–10, 2003, Yellowknife, Northwest Territories. Ottawa: Canadian Council on Ecological Areas.
Canadian Parks Council. n.d. "Aboriginal People and Canada's Protected Areas. Case Study 14." http://www.parks-parcs.ca/english/pdf/aboriginal/14PCAeng%20CPC%20CaseStudies.pdf. Last accessed October 29, 2009.
Carney, Judith. 1996. "Converting the Wetlands, Engendering the Environment: The Intersection of Gender and Agrarian Change in Gambia." In *Liberation Ecologies: Environment, Development, Social Movements*, edited by Richard Peet and Michael Watts, 165–87. London: Routledge.
Carr, Archie, III. 2004. "Utopian Bubbles: What Are Central America's Parks *for*?" *Wild Earth* Spring/Summer: 34–39.
Carruthers, Jane. 1995. *The Kruger National Park: A Social and Political History*. Pietermaritzburg: University of Natal Press.
Caruso, Emily. 2011. "Co-management Redux: Anti-politics and Transformation in the Ashaninka Communal Reserve, Peru." *International Journal for Heritage Studies* 17(6): 608–28.
———. 2012. "Being at the Centre: Self and Empire among Ashaninka People in Peruvian Amazonia." Ph.D. dissertation, University of Kent.
Carvill, Andy. 1998. *Speech Delivered at the Dedication of the Klondike Gold Rush International Historical Park, Bennett, BC*. Carcross, Yukon: Carcross-Tagish First Nation.
Castro, A. P., and E. Nielson. 2001. "Indigenous Peoples and Co-management: Implications for Conflict Management." *Environmental Science Policy* 4: 229–39.
Castro, William E. n.d. "Parque Cutivireni." Unpublished document, housed in the offices of the Central Ashaninka de Rio Ene, Satipo, Peru.
Catton, Theodore. 1995. *Land Reborn: A History of Administration and Visitor Use in Glacier Bay National Park and Preserve*. Anchorage, AK: National Park Service.
———. 1997. *Inhabited Wilderness: Indians, Eskimos and National Parks in Alaska*. Albuquerque: University of New Mexico Press.
———. 2009. *To Make a Better Nation: An Administrative History of the Timbisha Shoshone Homeland Act*. Report prepared under cooperative agreement with Rocky Mountain Cooperative Ecosystem Studies Unit for Death Valley National Park, California.

Centeno, M. 2001. "Comunicado de FUAC Llama 'A Seguir Luchando.'" *El Nuevo Diario*. http://archivo.elnuevodiario.com.ni/2001/julio/14-julio-2001/nacional/naciona122.html. Last accessed September 29, 2012.

Central American Commission on Environment and Development and the World Bank. 2002. *Nature, People, and Well-Being: Coordinating Sustainable Development in Mesoamerica, Business Plan (2003–2007)*. Paris: Conferencia de Socios y Donantes CBM and Comisión Centroamericana de Ambiente y Desarrollo (CCAD), World Bank.

Cernea, Michael. 2006. "Population Displacement Inside Protected Areas: A Redefinition of Concepts in Conservation Policies." *Policy Matters* 14: 8–26.

Cernea, Michael, and K. Schmidt-Soltau. 2005. "The End of Forcible Displacements?" *Policy Matters* 12: 42–51.

Cervone, Emma. 2002. "Engendering Leadership: Indigenous Women Leaders in the Ecuadorian Andes." In *Gender's Place: Feminist Anthropologies of Latin America*, edited by Rosario Montoya, Lessie Jo Frazier, and Janise Hurtig, 179–97. New York: Palgrave Macmillan.

Chambers, Cynthia M., and Narcisse J. Blood. 2009. "Love Thy Neighbour: Repatriating Precarious Blackfoot Sites." *International Journal of Canadian Studies* 39: 253–79.

Champagne, Duane. 2013. "UNDRIP (United Nations Declaration on the Rights of Indigenous Peoples): Human, Civil, and Indigenous Rights." *Wicazo Sa Review* 28(2): 60–86.

Chape, Stuart, Mark Spalding, and Martin Jenkins, eds. 2008. *The World's Protected Areas: Status, Values and Prospects in the Twenty-First Century*. Berkeley: University of California Press.

Chapin, Mac. 1990. "The Value of Biological and Cultural Diversity." *Cultural Survival Quarterly* 14(4): 2.

———. 1992. "The Co-existence of Indigenous Peoples and Environments in Central America." *Research and Exploration* 8(2): map supplement.

———. 2004. "A Challenge to Conservationists." *World Watch*, November/December: 17–31.

Chhatre, Ashwini, and Arun Agrawal. 2009. "Trade-offs and Synergies between Carbon Storage and Livelihood Benefits from Forest Commons." *Proceedings of the National Academy of Sciences* 106: 17667–70.

Cisneros, P., and J. McBreen. 2010. *Overlap of Indigenous Territories and Protected Areas in South America*. Quito, Ecuador: IUCN Sur.

Clark, Kim A. 1998. "Racial Ideologies and the Quest for National Development: Debating the Agrarian Problem in Ecuador (1930–50)." *Journal of Latin American Studies* 30: 373–93.

Cobb, Amanda J. 2005. "Understanding Tribal Sovereignty: Definitions, Conceptualizations, and Interpretations." *American Studies* 46(3/4): 115–32.

Colchester, Marcus. 1999. "Foreword." In *From Principles to Practice: Indigenous Peoples and Protected Areas in South and Southeast Asia*, IWGIA Document no. 97, edited by Marcus Colchester and Christian Erni, 10–17. Copenhagen: International Work Group for Indigenous Affairs.

———. 2003 [1994]. *Salvaging Nature: Indigenous Peoples, Protected Areas and Biodiversity Conservation*, rev. 2nd ed. Montevideo, Uruguay: World Rainforest Movement and Forest Peoples Programme.

———. 2004. "Conservation Policy and Indigenous Peoples." *Environmental Science and Policy* 7: 145–53.
Colchester, Marcus, Maurizio Farhan Ferrari, John Nelson, Chris Kidd, Peninnah Zaninka, Messe Vevant, Len Regpala, Grace T. Balawag, Borromeo Motin, and Banie Lasimbang. 2008. *Conservation and Indigenous Peoples: Assessing the Progress since Durban.* Interim Report: Discussion Draft, September 2008. FPP Series on Forest Peoples and Protected Areas. Montevideo, Uruguay: Forest Peoples Programme.
Coleman, Eric A. 2009. "Institutional Factors Affecting Biophysical Outcomes in Forest Management." *Journal of Policy Analysis and Management* 28(1): 122–46.
Comisión Centroamericana de Ambiente y Desarrollo y Unidad Regional de Asistencia Técnica. 2000. *Inventario de Proyectos Ambientales de Centroamérica: Informe Nacional Nicaragua, Versión Ejecutiva.* La Libertad, El Salvador: Comisión Centroamericana de Ambiente y Desarrollo (CCAD) y Unidad Regional de Asistencia Técnica (RUTA).
Commonwealth of Australia. 1996. *The National Strategy for the Conservation of Australia's Biological Diversity.* Canberra: Commonwealth Department of Environment, Sport and Territories.
Conference of the Parties to the Convention on Biological Diversity (CBD). 2004a. *Programme of Work on Protected Areas, Annex to COP 7 Decision VII/28 Protected Areas.* Seventh Conference of the Parties to the Convention on Biological Diversity, Kuala Lumpur, Malaysia.
———. 2004b. *Decision VII/28, Protected Areas.* Seventh Conference of the Parties to the Convention on Biological Diversity, Kuala Lumpur, Malaysia.
———. 2008. *COP 9 Decision IX/18, Protected Areas.* Ninth Conference of the Parties to the Convention on Biological Diversity, Bonn, Germany.
———. 2010. *COP 10 Decision X/2, Strategic Plan for Biodiversity 2011–20.* Tenth Conference of the Parties to the Convention on Biological Diversity, Nagoya, Japan.
———. 2012a. *COP 11 Decision XI/14, Article 8(j) and Related Provisions.* Eleventh Conference of the Parties to the Convention on Biological Diversity, Hyderabad, India.
———. 2012b. *COP 11 Decision XI/24, Protected Areas.* Eleventh Conference of the Parties to the Convention on Biological Diversity, Hyderabad, India.
Conservation Initiative on Human Rights. n.d. "Conservation and Human Rights Framework." http://www.iucn.org/about/work/programmes/social_policy/sp_themes_hrande/scpl_cihr/. Last accessed February 15, 2014.
Conservation International and Smithsonian Institution. 2001. "Rapid Assessment Program: Biological and Social Assessments of the Cordillera de Vilcabamba, Peru." SI/MAB Series 6/ RAP Working Papers. Washington, DC: Conservation International.
Conservation of Arctic Flora and Fauna (CAFF). 1994. *The State of Protected Areas in the Circumpolar Arctic, 1994.* CAFF Habitat Conservation Report no. 1. Trondheim, Norway: Directorate for Nature Management.
Cook, Bill, and Uma Kothari. 2001. *Participation: The New Tyranny?* London: Zed Books.
Coombes, Brad, and Stephanie Hill. 2005. "Na Whenua, Na Tuhoe. Ko D.o.C. te Partner: Prospects for Comanagement of Te Urewara National Park." *Society and Natural Resources* 18: 135–52.

Corredor Biológico del Atlántico. 2003. *Planes de Desarrollo Comunitario.* Managua, Nicaragua: Componente de Planificación y Monitoreo, Proyecto Corredor Biológico del Atlántico.

———. n.d. *Lista de Subproyectos Financiado por el Corredor Biológico del Atlántico (CBA).* http://www.cbanic.org. Last accessed May 1, 2005.

———. n.d. "Proyecto Corredor Biológico del Atlántico." [pamphlet]. Managua, Nicaragua.

Cranmer Webster, Gloria. 1992. "From Colonization to Repatriation." In *Indigena: Contemporary Native Perspectives,* edited by Gerald McMaster and Lee-Ann Martin, 25–37. Vancouver, BC: Douglas and McIntyre.

Cronon, William. 1986. "The Trouble with Wilderness; or, Getting Back to the Wrong Nature." In *Uncommon Ground: Re-thinking the Human Place in Nature,* edited by William Cronon, 69–90. New York: W. W. Norton.

Crosby, Alfred W. 1972. *The Columbian Exchange: Biological and Cultural Consequences of 1492.* Westport, CT: Greenwood.

———. 2004. *Ecological Imperialism: The Biological Expansion of Europe, 900–1900.* Cambridge, UK: Cambridge University Press.

Cruikshank, Julie. 1992. "Images of Society in Klondike Gold Rush Narratives: Skookum Jim and the Discovery of Gold." *Ethnohistory* 39(1): 20–41.

———. 1998. *The Social Life of Stories: Narrative and Knowledge in the Yukon Territory.* Lincoln: University of Nebraska Press.

Culp, Wanda, Richard Sheakley, Wilbur James, Kenneth Grant, Mary Rudolph, and Amy Marvin. 1995. "Presentation of the Huna Tlingits." In *Proceedings of the Third Glacier Bay Science Symposium, 1993,* edited by D. Engstrom, 302–8. Anchorage, AK: National Park Service.

Daniels, Amy E. 2002. "Indigenous Peoples and Neotropical Forest Conservation: Impacts of Protected Area Systems on Traditional Cultures." *Macalester Environmental Review.* http://lueci.clas.ufl.edu/southwood/grad-application/2002_Daniels%20-%20Neotropical%20forest%20conservation%20-%20indigenous%20peoples%20&%20protected%20areas.pdf. Last accessed December 31, 2013.

Dasmann, Raymond. 1991. "The Importance of Cultural and Biological Diversity." In *Biodiversity: Culture, Conservation, and Ecodevelopment,* edited by Margery L. Oldfield and Janis B. Alcorn, 7–15. Boulder, CO: Westview Press.

Dauenhauer, Nora Marks, and Richard Dauenhauer, eds. 1994. *Haa Kusteeyí, Our Culture: Tlingit Life Stories.* Seattle: University of Washington Press; Juneau, AK: Sealaska Heritage Foundation.

Davies, J., and E. Young. 1996. "Taking Centre Stage: Aboriginal Strategies for Redressing Marginalisation." In *Resources, Nations and Indigenous Peoples: Case Studies from Australasia, Melanesia and Southeast Asia,* edited by R. Howitt, J. Connell, and P. Hirsch, 152–71. Melbourne: Oxford University Press.

Dearden, Philip, and Steve Langdon. 2009. "Aboriginal Peoples and National Parks." In *Parks and Protected Areas in Canada: Planning and Management,* edited by Philip Dearden and Rick Rollins, 373–402. Don Mills, Ontario: Oxford University Press.

Deere, Carmen Diana, and Magdalena Leon. 2001. *Empowering Women: Land and Property Rights in Latin America.* Pittsburgh, PA: University of Pittsburgh Press.

De Janvry, Alain, Gustavo Gordillo, Jean-Phillippe Platteau, and Elizabeth Sadoulet. 2001. *Access to Land, Rural Poverty and Public Action*. Oxford, UK: Oxford University Press.

deKoninck, V. 2007. "Deconstructing the Stakeholder: A Case Study from Garig Gunak Barlu National Park, Australia." *The International Journal of Biodiversity Science and Management* 3(2): 77–87.

de la Cadena, Marisol. 1995. "'Women Are More Indian': Ethnicity and Gender in a Community near Cuzco." In *Ethnicity, Markets, and Migration in the Andes: At the Crossroads of History and Anthropology*, edited by Brooke Larson and Olivia Harris, 329–48. Durham, NC: Duke University Press.

De Lacy, Terry, and Bruce Lawson. 1997. "The Uluru-Kakadu Model: Joint Management of Aboriginal-Owned National Parks in Australia." In *Conservation through Cultural Survival: Indigenous Peoples and Protected Areas*, edited by Stan Stevens, 155–87. Washington, DC: Island Press.

de Laguna, Frederica. 1972. *Under Mount Saint Elias: The History and Culture of the Yakutat Tlingit*. Contributions to Anthropology no. 7. Washington, DC: Smithsonian Institution Press.

Deloria, Vine, Jr., and Lytle, Clifford M. 1984. *The Nations Within: The Past and Future of American Indian Sovereignty*. Austin: University of Texas Press.

Denevan, William M. 1992. "The Pristine Myth: The Landscape of the Americas in 1492." *Annals of the Association of American Geographers* 82(3): 369–85.

Dennis, Philip. 2004. *The Miskitu People of Awastara*. Austin: University of Texas Press.

Department of Conservation/Te Papa Atawhai, Tongariro/Taupō Conservancy (New Zealand). 2006. *Tongariro National Park Management Plan/Te Kaupapa Whakahaere mo Te Papa Rēhia o Tongariro*. http://www.doc.govt.nz/documents/about-doc/role/policies-and-plans/national-park-management-plans/tongariro-national-park/tongariro-national-park-management-plan.pdf. Last accessed February 15, 2013.

Department of Environment and Conservation (Papua New Guinea). 2010. *Papua New Guinea's Fourth National Report to the Convention on Biological Diversity*. http://www.sids2014.org/content/documents/141NBSAP.pdf. Last accessed March 1, 2014.

De Souza, Mike. 2007. "Harper Starts Northern Trek by Enlarging Nahanni National Park." *CanWest News* (August 9). http://proquest.umi.com/pqdweb?did=1318635671&Fmt=7&clientId=65345&RQT=309&VName=PQD. Last accessed March 7, 2008.

de Villiers, Bertus. 1999. *Land Claims and National Parks: The Makuleke Experience*. Pretoria: Human Sciences Research Council.

Dias, Braulio Ferreira de Souza. 2012. "Foreword." In *Recognizing and Supporting Territories and Areas Conserved by Indigenous Peoples and Local Communities: Global Overview and National Case Studies*, CBD Technical Series No. 64, edited by Ashish Kothari with Collen Corrigan, Harry Jonas, Aurelie Neumann, and Holly Shrumm, 6. Montreal: Secretariat of the CBD, ICCA Consortium, Kalpavriksh, and Natural Justice.

Diaz-Polanco, H. 1997. *Indigenous Peoples in Latin America: The Quest for Self-Determination*. Boulder, CO: Westview Press.

Diemberger, Hildegard Gemma Maria. 1997. "Beyul Khenbalung: The Hidden Valley of Artemesia—On Himalayan Communities and Their Sacred Landscape." In *Mandala and Landscape*, edited by A. W. MacDonald, 287–334. New Delhi: D. K. Printworld.

Diubaldo, Richard. 1998. *Stefansson and the Canadian Arctic*. Montreal: McGill-Queen's University Press.

Doberstein, Brent, and Sarah Devin. 2004. "Traditional Ecological Knowledge in Parks Management: A Canadian Perspective." *Environments* 32(1): 47–61.

Dodds, David. 1994. "The Ecological and Social Sustainability of Miskito Subsistence in the Rio Platano Biosphere Reserve, Honduras: The Cultural Ecology of Swidden Horticulturalists in a Protected Area." Ph.D. dissertation, University of California, Los Angeles.

Dowie, Mark. 2009. *Conservation Refugees: The Hundred-Year Conflict between Global Conservation and Native Peoples*. Cambridge, MA: MIT Press.

Dressler, Wolfram, Bram Büsher, Michael Schoon, Dan Brockington, Tanya Hayes, Christian A. Kull, James McCarthy, and Krishna Shrestha. 2010. "From Hope to Crisis and Back Again? A Critical History of the Global CBNRM Narrative." *Environmental Conservation* 37(1): 5–15.

Dudley, Nigel, ed. 2008. *Guidelines for Applying Protected Area Management Categories*. Gland, Switzerland: IUCN.

Dudley, Nigel, Shonil Bhagwat, Liza Higgins-Zogrib, Barbara Lassen, Bas Verschuuren, and Robert Wild. 2010. "Conservation of Biodiversity in Sacred Natural Sites in Asia and Africa: A Review of the Scientific Literature." In *Sacred Natural Sites: Conserving Nature and Culture*, edited by Bas Verschuuren, Robert Wild, Jeffrey McNeely, and Gonzalo Oviedo, 19–32. London: Earthscan.

Duran, Elvira, Jean-Francois Mas, and Alejandro Velasquez. 2005. "Land Use/Cover Change in Community-Based Forest Management Regions and Protected Areas in Mexico." In *The Community Forests of Mexico: Managing for Sustainable Landscapes*, edited by David Bray, Leticia Merino, and Deborah Barry, 215–38. Austin: University of Texas Press.

East, Ken M. 1991. "Joint Management of Canada's Northern Parks." In *Resident People and National Parks: Social Dilemmas and Strategies in International Conservation*, edited by Patrick C. West and Stephen R. Brechin, 333–45. Tucson: University of Arizona Press.

Eaton, P. 1997. "Reinforcing Traditional Tenure: Wildlife Management Areas in Papua New Guinea." In *Conservation through Cultural Survival: Indigenous Peoples and Protected Areas*, edited by Stan Stevens, 225–36. Washington, DC: Island Press.

Ecologist, The. 1993. *Whose Common Future? Reclaiming the Commons*. Philadelphia: New Society Publishers.

Eghenter, Cristina. 2000. *Mapping Peoples' Forests: The Role of Mapping in Planning Community-Based Management of Conservation Areas in Indonesia*. Washington, DC: Biodiversity Support Program.

Ekern, S. 2001. *Para Entender Totonicapán: Poder Local y Alcaldia Indigena*. FLACSO Dialogo 8. Guatemala City, Guatemala: FLACSO.

———. 2006. "Making Government: Community and Leadership in Mayan Guatemala." Ph.D. dissertation, University of Oslo.

Elias, S. 1997. *Autogestión Communitaria de Recursos Naturals: Estudio de Caso en Totonicapán.* Guatemala City, Guatemala: FLACSO.

Elias, S., and H. Wittman. 2005. "State, Forest and Community: Decentralization of Forest Administration in Guatemala." In *The Politics of Decentralization: Forests, Power and People,* edited by C. Pierce Colfer and D. Capistrano, 282–95. London: Earthscan.

Elias, S., A. Larson, and J. Mendoza. 2009. *Tenencia de la Tierra, Bosques y Medios de Vida en el Altiplano Occidental de Guatemala.* Guatemala City, Guatemala: CIFOR/PERT/USAC.

Ellis, Edward A., and Luciana Porter-Bolland. 2008. "Is Community-Based Forest Management More Effective than Protected Areas? A Comparison of Land Use/Cover Change in Two Neighboring Study Areas of the Central Yucatan Peninsula, Mexico." *Forest Ecology and Management* 256: 1971–83.

Ellis, Stephen C. 2005. "Meaningful Consideration? A Review of Traditional Knowledge in Environmental Decision Making." *Arctic* 58(1): 66–77.

Ellis, William. 2010. "The Khomani San Land Claim against the Kalahari Gemsbok National Park: Requiring and Acquiring Authenticity." In *Land, Memory, Reconstruction, and Justice: Perspectives on Land Claims in South Africa,* edited by C. Walker, A. Bohlin, R. Hall, and T. Kepe, 181–97. Athens: Ohio University Press.

Escobar, A. 1998. "Whose Knowledge, Whose Nature? Biodiversity, Conservation, and the Political Ecology of Social Movements." *Journal of Political Ecology* 5: 53–80.

Espinoza, Oscar. 1995. *Rondas Campesinas y Nativas en la Amazonia Peruana.* Lima: CAAAP.

Euraque, Dario. 1998. "The Banana Enclave, Nationalism, and Mestizaje in Honduras, 1910s–1930s." In *Identity and Struggle at the Margins of the Nation-State: The Laboring Peoples of Central America and the Hispanic Caribbean,* edited by Aviva Chomsky and Aldo Lauria Santiago, 151–68. Durham, NC: Duke University Press.

Executive Secretary of the Convention on Biological Diversity. 2009. "Advice on How Article 10(c) can be Further Advanced and Implemented as a Priority: Note by the Executive Secretary." Sixth meeting of the CBD Ad Hoc Open-Ended Intersessional Working Group on Article 8(j) and Related Provisions of the Convention on Biological Diversity, Montreal, November 2–6, 2009, Item 7 of the provisional agenda, UNEP/CBD/WG8J/add.1, June 12, 2009.

———. 2010. "In-Depth Review of the Implementation of the Programme of Work on Protected Areas." SBSTTA-14, UNDEP/CBD/SBSTTA/14/5/Add.1. www.cbd.int/cms/ui/forums/attachment.aspx?id=85. Last accessed February 15, 2014.

———. 2012. "Protected Areas: Progress in the Implementation of the Programme of Work and Achievement of Aichi Biodiversity Target 11." COP 11, UNEP/CBD/COP/11/26. https://www.cbd.int/doc/meetings/cop/cop-11/official/cop-11-26-en.pdf. Last accessed February 15, 2014.

Fairhead, James, Melissa Leach, and Ian Scoones. 2012. "Green Grabbing: A New Appropriation of Nature?" *The Journal of Peasant Studies* 39(2): 237–61.

Falla, Ricardo. 2001. *Quiche Rebelde: Religious Conversion, Politics, and Ethnic Identity in Guatemala.* Austin: University of Texas Press.

Farvar, M. Taghi. 2013. "Indigenous Peoples' and Community Conserved Territories and Areas" keynote presentation, World Indigenous Network Conference, June 6,

2013. Darwin, Australia. http://www.youtube.com/watch?v=pI4lueGYKdE. Last accessed February 25, 2014.

Fast, Helen B., Fikret Berkes, and Hudson Bay Programme. 1994. *Native Land Use, Traditional Knowledge and the Subsistence Economy in the Hudson Bay Bioregion*. Ottawa: Hudson Bay Programme.

Fay, Derick. 2005. "Kinship and Access to Land in the Eastern Cape: Implications for Land Tenure Reform." *Social Dynamics* 31(1): 182–207.

———. 2007. "Mutual Gains and Distributive Ideologies in South Africa: Theorizing Negotiations between Communities and Protected Areas." *Human Ecology* 35(1): 81–95.

———. 2011. "Migrants, Forests and Houses: The Political Ecology of Architectural Change in Hobeni and Cwebe, South Africa." *Human Organization* 70(3): 310–21.

———. 2012. "'The Trust Is Over! We Want to Plough!': Social Differentiation and the Reversal of Resettlement in South Africa." *Human Ecology* 40(1): 59–68.

Fay, Derick, Herman Timmermans, and Robin Palmer. 2002. "Competing for the Forests: Annexation, Demarcation and Their Consequences from c. 1878 to 1936." In *From Confrontation to Negotiation: Nature-Based Development on South Africa's Wild Coast*, edited by Robin Palmer, Herman Timmermans, and Derick Fay, 48–77. Pretoria: Human Science Research Council.

Fearon, Joclyn. 2010. "Population Assessments of Priority Plant Species Used by Local Communities in and around Three Wild Coast Reserves, Eastern Cape, South Africa." Master's thesis, Rhodes University.

Feit, Harvey A. 1988. "Self-Management and State Management: Forms of Knowing and Managing Northern Wildlife." In *Traditional Knowledge and Renewable Resource Management in Northern Regions*, International Union for the Conservation of Nature and Canadian Circumpolar Institute Occasional Publication no. 23, edited by Milton M. R. Freeman and Ludwig N. Carbyn, 72–91. Edmonton: Canadian Circumpolar Institute.

———. 2005. "Recognizing Co-management as Co-governance: Visions and Histories of Conservation at James Bay." *Anthropologica* 47(2): 267–88.

Feit, Harvey A., and Joseph J. Spaeder. 2005. "Co-management and Indigenous Communities: Barriers and Bridges to Decentralized Resource Management—Introduction." *Anthropologica* 47(2): 147–54.

Fenge, Terry. 1993. "National Parks in the Canadian Arctic: The Case of the Nunavut Land Claims Agreement." *Environments* 22(1): 20–63.

Ferguson, James. 1994. *Anti-Politics Machine: Development, Depoliticization, and Bureaucratic Power in Lesotho*. Minneapolis: University of Minnesota Press.

Ferrari, M. F. n.d. "Protecting Biodiversity and Indigenous Peoples/Local Communities' Rights: The Challenge in Southeast Asia." http://agris.fao.org/agris-search/search.do?f=2004%2FPH%2FPH04013.xml%3BPH2004000977. Last accessed February 24, 2014.

Finley-Brook, Mary. 2007. "Green Neoliberal Space: The Mesoamerican Biological Corridor." *Journal of Latin American Geography* 6(1): 101–24.

Finley-Brook, Mary, and Karl Offen. 2009. "Bounding the Commons: Land Demarcation in Northeastern Nicaragua." *Bulletin of Latin American Research* 28(3): 1–21.

Fisher, Roger, and William Ury. 1981. *Getting to Yes: Negotiating Agreement without Giving In*. New York: Houghton Mifflin.

Floyd, Troy. 1967. *The Anglo-Spanish Struggle for the Mosquitia*. Albuquerque: University of New Mexico Press.
Forest Peoples Programme. 2008. "Briefing for Media: Conservation and Indigenous Peoples—Assessing the Progress since Durban." http://www.forestpeoples.org/sites/fpp/files/news/2011/01/fpp_synthesis_briefing_oct08_eng.pdf. Last accessed April 20, 2011.
———. 2011a. "International Union for the Conservation of Nature to Review and Advance Implementation of the 'New Conservation Paradigm,' Focusing on Rights of Indigenous Peoples." January 14, 2011. http://www.forestpeoples.org/topics/participatory-resource-mapping/news/2011/01/press-release-international-union-conservation-na. Last accessed April 20, 2011.
———. 2011b. "Whakatane Assessments." http://www.forestpeoples.org/tags/whakatane-assessments. Last accessed August 31, 2012.
———. 2011c. "Whakatane Mechanism." http://www.forestpeoples.org/topics/environmental-governance/international-processes/whakatane-mechanism. Last accessed July 1, 2012.
———. 2012. "Wapichan People in Guyana Present Territorial Map and Community Proposals to Save Ancestral Forests." http://www.forestpeoples.org/topics/participatory-resource-mapping/news/2012/02/wapichan-people-guyana-present-territorial-map-an. Last accessed September 30, 2012.
Foster, Janet. 1998. *Working for Wildlife: The Beginning of Preservation in Canada*, 2nd ed. Toronto: University of Toronto Press.
Foucault, Michel. 1991. "Governmentality." In *The Foucault Effect: Studies in Governmentality*, edited by Graham Burchell, Colin Gordon, and Peter Miller, 87–104. Chicago: University of Chicago Press.
———. 1997. *Discipline and Punish: The Birth of the Prison*. Translated by A. Sheridan. London: Penguin Books.
———. 2010. *The Government of Self and Others: Lectures at the Collège de France, 1982–1983*. http://rauli.cbs.dk/index.php/foucault-studies/article/view/3127/3298.pdf. Last accessed June 27, 2013.
Fox, Jefferson, Pralad Yonzon, and Nancy Podger. 1996. "Mapping Conflicts between Biodiversity and Human Needs in Langtang National Park, Nepal." *Conservation Biology* 10(2): 562–9.
Franco, P. 2003. "Central America's Nature Reserves Imperiled." *Tierramerica*. http://www.ipsnews.net/2003/01/unprotected-nature-reserves/. Last accessed February 22, 2014.
Freeman, Milton M. R., and Ludwig N. Carbyn, eds. 1988. *Traditional Knowledge and Renewable Resource Management in Northern Regions*. International Union for the Conservation of Nature and Canadian Circumpolar Institute Occasional Publication no. 23. Edmonton: Canadian Circumpolar Institute.
Gagnon, Mariano. 2000. *Guerreros en el Paraiso*. Lima: Jaime Campodonico Editor.
Galvin, Mark, and Tobias Haller. 2008. *People, Protected Areas and Global Change: Participatory Conservation in Latin America, Africa, Asia and Europe*. Swiss National Centre of Competence in Research North-South, University of Bern, Vol. 3. Bern: Geographica Bernensia.
García, Alan. 2007a. "El Síndrome del Perro del Hortelano." *El Comercio*, October 28.
———. 2007b. "Receta para Acabar con el Perro del Hortelano." *El Comercio*, November 25.

———. 2008. "El Perro del Hortelano contra el Pobre." *El Comercio*, March 2.
Gedicks, Al. 1999. *The New Resource Wars: Native and Environmental Struggles against Multinational Corporations*. Boston: South End Press.
Geertz, Clifford. 1973. *The Interpretation of Cultures: Selected Essays*. New York: Basic Books.
Geisler, Charles. 2002. "Endangered Humans." *Foreign Policy* 130: 80–81.
———. 2003a. "A New Kind of Trouble: Evictions in Eden." *International Social Science Journal* 55: 69–78.
———. 2003b. "Your Park, My Poverty: Using Impact Assessment to Counter the Displacement Effects of Environmental Greenlining." In *Contested Nature: Promoting International Biodiversity Conservation with Social Justice in the Twenty-First Century*, edited by Stephen R. Brechin, P. R. Wilhusen, C. L. Fortwangler, and P. C. West, 217–29. Albany: State University of New York Press.
Geisler, Charles C., and Ragendra de Sousa. 2000. "From Refuge to Refugee: The African Case." Working Paper no. 38. Madison: Land Tenure Center, University of Wisconsin.
Gertsch, Frances, Graham Dodds, Micheline Manseau, and Joadamee Amagoalik. 2003. "Recent Experiences in Cooperative Management and Planning for Canada's Northernmost National Park: Quttinirpaaq National Park on Ellesmere Island." In *Making Ecosystem-Based Management Work: Proceedings of the Fifth International Conference on Science and Management of Protected Areas*, edited by N. W. P. Munro, J. H. M. Willison, T. B. Herman, K. Beazley, and P. Dearden, CD-ROM Proceedings, chapter 2. Wolfville, Nova Scotia: Science and Management of Protected Areas Association.
Ghai, D., ed. 1994. *Development and Environment: Sustaining People and Nature*. Oxford, UK: Blackwell.
Ghimire, Krishna B., and Michel P. Pimbert, eds. 1997. *Social Change and Conservation: Environmental Politics and Impacts of National Parks and Protected Areas*. London: Earthscan.
Ghimire, S. K., and D. B. Parajuli. 2001. "Indigenous Knowledge and Practice on Pasture Resource Management: Among the Pugmo People of the Shey Phoksundo National Park, Dolpa." *Wildlife Magazine* 3(1): 7–14.
Gibson, Clark C., John T. Williams, and Elinor Ostrom. 2005. "Local Enforcement and Better Forests." *World Development* 33(2): 273–84.
Glacier Bay National Park and Preserve. 2007a. "Glacier Bay National Park and Preserve." http://www.nps.gov/glba/index.htm. Last accessed April 7, 2007.
———. 2007b. "Glacier Bay as Homeland." http://www.nps.gov/glba/historyculture/glacier-bay-as-homeland.htm. Last accessed April 7, 2007.
Glass, Aaron. 2004. "Return to Sender: On the Politics of Cultural Property and the Proper Address of Art." *Journal of Material Culture* 9(2): 115–39.
Glavovic, Bruce. 1996. "Resolving People-Park Conflicts through Negotiation: Reflections on the Richtersveld Experience." *Journal of Environmental Planning and Management* 39(4): 483–506.
Global Environment Facility (GEF). 1997. *Nicaragua: Atlantic Biological Corridor Project*. Washington, DC: Global Environment Facility/World Bank.
———. 2011. "GEF Launches Process to Strengthen Partnership with Indigenous Peoples." Press release. http://www.thegef.org/gef/node/4753. Last accessed September 22, 2012.

Goetze, Tara C. 2005. "Empowered Co-management: Towards Power-Sharing and Indigenous Rights in Clayoquot Sound, BC." *Anthropologica* 47(2): 247–65.

Goldman, M. 2005. *Imperial Nature: The World Bank and Struggles for Social Justice in the Age of Globalization.* New Haven, CT: Yale University Press.

Gomez, F. 2010. "The Struggle for a Law on Sacred Sites in Guatemala." *Endogenous Development Magazine* 6: 26–29.

Gomez-Pompa, Arturo, and Andrea Kaus. 1992. "Taming the Wilderness Myth." *Bioscience* 42(4): 271–79.

Gordon, E. T., G. C. Gurdián, and C. R. Hale. 2003. "Rights, Resources, and the Social Memory of Struggle: Reflections on a Study of Indigenous and Black Community Land Rights on Nicaragua's Atlantic Coast." *Human Organization* 62(4): 369–81.

Gorenflo, L. J., Suzanne Romaine, Russell A. Mittermeier, and Kristen Walker-Painemilla. 2012. "Co-occurrence of Linguistic and Biological Diversity in Biodiversity Hotspots and High Biodiversity Wilderness Areas." *Proceedings of the National Academy of Sciences.* http://www.pnas.org/content/early/2012/05/03/1117511109.full.pdf+html. Last accessed September 22, 2012.

Gottesman, Dan. 1983. "Native Hunting and the Migratory Birds Convention Act: Historical, Political, and Ideological Perspectives." *Journal of Canadian Studies* 18(3): 67–89.

Govan, Hugh. 2009. "Achieving the Potential of Locally Managed Marine Areas in the South Pacific." *SPC Traditional Marine Resource Management and Knowledge Information Bulletin* 25: 16–25.

Government Communication and Information Systems (GCIS). 2009. "Decision on Kruger National Park Land Claims." http://www.gcis.gov.za/content/newsroom/media-releases/media-statements/decision-kruger-national-park-land-claims. Last accessed February 26, 2014.

Government of Canada. 1917. "An Act Respecting Game in the Northwest Territories of Canada." *Statues of Canada*, c. 36.

———. 1988. "Canada National Parks Act, 1988." *Statutes of Canada*, c. 48.

———. 2000. "Canada National Parks Act, 2000." *Statutes of Canada*, c. 32.

———. 2008. *Wood Buffalo National Park Game Regulations.* Vol. SOR/78-830. http://laws-lois.justice.gc.ca/PDF/SOR-78-830.pdf. Last accessed September 24, 2013.

Gow, Peter. 1991. *Of Mixed Blood: Kinship and History in Peruvian Amazonia.* Oxford, UK: Oxford University Press.

Graham, Maxwell. 1918. April 24, Letter to James Harkin. Vol. RG 85, vol. 665, file 3914, pt. 1, Library and Archives Canada.

Grandin, G. 2000. *The Blood of Guatemala: A History of Race and Nation.* Durham, NC: Duke University Press.

Gray, Andrew, Alejandro Parellada, and Helen Newing, eds. 1998. *From Principles to Practice: Indigenous Peoples and Biodiversity Conservation in Latin America.* IWGIA Document no. 87. Copenhagen: International Work Group for Indigenous Affairs.

Green, Carina. 2009. *Managing Laponia: A World Heritage Site as Arena for Sami Ethno-Politics in Sweden.* Uppsala Studies in Cultural Anthropology no. 47. Uppsala: Acta Universitatis Upsaliensis.

Greene, Shane. 2009. *Customizing Indigeneity: Paths to a Visionary Politics in Peru.* Stanford, CA: Stanford University Press.

Greenpeace. 1998. *Los Bosques de Totonicapán*. Guatemala City, Guatemala: Greenpeace.

Gregory, Derek. 2004. *The Colonial Present*. Malden, MA: Blackwell Publishing.

Greiber, Thomas, Melinda Janki, Marcos Orellana, Annalisa Savaresi, and Dinah L. Shelton. 2009. *Conservation with Justice: A Rights-Based Approach*. IUCN Environmental Law and Policy Paper no. 71. Gland, Switzerland: IUCN.

Griffith, Tom. 2001. "Latin America." In *A Survey of Indigenous Land Tenure*, Report for the Land Tenure Service of the Food and Agriculture Organization, edited by Marcus Colchester, 21–51. http://www.rightsandresources.org/documents/files/doc_1177.pdf. Last accessed September 21, 2013.

Grigsby, William. 2004. "The Gendered Nature of Subsistence and Its Effect on Customary Land Tenure." *Society and Natural Resources* 17(3): 207–22.

Grove, Richard. 1997. *Ecology, Climate and Empire: Colonialism and Global Environmental History, 1400–1940*. Cambridge, UK: White Horse Press.

Guha, Ramachandra. 1989. *The Unquiet Woods: Ecological Change and Peasant Resistance in the Himalaya*. Delhi: Oxford University Press.

Gurung, Harka B. 2003. *Trident and Thunderbolt: Cultural Dynamics in Nepalese Politics*. Lalitpur, Nepal: Social Science Baha. http://www.soscbaha.org/downloads/mcr12003.pdf. Last accessed September 24, 2013.

Gurung, Om. 2009. "Major Challenges for Implementing ILO Convention 169 in Nepal." Paper presented in the seminar "Should States Ratify Human Rights Conventions?" Center for Advanced Studies, Oslo, Norway. http://www.jus.uio.no/english/research/areas/intrel/projects/should-states-ratify-project/gurung-final-major-challenges-of-ilo-implemen.pdf. Last accessed February 13, 2014.

Haberfeld, S. 2000. "Government-to-Government Negotiations: How the Timbisha Shoshone Got Its Land Back." *American Indian Culture and Research Journal* 24(4): 127–65.

Hardt, Michael, and Antonio Negri. 2000. *Empire*. Cambridge, MA: Harvard University Press.

Harmon, David. 1996. "Losing Species, Losing Languages: Connections between Biological and Linguistic Diversity." *Southwest Journal of Linguistics* 15: 89–108.

———. 2002. *In Light of Our Differences: How Diversity in Nature and Culture Makes Us Human*. Washington, DC: Smithsonian Institution Press.

Harries, Patrick. 1987. "A Forgotten Corner of the Transvaal: Reconstructing the History of a Relocated Community through Oral Testimony and Song." In *Class, Community and Conflict*, edited by B. Bozzoli, 93–133. Johannesburg: Ravan Press.

Hartmann, B. 2004. "Conserving Racism: The Greening of Hate at Home and Abroad." *Different Takes* 27: 1–4.

Harvey, David. 2003. *The New Imperialism*. New York: Oxford University Press.

Hassall and Associates. 2003. "Evaluation of the NHT Phase 1 Facilitator, Coordinator and Community Support Networks." Report prepared for Environment Australia and Commonwealth Department of Agriculture, Fisheries, Forestry.

Hayes, Tanya M. 2006. "Parks, People, and Forest Protection: An Institutional Assessment of the Effectiveness of Protected Areas." *World Development* 34: 2064–75.

Hayes, Tanya M., and Elinor Ostrom. 2005. "Conserving the World's Forests: Are Protected Areas the Only Way?" *Indiana Law Review* 38: 595–617.

Hayes, Tanya, and Lauren Persha. 2010. "Nesting Local Forest Initiatives: Revisiting Community Forest Management in a REDD+ World." *Forest Policy and Economics* 12: 545–53.

Haynes, Chris. 2009. "Defined by Contradiction: The Social Construction of Joint Management in Kakadu National Park." Ph.D. dissertation, Charles Darwin University.

———. 2013. "Seeking Control: Disentangling the Difficult Sociality of Kakadu National Park's Joint Management." *Journal of Sociology* 49(2–3): 194–209.

Hazlewood, Julianne A. 2012. "CO_2lonialism and the 'Unintended Consequences' of Commoditizing Climate Change: Geographies of Hope Amid a Sea of Oil Palms in the Northwest Ecuadorian Pacific Region." *Sustainable Forestry* 31(1–2): 120–53.

Heatherington, Tracey. 2005. "How to Challenge a Green Giant: Ethnographic Critiques of Global Conservation." *Identities: Global Studies in Culture and Power* 12: 439–50.

Hecht, Susanna. 2004. "Invisible Forests: The Political Ecology of Forest Resurgence in El Salvador." In *Liberation Ecologies*, 2nd ed., edited by R. Peet and M. Watts, 64–103. London: Routledge.

Hecht, Susanna, and Alexander Cockburn. 2011. *The Fate of the Forest: Developers, Destroyers and Defenders of the Amazon*. Chicago: University of Chicago Press.

Heinen, Joel, and Jai N. Mehta. 1999. "Conceptual and Legal Issues in the Designation and Management of Conservation Areas in Nepal." *Environmental Conservation* 26(1): 21–29.

———. 2000. "Emerging Issues in Legal and Procedural Aspects of Buffer Zone Management with Case Studies from Nepal." *Journal of Environment and Development* 9(1): 45–67.

Heinen, Joel T., and Suresh K. Shrestha. 2006. "Evolving Policies for Conservation: An Historical Profile of the Protected Area System of Nepal." *Journal of Environmental Planning and Management* 49(1): 41–58.

Helms, Mary W. 1971. *Asang: Adaptations to Cultural Contact in a Miskito Community*. Gainesville: University of Florida Press.

Herlihy, Peter H. 1997. "Indigenous Peoples and Biosphere Reserve Conservation in the Mosquitia Rain Forest Corridor, Honduras." In *Conservation through Cultural Survival: Indigenous Peoples and Protected Areas*, edited by Stan Stevens, 99–129. Washington, DC: Island Press.

———. 2001. "Indigenous and Ladino Peoples of the Rio Platano Biosphere Reserve." In *Endangered Peoples of Latin America: Struggles to Survive and Thrive*, edited by Susan Stonich, 101–20. Westport: Greenwood Press.

Hernandez Castillo, R. Aida. 2005. "Between Complementarity and Inequality: Indigenous Cosmovision as an Element of Resistance in the Struggle of Indigenous Women." Paper presented at the conference Indigenous Struggles in the Americas and around the World: Land, Autonomy and Recognition, York University, Toronto, February 10–11, 2005. http://www.ucgs.yorku.ca/Indigenous%20 Conference/Aida_Hernandez.pdf. Last accessed September 21, 2013.

Hewitt, C. Gordon. 1972. *The Conservation of the Wild Life of Canada*. Toronto: Coles.

Hobson Herlihy, Laura. 2002. "The Mermaid and the Lobster Diver: Gender and Ethnic Identities among the Rio Platano Miskito Peoples." Ph.D. dissertation, Louisiana State University.

———. 2007. "Matrifocality and Women's Power on the Miskito Coast." *Ethnology* 46(2): 133–49.
Hockings, Marc, Sue Stolton, Fiona Leverington, Nigel Dudley, and José Courrau. 2006. *Evaluating Effectiveness: A Framework for Assessing Management Effectiveness of Protected Areas*, 2nd ed. Gland, Switzerland: IUCN.
Holdgate, Martin. 1999. *The Green Web: A Union for World Conservation*. London: Earthscan.
Hunn, Eugene S., Darryll R. Johnson, Priscilla N. Russell, and Thomas F. Thornton. 2003. "Huna Tlingit Traditional Environmental Knowledge, Conservation, and the Management of a 'Wilderness' Park." *Current Anthropology* 44 (Supp.): S79–103.
Huntington, Henry P., Patricia K. Brown-Schwalenberg, Kathryn J. Frost, Maria E. Fernandez-Gimenez, David W. Norton, and Daniel H. Rosenberg. 2002. "Observations on the Workshop as a Means of Improving Communication between Holders of Traditional and Scientific Knowledge." *Environmental Management* 30(6): 778–92.
Hutton, Jon, William M. Adams, and James C. Murombedzi. 2005. "Back to the Barriers? Changing Narratives in Biodiversity Conservation." *Forum for Development Studies* 2: 341–70.
Hvalkøf, Søren. 1994. "El Desastre Ashaninka y su Lucha." *Asuntos Indigenas* 2. Copenhagen: International Work Group for Indigenous Affairs.
Igoe, Jim. 2003. *Conservation and Globalization: A Study of National Parks and Indigenous Communities from East Africa to South Dakota*. Belmont, CA: Wadsworth/Thomson Learning.
Independent Evaluation Group of the World Bank. 2011. "The Mesoamerican Biological Corridor." *Regional Program Review* 5(2): 1–108.
Indian and Northern Affairs Canada, Government of the Northwest Territories, and Nunavut Tunngavik Incorporated. 1999–2000. *Annual Report: The Implementation of the Nunavut Land Claims Agreement*. Ottawa: Minister of Indian Affairs and Northern Development.
Indigenous Land Corporation (ILC). 1997. *Annual Report, 1996–1997*. Adelaide: ILC. http://www.ilc.gov.au/PDF/CorpPlan.pdf. Last accessed May 20, 2004.
———. 2003. *Corporate Plan, 2003–2006*. http://www.ilc.gov.au. Last accessed May 20, 2004.
Indigenous Peoples Ad Hoc Working Group for the World Parks Congress. 2003a. "Indigenous Peoples at the Vth World Parks Congress: A Summary Report and Assessment." http://www.swedbio.com/dokument/FPP%20wpc%20report.pdf. Last accessed April 24, 2011.
———. 2003b. *The Indigenous Peoples' Declaration to the World Parks Congress*. http://www.treatycouncil.org/section_211812142.htm. Last accessed April 24, 2011.
Ingold, Tim. 2000. *The Perception of the Environment: Essays in Livelihood, Dwelling and Skill*. London: Routledge.
INRENA. 2002. *Expediente Tecnico de Categorización de la Zona Reservada Apurimac: Reserva Comunal Ashaninka*. Lima: INRENA.
———. 2005. *Regimen Especial para la Administración de las Reservas Comunales*. Lima: INRENA.
———. 2007. "Mapa de la Reserva Comunal Ashaninka." Lima, Peru: Ministerio de Agricultura.

International Indigenous Forum on Biodiversity. 2008a. "Opening Statement at CBD Working Group on Protected Areas 2, Rome." http://www.indigenousportal.com/es/Diversidad-Biol%C3%B3gica/IIFB-Opening-Statement-at-CBD-Working-Group-on-Protected-Areas-2.html. Last accessed April 20, 2011.

———. 2008b. "Opening Statement at the Ninth Conference of the Parties to the Convention on Biological Diversity, Bonn, Germany." http://iifbmedia.blogspot.com/2008/05/iifb-opening-statement-in-cop9.html. Last accessed April 20, 2011.

International Union for Conservation of Nature (IUCN). 1969. *Resolution 1, National Park Definition*. 10th General Assembly of IUCN, New Delhi, India.

———. 1975. *Resolution 12.5 Protection of Traditional Ways of Life*. 12th IUCN General Assembly, Kinshasa, Zaire.

———. 1996. *Resolution 1.53 Indigenous Peoples and Protected Areas*. 1st World Conservation Congress, Montreal, Canada.

———. 2004a. *Resolution 3.049 Community Conserved Area*. 3rd World Conservation Congress, Bangkok, Thailand.

———. 2004b. *Resolution 3.055 Indigenous Peoples, Protected Areas, and the CBD Programme of Work*. 3rd World Conservation Congress, Bangkok, Thailand.

———. 2007. *State of Conservation of the Rio Platano Biosphere Reserve and World Heritage Site, Honduras, Central America*. Mission Report to UNESCO. http://whc.unesco.org/document/9013. Last accessed June 1, 2008.

———. 2008a. "Protected areas (Agenda item 4.7)." Position paper for the Ninth Meeting of the Conference of the Parties to the Convention on Biological Diversity (COP 9), Bonn, Germany, May 19–30, 2008. http://cmsdata.iucn.org/downloads/pas_cop9.pdf. Last accessed September 5, 2010.

———. 2008b. *Resolution 4.048 Indigenous Peoples, Protected Areas and Implementation of the Durban Accord*. 4th World Conservation Congress, Barcelona, Spain.

———. 2008c. *Resolution 4.049 Supporting Indigenous Conservation Territories and other Indigenous Peoples' and Community Conserved Areas*. 4th World Conservation Congress, Barcelona, Spain.

———. 2008d. *Resolution 4.050 Recognition of Indigenous Conservation Territories*. 4th World Conservation Congress, Barcelona, Spain.

———. 2008e. *Recommendation 4.127 Indigenous Peoples' Rights in the Management of Protected Areas Fully or Partially in the Territories of Indigenous Peoples*. 4th World Conservation Congress, Barcelona, Spain.

———. 2010. "Enhancing the Contribution of Protected Areas to Biodiversity Conservation: The Role of the CBD Programme of Work on Protected Areas (PoWPA)." Presented at the Tenth Meeting of the Conference of the Parties to the Convention on Biological Diversity, October 18–29, 2010, Nagoya, Japan. http://cmsdata.iucn.org/downloads/powpa_pp_sbstta14_final.pdf. Last accessed April 30, 2011.

———. 2011. "The IUCN Global Protected Areas Programme: Priorities and Opportunities." http://cmsdata.iucn.org/downloads/the_iucn_global_protected_areas_programme_16_october_2011.pdf. Last accessed September 20, 2012.

———. 2012a. *The IUCN Programme 2013–2016*. https://cmsdata.iucn.org/downloads/iucn_programme_2013_2016.pdf. Last accessed February 27, 2014.

———. 2012b. *Resolution 5.042 Proposing Goals for the Coverage of Protected Areas Based on Certification and Assessment Systems*. 5th World Conservation Congress, Jeju, South Korea.

———. 2012c. *Resolution 5.047 Implementation of the United Nations Declaration on the Rights of Indigenous Peoples in the Context of the UNESCO World Heritage Convention*. 5th World Conservation Congress, Jeju, South Korea.

———. 2012d. *Resolution 5.094 Respecting, Recognizing and Supporting Indigenous Peoples' and Community Conserved Territories and Areas*. 5th World Conservation Congress, Jeju, South Korea.

———. 2012e. *Resolution 5.099 IUCN Policy on Conservation and Human Rights for Sustainable Development*. 5th World Conservation Congress, Jeju, South Korea.

International Union for Conservation of Nature Commission on Environmental, Economic and Social Policy (IUCN CEESP). 2011. "Whakatane Assessments Are Moving Ahead." http://www.iucn.org/about/union/commissions/ceesp/?8011/Whakatane-Assessments-are-moving-ahead-and-looking-for-volunteers. Last accessed July 1, 2012.

———. 2012. "Progress Report of the Whakatane Mechanism." http://www.iucn.org/about/union/commissions/ceesp/?9764/Progress-Report-of-the-Whakatane-Mechanism. Last accessed September 30, 2012.

International Union for Conservation of Nature Commission on National Parks and Protected Areas (IUCN CNPPA). 1994. *Guidelines for Protected Areas Management Categories*. Gland, Switzerland: IUCN.

International Union for Conservation of Nature World Commission on Protected Areas (IUCN WCPA). 2003a. *The Durban Accord*. Vth World Parks Congress, Durban, South Africa.

———. 2003b. *Durban Action Plan*. Vth World Parks Congress, Durban, South Africa.

———. 2003c. *Message to the Convention on Biological Diversity*. Vth World Parks Congress, Durban, South Africa.

———. 2003d. *Recommendation V.16 Good Governance of Protected Areas*. Vth World Parks Congress, Durban, South Africa.

———. 2003e. *Recommendation V.24 Indigenous Peoples and Protected Areas*. Vth World Parks Congress, Durban, South Africa.

———. 2003f. *Recommendation V.26 Community Conserved Areas*. Vth World Parks Congress, Durban, South Africa.

———. 2010. "Putting Plans to Work: IUCN's Commitment to Protected Areas." http://www.cbd.int/cooperation/pavilion/iucn-wcpa-cop10-pa-booklet-en.pdf. Last accessed September 30, 2012.

International Union for Conservation of Nature (IUCN) and Forest Peoples Programme. 2012. "Concept Note for the Pilot Whakatane Assessments." http://www.forestpeoples.org/sites/fpp/files/publication/2011/08/fpp-iucn-en-concept-note-pilot-whakatane-assessments.pdf. Last accessed September 30, 2012.

International Working Group for Indigenous Affairs (IWGIA). 2009. "Identification of Indigenous Peoples." http://www.iwgia.org/sw641.asp. Last accessed December 30, 2013.

Jacknis, Ira. 1996. "Repatriation as Social Drama: The Kwakiutl Indians of British Columbia, 1922–1980." *American Indian Quarterly* 20(2): 274–86.

Jackson, Matthew. 1998. "The River of Returns? A New Mine May Soon Strike It Rich at the Expense of the South Nahanni." *Outdoor Canada* 26(4): 18.

Jacobs, Susie. 2002. "Land Reform: Still a Goal Worth Pursuing for Rural Women?" *Journal of International Development* 14: 887–98.

Jana, Sudeep, and Naya Sharma Paudel. 2010. *Rediscovering Indigenous Peoples' and Community Conserved Areas (ICCAs) in Nepal*. Kathmandu: ForestAction Nepal.

Jansen, Kees. 1998. *Political Ecology, Mountain Agriculture, and Knowledge in Honduras*. Thela Latin America Series. Amsterdam: Thela Publishers.

Jarosz, Lucy. 2001. "Feminist Political Ecology." In *International Encyclopedia of the Social and Behavioral Sciences*, edited by Neil J. Smelser and Paul B. Baltes, 5472–75. Oxford, U.K: Pergamon.

Jeanrenaud, Sally. 1999. "Introduction." In *Partnerships for Protection: New Strategies for Planning and Management for Protected Areas*, edited by Sue Stolton and Nigel Dudley, 126–34. London: WWF International and IUCN.

———. 2002. *People-Oriented Approaches in Global Conservation: Is the Leopard Changing Its Spots?* London: International Institute for Environment and Development and the Institute of Development Studies.

Johannes, R. E. 2002. "The Renaissance of Community-based Marine Resource Management in Oceania." *Annual Review of Ecology and Systematics* 33: 317–40.

Johnson, Martha, ed. 1992. *LORE: Capturing Traditional Environmental Knowledge*. Ottawa: Dene Cultural Institute and International Development Research Centre.

Jonas, Harry, J. Eli Makagon, Stephanie Booker, and Holly Shrumm. 2012. "International Law and Jurisprudence." Report No. 1 in *An Analysis of International Law, National Legislation, Judgements, and Institutions as They Interrelate with Territories and Areas Conserved by Indigenous Peoples and Local Communities*. Delhi: Natural Justice and Kalpavriksh.

Jonas, Holly, Harry Jonas, and Suneetha M. Subramanian, eds. 2014. *The Right to Responsibility: Resisting and Engaging Development, Conservation, and the Law in Asia*. Kota Kinabalu, Malaysia: United Nations Environment Programme and United Nations University–Institute of Advanced Studies.

Kaiser, J. 2001. "Bold Corridor Project Confronts Political Reality." *Science* 293(5538): 2196–99.

Kan, Sergei. 1989. *Symbolic Immortality: The Tlingit Potlatch of the Nineteenth Century*. Washington, DC: Smithsonian Institution Press.

Kandiyoti, Deniz. 1988. "Bargaining with Patriarchy." *Gender and Society* 2(3): 274–90.

Katz, C. 2001. "Vagabond Capitalism and the Necessity of Social Reproduction." *Antipode* 33(4): 709–28.

Keller, Robert H., and Michael F. Turek. 1998. *American Indians and National Parks*. Tucson: University of Arizona Press.

Kennett, Rod, Cathy Robinson, Ilse Kiessling, Djawa Yunupingu, Mr Munungurritj, and Djalalingba Yunupingu. 2004. "Indigenous Initiatives for Co-management of Miyapunu/Sea Turtle." *Ecological Management and Restoration* 5(3): 159–66.

Kepe, Thembela. 2008. "Land Claims and Comanagement of Protected Areas in South Africa: Exploring the Challenges." *Environmental Management* 41(3): 311–21.

———. 2010. "Land Claims and Comanagement of Protected Areas in South Africa: Exploring the Challenges." In *Land, Memory, Reconstruction, and Justice: Perspectives on Land Claims in South Africa*, edited by C. Walker, A. Bohlin, R. Hall, and T. Kepe, 235–54. Athens: Ohio University Press.

Kepe, Thembela, R. Wynberg, and W. Ellis. 2003. *Land Reform and Biodiversity Conservation in South Africa: Complementary or in Conflict?* Cape Town: Programme for Land and Agrarian Studies, University of the Western Cape.

Killick, Evan. 2007. "Autonomy and Leadership: Political Formations among the Ashéninka of Peruvian Amazonia." *Ethnos* 72(4): 461–82.

Kirsch, Stuart. 2006. *Reverse Anthropology: Indigenous Analysis of Social and Environmental Relations in New Guinea*. Stanford, CA: Stanford University Press.

Klondike Gold Rush National Historical Park. 2007. "Klondike Gold Rush National Historical Park." http://www.nps.gov/klgo. Last accessed April 7, 2007.

Klooster, D. 2003. "Forests Transitions in Mexico: Institutions and Forests in a Globalized Countryside." *The Professional Geographer* 55(2): 227–37.

Kockleman, Paul. 2007. "From Status to Contract Revisited: Value, Temporality, Circulation and Subjectivity." *Anthropological Theory* 7(2): 151–76.

Kofinas, Gary P. 2005. "Caribou Hunters and Researchers at the Co-management Interface: Emergent Dilemmas and the Dynamics of Legitimacy in Power Sharing." *Anthropologica* 47(2): 179–96.

Kothari, Ashish. 2006a. "Collaboratively Managed Protected Areas." In *Managing Protected Areas: A Global Guide*, edited by Michael Lockwood, Graeme L. Worboys, and Ashish Kothari, 528–48. London: Earthscan.

———. 2006b. "Community Conserved Areas." In *Managing Protected Areas: A Global Guide*, edited by Michael Lockwood, Graeme L. Worboys, and Ashish Kothari, 549–73. London: Earthscan.

———. 2006c. "Community Conserved Areas: Towards Ecological and Livelihood Security." *Parks* 16(1): 3–13.

———. 2006d. "Editorial." *Parks* 16(1): 1–2.

Kothari, Ashish, Colleen Corrigan, Harry Jonas, Aurélie Neumann, and Holly Shrumm, eds. 2012. *Recognising and Supporting Territories and Areas Conserved by Indigenous Peoples and Local Communities: Global Overview and National Case Studies*. CBD Technical Series No. 64. Montreal: Secretariat of the Convention on Biological Diversity, ICCA Consortium, Kalpavriksh, and Natural Justice.

Krahe, Diana L. 2005. "Last Refuge: The Uneasy Embrace of Indian Lands by the National Wilderness Movement, 1937–1965." Ph.D. dissertation, Washington State University.

Krech, Shepard. 1999. *The Ecological Indian: Myth and History*. New York: W. W. Norton and Co.

Krishnapillai, S. 2000. "Sharing the Land: The Deen Maar Indigenous Protected Area." *Arena Magazine* 48: 31–4.

Kulchyski, Peter Keith, and Frank J. Tester. 2007. *Kiumajut (Talking Back): Game Management and Inuit Rights, 1900–70*. Vancouver: University of British Columbia Press.

Kuper, Adam. 2003. "The Return of the Native." *Current Anthropology* 44(3): 389–95.

LAHURNIP (Lawyers Association for Human Rights of Nepalese Indigenous Peoples). n.d. "Indigenous Peoples in Nepal." http://www.lahurnip.org/page.php?id=2. Last accessed February 13, 2014.

Langdon, Steve, Rob Prosper, and Nathalie Gagnon. 2010. "Two Paths One Direction: Parks Canada and Aboriginal Peoples Working Together." *The George Wright Forum* 27(2): 222–33.

Langford, Cooper. 2003. "Draw the Line." *Up Here* 19(4): 52–58, 69.

Langton, Marcia. 1998. *Burning Questions: Emerging Environmental Issues for Indigenous Peoples in Northern Australia*. Darwin, Australia: Darwin Centre for Indigenous Natural and Cultural Resource Management, Northern Territory University.

———. 2003. "The 'Wild,' the Market, and the Native: Indigenous People Face New Forms of Global Colonization." In *Globalization, Globalism, Environments, and Environmentalism: Consciousness of Connections—The Linacre Lectures*, edited by S. Vertovec and D. Posey, 141–67. Oxford, UK: Oxford University Press.

———. 2012. "Lecture 4: The Conceit of Wilderness Ideology." Boyer Lectures. http://www.abc.net.au/radionational/programs/boyerlectures/2012-boyer-lectures-234/4409022#transcript. Last accessed February 9, 2014.

Langton, Marcia, Zane Ma Rhea, and Lisa Palmer. 2005. "Community-Oriented Protected Areas for Indigenous Peoples and Local Communities." *Journal of Political Ecology* 12: 23–50.

Larsen, Peter B. 2006. *Reconciling Indigenous Peoples and Protected Areas: Rights, Governance and Equitable Cost and Benefit Sharing*. Gland, Switzerland: IUCN.

Larson, A., D. Barry, G. Ram Dahal, and C. Pierce Colfer. 2010. *Forests for People: Community Rights and Forest Tenure Reform*. London: Earthscan.

Lasgorceix, Antoine, and Ashish Kothari. 2009. "Displacement and Relocation of Protected Areas: A Synthesis and Analysis of Case Studies." *Economic and Political Weekly* XLIV(49): 37–47.

Lausche, Barbara, and Françoise Burhenne. 2011. *Guidelines for Protected Areas Legislation*. IUCN Environmental Policy and Law Paper no. 81. Gland, Switzerland: IUCN.

Lawotri, Mahendra. 2001. "Racial Discrimination towards the Indigenous Peoples in Nepal: Non-Government Report for the Third World Conference against Racism (WCAR), 2001." http://www.mtnforum.org/resources/library/lawom01a.htm. Last accessed October 25, 2003.

Lawrence, David. 1996. "Managing Parks/Managing Country: Joint Management of Aboriginal Owned Protected Areas in Australia." Research Paper 2 1996–1997. Canberra: Department of the Parliament Library.

———. 2000. *Kakadu: The Making of a National Park*. Carleton: Miegunyah Press, Melbourne University Press.

Lee, Cathy, and Thomas Schaaf. 2003. *The Importance of Sacred Natural Sites for Biodiversity Conservation*. Proceedings of the international workshop held in Kunming and Xishuangbanna Biosphere Reserve, People's Republic of China, February 17–20, 2003. Paris: UNESCO.

Leenhardt, Pierre, Bertrand Cazalet, Bernard Salvat, Joachim Claudet, and Francois Feral. 2013. "The Rise of Large-Scale Marine Protected Areas: Conservation or Geopolitics?" *Ocean and Coastal Management* 85: 112–8.

Legislative Environmental Impact Statement. 2006. *Federal Register*, September 18, 2006, v. 70, no. 180, 54687.

Li, Tania. 2000. "Articulating Indigenous Identity in Indonesia: Resource Politics and the Tribal Slot." *Comparative Studies in Society and History* 42(1): 149–79.

———. 2003. "Masyarakat Adat, Difference, and the Limits of Recognition in Indonesia's Forest Zone." In *Race, Nature, and the Politics of Difference*, edited by D. Moore, J. Kosek, and A. Pandian, 380–406. Durham, NC: Duke University Press.

———. 2004. "Environment, Indigeneity and Transnationalism." In *Liberation Ecologies: Environment, Development, Social Movements*, 2nd ed., edited by R. Peet and M. Watts, 339–70. London: Routledge.

———. 2005. "Engaging Simplifications: Community-Based Natural Resource Management, Market Processes, and State Agendas in Upland Southeast Asia." In

Communities and Conservation: Histories and Politics of Community-Based Natural Resource Management, edited by J. Peter Brosius, Anna Tsing, and Charles Zerner, 427–57. Walnut Creek, CA: Rowman and Littlefield.

Lieberman, D. 1997. "Ethnobotanical Assessment of the Dwesa and Cwebe Nature Reserves." In *Indigenous Knowledge, Conservation Reform, Natural Resource Management and Rural Development in the Dwesa and Cwebe Nature Reserves and Neighboring Village Settlements*, edited by R. Palmer, H. Timmermans, K. Kralo, D. Lieberman, R. Fox, D. Hughes, K. Sami, N. Motteux, and U. Van Harmelen, 40–87. Grahamstown: ISER, Rhodes University.

Lim, Francis Khek Gee. 2008. *Imagining the Good Life: Negotiating Culture and Development in Nepal Himalaya*. Leiden: Brill.

Limbu, Shankar. n.d. "Summary of a Comparative Study of the Prevailing National Laws Concerning Indigenous Nationalities in Nepal and ILO Convention No. 169 on Indigenous and Tribal Peoples." http://www.ccd.org.np/pages/25%20Limbu%20 Comparative%20Analysis.pdf. Last accessed February 13, 2014.

Lockwood, Michael, Graeme L. Worboys, and Ashish Kothari, eds. 2006. *Managing Protected Areas: A Global Guide*. London: Earthscan.

Loo, Tina. 2001. "Making a Modern Wilderness: Conserving Wildlife in Twentieth-Century Canada." *Canadian Historical Review* 82(1): 92–121.

———. 2006. *States of Nature: Conserving Canada's Wildlife in the Twentieth Century*. Vancouver: University of British Columbia Press.

Luke, Timothy W. 1997. *Ecocritique: Contesting the Politics of Nature, Economy and Culture*. Minneapolis: University of Minnesota Press.

MacDonald, Theodore. 1997. *Conflict in the Galápagos Islands: Analysis and Recommendations for Management*. Cambridge, UK: Weatherhead Center for International Affairs.

MacEachern, Alan. 2001. *Natural Selections: National Parks in Atlantic Canada, 1935–1970*. Montreal: McGill-Queen's University Press.

MacKay, Fergus. 2007. "Indigenous Peoples, Protected Areas and the Right to Restitution: The Jurisprudence of the Inter-American Court of Human Rights." *Policy Matters* 15: 209–22.

———. 2011. "Indigenous Peoples' Forests and People: Property, Governance, and Human Rights and the Jurisprudence of the Inter-American Human Rights System." In *Forests and People: Property, Governance, and Human Rights*, edited by Thomas Sikor and Johannes Stahl, 33–46. New York: Earthscan.

MacKay, Fergus, and Emily Caruso. 2004. "Indigenous Lands or National Parks?" *Cultural Survival Quarterly* 28(1): 14–16.

MacKenzie, John M. 1988. *The Empire of Nature: Hunting, Conservation, and British Imperialism*. Manchester, UK: Manchester University Press.

MacLeod, H. 2004. "Taking Control in Chiapas." *New Internationalist* 374: 16–17.

Maffi, Louisa, ed. 2001. *On Biocultural Diversity: Linking Language, Knowledge, and the Environment*. Washington, DC: Smithsonian Institution Press.

———. 2007. "Biocultural Diversity and Sustainability." In *Sage Handbook on Environment and Society*, edited by J. Pretty, A. Ball, T. Benton, J. Guivant, D. Lee, D. Orr, M. Pfeffer, and H. Ward, 267–77. Los Angeles: Sage Publications.

Maffi, Louisa, and Ellen Woodley. 2010. *Biocultural Diversity Conservation: A Global Sourcebook*. London: Earthscan.

Magome, Hector, and James Murombedzi. 2003. "Sharing South African National Parks: Community Land and Conservation in a Democratic South Africa." In *Decolonizing Nature: Strategies for Conservation in a Post-Colonial Era*, edited by W. M. Adams and M. Mulligan, 108–34. London: Earthscan.

Mander, Jerry, and Victoria Tauli-Corpuz, eds. 2006. *Paradigm Wars: Indigenous Peoples' Resistance to Globalization*. San Francisco: Sierra Club.

Manore, Jean. 2007. "Contested Terrains of Space and Place: Hunting and the Landscape Known as Algonquin Park, 1890–1950." In *The Culture of Hunting in Canada*, edited by Jean Manore, 121–47. Vancouver: University of British Columbia Press.

Manseau, Micheline, Brenda Parlee, and G. Burton Ayles. 2005. "A Place for Traditional Ecological Knowledge in Resource Management." In *Breaking Ice: Renewable Resource and Ocean Management in the Canadian North*, edited by Fikret Berkes, Rob Huebert, Helen Fast, Micheline Manseau, and Alan Diduick, 141–64. Calgary: University of Calgary Press.

Manuel, George, and Michael Posluns. 1973. *The Fourth World: An Indian Reality*. Don Mills, Ontario: Collier-Macmillan.

Martin, Gary, Carlos del Campo, Claudia Camacho, Guadelupe Espinoza Sauceda, and Xóchitl Zolueta Juan. 2010. "Negotiating the Web of Law and Policy: Community Designation of Indigenous and Community Conserved Areas in Mexico." *Policy Matters* 17: 195–204.

Martin, Gary J., Claudia I. Camacho Benavides, Carlos A. del Campo García, Salvador Anta Fonseca, Francisco Chapela Mendoza, and Marco Antonio González Ortíz. 2011. "Indigenous and Community Conserved Areas in Oaxaca, Mexico." *Management of Environmental Quality: An International Journal* 22(2): 250–66.

Mascia, Michael B., and Sharon Pailler. 2011. "Protected Area Downgrading, Downsizing, and Degazettement (PADDD) and Its Conservation Implications." *Conservation Letters* 4(1): 9–20.

Mathias, E. 1994. "Indigenous Knowledge and Sustainable Development." IIRR Working Paper no. 53. Silang, Cavite, Philippines: International Institute of Rural Reconstruction.

———. 1995. "Recording Indigenous Knowledge: An Overview." In *Indigenous Knowledge in Conservation of Crop Genetic Resources*, edited by J. Schneider, 19–26. Bogor: Indonesia: CIPESEAP/CRIFC.

Matowanyika J., V. Garibaldi, and E. Musimwa, eds. 1995. *Indigenous Knowledge Systems and Natural Resource Management in Southern Africa*. Harare, Zimbabwe: IUCN.

Matthiessen, Peter. 2012. "In the Great Country." In *Artic Voices: Resistance at the Tipping Point*, edited by Subhankar Banerjee, 363–74. New York: Seven Stories Press.

Maundu, P. 1995. "Methodology for Collecting and Sharing Indigenous Knowledge: A Case Study." *Indigenous Knowledge and Development Monitor* 3(2): 3–5.

Mauss, Marcel. 1967. *The Gift: Forms and Functions of Exchange in Archaic Societies*. New York: W. W. Norton.

Mazel, O. 2006. "Returning Parna Wiru: Restitution of the Maralinga Lands to Traditional Owners in South Australia." In *Settling with Indigenous People*, edited by M. Langton, O. Mazel, L. Palmer, K. Shain, and M. Tehan, 159–81. Annandale, Australia: Federation Press.

MBC. 2002. *The Mesoamerican Biological Corridor: A Platform for Sustainable Development.* Managua: Comisión Centroamericana de Ambiente y Desarrollo and United Nations Development Programme/Global Environment Facility.

McCarthy, J. and S. Prudham. 2004. "Neoliberal Nature and the Nature of Neoliberalism." *Geoforum* 35: 275–83.

McCay, Bonnie J., and James M. Acheson, eds. 1987. *The Question of the Commons: The Culture and Ecology of Communal Resources.* Tucson: University of Arizona Press.

McElhinny, Vince. 2007. "Second Latin American Congress of National Parks and Protected Areas." *Info Brief*, November. Washington, DC: Bank Information Center. http://www.bicusa.org/wp-content/uploads/2013/01/InfoBrief_Nov2007.pdf. Last accessed September 21, 2013.

McGregor, Deborah. 2004. "Traditional Ecological Knowledge and Sustainable Development: Towards Co-existence." In *In the Way of Development: Indigenous Peoples, Life Projects, and Globalization*, edited by M. Blaser, H. A. Feit, and G. McRae, 72–91. New York: Zed Books.

McLean, Joanne. 1999. "Conservation and the Impact of Relocation on the Tharus of Chitwan, Nepal." *Himalayan Research Bulletin* 19(2): 38–44.

McLean, Joanne, and Steffen Straede. 2003. "Conservation, Relocation, and the Paradigms of Park and People Management: A Case Study of Padampur Villages and the Royal Chitwan National Park, Nepal." *Conservation and Society* 16: 509–26.

McShane, Thomas O., and Michael P. Wells, eds. 2004. *Getting Biodiversity Projects to Work: Towards More Effective Conservation and Development.* New York: Columbia University Press.

McSweeney, Kendra. 2004. "The Dugout Canoe Trade in Central America's Mosquitia: Approaching Rural Livelihoods through Systems of Exchange." *Annals of the Association of American Geographers* 94(3): 638–61.

Mendoza Vidaurre, René. 2002. "The New Ecology: Exploiting Forests to Preserve Them." *Envio* 21(253): 38–46.

Middleton, Beth Rose. 2011. *Trust in the Land: New Directions in Tribal Conservation.* Tucson: University of Arizona Press.

Middleton, Elisabeth. 2010. "A Political Ecology of Healing." *Journal of Political Ecology* 17: 1–28.

Miller, K., E. Chang, and N. Johnson. 2001. *Defining Common Ground for the Mesoamerican Biological Corridor.* Washington, DC: World Resources Institute.

Minc, G., D. Rodriguez, S. Sakai, R. Quiroga, L. Taber, and A. Rodríguez. 2001. *The Mesoamerican Biological Corridor as a Vector for Sustainable Development in the Region: The Role of International Financing, Preliminary Considerations.* Washington, DC: Inter-American Development Bank and World Bank.

Ministry of Forests and Soil Conservation, Nepal. 2007. *Sagarmatha National Park Management and Tourism Plan, 2007–2012.* Kathmandu: Ministry of Forests and Soil Conservation.

Minority Rights. 2012. "Two Years on from African Commission's Ruling, Kenya Continues to Drag Its Feet in Recognising Indigenous Peoples' Ownership of Wildlife Park, MRG Urges Government to Act." http://www.minorityrights.org/11191/press-releases/two-years-on-from-african-commissions-ruling-kenya-continues-to-drag-its-feet-in-recognising-indigenous-peoples-ownership-of-wildlife-park-mrg-urges-government-to-act.html. Last accessed June 1, 2012.

Mitchell, M. 1996. *From Talking Chiefs to a Native Corporate Elite: The Birth of Class and Nationalism among Canadian Inuit.* Montreal: McGill-Queen's University Press.

Mittermeier, Russell A., Cristina Goettsch Mittermeier, Patricio Robles Gil, John Pilgrim, and William R. Konstant. 2003. *Wilderness: Earth's Last Wild Places.* Mexico City: CEMEX.

Mollett, Sharlene. 2006a. "The Politics of Natural Resource Access: Indigeneity, Race and Property Rights in the Honduran Rio Platano Biosphere Reserve." Ph.D. dissertation, University of Toronto.

———. 2006b. "Race and Natural Resource Conflicts in Honduras: The Miskito and Garifuna Struggle for Lasa Pulan." *Latin American Research Review* 41(1): 76–101.

———. 2010. "*Esta Listo* (Are You Ready)? Gender, Race and Land Registration in the Río Plátano Biosphere Reserve." *Gender, Place and Culture* 17(3): 357–75.

Molnar, Augusta, Sara J. Scherr, and Arvind Khare. 2004. *Who Conserves the World's Forests? A New Assessment of Conservation and Investment Trends.* Washington, DC: Forest Trends and Ecoagriculture Partners.

Morel, Cynthia. 2010. "Conservation and Indigenous Peoples' Rights: Must One Necessarily Come at the Expense of the Other?" *Policy Matters* 17: 174–81.

Mosse, David. 2001. "'People's Knowledge,' Participation and Patronage: Operations and Representations in Rural Development." In *Participation: The New Tyranny?*, edited by B. Cooke and U. Kothari, 16–35. London: Zed Books.

Muller, Samantha. 2003. "Towards Decolonisation of Australia's Protected Area Management: The Nantawarrina Indigenous Protected Area Experience." *Australian Geographical Studies* 41(1): 29–43.

Müller-Böker, Ulrike. 1999. *The Chitawan Tharus in Southern Nepal: An Ethnoecological Approach.* Kathmandu: Nepal Research Centre Publications.

Mulrennan, Monica E., and C. H. Scott. 2005. "Co-management: An Attainable Partnership? Two Cases from James Bay, Northern Quebec and Torres Strait, Northern Queensland." *Anthropologica* 47(2): 197–213.

Munn, Nancy. 1996. "Excluded Spaces: The Figure of the Australian Aboriginal Landscape." *Critical Inquiry* 22(3): 446–65.

Murray, Grant, and Leslie King. 2012. "First Nations Values in Protected Area Governance: Tla-o-qui-aht Tribal Parks and Pacific Rim National Park Reserve." *Human Ecology* 40: 385–95.

Myers, Fred. 1989. "Burning the Truck and Holding the Country: Forms of Property, Time, and the Negotiation of Identity among Pintupi Aborigines." In *We Are Here: Politics of Aboriginal Land Tenure*, edited by E. Wilmsen, 15–42. Berkeley: University of California Press.

———. 1993. "Place, Identity, and Exchange: The Transformation of Nurturance to Social Reproduction over the Life-Cycle in a Kin-Based Society." In *Exchanging Products: Producing Exchange*, Oceania Monograph no. 43, edited by Jane Fajans, 33–57. Sydney: University of Sydney.

Nabhan, Gary P. 1997. *Cultures of Habitat.* Washington, DC: Counterpoint.

Nabokov, Peter. 2006. *Where the Lightning Strikes: The Lives of American Indian Sacred Places.* New York: Penguin

Nadasdy, Paul. 1999. "The Politics of TEK: Power and the 'Integration' of Knowledge." *Arctic Anthropology* 36(1–2): 1–18.

———. 2003a. *Hunters and Bureaucrats: Power, Knowledge, and Aboriginal-State Relations in the Southwest Yukon.* Seattle: University of Washington Press.

———. 2003b. "Reevaluating the Co-management Success Story." *Arctic* 56: 367–80.

———. 2005. "The Anti-politics of TEK: The Institutionalization of Co-management Discourse and Practice." *Anthopologica* 47(2): 215–32.

———. 2011. "'We Don't Harvest Animals; We Kill Them': Agricultural Metaphors and the Politics of Wildlife Management in the Yukon." In *Knowing Nature: Conservations at the Intersection of Political Ecology and Science Studies*, edited by M. J. Goldman, P. Nadasdy, and M. D. Turner, 135–51. Chicago: University of Chicago Press.

Nahual, Jorge, ed. 2009. *De Briloche a Barcelona: Pueblos Indigenas y Areas Protegidas por el Pleno Control de Sus Territorios.* Neuquen, Argentina: Impreso en Grafica Althabe.

Nash, June. 2001. *Mayan Visions: The Quest for Autonomy in an Age of Globalization.* New York: Routledge.

Natcher, David C., Susan Davis, and Clifford G. Hickey. 2005. "Co-management: Managing Relationships, Not Resources." *Human Organization* 64(3): 240–50.

National Native Title Tribunal. 2003. "What Does the Indigenous Land Corporation Do?" http://www.nntt.gov.au/publications/data/files/NTF_5f.pdf. Last accessed May 20, 2004.

National Park Service. 2010. *Harvest of Glaucous-Winged Gull Eggs by Huna Tlingits in Glacier Bay National Park and Preserve.* Record of Decision. August 2010. National Park Service, U.S. Department of the Interior, Glacier Bay Park and Preserve, Alaska.

———. 2012. "National Park Service, NAGPRA, Frequently Asked Questions." www.nps.gov/history/nagpra/FAQ/INDEX.HTM#How_many. Last accessed August13, 2012.

Navarro, R., and E. Rasmussen. 2005. "Cynical Trade." http://centralamerica.ms.dk/articles/English/cynicaltrade.htm. Last accessed July 13, 2005.

Negi, Chandra, and Sunil Nautiyal. 2003. "Indigenous Peoples, Biological Diversity and Protected Area Management: Policy Framework towards Resolving Conflicts." *International Journal of Sustainable Development and World Ecology* 10(2): 169–79.

Nelson, A., and K. M. Chomitz. 2011. "Effectiveness of Strict vs. Multiple Use Protected Areas in Reducing Tropical Forest Fires: A Global Analysis Using Matching Methods." *PloS ONE* 6(8): 1–14.

Nelson, Diane. 1999. *A Finger in the Wound: Body Politics in Quincentennial Guatemala.* Berkeley: University of California Press.

Nelson, Fred. 2010. "Democratizing Natural Resource Governance: Searching for Institutional Change." In *Community Rights, Conservation and Contested Land: The Politics of Natural Resource Governance in Africa*, edited by Fred Nelson, 310–33. London: Earthscan.

Nepstad, Daniel, S. Schwartzman, B. Bamberger, M. Santilli, D. Ray, P. Schlesinger, P. Lefebvre, A. Alencar, E. Prinz, Greg Fiske, and Alicia Rolla. 2006. "Inhibition of Amazon Deforestation and Fire by Parks and Indigenous Lands." *Conservation Biology* 20(1): 65–73.

Nettheim, G., G. Meyers, and D. Craig. 2002. *Indigenous Peoples and Governance Structures: A Comparative Analysis of Land and Resource Management Rights.* Canberra: Aboriginal Studies Press and AIATSIS.

Neufeld, David. 2001. "Parks Canada and the Commemoration of the North: History and Heritage." In *Northern Visions: New Perspectives on the North in Canadian History*, edited by Kerry Abel and Ken S. Coates, 45–76. Peterborough, Ontario: Broadview Press.

———. 2002. "The Commemoration of Northern Aboriginal Peoples by the Canadian Government." *George Wright Forum* 19(3): 22–33.

Neufeld, David, and Frank Norris. 1996. *Chilkoot Trail: Heritage Route to the Klondike*. Whitehorse, Yukon: Lost Moose Publishers.

Neumann, Roderick P. 1997. "Primitive Ideas: Protected Area Buffer Zones and the Politics of Land in Africa." *Development and Change* 28: 559–82.

———. 1998. *Imposing Wilderness: Struggles over Livelihood and Nature Preservation in Africa*. Berkeley: University of California Press.

———. 2004. "Nature-State-Territory: Towards a Critical Theorization of Conservation Enclosures." In *Liberation Ecologies: Environment, Development, Social Movements*, 2nd ed., edited by Richard Peet and Michael Watts, 195–217. London: Routledge.

———. 2005. *Making Political Ecology*. New York: Hodder Arnold.

Newcomer, Q. 2002. "Path of the Tapir: Integrating Biological Corridors, Ecosystem Management, and Socioeconomic Development in Costa Rica." *Endangered Species Update* 19(4): 186–93.

Nietschmann, Bernard Q. 1986. "Economic Development by Invasion of Indigenous Nations." *Cultural Survival Quarterly* 10(2): 2–12.

———. 1987. "The Third World War." *Cultural Survival Quarterly* 11(3): 1–16.

———. 1992a. "Conservation by Self-Determination." *Research and Exploration* 7(3): 372–4.

———. 1992b. *The Interdependence of Biological and Cultural Diversity*. Occasional Paper no. 21. Olympia, WA: Center for World Indigenous Studies.

———. 1994. "The Fourth World: Nations Versus States." In *Reordering the World: Geopolitical Perspectives on the Twenty-First Century*, edited by George J. Demko and William B. Wood, 225–42. Boulder, CO: Westview Press.

———. 1995. "Defending the Miskito Reefs with Maps and GPS: Mapping with Sail, Scuba, and Satellite." *Cultural Survival Quarterly* 18(4): 34–7.

———. 1997. "Protecting Indigenous Coral Reefs and Sea Territories, Miskito Coast, RAAN, Nicaragua." In *Conservation through Cultural Survival: Indigenous Peoples and Protected Areas*, edited by Stan Stevens, 193–224. Washington, DC: Island Press.

Niezen, Ronald. 2003. *The Origins of Indigenism: Human Rights and the Politics of Identity*. Berkeley: University of California Press.

Nolte, Christoph, Arun Agrawal, Kirsten M. Silvius, and Britaldo S. Soares-Filho. 2013. "Governance Regime and Location Influence Avoided Deforestation Success of Protected Areas in the Brazilian Amazon." *Proceedings of the National Academy of Science* 110(13): 4956–61.

Norgrove, Linda, and David Hulme. 2006. "Confronting Conservation at Mount Elgon, Uganda." *Development and Change* 37(5): 1093–116.

NotiCen: Central American and Caribbean Affairs. 2003. "Plan Puebla-Panama Fading, Even as Some Projects Advance." Latin America Data Base, University of New Mexico. http://ladb.unm.edu. Last accessed May 5, 2005.

———. 2005. "Honduras High Tech Land Solution Shows Low Regard for Garifunas." *Affairs* (April 7, 2005). Latin America Data Base, University of New Mexico. http://ladb.unm.edu. Last accessed May 5, 2005.

Nowlan, Linda. 2001. *Arctic Legal Regimes for Environmental Protection.* IUCN Environmental Policy and Law Paper no. 44. Gland, Switzerland: IUCN.

Ntshona, Z., M. Kraai, T. Kepe, and P. Saliwa. 2010. "From Land Rights to Environmental Entitlements: Community Discontent in the 'Successful' Dwesa-Cwebe Land Claim in South Africa." *Development Southern Africa* 27(3): 353–61.

Nustad, K. G. 2011. "Property, Rights and Community in a South African Land-Claim Case." *Anthropology Today* 27(1): 20–24.

Offen, Karl. 1999. "The Miskito Kingdom: Landscape and the Emergence of a Miskito Ethnic Identity, Northeastern Nicaragua and Honduras, 1600–1800." Ph.D. dissertation, University of Texas at Austin.

———. 2003. "The Territorial Turn: Making Black Territories in Pacific Columbia." *Journal of Latin American Geography* 2(1): 43–69.

Ogra, Monica. V. 2008. "Human-Wildlife Conflict and Gender in Protected Area Borderlands: A Case Study of Costs, Perceptions, and Vulnerabilities from Uttarakhand (Uttaranchal), India." *Geoforum* 39: 1408–22.

Ostrom, Elinor. 1990. *Governing the Commons: The Evolution of Institutions for Collective Action.* Cambridge, UK: Cambridge University Press.

Ostrom, Elinor, and H. Nagendra. 2006. "Insights on Linking Forests, Trees, and People from the Air, on the Ground, and in the Laboratory." *Proceedings of the National Academy of Sciences* 103(51): 19224–31.

Ostrom, Elinor, Thomas Dietz, Nives Dolšak, Paul C. Stern, Susan Stonich, and Elke U. Weber, eds. 2002. *The Drama of the Commons.* Washington, DC: National Academy Press.

Oviedo, Gonzalo, Luisa Maffi, and Peter B. Larsen. 2000. *Indigenous and Traditional Peoples of the World and Ecoregion Conservation: An Integrated Approach to Conserving the World's Biological and Cultural Diversity.* Gland, Switzerland: WWF International and Terralingua.

Oyono, René, R. P. Mbile, M. France, and S. Bandiaky. 2010. "Mapping Communities, Mapping Rights: Participatory Community Mapping as Rights Contestation in Cameroon." *Policy Matters* 17: 156–60.

Pacheco, P., D. Barry, P. Cronkelton, and A. Larson. 2012. "The Recognition of Forest Rights in Latin America: Progress and Shortcomings of Forest Tenure Reforms." *Society and Natural Resources* 25(6): 556–71.

PACTeam Canada, Inc. 2009. "Legislation, Sponsoring Agencies, and the Protected Areas Strategy." http://www.nwtpas.ca/documents/document-2009-legislative summaries.pdf. Last accessed September 14, 2009.

Pagdee, Adcharaporn, Yeon-Su Kim, and P. J. Daugherty. 2006. "What Makes Community Forest Management Successful: A Meta-Study from Community Forests throughout the World." *Society and Natural Resources* 19(1): 33–52.

Palmer, Lisa. 2004a. "Fishing Lifestyles: 'Territorians,' Traditional Owners and the Management of Recreational Fishing in Kakadu National Park." *Australian Geographical Studies* 42(1): 60–76.

———. 2004b. "Bushwalking in Kakadu: A Study of Cultural Borderlands." *Social and Cultural Geography* 5(1): 109–28.

Palmer, Robin, Derick Fay, Herman Timmermans, Fonda Lewis, and Johan Viljoen. 2002a. "Regaining the Forests: Reform and Development from 1994 to 2001." In *From Confrontation to Negotiation: Nature-Based Development on South Africa's*

Wild Coast, edited by Robin Palmer, Herman Timmermans, and Derick Fay, 111–43. Pretoria: Human Science Research Council.

Palmer, Robin, R. Kingwill, M. Coleman, and N. Hamer. 2006. *The Dwesa-Cwebe Restitution Claim: A Case Study as Preparation for a Field-Based Learning Programme*. Mowbray: Phuhlisani Solutions CC.

Palmer, Robin, Herman Timmermans, and Derick Fay, eds. 2002b. *From Confrontation to Negotiation: Nature-Based Development on South Africa's Wild Coast*. Pretoria: Human Science Research Council.

Palmer, Robin, Herman Timmermans, K. Kralo, D. Lieberman, R. Fox, D. Hughes, K. Sami, N. Motteux, and U. Van Harmelen. 1997. *Indigenous Knowledge, Conservation Reform, Natural Resource Management and Rural Development in the Dwesa and Cwebe Nature Reserves and Neighboring Village Settlements*. Grahamstown: ISER, Rhodes University.

Pannell, Sandra. 1994. "Mabo and Museums: The Indigenous (Re)appropriation of Indigenous Things." *Oceania* 65(1): 18–39.

Parenteau, Bill. 1998. "'Care, Control and Supervision': Native People in the Canadian Atlantic Salmon Fishery, 1867–1900." *Canadian Historical Review* 79(1): 1–35.

———. 2004. "A 'Very Determined Opposition to the Law': Conservation, Angling Leases, and Social Conflict in the Canadian Atlantic Salmon Fishery, 1867–1914." *Environmental History* 9(3): 436–63.

Parks Canada. 1979. *Parks Canada Policy*. Hull, Quebec: Parks Canada.

———. 1994. *Parks Canada Guiding Principles and Operational Policies*. Ottawa: Parks Canada.

———. 2007a. "Chilkoot Trail National Historic Site of Canada." http://pc.gc.ca/lhn-nhs/yt/chilkoot/activ/activ1c_n_e.asp. Last accessed December 30, 2007.

———. 2007b. "Taking Care of Nah?a dehé." Gatineau, Quebec: Parks Canada. http://dsp-psd.pwgsc.gc.ca/collection_2007/pc/R63-342-9-1-2006E.pdf. Last accessed March 7, 2008.

———. 2008. "Gwaii Haanas National Park Reserve and Haida Heritage Site." http://www.pc.gc.ca/pn-np/bc/gwaiihaanas/index_e.asp. Last accessed May 30, 2008.

Parlee, Brenda, and Micheline Manseau. 2005. "Using Traditional Knowledge to Adapt to Ecological Change: Denésoliné Monitoring of Caribou Movements." *Arctic* 58(1): 26–37.

Pathak, Neema, Seema Bhatt, Tasneem Balasinorwala, Ashish Kothari, and Grazia Borrini-Feyerabend. 2004. *Community Conserved Areas: A Bold New Frontier for Conservation*. IUCN/CEESP Briefing Note 5. Gland, Switzerland: IUCN.

Paudel, Naya Sharma, Sudeep Jana, and Jailab Kumar Rai. 2012. "Contested Law: Slow Response to Demands for Reformulating Protected Area Legal Framework in Nepal." *Journal of Forest and Livelihood* 10(1): 88–100.

Peepre, Juri, and Philip Dearden. 2002. "The Role of Aboriginal Peoples." In *Parks and Protected Areas in Canada: Planning and Management*, 2nd ed., edited by Philip Dearden and Rick Rollins, 323–53. Don Mills, Ontario: Oxford University Press.

Peepre, Juri, and Bob Jickling, eds. 1994. *Northern Protected Areas and Wilderness*. Proceedings from a Forum on Northern Protected Areas and Wilderness, Whitehorse, Yukon, November 1993. Whitehorse, Yukon: Canadian Parks and Wilderness Society and Yukon College.

Peet, Richard, and Michael Watts. 2004. *Liberation Ecologies: Environment, Development, Social Movements*. London: Routledge.

Peluso, Nancy Lee. 1992. *Rich Forests, Poor People: Resource Control and Resistance in Java*. Berkeley: University of California Press.

———. 1993. "Coercing Conservation? The Politics of State Resource Control." *Global Environmental Change* 3(2): 199–216.

———. 1995. "Whose Woods Are These? Counter-mapping Forest Territories in Kalimantan, Indonesia." *Antipode* 27(4): 383–406.

Peluso, Nancy Lee, and Peter Vandergeest. 2001. "Genealogies of the Political Forest and Customary Rights in Indonesia, Malaysia, and Thailand." *The Journal of Asian Studies* 60(3): 761–812.

Perez Chiriboga, Isabel. M. 2002. *Espíritus de Vida y Muerte: Los Miskitu Hondureños en Época de Guerra*. Tegucigalpa, Honduras: Guaymuras.

Perreault, T., and P. Martin. 2005. "Geographies of Neoliberalism in Latin America." *Environment and Planning A* 37: 191–201.

Persha, L., A. Agrawal, and A. Chhatre. 2011. "Social and Ecological Synergy: Local Rulemaking, Forest Livelihoods, and Biodiversity Conservation." *Science* 331: 1606–8.

Phillips, Adrian. 2003. "Turning Ideas on Their Head: The New Paradigm for Protected Areas." *The George Wright Forum* 20(2): 8–32.

Pimbert, Michel. 2002. "Preface." In *People-Oriented Approaches in Global Conservation: Is the Leopard Changing Its Spots?* by Sally Jeanrenaud, vi–xi. London: International Institute for Environment and Development and the Institute of Development Studies.

Pimbert, Michel P., and Jules Pretty. 1995. *Parks, People and Professionals: Putting 'Participation' into Protected Area Management*. UNRISD Discussion paper No. 57. Geneva: United Nations Research Institute for Social Development. http://www.ibcperu.org/doc/isis/6931.pdf. Last accessed February 15, 2014.

Piper, Liza, and John Sandlos. 2007. "A Broken Frontier: Ecological Imperialism in the Canadian North." *Environmental History* 12(4): 759–95.

Plant, Roger, and Søren Hvalkøf. 2001. *Land Titling and Indigenous Peoples*. Sustainable Development Department Technical Papers Series. Washington, DC: Inter-American Development Bank. http://idbdocs.iadb.org/wsdocs/getdocument.aspx?docnum=363808. Last accessed September 21, 2013.

Porsild, Alf Erling. 1936. "The Reindeer Industry and the Canadian Eskimo." *The Geographical Journal* 88(1): 1–17.

Porter, L. 2004. "Planning's Colonial Culture: An Investigation of the Contested Process of Producing Place in (Post)colonial Victoria." Ph.D. dissertation, The University of Melbourne.

Porter-Bolland, Luciana, Edward A. Ellis, Manuel R. Guariguata, Isabel Ruiz-Mallen, Simoneta Negrete-Yankelevich, and Victoria Reyes-Garcia. 2012. "Community Managed Forests and Forest Protected Areas: An Assessment of Their Conservation Effectiveness across the Tropics." *Forest Ecology and Management* 268: 6–17.

Posey, Darrell A., ed. 1999. *Cultural and Spiritual Values of Biodiversity*. London: Intermediate Technology Publications and UNEP.

———. 2003. "Fragmenting Cosmic Connections: Converting Nature into Commodity." In *Globalization, Globalism, Environments, and Environmentalism:*

Consciousness of Connections—The Linacre Lectures, edited by S. Vertovec and D. Posey, 123–40. Oxford, UK: Oxford University Press.

Posey, Darrell A., and Graham Dutfield. 1996. *Beyond Intellectual Property: Toward Traditional Resource Rights for Indigenous Peoples and Local Communities*. Ottawa: International Development Research Centre.

Povinelli, Elizabeth. 1993. *Labor's Lot: The Power, History, and Culture of Aboriginal Action*. Chicago: University of Chicago Press.

———. 2002. *The Cunning of Recognition: Indigenous Alterities and the Making of Australian Multiculturalism*. Durham, NC: Duke University Press.

Power, T. 2002. "Joint Management at Uluru-Kata Tjuta National Park." *Environmental and Planning Law Journal* 19(4): 284–302.

Pretty, Jules. 2007. *The Earth Only Endures: On Reconnecting with Nature and Our Place in It*. London: Earthscan.

Pretty, Jules, Bill Adams, Fikret Berkes, Simone Ferreira De Athayde, Nigel Dudley, Eugene Hunn, Luisa Maffi, Kay Milton, David Rapport, Paul Robbins, Eleanor Sterling, Sue Stolton, Anna Tsing, Erin Vintinnerk, and Sarah Pilgrim. 2009. "The Intersections of Biological Diversity and Cultural Diversity: Towards Integration." *Conservation and Society* 7(2): 100–12.

Pryde, Philip R. 1991. *Environmental Management in the Soviet Union*. Cambridge, UK: Cambridge University Press.

Pungetti, Gloria, Gonzalo Oviedo, and Della Hooke, eds. 2012. *Sacred Species and Sites: Advances in Biocultural Conservation*. Cambridge, UK: Cambridge University Press.

Pyrillis, Rita. 2000. "Repatriation's Open Door Helps Museums as Well as Native Communities." *National Museum of the American Indian Quarterly* Winter: 10–11.

Radcliffe, Sara, and Sallie Westwood. 1996. *Remaking the Nation: Identity and Politics in Latin America*. London: Routledge.

Rankin, Katharine. 2003. "Cultures of Economies: Gender and Socio-spatial Change in Nepal." *Gender, Place and Culture* 10(1): 111–29.

Reddy, S. 2002. "Communal Forests, Political Spaces: Territorial Competition between Common Property Institutions and the State in Guatemala." *Space and Polity* 6(3): 271–87.

Redford, Kent. 1991. "The Ecologically Noble Savage." *Cultural Survival Quarterly* 15(1): 46–48.

Redford, Kent, and S. E. Sanderson. 2000. "Extracting Humans from Nature." *Conservation Biology* 14: 1362–4.

Regmi, Mahesh C. 1975. "Landholding, Trade, and Revenue Collection in Solukhumbu." *Regmi Research Series* 7: 122–6. http://himalaya.socanth.cam.ac.uk/collections/journals/regmi/pdf/Regmi_07.pdf. Last accessed September 22, 2013.

Reid, Hannah. 2001. "Contractual National Parks and the Makuleke Community." *Human Ecology* 29(2): 135–55.

Republica de Honduras. 1992. *Ley para la Modernización y el Desarrollo del Sector Agrícola*. Tegucigalpa, Honduras: MDC.

Riascos, Juan Carlos Riascos de la Peña, Paulina Ormanza, Gonzalo Zambrana, and Cynthia Silva. 2008. *Caracterización de las Áreas Indígenas y Comunitarias para la Conservación en Bolivia, Ecuador y Colombia*. http://cmsdata.iucn.org/downloads/andes_regional_icca_review.pdf. Last accessed February 10, 2014.

Ribot, Jesse C. 2004. *Waiting for Democracy: The Politics of Choice in Natural Resource Decentralization*. Washington, DC: World Resources Institute.
———. 2008. *Authority over Forests: Negotiating Decentralization in Senegal*. Representation, Equity, and Environment Working Paper no. 36. Washington, DC: World Resources Institute.
Richards, P. 1995. *Indigenous Agricultural Revolution: Ecology and Food Crops in West Africa*. London: Hutchinson.
Rinne, Pia. 2007. "Struggles over Resources and Representations in Territorial Conflicts in the Northern Autonomous Atlantic Region (RAAN), Nicaragua." Ph.D. dissertation, University of Helsinki.
Rivas D., T. 1938. *Mensajes, Memorias, Acuerdos, Decretos y Comunicaciones Oficiales para la Mosquitia Hondureña*. Tegucigalpa, Honduras: Biblioteca de Juan Enrique Cardona.
Robins, Steve, and Kees van der Waal. 2008. "'Model Tribes' and Iconic Conservationists? The Makuleke Restitution Case in Kruger National Park." *Development and Change* 39(1): 53–72.
———. 2010. "'Model Tribes' and Iconic Conservationists? Tracking the Makuleke Restitution Case in Kruger National Park." In *Land, Memory, Reconstruction, and Justice: Perspectives on Land Claims in South Africa*, edited by C. Walker, A. Bohlin, R. Hall, and T. Kepe, 163–80. Athens: Ohio University Press.
Robinson, C., and N. Mununggurtij. 2001. "Sustainable Balance: A Yolngu Framework for Cross-Cultural Collaboration." In *Working on Country: Contemporary Indigenous Management of Australia's Lands and Coastal Regions*, edited by R. Baker, J. Davies, and E. Young, 92–107. Melbourne: Oxford University Press.
Rocheleau, Diane, Barbara Thomas-Slayter, and Ester Wangari. 1996. "Gender and Environment: A Feminist Political Ecology Perspective." In *Feminist Political Ecology: Global Issues and Local Experiences*, edited by Diane Rocheleau, Barbara Thomas-Slayter, and Ester Wangari, 3–23. London: Routledge.
Rodon, Thierry. 1998. "Co-management and Self-determination in Nunavut." *Polar Geography* 22(2): 119–35.
Rosales, Hawk. 2012. "The InterTribal Sinkyone Wilderness: Ten Tribes Reclaiming, Stewarding, and Restoring Ancestral Lands." In *Protecting Wild Nature on Native Lands: Case Studies by Native Peoples from Around the World*, Volume II, edited by Vance G. Martin and Sharon Shay Sloan, 140–7. Boulder, CO: The Wild Foundation.
Rose, Deborah Bird. 1996. "Land Rights and Deep Colonising: The Erasure of Women." *Aboriginal Law Bulletin* 3(85): 6–13.
Rose, Laurel. 1991. *The Politics of Harmony: Land Dispute Strategies in Swaziland*. Cambridge, UK: Cambridge University Press.
Ross, Anne, Kathleen Pickering Sherman, Jeffrey G. Snodgrass, Henry D. Delcore, and Richard Sherman. 2011. *Indigenous Peoples and the Collaborative Stewardship of Nature: Knowledge Binds and Institutional Conflicts*. Walnut Creek, CA: Left Coast Press.
Ross, Helen, Chrissy Grant, Cathy J. Robinson, Arturo Izurieta, Dermot Smyth, and Phil Rist. 2009. "Co-management and Indigenous Protected Areas in Australia: Achievements and Ways Forward." *Australasian Journal of Environmental Management* 16: 242–52.

Rossiter, D., and P. K. Wood. 2005. "Fantastic Topographies: Neo-liberal Responses to Aboriginal Land Claims in British Columbia." *The Canadian Geographer* 49(4): 352–66.

Rubin, Jeffrey. 1994. "Models of Conflict Management." *Journal of Social Issues* 50(1): 33–46.

Runte, Alfred. 1993. *Yosemite: The Embattled Wilderness*. Lincoln: University of Nebraska Press.

Ruru, Jacinta. 2008. "A Maori Right to Own and Manage National Parks?" *Journal of South Pacific Law* 12(1): 105–10.

Rutherford, John, James McLean, and James Harkin. 1922. *Report of the Royal Commission Appointed by Order in Council of Date May 20, 1919 to Investigate the Possibilities of the Reindeer and Musk-Ox Industries in the Arctic and Sub-Arctic Regions of Canada*. Ottawa: King's Printer.

Rutherford, Stephanie. 2007. "Green Governmentality: Insights and Opportunities in the Study of Nature's Rule." *Progress in Human Geography* 31(3): 291–307.

Rylands, A. B., M. T. da Fonseca, R. B. Machado, L. P. de S. Pinto, and R. B. Cavalcanti. 2008. "Brazil." In *The World's Protected Areas: Status, Values and Prospects in the Twenty-First Century*, edited by Stuart Chape, Mark Spalding, and Martin Jenkins, 208–17. Berkeley: University of California Press.

Sabin, Paul. 1995. "Voices from the Hydrocarbon Frontier: Canada's Mackenzie Valley Pipeline Inquiry (1974–1977)." *Environmental History Review* 19(1): 17–48.

Safa, Helen I. 2005. "Challenging Mestizaje: A Gender Perspective on Indigenous and Afrodescendant Movements in Latin America." *Critique of Anthropology* 25(3): 307–30.

Said, Edward. 1979. *Orientalism*. New York: Vintage Books.

———. 1993. *Culture and Imperialism*. New York: Vintage Books.

Sandlos, John. 2001. "From the Outside Looking In: Aesthetics, Politics, and Wildlife Conservation in the Canadian North." *Environmental History* 6(1): 6–31.

———. 2002. "Where the Scientists Roam: Ecology, Management and Bison in Northern Canada." *Journal of Canadian Studies* 37(2): 93–129.

———. 2005. "Federal Spaces, Local Conflicts: National Parks and the Exclusionary Politics of the Conservation Movement in Ontario, 1900–1935." *Canadian Historical Association Journal* 16: 293–318.

———. 2007. *Hunters at the Margin: Native People and Wildlife Conservation in the Northwest Territories*. Vancouver: University of British Columbia Press.

Santos-Granero, Fernando. 2004. "Arawakan Sacred Landscapes: Emplaced Myths, Place Rituals, and the Production of Locality in Western Amazonia." In *Kultur, Raum, Landschaft: Zur Bedeutung des Raumes in Zeiten der Globalität*, edited by Ernst Halbmayer and Elke Mader, 93–122. Frankfurt am Main: Brandes and Apsel Verlag.

Schaaf, Thomas, and Cathy Lee. 2006. *Conserving Cultural and Biological Diversity: The Role of Sacred Natural Sites and Cultural Landscapes*. Proceedings of UNESCO-IUCN International Conference, Tokyo, Japan. Paris: UNESCO.

Schaller, George. 2012. "Saving the Arctic National Wildlife Refuge." In *Artic Voices: Resistance at the Tipping Point*, edited by Subhankar Banerjee, 439–49. New York: Seven Stories Press.

Scott, James C. 1998. *Seeing Like a State: How Certain Schemes to Improve the Human Condition Have Failed*. New Haven, CT: Yale University Press.

Secaira, E. 2000. *La Conservacion de la Naturaleza, el Pueblo y Movimiento Maya, y la Espiritualidad en Guatemala: Implicaciones para Conservacionistas*. Guatemala City, Guatemala: The Nature Conservancy.

Seider, Rachel. 2002. "Introduction." In *Multiculturalism in Latin America: Indigenous Rights, Diversity and Democracy*, edited by Rachel Seider, 1–23. London: Palgrave MacMillan.

Sellars, Richard West. 2009 [1997]. *Preserving Nature in the National Parks: A History*. New Haven, CT: Yale University Press.

Sherpa, Lhakpa Norbu. 2003. "Sacred Beyuls and Biodiversity Conservation in the Himalayas." In *The Importance of Sacred Natural Sites for Biodiversity Conservation*, edited by Cathy Lee, 101–5. Paris: UNESCO. http://unesdoc.unesco.org/images/0013/001333/133358e.pdf. Last accessed September 21, 2013.

Shrumm, Holly. 2010. "Exploring the Right to Diversity in Conservation Law, Policy, and Practice." *Policy Matters* 17.

Sikor, Thomas, and Johanes Stahl. 2011. *Forests and People: Property, Governance, and Human Rights*. New York: Earthscan.

Sitka National Historical Park. 2007a. "Sitka National Historical Park. Southeast Alaska Indian Cultural Center." http://www.nps.gov/sitk/parkilometersgmt/southeast-alaska-indian-cultural-center.htm. Last accessed April 5, 2007.

———. 2007b. "Sitka National Historical Park. Kayaaní Commission." http://www.nps.gov/sitk/historyculture/the-tlingit.htm. Last accessed November 21, 2007.

———. 2007c. "The First Annual Centennial Strategy for Sitka National Historical Park." http://www.nps.gov/sitk/parkmgmt/upload/SITK_Centennial_Strategy.pdf. Last accessed February 8, 2014.

Sivaramakrishnan, K. 1999. *Modern Forests: Statemaking and Environmental Change in Colonial Eastern India*. Stanford, CA: Stanford University Press.

———. 2008. "Science, Environment and Empire History: Comparative Perspectives from Forests in Colonial India." *Environment and History* 14(1): 45–61.

Smith, Carol. 1997. "The Symbolics of Blood: Mestizaje in the Americas." *Identities: Global Studies in Culture and Power* 3(4): 495–521.

Smith, Delores, producer. 1999. "Keish: Skookim Jim Mason, a Man Standing in Two Worlds." Video produced for Northern Native Broadcasting Yukon. Whitehorse, Yukon: Skookum Jim Friendship Centre.

Smyth, D., and J. Sutherland. 1996. *Indigenous Protected Areas: Conservation Partnerships with Indigenous Landholders*. Canberra: Environment Australia.

Smyth, Dermot. 1995. "Protecting Country: Indigenous Protected Areas Phase Two Report." Consultancy report prepared for the Australian Nature Conservation Agency, Canberra.

———. 2001. "Joint Management of National Parks." In *Working on Country: Contemporary Indigenous Management of Australia's Lands and Coastal Regions*, edited by R. Baker, J. Davies, and E. Young, 60–74. Melbourne: Oxford University Press.

Sneed, Paul G. 1997. "National Parklands and Northern Homelands: Toward Co-management of National Parks in Alaska and the Yukon." In *Conservation through Cultural Survival: Indigenous Peoples and Protected Areas*, edited by Stan Stevens, 135–54. Washington, DC: Island Press.

Sobrevila, Claudia. 2008. *The Role of Indigenous Peoples in Biodiversity Conservation: The Natural But Often Forgotten Partners.* Washington, DC: International Bank for Reconstruction and Development/The World Bank.

Spaeder, Joseph J. 2005. "Co-management in a Landscape of Resistance: The Political Ecology of Wildlife Management in Western Alaska." *Anthropologica* 47(2): 165–78.

Spak, Stella. 2005. "The Position of Indigenous Knowledge in Canadian Co-management Organizations." *Anthropologica* 47(2): 233–46.

Spence, Mark. 1999. *Dispossessing the Wilderness: Indian Removal and the Making of the National Parks.* Oxford, UK: Oxford University Press.

Spierenburg, Marja, Conrad Steenkamp, and Harry Wels. 2008. "Enclosing the Local for the Global Commons: Community Land Rights in the Great Limpopo Transfrontier Conservation Area." *Conservation and Society* 6(1): 87–97.

Spoon, Jeremy, and Lhakpa Norbu Sherpa. 2008. "Beyul Khumbu: The Sherpa and Sagarmatha (Mount Everest) National Park and Buffer Zone, Nepal." In *Values of Protected Landscapes and Seascapes*, edited by Josep-Maria Mallarach, 68–79. Gland, Switzerland: IUCN.

Springer, Jenny, Jorge Gastelumendi, Gonzalo Oviedo, Kristen Walker Painemilla, Michael Painter, Kemi Seesink, Helen Schneider, and David Thomas. 2010. "The Conservation Initiative on Human Rights: Promoting Increased Integration of Human Rights in Conservation." *Policy Matters* 17: 81–83.

Standlea, David M. 2006. *Oil, Globalization, and the War for the Arctic Refuge.* Albany: State University of New York Press.

Stanley, Thomas R. 1995. "Ecosystem Management and the Arrogance of Humanism." *Conservation Biology* 9(2): 255–62.

Steenkamp, Conrad. 2001. "The Makuleke Land Claim: An Environmental Conflict." Ph.D. dissertation, University of the Witwatersrand.

Steenkamp, Conrad, and David Grossman. 2001. *People and Parks: Cracks in the Paradigm.* Pretoria: IUCN South Africa.

Steenkamp, Conrad, and Jana Uhr. 2000. *The Makuleke Land Claim: Power Relations and Community-Based Natural Resource Management.* Evaluating Eden Series Discussion Paper no. 18. London: International Institute for Environment and Development.

Stefansson, Vihjalmur. 1921. *The Friendly Arctic: The Story of Five Years in Polar Regions.* New York: Macmillan.

———. 1924. *The Northward Course of Empire.* New York: Macmillan.

Stefansson, Vihjalmur, and Rudolph Martin Anderson. 1913. *My Life with the Eskimo.* New York: Macmillan.

Stegner, Wallace. 1997 [1969]. "Coda: Wilderness Letter." In *Sound of Mountain Water*, by Wallace Stegner, 145–53. New York: Penguin.

Stevens, Stan. 1986. "Inhabited National Parks: Indigenous Peoples in Protected Landscapes." East Kimberley Impact Assessment Project, Working Paper no. 10. Canberra City: Australia National University.

———. 1993. *Claiming the High Ground: Sherpas, Subsistence, and Environmental Change in the Highest Himalaya.* Berkeley: University of California Press.

———, ed. 1997a. *Conservation through Cultural Survival: Indigenous Peoples and Protected Areas.* Washington, DC: Island Press.

———. 1997b. "Consultation, Co-management, and Conflict in Sagarmatha National Park, Nepal." In *Conservation through Cultural Survival: Indigenous Peoples and Protected Areas*, edited by Stan Stevens, 63–97. Washington, DC: Island Press.

———. 2005. "Wilderness, Social Nature, and Protected Areas: IUCN's Encounter with the Indigenous World." Paper presented at the Annual Meeting of the Association of American Geographers, Denver.

———. 2006. "Towards a (Post)colonial Protected Area in the Mt. Everest/Chomolungma Region of Nepal?" Paper presented at the Annual Meeting of the Association of American Geographers, Chicago.

———. 2007. "Theorizing Protected Areas: Fourth World and (Post)colonial Perspectives on Conservation Enclosures, Commons, and Liberation Ecologies." Paper presented at the Annual Meeting of the Association of American Geographers, San Francisco.

———. 2008a. "Nepal: Indigenous and Community Conserved Areas (ICCA) National Legal Survey." http://www.iccaconsortium.org. Last accessed September 30, 2012.

———. 2008b. "The Mount Everest Region as an ICCA: Sherpa Conservation Stewardship of the Khumbu Sacred Valley, Sagarmatha (Chomolungma/Mt. Everest) National Park and Buffer Zone." http://www.iccaconsortium.org. Last accessed September 30, 2012.

———. 2009. "Seeking Respect for a Sherpa Community Conserved Area: Responsibility, Recognition, and Rights in the Mt. Everest Region of Nepal." In *Rights-Based Approaches: Exploring Issues and Opportunities for Conservation*, edited by Jessica Campese, Terry Sunderland, Thomas Greiber, and Gonzalo Oviedo, 203–27. Bogor, Indonesia: Center for International Forestry.

———. 2010. "Implementing the UN Declaration on the Rights of Indigenous Peoples and International Human Rights Law through the Recognition of ICCAs." *Policy Matters* 17: 181–94.

———. 2013. "National Parks and ICCAs in the High Himalaya of Nepal: Challenges and Opportunities." *Conservation and Society* 11(1): 29–45.

———. 2014. "Defending and Strengthening Sherpa ICCAs and Rights in Sagarmatha (Mt. Everest) National Park, Nepal." In *The Right to Responsibility: Resisting and Engaging Development, Conservation, and the Law in Asia*, edited by Holly Jonas, Harry Jonas, and Suneetha M. Subramanian, 71–98. Kota Kinabalu, Malaysia: Natural Justice and United Nations University–Institute of Advanced Studies.

Stevenson, Marc. 2004. "Decolonizing Co-management in Northern Canada." *Cultural Survival Quarterly* 28(1). http://www.culturalsurvival.org/publications/cultural-survival-quarterly/canada/decolonizing-comanagement-northern-canada. Last accessed September 14, 2013.

———. 2006. "The Possibility of Difference: Rethinking Co-management." *Human Organization* 65(2): 167–80.

Stocks, Anthony. 2003. "Mapping Dreams in Nicaragua's Bosawás Biosphere Reserve." *Human Organization* 62(4): 344–56.

Stocks, Anthony, Benjamin McMahan, and Peter Taber. 2007. "Indigenous, Colonist, and Government Impacts on Nicaragua's Bosawás Reserve." *Conservation Biology* 21(6): 1495–505.

Struzik, Ed. 2008. "East Arm National Park a Long Time in Coming." *Edmonton Journal* (January 20): E6.
Style, S. 2001. "Down Mexico Way." *The Ecologist* 31(5): 50–52.
Sundberg, Juanita. 2003. "Strategies for Authenticity and Space in the Maya Biosphere Reserve, Petén, Guatemala." In *Political Ecology: An Integrative Approach to Geography and Environment-Development Studies*, edited by Karl S. Zimmerer and T. J. Bassett, 50–69. New York: Guilford.
———. 2004. "Identities in the Making: Conservation, Gender and Race in the Maya Biosphere Reserve, Guatemala." *Gender, Place and Culture* 11(1): 43–66.
———. 2006. "Conservation Encounters: Transculturation in the 'Contact Zones' of Empire." *Cultural Geographies* 13: 239–65.
Surallés, Alexander, and Pedro García Hierro. 2005. *The Land Within: Indigenous Territory and the Perception of the Environment*. Copenhagen: International Work Group for Indigenous Affairs.
Szabo, S., and Smyth, D. 2003. "Indigenous Protected Areas in Australia: Incorporating Indigenous Owned Land into Australia's National System of Protected Areas." In *Innovative Governance: Indigenous Peoples, Local Communities and Protected Areas*, edited by H. Jaireth and D. Smyth, 145–64. New Delhi: Ane Books.
Tamang, Parshuram. 2003. "Customary Law and Conservation in the Himalaya: The Case of Nepal." Paper presented at the Vth World Parks Congress, Durban, South Africa. http://www.earthlore.ca/clients/WPC/English/grfx/sessions/PDFs/session_1/Tamang.pdf.
Tanner, Terry. 2008. "The Mission Mountains Tribal Wilderness Area." In *Protecting Wild Nature on Native Lands: Case Studies by Native Peoples from Around the World*, Vol. 1, edited by Julie Cajune, Vance G. Martin, and Terry Tanner, 1–24. Boulder, CO: Fulcrum Publishing.
Taylor, P. J., and F. H. Buttel. 1992. "How Do We Know We Have Global Environmental Problems? Science and the Globalization of Environmental Discourse." *Geoforum* 23(3): 405–16.
Tehan, M. 2003. "A Hope Disillusioned, an Opportunity Lost? Reflections on Common Law Native Title and Ten Years of the Native Title Act." *Melbourne University Law Review* 27(2): 523–71.
Terblanche, André, and Mcebisi Kraai. 1996. *Dwesa and Cwebe: Enduring, Democratic Conservation after Apartheid's Abuses*. Mthatha: Transkei Land Service Organization.
Terborgh, John. 1999. *Requiem for Nature*. Washington, DC: Island Press.
———. 2004. "Reflections of a Scientist on the World Parks Congress." *Conservation Biology* 18(3): 619–20.
Tester, Frank J., and Peter Kulchyski. 1994. *Tammarniit (Mistakes): Inuit Relocation in the Eastern Arctic, 1939–63*. Vancouver: University of British Columbia Press.
Thompson, Doug. 2001. "Frontiers of Identity: The Atlantic Coast and the Formation of Honduras and Nicaragua, 1786–1894." Ph.D. dissertation, University of Florida.
Thornton, Thomas F. 1998. *Traditional Tlingit Use of Sitka National Historical Park*. Final Report, NPS contract 14443PX970095345. Sitka: Sitka National Historical Park.

———. 2000. "A Time of Gathering: Tlingit Berry Picking in Glacier Bay National Park." Video produced by Thomas F. Thornton and University of Alaska Southeast Media Services. Distributed by Glacier Bay National Park, Bartlett Cove, Alaska, and Hoonah Indian Association, Hoonah, Alaska.

———. 2004a. "The Geography of Tlingit Character." In *Coming to Shore: Northwest Coast Ethnology—Traditions and Visions*, edited by M. Harkin, S. Kan, and M. Mauze, 363–84. Lincoln: University of Nebraska Press.

———. 2004b. *Klondike Gold Rush National Historical Park: Ethnographic Overview and Assessment.* Anchorage, AK: National Park Service, Department of the Interior.

———. 2007. "Alaska Native Corporations and Subsistence: Paradoxical Forces in the Construction of Sustainable Communities." In *Sustainability and Communities of Place*, edited by Carl Maida, 41–62. New York: Berghahn Books.

———. 2008. *Being and Place among the Tlingit.* Seattle: University of Washington Press.

Tilley, Virginia. 2005. *Seeing Indians: A Study of Race, Nation, and Power in El Salvador.* Albuquerque: University of New Mexico Press.

Timmermans, Herman. 1997. "Workshops." In *Indigenous Knowledge, Conservation Reform, Natural Resource Management and Rural Development in the Dwesa and Cwebe Nature Reserves and Neighboring Village Settlements*, edited by Robin Palmer and Herman Timermans, 165–281. Grahamstown: ISER, Rhodes University.

———. 2002. "Natural Resource Use at Dwesa-Cwebe." In *From Confrontation to Negotiation: Nature-Based Development on South Africa's Wild Coast*, edited by Robin Palmer, Herman Timmermans, and Derick Fay, 173–98. Pretoria: Human Science Research Council.

———. 2004. "Rural Livelihoods at Dwesa/Cwebe: Poverty, Development and Natural Resource Use on the Wild Coast, South Africa." M.Sc. thesis, Rhodes University.

Tiu, R., and P. Garcia. 2003. *Los Bosques Comunales de Totonicapán: Historia, Situación Juridica y Derechos Indigenas.* Guatemala City, Guatemala: FLACSO.

Tober, James A. 1981. *Who Owns the Wildlife? The Political Economy of Conservation in Nineteenth-Century America.* Westport, CT: Greenwood Press.

Tofa, Matalena. 2007. "Justice in Collaboration? Indigenous Peoples and Postcolonial Conservation Management." Master's thesis, University of Auckland.

Toly, N. J. 2004. "Globalization and the Capitalization of Nature: A Political Ecology of Biodiversity in Mesoamerica." *Bulletin of Science, Technology and Society* 24(1): 47–54.

Transkei Land Service Organization. 1995. *Planning and Progress Summary of Tralso Research Programme 1995/96: People and Parks—The Transkei Wild Coast in Perspective.* Mthatha: Transkei Land Service Organization.

Treude, Erhard. 1968. "The Development of Reindeer Husbandry in Canada." *Polar Record* 14(88): 15–19.

Tropp, J. A. 2006. *Natures of Colonial Change: Environmental Relations in the Making of the Transkei.* Athens: Ohio University Press.

Truth and Reconciliation Commission. 2002. "Final Report." http://www.cverdad.org.pe/ingles/ifinal/index.php. Last accessed April 12, 2011.

Tsing, Anna L. 2005. *Friction: An Ethnography of Global Connections.* Princeton, NJ: Princeton University Press.

Tsing, Anna L., J. Peter Brosius, and Charles Zerner. 2005. "Introduction: Raising Questions about Communities and Conservation." In *Communities and Conservation: Histories and Politics of Community-Based Natural Resource Management*, edited by J. Peter Brosius, Anna Tsing, and Charles Zerner, 1–34. Walnut Creek, CA: Rowman and Littlefield.

Tuan, Yi Fu. 1974. *Topophilia: A Study of Environmental Perception, Attitudes, and Values*. Englewood Cliffs, NJ: Prentice-Hall.

Turner, Stephen. 2002. "The Governance of Nature Conservation in South Africa." In *Contested Resources: Challenges to the Governance of Natural Resources in Southern Africa*, edited by T. A. Benjaminsen, Ben Cousins, and Lisa Thompson, 165–80. Bellville: University of the Western Cape Programme in Land and Agrarian Studies.

United Nations Department of Economic and Social Affairs, Division for Social Policy and Development, Secretariat of the Permanent Forum on Indigenous Issues. 2009. *State of the World's Indigenous Peoples*. New York: United Nations.

United Nations Educational, Scientific and Cultural Organization. 2008. "Man and the Biosphere Program." www.unesco.org/mab. Last accessed October 6, 2008.

United Nations Subcommission on Prevention of Discrimination and Protection of Minorities. 1986/1987. UN Doc. E/CN.4/Sub.2/1986/7 and Add. 1–4.

Universidad del Valle de Guatemala. 2003. "Mapa de Cobertura Forestal de la Republica de Guatemala."

Upreti, Bishnu Raj, and Jagannath Adhikari. 2006. "A Case Study on Marginalized Indigenous Communities' Access to Natural Resources in Nepal: National Laws, Policies and Practices." http://www.icarrd.org/en/icard_doc_down/case_Nepal.pdf. Last accessed November 15, 2011.

Usher, Peter. 1987. "Indigenous Management Systems and the Conservation of Wildlife in the Canadian North." *Alternatives* 14(1): 3.

———. 2004. "Caribou Crisis or Administrative Crisis? Wildlife and Aboriginal Policies on the Barren Grounds of Canada, 1947–60." In *Cultivating Arctic Landscapes: Knowing and Managing Animals in the Circumpolar North*, edited by David G. Anderson and Mark Nutall, 172–99. New York: Berghahn Books.

Utting, P. 1993. *Trees, People and Power: Social Dimensions of Deforestation and Forest Protection in Central America*. London: Earthscan.

Valente, Marcela. 2007. "Environment: Conservation Expands in Latin America." *Tierraamerica: Inter Press Service News Agency*. November 2, 2007. http://ipsnews.net.

Vandergeest, Peter, and Nancy L. Peluso. 1995. "Territorialization and State Power in Thailand." *Theory and Society* 24(3): 385–426.

Veber, Hanne. 1998. "Salt of the Montaña: Interpreting Indigenous Activism in the Rain Forest." *Cultural Anthropology* 13(3): 382–413.

———. 2000. "An Introduction to Eight Essays on the Structures of a Social Order in the Upper Amazon." In *Gendered Spaces and Interethnic Politics: The Pajonal Ashéninka Case*, edited by Hanne Veber. Copenhagen: University of Copenhagen Press.

Veblen, T. T. 1975. "The Ecological, Cultural and Historical Bases of Forest Preservation in Totonicapán, Guatemala." Ph.D. dissertation, University of California, Berkeley.

———. 1978. "Forest Preservation in the Western Highlands of Guatemala." *The Geographical Review* 68: 417–34.
Verschuuren, Bas, Robert Wild, Jeffrey A. McNeely, and Gonzalo Oviedo, eds. 2010. *Sacred Natural Sites: Conserving Nature and Culture*. London: Earthscan.
Villalba, Fernando. 2010. "Un-discovering Wilderness: Protecting Traditional Resource Use Rights in National Parks." *Policy Matters* 17: 126–34.
Wade, Peter. 1997. *Race and Ethnicity in Latin America*. London: Pluto Press.
Walker, C. 2008. *Landmarked: Land Claims and Restitution in South Africa*. Athens: Ohio University Press.
Wallace, Anthony F. C. 2005. "The Consciousness of Time." *Anthropology of Consciousness* 16(2): 1–15.
Warren, K. 2008. "The Dynamic and Multi-faceted Character of Pan-Mayanism in Guatemala." In *Indigenous Peoples: Self-Determination, Knowledge, Indigeneity*, edited by H. Minde, 107–32. Delft, The Netherlands: Eburon.
Warren, Louis S. 1997. *The Hunter's Game: Poachers and Conservationists in Twentieth-Century America*. New Haven, CT: Yale University Press.
Warrior, Robert A. 1995. *Secrets: Recovering American Indian Intellectual Traditions*. Minneapolis: University of Minnesota Press.
Watanabe, Yoko. 2008. *Indigenous Communities and Biodiversity*. Washington, DC: Global Environment Facility.
Watkins, Mel. 1977. *Dene Nation, the Colony Within*. Toronto: University of Toronto Press.
Watt, Laura A. 2002. "The Trouble with Preservation, or, Getting Back to the Wrong Term for Wilderness Protection: A Case Study at Point Reyes National Seashore." *The Yearbook of the Association of Pacific Coast Geographers* 64: 55–72.
Weaver, Sally M. 1991. "The Role of Aboriginals in the Management of Australia's Cobourg (Gurig) and Kakadu National Parks." In *Resident Peoples and National Parks: Social Dilemmas and Strategies in International Conservation*, edited by Patrick C. West and Steven R. Brechin, 311–33. Tucson: University of Arizona Press.
Weiner, Annette. 1985. "Inalienable Wealth." *American Ethnologist* 12(2): 210–27.
———. 1992. *Inalienable Possessions: The Paradox of Keeping while Giving*. Berkeley: University of California Press.
Weiner, Douglas R. 2002. *A Little Corner of Freedom: Russian Nature Protection from Stalin to Gorbachev*. Berkeley: University of California Press.
Weiss, Gerald. 1975. *Campa Cosmology: The World of a Forest Tribe in South America*. Anthropological Papers of the American Museum of Natural History no. 52, part 5. New York: American Museum of Natural History.
Weitzner, Viviane, and Micheline Manseau. 2001. "Taking the Pulse of Collaborative Management in Canada's National Parks and National Park Reserves: Voices from the Field." In *Crossing Boundaries in Park Management: Proceedings of the Eleventh Conference on Research and Resource Management in Parks and on Public Lands*, edited by D. Harmon, 253–9. Hancock, MI: The George Wright Society.
Welsh, Peter. 1997. "The Power of Possession: The Case against Property." *Museum Anthropology* 21(3): 12–18.
West, Paige. 2006. *Conservation Is Our Government Now: The Politics of Ecology in Papua New Guinea*. Durham, NC: Duke University Press.

West, Paige, James Igoe, and Dan Brockington. 2006. "Parks and Peoples: The Social Impacts of Protected Areas." *Annual Review of Anthropology* 35: 251–77.
West, Patrick C., and Steven R. Brechin, eds. 1991. *Resident Peoples and National Parks: Social Dilemmas and Strategies in International Conservation*. Tucson: University of Arizona Press.
Western, David, R. M. Wright, and S. C. Strum, eds. 1994. *Natural Connections: Perspectives in Community-Based Conservation*. Washington, DC: Island Press.
Whande, Webster. 2010. "Windows of Opportunity or Exclusion? Local Communities in the Great Limpopo Transfrontier Conservation Area, Africa." In *Community Rights, Conservation and Contested Land: The Politics of Natural Resource Governance in Africa*, edited by Fred Nelson, 147–73. London: Earthscan.
White, Andy, and Alejandra Martin. 2002. *Who Owns the World's Forests? Forest Tenure and Public Forests in Transition*. Washington, DC: Forest Trends and Center for International Law.
Whitten, Norman, Jr., and Arlene Torres. 1998. "To Forge the Future in the Fires of the Past." In *Blackness in Latin America and the Caribbean: Social Dynamics and Cultural Transformations*, edited by Norman Whitten Jr. and Arlene Torres, 3–33. Bloomington: Indiana University Press.
Wiener, James F. 2001. *Tree Leaf Talk: A Heideggerian Anthropology*. New York: Berg.
Wiersma, Yolanda F., Thomas J. Beechy, Bas M. Oosenbrug, and John C. Meikle. 2005. *Protected Areas in Northern Canada: Designing for Ecological Integrity, Phase 1 Report*. CCEA Occasional Paper no. 16. Ottawa: Canadian Council on Ecological Areas.
Wild, Robert, and Christopher McLeod, eds. 2008. *Sacred Natural Sites: Guidelines for Protected Area Managers*. Best Practice Protected Area Guidelines Series No. 16. Gland, Switzerland: UNESCO, and Paris: IUCN.
Wilkins, David. 1997. *American Indian Sovereignty and the U.S. Supreme Court: The Masking of Justice*. Austin: University of Texas Press.
Wilshusen, Peter R., Steven R. Brechin, Crystal L. Fortwangler, and Patrick C. West. 2002. "Reinventing a Square Wheel: Critique of a Resurgent 'Protection Paradigm' in International Biodiversity Conservation." *Society and Natural Resources* 15: 17–40.
Wittman, H., and C. Geisler. 2005. "Negotiating Locality: Decentralization and Communal Forest Management in the Guatemalan Highlands." *Human Organization* 64(1): 62–74.
World Rainforest Movement. 2003. "Corredor Biológico Mesoamericano: ¿Conservación o Apropiación?" http://www.prodiversitas.bioetica.org/panama.htm. Last accessed May 29, 2005.
World Resources Institute, United Nations Environment Programme, United Nations Development Programme, and World Bank. 2003. "Proposed Elements of the Mesoamerican Biological Corridor." http://earthtrends.wri.org/text/environmental-governance/map-478.html. Last accessed on May 1, 2006.
World Wide Fund for Nature (WWF International). 2008. *Indigenous Peoples and Conservation: WWF Statement of Principles*. Gland, Switzerland: WWF International.
Worster, Donald. 1994. *Nature's Economy: A History of Ecological Ideas*, 2nd ed. Cambridge, UK: Cambridge University Press.

Wynberg, Rachel, and Thembela Kepe. 1999. *Land Reform and Conservation Areas in South Africa: Towards a Mutually Beneficial Approach.* Pretoria: IUCN South Africa.

Zimmerer, Karl S. 2006a. "Cultural Ecology at the Interface with Political Ecology: The New Geographies of Environmental Conservation and Globalization." *Progress in Human Geography* 30(1): 63–78.

———. 2006b. "Geographical Perspectives on Globalization and Environmental Issues: The Inner-Connections of Conservation, Agriculture, and Livelihoods." In *Globalization and New Geographies of Conservation*, edited by Karl Zimmerer, 1–43. Chicago: University of Chicago Press.

Zimmerer, Karl S., and D. Carter. 2002. "Conservation and Sustainability in Latin America and the Caribbean." In *Latin America in the Twenty-First Century: Challenges and Solutions*, edited by Gregory Knapp, 207–49. Austin: University of Texas Press.

Zimmerer, Karl S., R. E. Galt, and M. V. Buck. 2004. "Globalization and Multi-spatial Trends in the Coverage of Protected-Area Conservation (1980–2000)." *Ambio* 33(8): 520–9.

Zingapan, Kail, and Dave De Vera. 1999. "Mapping the Ancestral Lands and Waters of the Calamian Tagbanwa of Coron, Northern Palawan." http://www.iapad.org/publications/ppgis/coron_best_practice_paper.pdf. Last accessed July 15, 2013.

Editor and Contributors

About the Editor

Stan Stevens, Ph.D., is a faculty member in geography at the University of Massachusetts Amherst. He is the editor (and contributing author) of *Conservation through Cultural Survival: Indigenous Peoples and Protected Areas* (1997) and the author of *Claiming the High Ground: Sherpas, Subsistence, and Environmental Change in the Highest Himalaya* (1993). Stevens's research in cultural and political ecology has focused on Indigenous peoples, land use, and conservation in Nepal. Since the early 1980s, he has worked with Sharwa (Sherpa) leaders on Indigenous rights and community conservation issues, including respect and recognition of Sharwa Indigenous Peoples' and Community-Conserved Territories and Areas (ICCAs) within Sagarmatha (Mount Everest) National Park, Nepal. He is active in international efforts to promote rights-based conservation, community conservation, and the new protected area paradigm through his participation in the IUCN's Commission on Environmental, Economic, and Social Policy and the intercommission group Theme/Strategic Direction on Governance, Communities, Equity, and Livelihood Rights in Relation to Protected Areas and as an officer and steering committee member of the ICCA Consortium, a Switzerland-based association of sixty Indigenous peoples and Indigenous peoples organizations, community organizations, and conservation organizations that works worldwide on behalf of conservation and human rights through appropriate recognition and support for ICCAs. Stevens's recent work has focused on Indigenous peoples, protected areas, ICCAs, and rights, particularly in the high Himalaya of Nepal and Sagarmatha National Park. Recent publications include articles in *Policy Matters* and *Conservation and Society* and chapters in two edited books, *Rights-based Approaches: Exploring Issues and Opportunities for Conservation* (2009) and *The Right to Responsibility: Resisting and Engaging Development, Conservation, and the Law in Asia* (2014).

About the Contributors

Emily Caruso, Ph.D., received her doctorate in anthropology at the University of Kent, United Kingdom, after conducting field research with the Ashaninka people in eastern Peru. She has worked on Indigenous peoples' rights as a staff member at Forest Peoples Programme (UK) and on collaborative research and community conservation in her current position as regional programmes director of the Global Diversity Foundation. She has published on Indigenous peoples' rights and conservation and the politics of protected area comanagement.

Brian W. Conz, Ph.D., is an assistant professor of geography and regional planning at Westfield State University, Westfield, Massachusetts. He has conducted geographic research in Central America since 2003, working principally with K'iche' Maya people in highland Guatemala as well as with peoples of the African Diaspora in Belize and Caribbean Guatemala. As a student of Indigenous and traditional land-use and conservation practices, his research focuses on the intersection of such practices with local and regional ecologies, social movements, environmentalism, and conservation policy.

Derick A. Fay, Ph.D., is an assistant professor of anthropology at the University of California, Riverside. His research, based in South Africa, examines the relationships between the end of apartheid and postapartheid transformations and rural Xhosa peoples' access to land and natural resources, focusing on resettlement, land tenure, and community relations with protected areas. He is the coeditor of two books: *The Rights and Wrongs of Land Restitution: 'Restoring What Was Ours'* (2009), with Deborah James, and *From Conflict to Negotiation: Nature-Based Development on South Africa's Wild Coast* (2003), with Robin Palmer and Herman Timmermans.

Mary Finley-Brook, Ph.D., is an associate professor of geography, environmental studies, and international studies at the University of Richmond in Richmond, Virginia. Her research critiques market-oriented conservation and development programs in Indigenous peoples' territories across Latin America and has been published in journals such as *AlterNative*, *Annals of the Association of American Geographers*, *The Canadian Geographer*, and *Water Alternatives*.

Marcia Langton, Ph.D., is a renowned Aboriginal rights activist and geographer and holds the Foundation Chair in Australian Indigenous Studies at the University of Melbourne, Australia. She has a Ph.D. in geography (Macquarie University). Langton has been awarded the Order of Australia and the Neville Bonner Award for Indigenous Teacher of the Year and is a fellow of the Academy of Social Sciences in Australia. She is the author of *Burning Questions: Emerging Environmental Issues for Indigenous Peoples in Northern Australia* (1998) and coeditor of *Honour among Nations? Treaties and Agreements with Indigenous Peoples* (2004), *Settling with Indigenous Peoples: Modern Treaty and Agreement Making* (2006), *First Australians: An Illustrated History* (2008), and *Community Futures, Legal Architecture: Foundations for Indigenous People in the Global Mining Boom* (2012).

Sharlene Mollett, Ph.D., is an assistant professor in the Centre for Critical Development Studies at the University of Toronto, Scarborough. Her work examines the entanglement of race and natural resource conflicts in Honduras, with long-standing projects and collaborations with Miskito and Garifuna peoples. Her research has been published in such journals as *Annals of the Association of American Geographers*; *Geoforum*; *Gender, Place and Culture*; *Cultural Geographies*; *Latin America Research Review*; and *Latin American Perspectives*.

Lisa Palmer, Ph.D., is a faculty member in the School of Land and Environment, University of Melbourne, Australia. Palmer's dissertation research examined Aboriginal and non-Aboriginal land management interests in Kakadu National Park, the comanaged protected area that is Australia's largest national park and a World Heritage site. She has also conducted research on resource management in Timor Leste and Indigenous peoples' land claims in Australia and New Zealand. She is a coeditor of *Honour among Nations? Treaties and Agreements with Indigenous Peoples* (2004) and *Settling with Indigenous Peoples: Modern Treaty and Agreement Making* (2006).

Zane Ma Rhea, Ph.D., has worked with Indigenous people over the last thirty-five years in various capacities. She is recognized internationally for her expertise in comparative education and for improving the quality of education and other human services to Indigenous people using a rights-based framework, focusing on organizational change management, professional development, and the recognition and preservation of Indigenous knowledge in mainstream organizations through meaningful partnerships with Indigenous families and communities. She teaches across the Indigenous Education and Leadership Programs at Monash University in Melbourne, Australia, and undertakes research in Indigenous education, Indigenous-settler studies, and organizational development.

John Sandlos, Ph.D., teaches history at Memorial University of Newfoundland in St. John's, Canada. His research has focused on the history of wildlife conservation and protected areas in the Canadian North and more recently on the environmental and social issues associated with abandoned mines in northern Canada. He is the author of *Hunters at the Margin* (2007) and many articles in refereed journals.

Stan Stevens, Ph.D., is a faculty member in geography at the University of Massachusetts Amherst. For information about his work see "About the Editor."

Thomas F. Thornton, Ph.D., is director of the master's program in environmental change and management at the Environmental Change Institute, School of Geography and the Environment, University of Oxford. He has worked extensively with Indigenous peoples in the Pacific Northwest and especially in Alaska, including research in and around several Alaskan and Canadian protected areas. He is the author of *Being and Place among the Tlingit* (2008) and editor of *Haa Léelk'w Hás Aaní Saax'ú: Our Grandparents' Names on the Land* (2012) and *Haa Aaní: Our Land. Tlingit and Haida Land Rights and Use* (1998).

Illustration Credits

Figure I.1. Cartography by Piper R. Gaubatz

Figure 1.1. Adapted from IUCN and UNEP-WCMC (2012). The World Database on Protected Areas (WDPA). February 2012. Cambridge, UK: UNEP-WCMC. www.protectedplanet.net

Figure 1.2. Adapted from IUCN and UNEP-WCMC (2012). The World Database on Protected Areas (WDPA). February 2012. Cambridge, UK: UNEP-WCMC. www.protectedplanet.net

Figure 1.3. Adapted from IUCN and UNEP-WCMC (2012). The World Database on Protected Areas (WDPA). February 2012. Cambridge, UK: UNEP-WCMC. www.protectedplanet.net

Figure 1.4. Adapted from Dudley (2008). IUCN

Figure 2.1. ISD/Earth Negotiations Bulletin

Figure 2.2. Stan Stevens

Figure 2.3. Stan Stevens

Figure 2.4. Stan Stevens

Figure 2.5. Stan Stevens

Figure 2.6. Stan Stevens

Figure 3.1. Adapted from Commonwealth of Australia, Department of Sustainability, Environment, Water, Population and Communities (2013). www.environment.gov.au/indigenous/ipa/map.html

Figure 3.2. Dhimurru Aboriginal Corporation

Figure 3.3. Dhimurru Aboriginal Corporation

Figure 4.1. Cartography by Diana Mastracci

Figure 5.1. Cartography by Cassandra Lee

Figure 6.1. Adapted from INRENA (2007). Cartography by Piper R. Gaubatz and Leif Stevens

Figure 6.2. Emily Caruso

Figure 7.1. Mary Finley-Brook
Figure 7.2. Mary Finley-Brook
Figure 7.3. Adapted with permission from World Resources Institute. Cartography by Joseph Stoll. Reprinted with permission from the *Journal of Latin American Geography*
Figure 7.4. Adapted from Corredor Biológico del Atlántico (n.d.). Illustration by Piper R. Gaubatz
Figure 8.1. Cartography by Sharlene Mollett. Reprinted courtesy of *Latin American Research Review*
Figure 9.1. Cartography by Derick Fay
Figure 9.2. Adapted from Timmermans (2004)
Figure 9.3. Derick Fay
Figure 9.4. Derick Fay
Figure 10.1. Adapted from Universidad del Valle de Guatemala (2003). Cartography by Brian Conz
Figure 10.2. Brian Conz
Figure 10.3. Brian Conz
Figure 11.1. Adapted from IUCN and UNEP-WCMC (2012). The World Database on Protected Areas (WDPA). February 2012. Cambridge, UK: UNEP-WCMC. www.protectedplanet.net. Reprinted courtesy of Natural Justice and United Nations University–Institute of Advanced Studies. Cartography by Piper R. Gaubatz and Stan Stevens
Figure 11.2. Adapted from IUCN and UNEP-WCMC (2012). The World Database on Protected Areas (WDPA). February 2012. Cambridge, UK: UNEP-WCMC. www.protectedplanet.net. Reprinted courtesy of Natural Justice and United Nations University–Institute of Advanced Studies. Cartography by Piper R. Gaubatz and Stan Stevens
Figure 11.3. Stan Stevens
Figure 11.4. Stan Stevens. Reprinted courtesy of IUCN, IUCN CEESP, CIFOR, *Conservation and Society*, Natural Justice, and United Nations University–Institute of Advanced Studies

Index

Aboriginal and Torres Straits Islanders, 89. *See also* Adnyamathanha community; Yolngu
adaptive management, 76, 148
Adnyamathanha community, 94. *See also* Nantawarrina IPA
advisory boards, and Canadian wildlife, 141–42, 146–47; Canadian protected area, 143
African Commission on Human and Peoples' Rights: and Endorois decision, 292, 309n3; and identifying Indigenous peoples, 17; and new paradigm implementation, 288
Alaska, protected areas, 4, 34, 45n35, 78, 109, 110f, 112–13, 118, 129n1. *See also individual protected areas*
Alcaldes Auxiliares, 246, 248–49
Alcaldes Comunales de los 48 Cantones (Communal Mayors of the 48 Towns; AC48), 248–49, 252–58, 254f; relations with UCJ, 249, 253–54
Alcorn, Janis, 11n3, 267
Alfred, Taiaiake, 168–69
Allen, John, 178–79
Amazon: conservation by Indigenous peoples in Brazil, 25; national integration and territorialization in Peru, 151; protected areas in Peru, 151; resource region in Peru, 150–51
Amarakaeri Communal Reserve: petroleum exploration in, 159–60; shared governance issues, 160; state territorialization, 160

Anaya, James, 45n35, 264–66
Arctic National Wildlife Refuge, 4, 11n4. *See also* Gwitch'in; Inupiat
Ashaninka, 152, 170n10; and anti-anti-politics, 167; awareness of Ashaninka Communal Reserve, 152, 162; as "masters of the universe," 151, 167; hunting 163; identity and territory, 161–63; practices of self-determination, 164–67; sovereignty, 151, 167–69
Ashaninka Communal Reserve, 152, 153f, 162f; Ashaninka counter narratives of, 161–64; Ashaninka park guards, 157–59, 166; Ashaninka self-determination, 164–67; Ashaninka sovereignty, 168–69; as Ashaninka territory and place, 163–65; contention over, 157, 164–65; federations and governance of, 157–59, 165, 167; governmentalizing of, 157–60; shared governance of, 157–59, 165, 168–69; state imaginaries of, 151, 154–55; state territorialization of, 151, 156, 164–65
Atlantic Biological Corridor, 173, 185–94; and colonists, 191; and decision-making, 187–88, 190–91, 194; donors of, 186, 190–92; and Indigenous peoples, 186, 188–89; land tenure issues, 190–92; projects, 188–90, 189t, 191–92; and rights, 190, 192. *See also* biological corridors; Mesoamerican Biological Corridor

367

atlas of eternity. See *historia*
Australia: overlap of protected areas and Indigenous peoples' territories in, 34–35; shared governance of protected areas in, 77. *See also* IPAs
Awas Tingni decision, 193

Badlands National Park: hunting in, 45n35; and proposed tribal national park, 45n35; shared governance of, 78
Berkes, Fikret, 42n22, 88, 302, 303, 304
beyul (hidden valley), 269, 269f, 270–71, 281n11
biocultural diversity: concept of, 22; ICCAs and, 71, 296s; Indigenous peoples and, 22–26; new paradigm and, 283, 303, 305, 306, 308
biodiversity: association with Indigenous peoples, 3, 16, 22–26, 102, 104, 274, 308, 311n17; conceptions of, 11n2, 43n24, 87, 89; geography of, 22–23, 42nn18–19; and ICCAs, 70, 71; and new paradigm, 7, 8, 10, 11n2, 26, 53, 60, 62t, 65, 102,104, 172, 308, 311n17; and old paradigm, 36, 48, 62t; and protected areas, 3, 11n2, 38, 43n24, 43n27, 62t, 87, 133, 305
biological corridors, 43n26, 177–79; national corridors, 184–85; and neoliberalism, 172–80, 194–95; and new paradigm, 172; and regional development planning, 173, 175; top-down planning of, 172, 178, 194. *See also* Atlantic Biological Corridor; Mesoamerican Biological Corridor
biosphere reserves: as inhabited protected areas, 197, 200; and protection of cultural diversity and cultural landscapes, 197, 213n2
Bolivia, overlap of protected areas and Indigenous peoples' territories, 34
Bon, 271, 281n10
Borrini-Feyerabend, Grazia, 32s, 67, 71, 76, 81nn8–9, 277
Bosawás Biosphere Reserve, 25, 187; colonists, 187; extension into Corazón Transboundary Biosphere Reserve, 192; Indigenous peoples in, 187; land titling, 187; and restitution, 292

Buddhism, and conservation, 270–71, 274, 281n10
buffer zones, 34, 64, 72; Ashaninka Communal Reserve, 153f; and biological corridors, 180, 182f, 184, 187, 194; Kruger National Park, 222–24, 249; Los Altos de San Miguel Regional Municipal Park, 249; in Nepal, 263, 267, 279, 281n2, 281nn5–6; Río Plátano Biosphere Reserve, 198; Sagarmatha National Park, 75f, 268, 269f, 271f, 273, 282nn13–15
Burhenne, Françoise, 81n7, 290

Cadastral and Land Regularization Project. *See* El Proyecto de Catastro y Regularización
CAFTA. *See* Central American Free Trade Agreement
Calmegane, Ida, 121
Canada: colonialism in northern, 135–36, 144–45, 148; conservation paradigm shift in, 141–42; critiques of protected area policies in, 143–48; devolution, 148; displacement from protected areas, 134, 139, 142; early protected area history, 137; Fourth World conditions, 134–35; harvesting in national parks in, 142–44, 149n2; legislative change and national parks, 142; national park reserves, 142; northern national parks, 142–43, 149n2; overlap of protected areas and Indigenous peoples' territories, 34; protected area reform recommendations, 148; rights violations in protected areas, 134, 139; shared governance of protected areas, 77, 127, 141, 143–49
Canyon de Chelly National Monument, 78
Carcross-Tagish First Nation, 119
Carr, Archie III, 173,182
Carvill, Andy, Chief of Carcross-Tagish First Nation, 119, 127
CBD, 58–60, 87; decisions of, 27; executive secretary of, 60, 71; and ICCAs, 60, 69, 70, 71, 277, 294–96, 311n16; and new paradigm 7, 22, 47,

Index • 369

58–60, 285–86, 288; and rights, 59, 66, 68, 80n5. *See also* Programme of Work on Protected Areas
Central America, overlap of protected areas and Indigenous peoples' territories, 33
Central American Commission on Environment and Development (CCAD), 181–82, 192
Central American Free Trade Agreement (CAFTA), 175, 193
Chapin, Mac, 22, 23, 87
Chilkoot Trail, 118–120, 127
Chomolungma, 271f. *See also* Mount Everest
Colchester, Marcus, 5, 38, 44n32, 286
collective tenure: and biodiversity, 23; and community-based natural resource management, 64; and displacement, 38t; in Honduras, 198, 199, 201, 206, 207, 210; and ICCAs, 75f, 82n17, 296s; and IPAs, 98; lack of recognition of, 201, 207, 262, 263, 265, 293, 293s; mapping and recognition of, 41n10; in Nepal, 262, 263, 265; and new paradigm, 284s, 307; in Nicaragua, 193, 195; and protected areas, 35; and restitution, 55; rights to, 20, 21, 49, 277, 284s; and shared governance of protected areas, 300s. *See also* commons; community forests; land tenure; land title
Colombia: cogovernance of national parks in, 78; overlap of protected areas and Indigenous peoples' territories in, 34
colonists: in Honduras, 206, 213n3; in Nicaragua, 187, 191; in Peru, 150, 161, 164, 166, 191
comanagement. *See* shared governance
comanagement boards, 299, 301s, 304; in Canada, 141, 144–45
Commission on Environmental, Economic, and Social Policy (CEESP), 12, 290
Commission on Environmental Law, 81n7, 290
commons, 42n22, 268, 270, 271f, 272–74; conservation significance of, 274; and displacement, 38t; and ICCAs, 70–71, 73–74, 82n15; in Guatemala, 244, 250, 251, 257, 259; management of, 24, 42n22, 261, 265; in Nepal, 261, 265, 266, 267, 272, 282n12; and rights, 261; state policies toward, 39, 46n39, 261, 265, 275; tragedy of, 42n22. *See also* enclosure; expropriation
communal conservancies, 72, 294
communal reserves: Indigenous peoples' ownership of territory in, 152; in Peru, 151–52
community, 11n1, conceptions of, 88
community-based conservation, 61, 88; shortcomings of, 61, 64
community-based natural resource management (CBNRM): shortcomings of 61, 64; and social justice, 61, 64
community-conserved areas. *See* ICCAs
community forests, 24–26, 75f, 242–43, 245, 246, 247, 248, 256–57, 271f, 272–3, 282n14
community-oriented protected areas, 84, 102. *See also* ICCAs; IPAs
community–protected area negotiations, 235–38, 239n5
COMPAS, 257
Confederated Salish and Kootenai tribes, 72
Conferences of the Parties to the CBD (COPs), 59–60. *See also* CBD
conservation, conceptions of, 11n2, 24, 43n24, 155
Conservation Initiative on Human Rights, 291, 309n2
Conservation International, 42n19, 154, 182, 183t, 309n2
conservation organizations: and community-based conservation, 61; and conservation corridors, 178, 182, 183t, 184–86; and ICCAs, 277, 295; and new paradigm, 64, 79–80, 200, 306–8; and protected areas, 29, 35, 53, 64–65, 247–48; relations with Indigenous peoples, 6, 45n36, 48, 185–86, 298, 302–3, 307, 310n8, 310n10; and rights, 6, 291, 306–8, 309n2
conservation refugees, 37, 45n37

Conservation Through Cultural Survival: Indigenous Peoples and Protected Areas (Stevens), 9, 259
Conservation with Justice: A Rights-Based Approach (Greiber), 81n7
contractual national parks, 226
Convention on Biological Diversity. *See* CBD
Convention on the Elimination of All Forms of Racial Discrimination (CERD), 42n15, 81n13
country, conceptions of, 107n23
Cronon, William, 126
cultural foods, 115, 163
cultural landscapes, 1, 8, 42n19, 129n1, 161–62; in Himalaya, 267
customary law: and biodiversity, 23, 24; and deep colonizing, 310n9; and displacement, 38t; and forest conservation, 272, 273f, 282n14; and Fourth World, 19; and ICCAs, 70, 296, 296s; and IPAs, 275, 96; in Nepal, 262, 266–67, 272, 273f, 275, 279; and new paradigm 284s; and rights, 21
customary tenure, 201, 292, 293, 293–94s. *See also* collective tenure; land tenure; land title

Dalton, Richard, 116
Death Valley National Park, 79f, 292
deep colonizing, 302, 310n9
deforestation, reduced in Indigenous peoples' territories, 25–26
Department of National Parks and Wildlife Conservation, Nepal, 267, 275; and ICCAs, 276, 278–80; and new paradigm, 278–79; relations with Indigenous peoples, 266–67, 275–76, 278–80, 281n2; relations with Sharwa, 276, 282nn13–16
Deutsche Gesellschaft f r Technische Zusammenarbeit (GtZ, Society for Technical Cooperation), 223–25, 233. *See also* Transform project
Dhimurru IPA, 93f, 96–101, 99f, 100f
Dias, Braulio Ferreira de Souza, 60, 71
Diné, and Navajo tribal parks, 72, 74f
displacement, 3, 6–7, 37, 44n34, 48, 134, 221, 222, 265, 281n5; data quality issues, 45n36; and new paradigm, 63t, 284s; number of people displaced globally, 37, 45n36; and rights, 48, 55, 65, 66, 68, 278, 309n3; types of displacement, 37, 38t
dispossession, 37, 117
distributive negotiations, 218–21, 225, 230, 237–38; and morality, 220
doctrine of discovery, 41n8
Dolpo-pa, 264, 270, 271, 274
Dowie, Mark, 45n37
Dudley, Nigel, 33
Durban Parks Congress. *See* World Parks Congress
Durban Accord, 51–53; main targets of, 53, 57
Durban Action Plan, 51–55, 57
Dutfield, Graham, 42n15
Dwebe Project, 230–31, 233; and mutual gains negotiations, 231, 233
Dwesa-Cwebe claim and negotiations, 227–35, 237, 292
Dwesa-Cwebe Nature Reserve, 217, 223f, 227, 228f, 229f; eviction and exclusion, 227; history of, 227–29; mass protests in, 228; proposed shared governance of, 231–34; and restitution, 292; settlement, 232, 234–35; settlement implementation problems, 227, 230, 233; subsistence in, 235f, 227, 229; subsistence rights issues, 234, 235f, 239n3

Eastern Cape Nature Conservancy (ECNC), 228–29, 234
Eco-Ashaninka, 157; changing relationships and roles, 158, 167; and shared governance of Ashaninka Communal Reserve, 158, 165
eco-corridors. *See* biological corridors
ecoregion, 42n20
ecologically noble savage, 11n3
El Proyecto de Catastro y Regularización (Cadastral and Land Regularization Project), 198, 206–8, 210–12; contestation by RAYAKA and TASBA, 207, 212
Empire, concept of, 168, 171n15. *See also* Hardt, Michael; Negri, Antonio

enclosure, and conservation, 39, 113, 126
Endorois, 292, 309n3
Ene Ashaninka Federation (CARE), 167; and shared governance, 167
engaged universals, 70, 89, 104, 268–69
England, inhabited national parks, 36
environmentality, 45n38, 303, 310nn11–12; adverse conservation outcomes of, 303; and rights, 303; and shared governance, 301, 303; and territorialization, 303
Escobar, Arturo, 104, 255
European protected areas, 44n32
eviction. *See* displacement
expropriation, 18, 19, 41n8, 262–63; and protected areas, 3, 22, 39–40, 44n34, 49, 261, 292

Farvar, Taghi, 47
Fifth World Parks Congress, Durban, South Africa: challenging old paradigm at, 47; controversy at, 51; Indigenous peoples' participation in, 47, 51; and new paradigm policies, 52–53, 53t; significance of, 47, 49
Flora and Fauna International, 183t, 309n2
Forest Peoples Programme, 5, 286, 288, 290
fortress conservation, 6, 36, 44n33, 126, 197, 200. *See also* displacement
Fourth World, 18–19, 86, 135; and Canada, 135; and displacement, 134; and ICCAs, 295; and Nepal, 262–63; and new paradigm, 65, 295, 306; and protected areas, 19, 39, 40, 65
France, regional parks of, 36
free, prior, and informed consent, 7, 8, 21, 50s, 53, 55, 58, 61–63, 62t, 66, 68, 69, 264–65, 267, 275, 277, 282n17, 284s
free-market environmentalism, 193
Friends of Makuleke, 226, 236
frontier dynamics, 18, 19, 39, 44n28, 118, 139, 150

Garifuna, 185, 189, 198; and swidden, 187, 203, 213n9
Geisler, Charles, 37, 45n37

gender bias, 96
Glacier Bay National Park, 116–18, 124–25; glaucous-winged gull eggs harvest strategy, 124–25, 126; Tlingit identity, repatriation, and reconciliation, 138
Global Environment Facility: support for ICCAs, 288; support for protected areas, 29, 43n28, 64
Goldman, Michael, 179
governmentality, 39, 45n38, 159, 303, 310nn11–12; adverse conservation outcomes of, 303; and rights, 303
governance, of protected areas, 67; and CBD, 59, 68, 81n10, 288; good governance, 54t, 67, 81n9; governance types, 30–33, 33s, 69–79; Indigenous peoples' participation in, 52–53, 149, 160, 186, 194, 195, 227, 298, 301, 302–4; and IUCN, 52, 54t, 56, 58, 66, 81n10; and new paradigm, 7, 50s, 62t, 284s, 288, 293, 296s, 300s; and PoWPA, 43n28, 60, 68, 285; and rights, 21, 52–55, 66, 67, 284s, 307. *See also* ICCAs; IPAs; shared governance
Governance of Protected Areas: From Understanding to Action (Borrini-Feyerabend), 81n8, 289
Grand Canyon National Park and World Heritage Site, 34
Great Limpopo Transfrontier Conservation Area, 227
green grabbing, 39
green neoliberalism, 172, 177; Indigenous participation in, 179; power and spatial dynamics of, 178–79; role of development banks and aid agencies in, 173
Greiber, Thomas, 81n7
Gros Morne National Park, displacement from, 142
Guatemala, protected areas in, 242–43
Guatemala National Forestry Agency (INAB), 252, 253, 256
Guidelines for Applying Protected Area Management Categories (Dudley), 33, 43n24, 289
Guidelines for Protected Area Legislation (Lausche and Burhenne), 87n7, 290
Guyana, ICCAs in, 72

Gwaii Haanas National Park Reserve and Haida Heritage Site, 127, 144, 298, 299
Gwitch'in, 11n4

Haida Heritage Sites, 72, 127, 298, 299
Haida Nation, and conservation, 72, 127
Hardt, Michael, 171n15
Harvey, David, 18
Hazlewood, Julianne, 311n17
Himalayan National Park Regulations, 266–67
historia, 108, 115–18, 120, 124, 126, 128
Hobson Herlihy, Laura, 204, 213n8
hunting and gathering, 86, 109, 124–26, 128. *See also* subsistence

ICCA Consortium, 257, 260n4, 288, 289, 296, 361
ICCA Network Nepal, 276
ICCA Registry, 71, 289
ICCAs, 30, 33s, 44n31, 54t, 56, 58, 60, 69–75, 82n15; appropriate recognition of, 74–75, 81n13, 277–78, 284s, 287, 294–96, 296s, 309n5; and biocultural diversity, 71, 296s; in Canada, 72; characterizations of, 70–71; as commons, 70; conservation effectiveness of, 82n15; and Convention on Biological Diversity, 60, 69, 70, 71, 277, 294–96, 311n16; as engaged universal, 268–69; examples of, 72–73; in Guatemala, 256–57, 259, 260n4; in Guyana, 72; and ILO, 169, 296s; and IUCN, 69, 70, 71, 73, 75, 277, 294–96; and livelihood security, 70, 284s, 297s; in Mexico, 82n17; in national protected area systems, 30, 35, 56, 70, 69, 72, 75, 81n12, 82n17, 84, 282n17, 284s, 288, 294, 297s6, 310n; in Nepal, 261, 265, 267–75, 281nn7–8; number of, 71; overlap with protected areas, 74–75, 268–275, 277–79, 284s, 287, 295, 297s; in Papua New Guinea, 82n17; as protected area governance type, 33s, 70; as protected areas, 72, 81n12, 295, 297s; and restitution, 294s; and rights, 74, 277, 282nn17–18; and sacred natural sites, 70; and shared governance of protected areas, 278, 295; standardization of, 279, 282n17, 295, 297s; state conflict with, 276–79, 294–96; and tenure security, 295–96, 296s; as umbrella term, 70, 258; and UNDRIP, 277, 282n17, 296s; in United States, 72, 73f, 74f
ILO 169, 20–21, 56, 200, 207, 210; and Nepal, 263, 279
India, overlap of protected areas and Indigenous peoples' territories in, 35
Indigenous Conservation Territories, 71, 73, 270
Indigenous knowledge, 42n22, 56, 85, 87, 102, 104, 124; and conservation, 24, 26, 51, 56, 76, 141; and Convention on Biological Diversity, 56, 81n5; and coproduction of knowledge, 76, 303–4; and ICCAs, 70, 84, 277, 278; and intergenerational transfer, 102; and IPAs, 85, 89, 98, 102, 104; and new paradigm, 6, 10, 53, 62t, 64, 77, 84, 104; and protected areas, 53, 56, 62t, 301s; and shared governance, 76, 136, 144–46, 147, 148, 301s; and tenure security, 103. *See also* science, Indigenous
Indigenous languages, 15, 42n18
Indigenous peoples: as assumed threats to conservation, 3, 36, 40, 154, 155, 201; authenticity, 155–56; and biodiversity, 3, 16, 22–26, 89; conservation contributions of, 4, 24–26; cultural diversity contributions of, 15; identification of, 16, 40n1, 40nn4–5; as keyword, 15; market-based economic activities of, 89; number of, 15; population of, 15; and protected area management categories, 30, 65–66; rights violations against, 3, 17; and subsistence, 85, 200; and territorial overlap with protected areas, 3, 33–35, 44n32; worldviews of, 11n2. *See also* Fourth World; Indigenous knowledge; Indigenous languages
Indigenous Peoples Ad Hoc Working Group for the World Parks Congress, 44n32, 48

Indigenous Peoples' and Community-Conserved Territories and Areas. *See* ICCAs

Indigenous Peoples' Declaration to the World Parks Congress, 48, 50s

Indigenous Protected Areas. *See* IPAs

Indigenous rangers, 301s; in Australia, 97, 99–101; in Peru, 157–59, 166

Indigenous rights, 19–22, 87, 263–67, 275, 308; and CBD, 81n13; and ICCAs, 277–80, 282nn17–19; and protected areas, 49, 53, 55–59, 65–66, 261, 266–67, 283, 284s, 308; red flags, 267. *See also* ILO 169; IUCN; new paradigm; UNDRIP

Integrated Conservation and Development Projects (ICDP), 61; shortcomings of, 61, 64; and social justice, 61, 64

Inter-American Commission on Human Rights, 288

International Indigenous Forum on Biodiversity, 285

International Labour Organization Convention 169 (ILO 169). *See* ILO 169

International Union for Conservation of Nature. *See* IUCN

Inter-Tribal Sinkyone Wilderness, 72

Inuit: land claims settlement of, 143; shared governance by, 143–44

Inupiat, 11n4

IPAs, 34, 72, 84–85; achievements and significance of, 94–95, 101–4, 310n6; agreements and management plans, 92, 95, 103, 107n22, 310n6; as decolonization, 94; establishment of, 90, 92, governance of, 84–85; 97, 294; Indigenous peoples' concerns with, 91, 95–97; and knowledge, 85, 87, 102, 104; and livelihoods and biodiversity, 85–87; monitoring and research by, 98; number and area of, 34, 92, 93f, 103; partnerships, 93–94, 96–97, 99; rangers, 97, 99f, 100f, 101; restoration, 98; staff, 99–101; subsistence and market economy activities, 85, 101–2, 104. *See* Dhimurru IPA; Nantawarrina IPA

Iran, nomadic peoples' territories, 73

IUCN: and ICCAs, 69, 70, 71, 73, 75, 277; and new paradigm, 7, 47–58, 285–86, 289–91; protected area management categories, 30, 32s; protected area matrix, 31f; protected area policies of, 27, 29–30, 51–58, 54t, 68, 289–91; and rights, 66, 68, 81nn 6–7; and UNDRIP, 56, 57–58, 66, 68, 291; and *World Conservation Strategy*, 43n24

IUCN Environmental Law Centre, 290

Johnnie, Jessie, 121
Jomo Miyolangsangma, 271f

Kaa-Iya del Gran Chaco National Park and Integrated Management Area, 77–78

Kakadu National Park and World Heritage Site, 34, 90; and restitution, 292

Kalahari Gemsbok National Park, and restitution, 292

Karen people, 290

Katz, Cindi, 178

Kayapo people, 173

Kgalagadi Transfrontier Park, shared governance of, 78

Khumbu, 268, 269f; *beyul*, 269f, 270–71; ICCAs, 268–76; as Indigenous Conservation Territory, 270; sacred natural sites in, 270–71, 271f, 273f. *See also* Sharwa

Khumbu Yul Lha, 271f, 272

K'iche' Maya, 244–46; forest conservation by, 251; forest use by, 244, 246, 250–52; forest management by, 245–47, 257; ICCAs, 256–57; livelihoods of, 244; self-governance by, 245–46, 248–49

Klondike Gold Rush International Historical Park, 118–21

Kluane National Park Reserve, 142, 143, 149n2

Konashen Community-owned Conserved Area, 72

Kothari, Ashish, 69, 71

Kouchibouguac National Park, displacement from, 142
Kruger National Park, 78, 223f; history, 222; land claims in, 218, 221–27; and restitution, 226–27, 292, 309n3. *See also* Makuleke; Pafuri Triangle

Lake Bogoria National Reserve, 292, 309n3
Lakota, 78; proposed tribal national park, 45n35
land claims, 200, 201; in Australia, 90; in Alaska, 109–10, 112, 115, 127; in Canada, 141–43, 147, 149n2; in Nicaragua, 191–92; in South Africa, 217, 221–27; 226–35, 239n7
land grabbing, 258
land management (customary), 98, 102. *See also* ICCAs
land tenure, 89, 94, 105n4, 190–92, 198–99, 201; usufruct, 38t, 207, 293s; and women, 199, 201–5; 210. *See also* collective tenure; El Proyecto de Catastro y Regularización; land title
land title: in Alaska, 109, 110, 112; in Australia, 89, 90, 91, 94, 102, 105nn4–6, 105–6n8; in Canada, 142; and Garifuna, 185; and IPAs, 102; in Latin America, 200–201; mapping, 41n10, 309n4; native title, 89–90, 105n6; and new paradigm, 293; in Nicaragua, 187, 189t, 190, 193, 292; and protected areas, 34, 44n28, 55, 200–201, 292, 293, 309n4; and Río Plátano Biosphere Reserve, 198–99, 206–7, 209–12, 292; and women, 201, 209, 212. *See also* collective tenure; land tenure
Langtang National Park, 264, 264f; *beyul*, 271
Laponia World Heritage Site, shared governance of, 77
Lausche, Barbara, 81n7, 290
Lhomi people, 264
livelihoods: and biodiversity, 85–87; and new paradigm, 284s. *See also* protected areas; subsistence
local communities. *See* community
Locally Managed Marine Areas, 26, 72

Los Altos de San Miguel Regional Municipal Park, 243, 247; and CONAP, 249, 253, 256; demand for dissolution of, 247, 249; establishment and history, 243, 248, 255; and NGOs, 247–49; overlap with community forests and lands, 243; and restrictions on livelihoods, 249–251; and shared governance, 243, 249. *See also* UCJ
Lunaat' (Tlingit leader), 119–20

Makalu-Barun National Park, 264, 264f, 271; *beyul*, 271
Makuleke people, 217; eviction from Kruger National Park, 222; land claim, 221–37; restitution, 309n3. *See also* Kruger National Park
Maluleke, Gibson, 224
Man and the Biosphere Programme (UNESCO). *See* biosphere reserves.
Mander, Jerry, 19
Maori people, 35, 49, 77, 78f
mapping, 41n10, 155, 162, 165, 180, 185, 194, 206, 257, 309n4. *See also* El Proyecto de Catastro y Regularización
Matthiesen, Peter, 4
Maya, 242, 244; pan-Maya rights movement, 242, 244, 255
Mayangna people, 187, 193
Mesoamerican Biological Corridor, 43n26, 180, 192; donors and partners of, 181–83, 183t; Indigenous peoples' lack of participation and benefits, 195; and land "regularization," 176; megaproject environmental managerialism and, 178; and neoliberalism, 176, 195; protected areas and buffer zones, 180, 181f, 182f, 184. *See also* Atlantic Biological Corridor; biological corridors
Mesoamerican Project (MP), 175, 193
mestizaje, 207–8
Mexico: community forests in, 24–25; and ICCAs, 72, 82n17
mobile Indigenous peoples, 80n3
Mead, Aroha, 49
Miskito, 198, 202, 213n5; contestation of land titling process, 207; land tenure, 202–3; economic activities, 203–5;

matrifocality and family land, 202–5; patriarchy and status of women, 203–4, 209–12; settlement within Río Plátano Biosphere Reserve, 198; subsistence use rights in Río Plátano Biosphere Reserve, 206, 213n9; women and economic activities, 203–5
Miskitu people, 179, 186–87, 195, 196n2
Mission Mountains Tribal Wilderness, 72, 73f
Monument Valley Navajo Tribal Park, 74f
Mount Elgon National Park, 290
Mount Everest, 269f, 271f, 281n3
Movimiento Maya (Mayan Movement), 244
Muller, Samantha, 94
mutual gains negotiations, 217–19, 237–38; ideology of, 220, 226–27; and morality, 220, 231

Namibia: communal conservancies in, 272, 94; shared governance protected areas in, 78
Nantawarrina IPA, 92, 93f, 94–96
nation, concept of, 40n6
national forests, displacement from, 44n34
national parks, 32s; definition of, 29, 33–34; plant-harvesting agreements in, 45n35; hunting in, 45n35; U.S., 34, 36, 45n35, 108–9
nation-states, unitary, 17, 18, 42n17, 46n39
Native American Land Conservancy, 72
Native American Graves Protection and Repatriation Act (NAGPRA), 109, 113–15, 125
native title, in Alaska, 110; in Australia, 89–91, 105nn5–6; in Canada, 142
natural resources: conceptions of, 11n2, 109; and conflict, 191, 198, 200–201, 207, 243; and displacement, 37, 38t; and new paradigm, 61, 61t, 109, 126, 128, 284s; and old paradigm, 22, 36, 81n11, 109; and repatriation, 115, 124–28; sustainable use and conservation of, 24, 43n24; and sustainable use in protected areas, 30, 32s, 65, 81n11, 266; and rights, 21, 48, 53, 57, 66, 191, 266; and territorialization, 17, 22, 41n11
Nature Conservancy, The, 182, 183t, 184, 256, 309n2
Navajo. *See* Diné
nawa (guardian), 272, 282n14
negotiation theory, 217; ideologies, 220, 238; morality, 220. *See also* distributive negotiations; mutual gains negotiations
Negri, Antonio, 171n15
Nepal: and displacement from protected areas, 265; high Himalayan protected areas in, 263–64; ICCAs in, 267–76, 278–80; Indigenous peoples' movement in, 263; Indigenous peoples' status in, 262–63, 278–79; Indigenous peoples' territories in, 262–63; national park regulations in, 266–67; protected areas in, 263–64, 264f, 267, 281n2, 281n8; protected area overlap with ICCAs, 265, 268; protected area overlap with Indigenous peoples' territories, 35, 261, 265; rights in, 264–67; as unitary nation-state, 263
new paradigm, 7, 8–9, 36–40, 60–69, 80n2, 87–89, 103, 241, 283, 284s, 305–8; and biodiversity, 53, 60, 62t, 65, 102, 104, 172, 308, 311n17; and community-oriented protected areas, 103–4; conceptualization of, 7, 8–9, 60–63, 63t; contrasts with old paradigm, 61–63, 62t; as decolonization, 8, 22, 41n10, 48, 94, 148, 306, 311n14; as "geography of hope," 308, 311n17; and governance, 67–69; implementation of, 283–92, 306–8; key approaches of, 69–79; and livelihoods, 8, 62t, 66, 283, 284s, 286, 305–6; policies of, 47, 51–60; principles and assumptions of, 36, 44n34, 48–50, 60–69; and reconciliation, 8, 56, 77, 125–28, 283, 298, 306, 308; and restitution, 53, 55, 56, 92–93, 283, 284s, 306; and rights, 22, 61, 65–66, 283, 284s, 308; significance of, 7, 8–9, 283, 305–6, 308. *See also* ICCAs; IPAs, rights-based conservation; shared governance

New Zealand, overlap of protected areas and Indigenous peoples' territories in, 35
Nietschmann, Bernard Q., 18, 19, 23, 185–86, 259

Ob Luang National Park, 290
Ogiek people, 290
old paradigm: characteristics of, 3, 6–7, 36–40, 44nn33–34, 62–63t; Indigenous peoples' denunciation of, 47–50, 49f, 50s; key assumptions of, 36; persistence of, 7, 285. *See also* displacement; fortress conservation
Old Woman Mountains Preserve, 72
Oxlajuj Ajpop, 257

Pafuri Triangle, 217, 222–23, 225–26; biodiversity in, 222; restitution of, 226, and shared governance, 226–27
paper parks, 4
Papua New Guinea: and ICCAs, 72, 82n17; overlap of protected areas and Indigenous peoples' territories in, 35; wildlife management areas in, 35, 72
paradigm wars, 19
Paseo Pantera, 180, 182
Peru: communal reserves in, 151–52; protected area system, 151–52
Pharak, 268, 269f
Philippines, overlap of protected areas and Indigenous peoples' territories in, 35
pluri-national states. *See* states
political economy of conservation funding, 64–65
Posey, Darrell, 42n15
Programme of Work on Protected Areas, 27, 59–60, 285; Element 2, 43n28, 60, 285, 286–87
protected areas: assessment and evaluation of, 69, 287, 289–90, 295; benefit sharing, 7, 52, 56, 60, 284s; biodiversity conservation significance of, 24–26, 133; and "civilizing mission" of, 39; as conservation enclosures, 39; and Convention on Biological Diversity, 27; critiques of, 5–6, 39; definitions of, 26, 29, 43n24; extent of, 27, 27f, 28f; downgrading, downsizing, and degazettement of, 4; ecological compromise of, 4–5; extractive industries in, 4, 5, 12n5; and frontier pacification, 39; funding of, 29, 64–65; and governmentality, 39; governance of, 67–68, 81nn8–9, 289–90; and governance types, 30–32, 33s; as green grabbing, 39; as high modernism, 39; history of, 44n29, 44n34; as imperialism, 39; Indigenous peoples' participation in governance of, 53, 56, 60, 66, 301–3; and IUCN, 27; and livelihoods, 203, 205, 226, 227, 229, 249–52, 257, 265–66, 266–67; management of, 67–69, 267; and management categories, 30, 32s, 65–66, 81n11, 91; matrix, 31f; and modernism, 39, 46n39; number of, 26, 27f, 28f; and power relations, 5, 38, 40, 67, 76, 77, 93, 94–95, 126, 136, 144–49, 159–60, 167–69, 178–79, 209–11, 249, 279, 298, 301–5, 308; and racialization, 39, 301, 304, 305; and reconciliation, 39, 283, 305–6; rights recognition in, 52–61, 65–66, 68, 305–6, 308; rights violations by, 3, 7, 37, 40, 48, 285; as "spaces of exception," 211; significance of, 27; and state building, 46n39; and *terra nullius*, 39; as territorialization, 39. *See also* ICCAs; IPAs, new paradigm; old paradigm; shared governance
Puebla-Panama Plan (PPP), 175–76

racialization: and discourses in Honduras, 198, 199, 207–9, 212, 214nn11–12; and Indigenous peoples, 17, 39, 40; and shared governance, 298, 301, 304, 305. *See also mestizaje*
Rai people, 264, 281n4
RAYAKA ("life," Miskito organization), 207, 212
reconciliation. *See* new paradigm
relocation. *See* displacement
repatriation, 109, 114–15, 125–28. *See also* Native American Graves Protection and Repatriation Act

resistance, 19, 118, 168, 202, 212, 255; conceptual limitations of, 167; as territorial defense, 19
resource wars, 19
responsibility, in relation to rights, 26, 126, 128, 284s
restitution, 49, 53, 55, 58, 79f, 218, 226–27, 292–93, 293–94s; and Endorois case, 292, 309n3; and IUCN policy, 53, 54t, 55, 58, 292; and mediation by NGOs, 218, 221–26, 236–37; in Nepal, 266; and new paradigm, 283, 284s, 287, 292–93, 294s, 308; in South Africa, 292, 309n3. See also Dwesa-Cwebe Nature Reserve; Kruger National Park; new paradigm
Richtersveld National Park, shared governance in, 78
rights-based conservation, 8, 12n6, 22, 61, 241–42, 255, 259, 309nn1–2; in Nepal, 266, 277–79
Río Plátano Biosphere Reserve, 197, 199f; buffer zone, 198; cultural zone of, and Indigenous peoples, 198; cultural zone of, and land title, 207, 212; *ladino* colonists in, 198; land tenure and titling in, 198, 206–7; Miskito women and land tenure issues in, 198; and racialization of land title regularization, 198; and restitution, 292; UNESCO biosphere reserve and World Heritage Site, 197; zonation, 198

Saami, 77
sacred forests: in Guatemala, 257; in Sagarmatha National Park, 269, 271f, 272, 273f, 274
sacred natural sites: conservation significance of, 24, 26, 42n22; custodianship of, 56, 261, 267; in Guatemala, 256–57; and ICCAs, 70, 71, 72, 73, 74, 82n15, 256–57, 261, 264, 268–72, 271f, 273f, 274; IUCN policy on, 54t, 56, 58, 66; in Nepal, 261, 265, 269–72, 271f, 273f, 274; and restitution, 294s; and rights, 66, 277
Sagarmatha National Park and World Heritage Site (SNP), 75f, 264, 264f,
269f, 271, 271f, 274–75; and *beyul*, 271; and ICCAs, 267–76; and Sharwa, 268, 270, 272, 275–76. *See also* Sharwa
Sagarmatha National Park Buffer Zone (SNPBZ), 75f, 268, 269f, 271f, 273, 282nn13–14
science, Indigenous, 62t. *See also* Indigenous knowledge
science, Western: and "anti-politics machine," 304–5; and coproduction of knowledge, 303–4; and decision-making, 145–46, 156, 303; and "green science," 194; and Indigenous knowledge, 97, 145–46, 156, 303–5; and new paradigm, 62t; and old paradigm, 62t; and techno-managerialism, 156, 304
sea management, 98
Secaira, Estuardo, 256
Servicio Nacional de Áreas Naturales Protegidas (SERNANP): and administration protected areas in Peru, 152; advocacy of techno-managerialism, 157, 168; and anti-politics, 157–60; and governmentality, 159–60; and narratives of the Ashaninka and the Ashaninka Communal Reserve, 155–57; and resource extraction in protected areas, 156, 159–60; role in Ashaninka Communal Reserve governance, 157
shared governance (of protected areas), 54t, 56, 76–79, 90, 143–45; and "anti-politics machine," 146, 304–5, 310n13; benefits of, 76–77, 298; cooptation of, 136, 146, 169, 302–3; and coproduction of knowledge, 303–4; critiques of, 77, 98, 106n13, 106n21, 136, 144–47, 298–300, 301–5; and decision-making, 299–301, 300s; and deep colonizing, 302, 310n9; and environmentality, 301, 303, 310nn11–12; epistemological issues of, 145–46, 299, 300, 303–5; governmentalizing of, 157–60; and ICCA overlap, 278, 301s; and legitimization of state intervention, 146–47; marginalization and, 144–45, 147; and new paradigm,

shared governance (*continued*)
76, 284s, 298–301, 300–301s; and paternalism, 136, 139, 147, 302, 305; power dynamics, 77, 136, 144, 145, 147, 298, 301–5, 310nn7–9, 310n13; and racialization, 298, 301, 304, 305; and sovereignty, 77, 169, 310n13; structural issues, 227, 301–5; and techno-managerialism, 145, 303, 304, 310n10

Sharwa (Sherpa), 264, 268, 269f, 281n3, 281n9–10; and biodiversity, 274; community land management by, 75f, 268–75, 272–74; community forests, 75f, 268, 269, 270, 271f, 272–74; community grazing management, 268, 270, 272; firewood collection management system, 272–74, 282nn13–15; ICCAs and overlap with Sagarmatha National Park, 268–275; ICCA recognition efforts, 275–76; *nawa*, 272, 282n14; sacred natural sites, 268, 269, 270–74, 273f; and Sagarmatha National Park, 268, 270, 272, 274, 275–76; territory, 268, 269f; village assemblies, 75f, 82nn13–14, 270, 271f, 272; village law, 270, 272, 282n14; wildlife protection, 271, 274. *See also* Khumbu; Pharak; Sagarmatha National Park; Sagarmatha National Park Buffer Zone

Shey-Phoksundo National Park, 264, 264f, 271; sacred valley, 271. *See also* Bon; Dolpo-pa

Sherpa. *See* Sharwa

Sitka National Historical Park, 121–24; and Southeast Alaska Indian Cultural Center, 122–23

Skagway Traditional Council, 121; plant walk, 121

Sneed, Paul, 76

Sobrevilla, Claudia, 44n32

South America, overlap of protected areas and Indigenous peoples' territories in, 33

socio-ecological systems, 42n22

South Africa, shared governance of protected areas in, 78

South Africa National Parks (SANP), 226–27

sovereignty, 19, 20, 21, 41n9, 77, 144; Ashaninka, 151, 167, 168–69; conceptions of, 168–69; in new paradigm, 7; as right, 20–21, 41n13

Soviet Union, protected areas in, 37

Specialist Group on Indigenous Peoples, Customary and Environmental Laws and Human Rights (SPICEH), 290

Spence, Mark, 37

states, 41n7; and conservation record 4, 5, 11n2; myth of noble state, 11n3; pluri-national, 22, 42n17; and rights, 17–18, 20, 307–8; unitary, 17, 18, 42n17, 46n39. *See also* displacement; expropriation; Fourth World; frontier; old paradigm; territorialization

Steenkamp, Conrad, 225–26

Stegner, Wallace, 308, 311n17

Stevens, Stan, 9, 113, 129n1

subsidiarity, 81n8

subsistence: in Alaska, 109, 112–13, 116–17; in Australia, 85–87, 104; in Guatemala, 250–51; in Nepal, 264, 266–67, 272–74; in South Africa, 222; state restrictions on, 134–35, 139

Subsistence Resource Commissions (Alaska), 78; and use rights, 45, 112–13, 206, 266–67

swidden, 161, 213n9, 266

Tamang, 264

TASBA ("land," Miskito organization), 207, 212

Tauli-Corpuz, Vicki, 19

terra nullius, 18, 39

territory, 11n4, 21, 83n20, 89, 102, 118, 105n6, 129n1, 156–57, 164–66, 255; conceptions of, 46n39, 163, 201; defense of, 19, 77; and displacement, 38; and ICCAs, 70; and identification of Indigenous peoples, 16, 17; and new paradigm, 7–8, 283, 284s; and rights, 8, 21–22, 66–67. *See also* country; territorialization

territorialization, 19, 164, 207; and conservation, 303; and

environmentality, 301, 303; and Fourth World, 19; and power relations, 304–5; and protected areas, 19, 39, 164, 311n13; and shared governance, 301, 311n13
Thelan Game Sanctuary, displacement from, 139
Theme on Governance, Equity, and Rights (TGER), 51, 291
Theme on Indigenous and Local Communities, Equity, and Protected Areas (TILCEPA), 51, 291
Third World War, 19
Timbisha Shoshone, restitution, 79f
Timbisha Shoshone Natural and Cultural Preservation Area, 79, 79f
Tla-o-qui-aht First Nation, tribal parks, 72, 83n18
Tlingit, 108–9; *at.óow* (valued or sacred possessions), 110–11, 114–15, 128; cultural foods, 115, 124; gifts, 114; potlatch, 113; *shagoon* (heritage-destiny), 110, 117, 120–21, 126; subsistence, 124–25, 129n1; totem poles, 121–22, 123
Tongariro National Park and World Heritage Site, shared governance of, 77, 78f, 83n22
Tongass National Forest, 109
topophilia, 108, 116
Torre, Luz María de la, 49f
Torngats National Park, shared governance of, 144–45
Totonicapán, 243, 260n1; beetle impacts on forests in, 246, 252nn3–4, 253f; forest cover and change, 244–46, 251; Indigenous governance of, 243–46, 248–49, 253–54, 254f; K'iche' Maya population of, 246; municipal government and conservation, 243, 257; NGOs in, 247–49, 252–54; protected areas, 242, 243. *See also* K'iche' Maya; UCJ
Transkei Land Service Organization (Tralso), 227, 230, 233
Transform project, 222–26, 233
tribal national parks, 45n35
tribal parks: in Canada, 72, 83n18; in United States, 72–73, 73f, 74f

truth and reconciliation commission, 54t, 56, 287, 307
Tsing, Anna Lowenhaupt, 88, 104

UCJ (Ulew Che' Ja'), 247–49, 252–54
Ulew Che' Ja'. *See* UCJ.
Uluru-Kata Tjuta National Park and World Heritage Site, 35, 90; and restitution, 292
UN Declaration on the Rights of Indigenous Peoples (UNDRIP). *See* UNDRIP
UN Development Programme (UNDP), 29, 183t, 191
UNDRIP, 8, 16, 20–22, 41nn12–13, 56, 66, 87; and good governance, 68; and ICCAs, 81n13, 277–78, 282n17; and IUCN, 56, 57–58, 66, 68; as minimal standard, 68; and Nepal, 263, 267; and new paradigm, 54, 56, 66, 68, 289, 291
UN Educational, Scientific, and Cultural Organization (UNESCO), 197, 200
UN Environment Programme (UNEP), 29, 32, 71, 183t, 281n2, 289. *See also* World Conservation Monitoring Centre; World Database on Protected Areas
UN Expert Mechanism on the Rights of Indigenous Peoples (EMRIP), 56, 289, 307
UN human rights monitoring mechanisms, 56, 66, 288, 306, 307
UN Permanent Forum on Indigenous Issues (UNPFII), 15, 56, 289, 307
UN Special Rapporteur on the Rights of Indigenous Peoples, 41n15, 45n35, 56, 266, 288, 307, 309n3
U.S. National Park Service: and Alaska national parks, 109, 112, 113, 117, 118, 122, 123, 125, 126; and changing policies and practices, 36, 45n35, 78, 79
Ute Mountain Park, 72

Village Planner (TVP), 227, 230, 232–33; and distributive negotiations, 230, 232

Wales, inhabited national parks in, 36
Wapichan Conserved Forest, 82n17

Weaver, Sally, 76
Whakatane Assessment, 56, 289–90
Whakatane Mechanism, 128, 289–90
wilderness: and Alaska, 4, 108, 112–13, 117–18, 121, 125; area, 42n19; and Ashaninka Communal Reserve, 155; and biodiversity, 22; concept of, 4, 11n2, 42n19, 108, 117, 125–26, 128, 155, 308, 311n17; and cultural diversity, 42n18; and cultural erasure, 39, 117; as cultural landscape, 4, 39, 42n19, 129n1; displacement from, 37, 39; as enclosure, 113, 126; extent of, 42n19; and Glacier Bay, 117, 121, 128; and Kruger National Park, 223; and new paradigm, 8; as protected area management goal, 5, 30, 32s, 36, 43, 133–34, 155, 223, 308; and old paradigm, 36–37, 39, 46n39, 48; *terra nullius*, 39; tribal, 72, 73f
Wildlife Conservation Society, 183t, 309n2
wildlife management: in Canada, 134–36; state appropriation of, 139–40; state promotion of commercialization of, 136, 140; policies and regulations, 137–38; and wildlife ranching, 139–40
wildlife management area, 35, 72
win-win negotiations, 217, 219, 225, 237–38. *See also* mutual gains negotiations
women: economic activities of, 203, 204–5; and gender discrimination in land titling programs, 201–2; and land management, 96; and land tenure, 201–5, 210; and subsistence practices, 203
Wood Buffalo National Park: advisory committee of, 143, 146–47, 149n2; commercialization of wildlife at, 140

World Commission on Protected Areas (WCPA), 23, 27, 32, 47, 53, 81n7, 289–90
World Conservation Congress (WCC), 23, 27, 57–58, 73, 75, 80n2, 81n6, 277, 289–90, 295–96
World Conservation Monitoring Centre (WCMC), 32, 67, 289
World Conservation Strategy, 43n24
World Database on Protected Areas (WDPA), 31, 32, 44n30, 44n32, 71, 72, 281n2, 289
World Parks Congress (WPC), 27, 44n32, 290; in Durban, South Africa, 47–57, 49f, 80n1
World Bank, 25; and Atlantic Biological Corridor, 191–92; and Mesoamerican Biological Corridor, 175, 184t, 185, 193; and protected area support, 29, 43n28, 44n28, 64
World Heritage Site (UNESCO), 43n25; and free, prior, and informed consent, 309n3; ICCA in, 75f; shared governance of, 77, 78f, 83n22. *See also individual World Heritage sites*
World Wide Fund for Nature, 22, 23, 42n20, 99, 230, 309n2
World Wildlife Fund (WWF), 182, 183t, 309n2

Yekuana people, 73
Yellowstone model, 36
Yellowstone National Park and World Heritage Site, 34
Yolmo people, 264, 271
Yolngu people, 96
Yosemite National Park and World Heritage Site, 12n5, 34